新闻学与传播学经典丛书·大师系列

新闻伦理学
The Ethics of Journalism
中文·英文（双语版）

［美］纳尔逊·安特宁·克劳福德
(Nelson Antrim Crawford) 著
江作苏　王　敏　译

中国传媒大学出版社
·北京·

新闻学与传播学经典丛书·大师系列

- 社会传播的结构与功能
- 变化中的时间观念
- 新闻学原理
- 帝国与传播
- 传播的偏向
- **新闻伦理学**
- 个性动力论
- 控制论（第二版）

出版说明

《新闻伦理学》是美国较早提出新闻媒介伦理的著作。

本书作者纳尔逊·安特宁·克劳福德强调，新闻从业者应当具备新闻学、政治学、文学等专业知识，各种新闻伦理问题，需要在法律、历史、社会学和文学等领域作进一步探讨。本书还收纳了20世纪初美国各大报纸的媒体规范与条例，于新闻媒介研究者而言，这些资料弥足珍贵。

20世纪初的美国，新闻审查制度较严，学界对于新闻自由和党派宣传的观点稍显偏激，本书的某些表述甚至是不恰当的。为了保持原貌，我们在出版时未作处理。请您阅读时细加甄别，取其精华，去其糟粕。

总　序

　　新闻与大众传播事业在现当代与日俱增的影响与地位，呼唤着新闻学与传播学学术研究的相应发展和跟进。而知识的传承、学术的繁荣、思想的进步，首先需要的是丰富的思想材料的积累。

　　"新闻学与传播学经典丛书·大师系列"的创设，立意在接续前辈学人传译外国新闻学与传播学经典的事业，以一定的规模为我们的学术与思想界以及业界精英人士理解和借鉴新闻学与传播学在西方方兴未艾之际的精华，提供基本的养料，便于站在前人的肩膀上作进一步的探究，以免长期在黑暗中自行低效摸索。

　　将近十年前，在何道宽教授与我的发起和主持下以及在司马兰女士的大力支持下，"新闻学与传播学丛书·大师系列"开始启动，至今已推出十来种名著的中译本，在学界也较有影响。这首先是何道宽教授的贡献，他作为英语科班出身、口译笔译俱佳的高手，依然投身于传播学经典的引进；退休后更是一发不可收，每天清晨起床开始工作，每年推出好几本译著，而且专攻技术学派（何老师称之为"环境学派"），不但包办了哈罗德·伊尼斯、马歇尔·麦克卢汉著作的所有中译本，而且还延伸到了保罗·莱文森等当代名家的著作。

　　记得何老师说过，他热爱传播学学术翻译到了这样的程度："不给我钱（稿费）我也愿意翻译。"我当时就感慨，新闻传播学界要是多一些像何老师这样外语水平高、热衷翻译的专才就好了。可是在目前的学术考核体制下，译著辛苦和稿费低暂且不提，在多数学校译著还不能算作科研成果。这也妨碍了许多为教学科研和生活所累的年轻学人接续这一事业。

好在随着新闻传播学的发展,越来越多的学人意识到了我九年多前说的两个80%:新闻学与传播学是舶来品,80%的学术和思想资源不在中国;而日见人多势众的研究队伍将80%以上的精力投放到虽在快速发展,但是仍处于"初级阶段"的国内新闻与大众传播事业的研究上。这两个80%倒置的现实,导致了学术资源配置的严重失衡和学术研究的肤浅化、泡沫化;专业和学术著作的翻译虽然在近几年渐成气候,但是其水准、规模和系统性不足以摆脱"后天失调"的尴尬。

如果说当年启动时,我们深感百余年前梁启超呼吁"国家欲自强,以多译西书为本;学子欲自立,以多读西书为功"对于当代新闻传播学的意义,如果说任公所言西学著述"今之所译,直九牛之一毛耳"的巨大落差,如果说新闻学与传播学相关典籍的译介比其他学科还要滞后许多,以至于我们的学人们对这些经典知之甚少,眼界相当狭窄,那么这种状况已经有所改观。如今的新闻传播学,虽然仍属小学科,但是近十年出版的图书数量猛增,其中译著的大量问世是最为引人瞩目的现象。

这些新闻传播学译著可能并非本本经典,事实上也出现了些许重复翻译,一些译本的翻译质量存在问题,译校也比较粗糙,但是总体而言,它们对于学术的推动和学科地位的提升功不可没,尤其是比较媒介理论、传播研究方法类译著,直接滋养了年轻学子,使得他们的研究水准迅速提升。回想十年前,尽管几乎所有新闻传播专业学生言必称传播学"四大奠基人"或"四大先驱",可是当时他们的传播学译著一本也没有被翻译成中文。

本译丛将奉献新闻学与传播学大师的经典之作,如哈罗德·拉斯韦尔、埃尔·塔尔德、哈罗德·伊尼斯、马歇尔·麦克卢汉、库尔特·卢因、卡尔·霍夫兰等人的佳作。大部分名著是新近翻译出版的,部分名著是中文版的修订本。"译事之艰辛,惟事者知之。"从事这种恢弘迫切而又繁难备至的工作,需要好几代人做出不懈努力,幸赖同道和出版者的大力扶持。我们自知学有不逮,力不从心,因此热忱欢迎中青年学人加入译者队伍,我们也将虚心聆听各界读者提出的批评和建议。

主编

目　录

序言一	1
序言二	3
前　言	11
第一章　出版的商业伦理	13
第二章　作为一种职业的新闻	30
第三章　公众对报纸的指控	41
第四章　报业的缺陷：唯物主义的控告	59
第五章　报业的缺陷：现实主义的解释	66
第六章　客观性原则的应用：平衡与比例	81
第七章　客观性原则的应用：煽情主义	86
第八章　客观性原则的应用：社论引导	95
第九章　建立专业标准：法律措施	103

第十章　建立专业标准：记者组织　　　　　　　　　　　　　　*111*

第十一章　建立专业标准：报纸职责　　　　　　　　　　　　　*118*

第十二章　建立专业标准：教育机构　　　　　　　　　　　　　*125*

附录 A　记者组织、报纸杂志所遵循的新闻伦理准则与规范　　　*132*
附录 B　参考文献选辑　　　　　　　　　　　　　　　　　　　*167*
附录 C　新闻伦理学词汇索引　　　　　　　　　　　　　　　　*174*
译者跋　　　　　　　　　　　　　　　　　　　　　　　　　　*188*

The Ethics of Journalism　　　　　　　　　　　　　　　　　　*193*

Preface　　　　　　　　　　　　　　　　　　　　　　　　　　*195*

I　The Business Ethics of Publishing　　　　　　　　　　　　*197*

II　Journalism as a Profession　　　　　　　　　　　　　　　*218*

III　Public Charges Against the Newspaper　　　　　　　　　*231*

IV　Deficiencies of the Press: The Materialistic Indictment　*255*

V　Deficiencies of the Press: A Realistic Explanation　　　　*265*

VI　The Principle of Objectivity Applied: Balance and Proportion　*289*

VII　The Principle of Objectivity Applied: Sensationalism　　*297*

VIII　The Principle of Objectivity Applied: Editorial Leadership　*311*

IX　Setting Professional Standards: Legal Measures　　　　　*323*

X　Setting Professional Standards: Organizations of Journalists　*335*

XI　Setting Professional Standards: The Newspaper's Part　　*345*

XII Setting Professional Standards: Educational Agencies   356

Appendix A   Codes of Ethics and Rules Adopted by Organizations of

Journalists and by Newspapers   367

Appendix B   A Selective Bibliography   413

Appendix C   INDEX   423

A PARTIAL LIST OF BORZOI TEXTS   435

序言一

The Ethics of Journalism is the first book to work out an ethics of the news media, and its translation is of historic importance to our field. Choosing this book for translation shows an intelligent understanding of journalism history, and challenges us today to match the quality and depth of this landmark book. The translation is accurate, clear and precise in its content, and thorough in all its details. The importance of this selection, and the quality of the translation, make this new book an especially valuable contribution to media ethics scholarship worldwide.

Crawford was the first in the United States to recognize that journalism ethics required a liberal arts degree in journalism or a related field such as literature or political science. He was an award—winning journalist, but he dedicated most of his life to university and college education. The issues in journalism ethics that he emphasized in his book, Crawford saw as requiring further study in law and history and sociology and literature. Crawford wanted journalists to ask important questions and identify important issues in society and government. This broad educational framework is taught in this book, and therefore is an inspiration and ideal for journalism theory and practice yet today.

《新闻伦理学》是第一本提出新闻媒介伦理的著作，其译作具有历史性意义。选择翻译此书，显示出译者对新闻史的睿智理解。并且，这本里程碑式著作的品质与深度，对我们现今的知识水平和理解能力也是一种挑战。所幸，译文在整体把握和细节处理上做到了精确、明晰和规范。选择的睿智和翻译的品质，使得这本新书对世界范围内的媒介伦理研究卓有贡献。

　　在美国，克劳福德第一个意识到，从新闻职业伦理的要求出发，从业者应具备新闻、文学或政治学专业的学位。克劳福德是一位获奖无数的记者，却将一生的多数光阴奉献给了大学教育。克劳福德认为，他在书中强调的各种新闻伦理问题，需要在法律、历史、社会学和文学等领域作进一步探讨。他希望记者能发现并提出关于社会和政府的重要问题以及重大议题。这种具有教益的宏大框架，时至今日，依然对新闻理论和实践具有启示意义。

〔美〕克利福德·G·克里斯琴斯
2016年3月于美国伊利诺伊大学厄巴纳-香槟分校

# 序言二

每个问题都有两面,缺一不可
——读克劳福德《新闻伦理学》

新闻学是一门应用学科,必须建立在丰富的新闻实践基础之上。1690年第一篇新闻学博士论文,如今看起来可能还不如现在本科论文的水平,但那毕竟是300多年前对新闻实践理性思考的结果,那时在欧洲几个国家总共只有二三十家发行量很小的周报。直到19世纪中叶,大众报刊兴起,才奠定了新闻学得以形成的基础。于是19世纪末,瑞士和德国的大学出现了新闻学的课程,20世纪初美国的大学建立了新闻学的院系。

既然新闻学的初创在美国形成体系,那就必须得有代表作,故1922年报刊专栏作家沃尔特·李普曼(Walter Lippmann,1889—1974)的《舆论学》(*Public Opinion*)、1924年新闻学者卡斯珀·约斯特(Casper Salathiel Yost,1863—1941)的《新闻学原理》(*Principles of Journalism*)和美国记者、教育家纳尔逊·安特宁·克劳福德(Nelson Antrim Crawford,1888—1963)的《新闻伦理学》(*The Ethics of Journalism*)构成了较早的学科代表作。

由于历史的原因,约斯特的《新闻学原理》早在20世纪60年代就在中国人民大学新闻系作为批判材料被翻译了出来，有油印本，但人们只能通过批判文章了解这本书的某些被歪曲的观点。改革开放以后，人们直接接触到较新的传播学，反而遗忘了这本书，直到2013年才出版中译本。"文化大革命"后期，中国人民大学新闻系教师林珊翻译了李普曼的《舆论学》，她赶上了改革开放的春天，译稿于1980年由中国人民大学新闻系铅印，传播很广，估计印了上万册，以至于1989年华夏出版社正式出版时，反而卖不动了。克劳福德的《新闻伦理学》遭到冷遇，因为在1949年以后的几十年内，中国的新闻业不再是一个行业，而是党政机关的一个部门，因而也就谈不上新闻职业道德，只需要宣传纪律就够了。直到改革开放后，该书才在一些教材里被提及。这本书的意义在于，它是确认新闻传播业是一个社会行业的最早的职业道德的基础之作。

改革开放后的中国新闻传播业，经历了从计划经济体制向市场经济体制的漫长过渡，我们没有及时总结世界新闻传播业的历史的经验，结果几乎重走了美国百年前媒体从职业道德无序到比较有序的历史进程。上世纪90年代我多次提到我国的媒体在重复美国百年前黄色新闻潮的做法，但苦于没有像这本书那样系统的论据来说服媒体遵循职业道德。2003年起至今，我国新闻传播业界持续展开了"三项学习教育"，三项学习的内容之一，便是新闻职业道德，因为落实很不够，至今一再被强调。在这个形势下，江作苏、王敏翻译的克劳福德《新闻伦理学》中译本，便有了现实意义。而我觉得其学术意义应该更大些，因为我国缺乏现代新闻职业道德的传统根基。

克劳福德做过记者，还是多个杂志的主编，一生出版了多本社会科学的论著，并为大英百科全书、社会科学百科全书、美国传记词典撰稿。由他来评述美国新闻业的德行和恶行、论证新闻伦理，较为客观并具有学术深度。阅读这本近百年前的书，我感觉好像在讨论今天发生在中国的事情，因为那时的许多违反新闻职业道德和规范的事情，在中国差不多都有，甚至为非道德行为辩护的理由都差不多。在这个意义上，我推荐我国的新闻工作者读一读此书，汲取那时的教训，不要重走美国同行曾经走过的老路。

这本书的附录 A 是美国当时不同层次和地区的 17 个新闻职业准则文件，包括 1923 年刚制定的美国编辑人协会《新闻业信条》（全国性的），以及 5 个州、9 家报纸、1 位学者制定的新闻职业准则文件。附录 B 是"参考文献选辑"共 83 本（篇），还有各章（共 12 章）篇尾提供的"补充阅读"（共 106 本或篇）。这些历史文献囊括了当时并不多的、从不同方面和角度涉及新闻职业道德与规范的文献（论著、相关论著的某些章节、论文、道德自律文件、各种公告和通知）。各章的"补充阅读"＋书后的"参考文献选辑"，去除重复的，共计近 100 本（篇），基本集中在作者写这本书之前的 10 年内，包括李普曼的《自由与新闻》《舆论学》和帕克的《移民报刊及其控制》，均是 1920－1923 年的论著。这些都是当时人们对这个问题认识的宝贵历史资料，由此可以研究为什么新闻职业道德问题那时会被提上日程，以及当时人们是怎样思考这个问题的。当时美国的新闻传播学界和业界，以及相关的社会领域，共同为新闻传播业形成职业道德和规范而努力的印记，清晰可见。

我在这里挑一则新闻职业准则谈谈体会，它是克劳福德提供的 9 家报纸新闻职业准则文件中最短的一则，只有 11 句话，作者是 1921－1923 年在任的美国总统沃伦·甘梅利尔·哈定（Warren Gamaliel Harding，1865－1923）。哈定 12－14 岁时，在一家摇摇欲坠的印刷所做过学徒。1881 年，他随父亲定居俄亥俄州的马里恩小镇。1884 年，19 岁的哈定与两位朋友筹资 300 美元买下了当地的《马里恩星报》（The Marion Star）。这是一份很小的日报，恐怕不比一张传单大多少，报社的主要财产是一架凑合能用、手工操作的印刷机。年内，他从朋友手中买下了该报的所有股份。后来该报成为俄亥俄州出类拔萃的城镇小报之一。俄亥俄州的人不仅喜欢读哈定办的报纸，也开始注意起报纸的老板哈定。尽管哈定曾被评为最差的美国总统，但他办的乡镇小日报《马里恩星报》严格遵循新闻职业道德准则，值得我们认真研究他办报的成功之道：以公信力换取影响力。

该文件前五句和最后一句依次是：

记住：每个问题都有两面，缺一不可（Remember there are two sides to every question. Get them both）。

确保真实（Be truthful）。

获取事实。错误在所难免，但务必尽力追求准确。我宁愿要1个完全准确的故事，也不要100个一半差错的故事（Get the facts. Mistakes are inevitable, but strive for accuracy. I would rather have one story exactly right than a hundred half wrong）。

正直、公正、宽容（Be decent. Be fair. Be generous）。

以鼓励代替批评。每个人都有好的一面，发掘其善而不要对任何人的感情造成不必要的伤害（Boost-don't knock. There's good in everybody. Bring out the good and never needlessly hurt the feelings of anybody）。

……

我希望这份报纸进入每个家庭，而不会破坏任何一个孩子的纯真（I want this paper to be so conducted that it can go into any home without destroying the innocence of any child）。

哈定确定的职业道德第一句用现在的说法即"全面"，同类的表述如当时《堪萨斯城市邮报》(*The Kansas City Journal-post*) 职业规范的第一句"每个故事都有两面，报道时缺一不可"（There are two sides to every story. Get them both）。这个道理不言而喻，但做到全面看问题却不容易。他们都抓住了记者采写时最容易发生的情形：只写自己想到（上级要求）的或只想讲述的一面，这是最为普遍且被人们忽视的不真实。

第二句"确保真实"，这种强调性的说法对正处于美国黄色新闻潮时期（19世纪80至90年代）的报纸主办者来说，没有道德定力是不敢确保的。

第三句用现在的话概括即"准确"。这是从另一个角度对新闻真实的追求，哈定知道做到准确不容易，但仍然顽强地要求尽可能做到。同类的话还有当时《萨克拉门托蜜蜂报》(*The Sacramento Bee*) 的准则第一句话："宁可失去一篇报道，也不要浪费第二天的时间去更正它"（Better lose an item than make a splurge one day and correct it next）。

第四句是对正直、公正、宽容的要求,这些主要基于人的良心(相当于中国的俗话"人心均有一杆秤"),前两者我们至少字面上熟悉,但"宽容"似乎现在被忽略了,对新闻工作者来说,即不要追求用同一个标准看人视物,容忍多样与多元。

第五句似乎有些像我们常说的以正面报道为主,其实不然,这主要是针对法警新闻的。同类的法警报道案例在中国几乎每天都在发生,因而这一句对我们的借鉴意义很现实。

最后一句(第十一句),实际上主要谈的是媒体的涉性涉暴问题,如同当时《西雅图时报》(The Seattle Times)准则文件的第一句"记住,年轻女孩也读《西雅图时报》"。媒体的近半受众是女性、三分之一受众是未成年人,这个受众比例在新闻媒体的运作中和媒体人的实际工作中,其实是常被忽视的。

鉴于中国新闻传播业的起步与美国存在发展阶段的差异,克劳福德的这本书在一定程度上反而更适合现在的中国新闻传播界借鉴。读这本书,给我一种强烈的感觉:近百年过去了,关于新闻职业道德和规范的基本原则没有发生根本变化,仍然还是真实(准确)、客观、公正、全面,以及体现人性的维护公民隐私权、保护妇女儿童合法权益和拒绝广告商对报纸的控制(包括不得把广告冒充新闻)等内容,只是现在的表现的花样更多或更隐蔽了。有鉴于此,这本书提供了认识新闻职业道德的基础。

克劳福德的《新闻伦理学》把美国新闻学形成时期的思想活动,完整、真实地留给了后人。中国最早的学术新闻学论著是1919年出版的徐宝璜的《新闻学》,他是在密苏里新闻学院学过新闻学的中国留学生之一;邵飘萍的《实际应用新闻学》(1923年)的基本原理直接来自日本,而日本早期新闻学也来自美、英(后来德国新闻学一度占据主导地位)。两相对照,他们很好地将美国新闻学的基本原理与中国新闻实践相结合,写得颇为中国化。他们的论著在中国最早确定新闻学理论的基本框架,新闻职业道德的思想自然地融入其中,但没有作为论证主题。这次克劳福德《新闻伦理学》中文版的出版,集中展现了新闻职业道德理念如何形成、发展的脉络,对新闻理论的框架中补充职业道德这一部分,具有重要的学术意义。

如果梳理我国实行市场经济以来新闻传播界遵循职业道德的情形,恐怕基本是一部他律不断加强、自律形同虚设的历史。不要说一些基本的职业理念被做了相反的认识(例如隐形采访被认为是媒体竞争的秘密武器、记者写软文成为基本工作),就是新闻要真实这样的要求,大多是通过相关党政部门下达文件或行政规章来约束的,自我纠正的情形只有两家报纸(《南方都市报》和《新京报》)坚持下来,多数媒体没有主动纠错的机制。为什么以自律为特征的新闻职业道德在中国却必须要通过他律来约束?

从克劳福德的论述和他提供的近百本(篇)文献看,美国新闻职业道德形成的根基是协商精神,这个传统可以追溯到17世纪的《"五月花号"公约》,这种协商精神存在于美国文化形成的全过程,潜在地发挥着作用。协商意味着存在各种意见,几乎所有美国的新闻职业规范均从具象问题出发,以娓娓道来的叙事方式呈现,没有强行的定论和先验的理念。其中舆论也起到了重要作用,本书各章提供的"补充阅读"重复率最高的参考文献是李普曼的《舆论学》,李普曼就观察到这一点并很重视。

具象讨论新闻职业道德,不可避免会纠缠于具体实务和缺少超越,因而协商需要引领。美国新闻职业道德的超越来源于新教伦理,《新闻伦理学》附录A提供的《华盛顿州伦理道德规范》一共15行,听起来像是基督教爱欲和自律的转述。

I will be 我将(做到)

Truthful in News 新闻真实

Truthful in Editorials 社论真实

Truthful in Advertising 广告真实

True to all my Obligations 切实履行所有责任

Honest with my Competitors 诚实对待对手

True to the Ideals of Journalism 践行新闻理想

Mindful to the Value of Sincerity 铭记诚信价值

Faithful to Community, State, Nation 忠于社区，忠于国家，忠于民族

Firm in Publication of Clean News 确保报道透明

Honorable in all of my Dealings 保证业务信誉

Thorough in all of my Studies 调查力求彻底

Unselfish in all my Services 无私奉献

Faithful to all my Friends 忠于朋友

Fair to all my Critics 直面批评

这样的自律传统，在同样新教伦理笼罩的19世纪40年代的德国亦然。那时德国报纸刊登不真实新闻的情况时有发生，即使反对专制制度的报纸也会由于素材符合自己的观点而匆忙刊登各种传闻。马克思曾就《莱比锡总汇报》被普鲁士当局查禁一事写道："我们承认《莱比锡总汇报》被指摘的那些缺点并不是纯粹捏造的。但我们认为，这是由人民报刊的实质本身所产生的一些缺点，因此，如果人们还打算容许报刊有一个发展过程，那就应该容许它在发展过程中产生这些缺点。""报刊的本质总是真实的和纯洁的，这种毒素会在报刊的永不停息的滚滚激流中变成真理和强身健体的药剂。""自由报刊是人民在自己面前的毫无顾虑的忏悔，大家知道，坦白的力量是可以使人得救的。自由报刊是人民用来观察自己的一面精神上的镜子，而自我审视是智慧的首要条件。"显然，他对报纸职业道德意识的形成，寄托于德国新教伦理式的自律，后来欧美新闻传播业的自律也确实是在这种文化氛围中形成。

美国与中国的文化传统、精神气质差异较大。中国没有美国那样的协商精神传统，加上后来的革命传统，中国的新闻传播业出现与美国百年前那些新闻职业道德的病症，其解决路径会有不同吗？就新闻职业道德意识的形成而言，中国尚缺少美国的那种文化氛围，美国不是他山之石。但是，既然现在世界新闻传播业已经有了基本认可的职业道德要求，中国新闻传播界只能由各种他律来监督着遵守职业道德吗？

韩国1987年通过"6·29"民主化宣言以后，其新闻传播业一下子

就获得了新闻自由，但同时也发生了记者普遍受贿的现象，红包新闻几乎人人难免。那时笔者认为，韩国历史上属于中国的文化圈，新闻传播行业可能就得依靠各种他律来管束，才能遵守规则，内化的自律式道德很难实现。笔者多次询问到韩国访学归来的学者，初期确实如笔者所想象的那样，韩国的新闻红包现象与中国的差不多，很普遍。但最近十多年，得到的答复逐渐相反了，韩国新闻传播业界的红包问题已基本消除。因为韩国社会整体上完善了民主与法治，当社会整体处于民主与法治状态时，新闻传播业作为社会一部分，而且是社会比较彰显的一部分，新闻自律水到渠成，没有谁一再强调，步入了自律的状态。

现在中国的情景，尚处于推进民主与法治的进程中，当整体性问题尚未得到解决时，就要求新闻传播业一个行业自觉地遵循职业道德，是比较困难的事情。

谈以上问题，并非说我们无所作为，干等美好未来，而是说要认识到问题的复杂性与韧性，从眼下能做的工作做起。例如，翻译出版克劳福德的《新闻伦理学》一书便是一项学术研究方面的基础工作。还要不予余力地反复讲述新闻职业道德的基本要求，从辨清是非做起。不要小看那几个价值判断，现在相当多的新闻传播从业者不知道怎样做是对的，怎样做是错的。我们要做的，如毛泽东所说，"经常讲，反复讲"。

可能在未来某个阶段，随着中国社会整体民主与法治的完善，新闻传播业的职业道德自律会成为常态，那时我们享受的是一种"它在丛中笑"幸福感，因为我们为此努力过。

陈力丹
2017 年 4 月 2 日于北京时雨园

前　言

众所周知，应对社会的善与恶时，没有哪种机构比新闻报刊更加行之有效。因此，不仅对记者而言，对于普罗大众也至关重要的一点是，新闻实践的标准在于实现社会利益的最大化。

本书旨在促进这种标准的形成、发展以及被广为接受，力图以关照现实而非理论阐述的方式，呈现当下新闻界的现状及其成因。书中，作者畅所欲言，旁征博引，但并非把这些观点作为相关议题的定论抛给读者。相反，他希望借此引发读者进一步独立思考。本书并非试图为年轻记者提供一套行动指南，而是希望有助于他们形成自己的职业伦理观。这种伦理观应该益于实践、易于评判、忠于理智，并且适用于作为社会机构的新闻报刊。对于任何职业而言，如果多数从业者都能秉持和遵循这种伦理哲学，这一职业就已经（至少潜移默化中）实现了匡时济俗的社会意义。

读者将会看到，本书从头至尾参考了大量相关新闻以及报纸的具体实践准则。有些地方，作者引用了长篇大论，目的是为那些平日不太容易接触、阅读到这些资料的读者提供方便。因此，对于某些读者而言，或是在限时探讨新闻伦理问题的课堂之上，本书可以作为一个快速阅读的单元。而对于那些会花整个学期的时间来研究这一问题的课程而言，这本书又可作为基础的教材,其中以引用文献的形式阐释了多个子课题。

作者非常感激匿名或知名人士对本书提出了不计其数的宝贵建议。在本书筹备之际,这些建议给予作者极大的帮助。作者尤其要感谢的是许多新闻记者以及讲授新闻学的老师,特别是哥伦比亚大学新闻学院院长J·W·坎利夫博士以及华盛顿大学新闻学院院长M·L·斯潘塞博士所赐予的真知灼见。对于那些同意引用文章的原作者,以及《国家》(The Nation)、《华盛顿报》(The Washington Newspaper)、《心理卫生》(Mental Hygiene)等报刊——允许本书作者使用其刊载的文章,作者也致以诚挚的谢意。

纳尔逊·安特宁·克劳福德

第一章　出版的商业伦理

显然，报纸是一种商品。各种各样的报纸在市场上流通，被出售和购买。为了在报纸上登广告，无论是迫不得已还是心甘情愿，广告商都需要支付一大笔费用。

稳定而合法经营的报纸，除了发行和广告收入之外，没有其他实质性的收入来源。世界各地都有一些报纸因经营不善而出现财务赤字，出版商只得通过零件印刷（job printing）来补救。世界各地也有少数报纸，通过收受甚至招揽个人、公司或政党的赞助，作为对出版商资助的一种补偿。但是，大多数的美国报纸并非此类。典型的美国报纸的收入源自发行和广告，还有一小部分报纸通过售卖废弃的新闻纸以及其他类似物品的方式获取补贴。

直至目前，报纸都还是一种商业企业。持有这种看法的人，称出版是"报纸生意"，就好比年轻的新人记者把出版称作"报纸游戏"一样。报纸被视作商业企业，其运营取决于直接相关者，即广告商、订阅者和买报人，任何商业企业都存在这种责任关系，只是因为报纸与其他商业企业的内在差异而略有不同。

订户一旦订阅报纸，就有权知道自己能获得什么。募捐者或其他人都无权歪曲报纸的内容、派发的奖励或者交易中的其他因素。"购者自慎"①，如同一位开明的商人在商品交易中常把这句话挂在嘴边一样，报纸若要遵循普通生意的标准，也只能按照这句话去做。我们不能指望募捐者或报刊经销商能够细致深入地探讨新闻要点、特写报道或编辑方针。但是，他们至少可将报纸的本来面貌大体描述出来。极少有报纸会刻意向潜在的订阅者撒谎。如果在寻求赞助的过程中出现不实的情况，通常是因募捐者的无知或不诚信造成的。

当获得了订阅之后，报纸有义务保证订阅者及时、定期收到报刊，并确保报刊版本、新闻内容、派发时间以及其他因素都令人满意。所有严肃的大报都会不遗余力地履行这些义务。这不仅是一种商业伦理，亦是一种商业策略。

例如，一些大型的都市日报，尽管发行量巨大，但是仍属于美国报纸中的少数派。对于这些报纸而言，订阅量的影响力甚微。由于报纸每日售出，买报人持续购买的习惯使得他们与订阅者几无二致，其姓名是否由报社记录在案，并不十分要紧。报纸应把这些持续买报者和订阅者等同视之，所尽义务不应有别。

一些大型报纸对售卖的份额有限定，多则不卖，因为担心被人利用而达到宣传之目的。不止一家报社内部存在这样一条规定，即达到或超过20份的购买量就必须向总经理报告。总经理会调查这个买家为何需要这么多份报纸。这种规定可追溯至报刊受公司或个人资助的时期。彼时，具体的资助方式便是超额购买某份报纸，而这些报纸中往往包含吹捧资助者的内容。如今，许多人认为报纸被过度资助了。譬如，一家铁路公司大量购进某份报纸，而该报的某个版面恰恰刊有维护铁路公司利益的社论文章时，公众会更加坚信这一点。他们无法相信，该社论文章是真实且毫无偏袒的。因此，报社应当拒绝把报纸卖给这家铁路公司，才会显得刚直不阿，甚至还能因此规避恶行。有时，也有对立的观点认为，铁路公司可以翻印这篇社论并且广为传播，但是，如果该报的版权是受到保护的，这种说法便不能成立。而大部分都市日报的版权确实受

---

① Caveat emptor，拉丁语，意为"货物出门概不退换，买主须自行当心"。——译者注

到保护。

在扩大发行的过程中,报纸同样对广告商担负某种义务。从财务的角度看,报纸扩大发行的主要目的是获得更高的广告费。都市日报的收入中至少有80%源自广告,因为通过发行所获的收益还不够支付其印刷及纸张的费用,因此,除非广告费有所提升,否则,发行量越大就意味着报纸营收的亏损越大。而稍小规模的报纸,尽管可以通过订阅来获取利润,但它们也承认,通过增加发行量来提升广告收益,是一种更为重要的盈利途径。

显然,扩大发行的策略对于广告商非常重要。某人选择了订阅一份报纸,是因为他的一位年轻女性朋友希望在该报举行的抽奖活动中获奖,赢得一辆汽车或一架钢琴;而另一个人只是因为喜欢阅读这份报纸而订阅。两个订阅者表现出来的阅读兴趣大相径庭。为了获得一套银器的奖励而订阅报纸的家庭主妇,并不会成为一个真正对报纸感兴趣的读者。她对这份报纸兴趣的大小会随着奖励价值的变化而变化,甚至有时会出现这样的情况:订阅者发现报纸有误导性信息,原本奖品应该是银器,而实际上只是铜器,她很可能因此对这份报纸失去兴趣,甚至转而讨厌它。

无论是报社举办抽奖活动还是实施奖励计划,都不能被认定有违伦理,除非活动确实存在不当之处。然而,最终的事实是,不采取这两种做法的报纸,在与广告商打交道的过程中更加游刃有余。即使根据现代发行报表和审计方法,广告商知道发行量是怎么获得的,这一点依然如此。

当然,报纸对广告商所担负的最基本的伦理责任在于,不可虚报其发行量。需要反复强调的是,广告商购买报纸版面,不仅仅是需要一个空间,更是需要一个通过报纸向读者传递讯息的机会。

近年来,发行量数据的可信度得到提升。不久前,一些广告商和广告代理建议把可信的报纸发行量数据公布出来,并经过第三方的核实。对此,出版商显得愤愤不平。第一个尝试公布发行量数据的人是乔治·P·罗威尔(George P. Rowell)。他于1870年首次出版了《美国报纸名录》（American Newspaper Directory，以下简称《名录》）。在《名录》出版后的第九个年头，他找出了一个能够决定报纸发行量排行的关键因素。在某些情况下，在这一关键因素的作用下，报纸的发行量会有50,000份的上下浮动，尽管罗威尔先生表示，他希望此关键因素，较之于先前计划公布的实际发行数量，"更能满足所有相关人员的需求"。在1879年的《名录》中，他写道：

> 1870年，我们首次决定公布这方面的信息时，编辑通过报纸的经营者来获取报表，于是在公布的数据之前插入了"号称"一词。一段时间后，对于"号称"这一表述出现了越来越多的反对声音，并且，为了拿掉这个词，出版商通过宣誓书等形式提供了各种证明报告。同时，也有许多人赞同"号称"这种说法，并指出任何"号称"都是一样的，提出的都是无法证实的主张。显然，如果《名录》要变得具有权威性，必须杜绝出现这种"号称"的发行量。其后，那些由经营者提供了证明材料的报纸，其发行量的数值显得真实可信，发布时没有任何前缀修饰语；而对于其他报纸，通常在公布的数值之前加上"估计"一词。
>
> 在一到两年的时间内，"估计"一词也变得令人反感，报纸发行商经常要求删去它。对于这一要求，编辑们统一的回复是，只有提供了可证明发行报表准确性的材料，"估计"这个词才能被删除。
>
> 这一做法惹恼了许多人。这本是一个辨别发行商是否诚实的方法。刚被采用时，它似乎卓有成效。毫无疑问，它适时地满足了当时的某些需求，但却逐渐招来了外界太多的不满，以致最终被摒弃。
>
> 我们现在唯一需要的，就是一份涵盖了发行数目的详细报表，发行商可以采用任何便捷的方式提供给我们。如果这份报表中存在纰漏，并招来异议和骂名，它将被废弃。在任何情况

下,报社都有义务接受来自竞争对手的严格审查,这能为发行量的统计提供许多真实信息。①

在很大程度上,基于广告商和广告代理的需求,发行量的数据统计问题已经逐步得到改善。在这一过程中,美国发行审计局(Audit Bureau of Circulations)发挥了很大的作用。这是一个非营利机构,由发行商、广告商以及广告代理组成,通常被称作"A. B. C."。它提出并采用了"净付款发行量"(net paid circulation)的定义,并制订了一个方案,以确保发行商提供的数据受到独立的审计。这样就能够有力地确保隶属于审计局的所有发行物均可基于同一排名体系进行比较。实际上,几乎所有的大型报纸都隶属于该审计局,因此,目前报纸的发行量仍在不断扩大,而谎报虚假发行量的情况已大大减少。

然而,在近期的一次编辑者大会上,作者听到一位乡村报纸编辑严肃地提出这样一个问题:对于某些正处于商讨中的出版计划,发行量到底应该以"实际"的为准,还是以"号称"的为基础。当前存在的一个事实是,小规模报纸的发行量经常被歪曲(尽管今昔歪曲程度已有不同),这是此类报纸获得的全国性广告少之又少的主要原因之一。不少乡村报纸仍然把印刷的报纸数量当作实际的发行量。

除了发行数量之外,广告商或广告代理也必须考虑发行质量,也就是说,他们必须考虑报纸读者的购买力及其购买意向问题。衡量发行质量,并没有固定标准,即使存在这样的衡量标准,运用起来也不切实际。显然,都市日报要想确定每位订阅者的收入和需求几乎不可能。因此,对于发行数量的衡量也必定是综合考虑的。在招揽广告的过程中,报纸有义务确保发行质量,须呈现准确而公正的数据,并据此得出真实可靠的结论。但是,对报纸和杂志刊载的自我宣传性内容,不管是谁看了,都难免会怀疑其声称的发行质量是否有所夸张。至少从理论上讲,公布这些信息的时候,报纸有义务确保其准确性。

---

① 《美国报纸名录》序言,1879年。

报纸的另一个义务是，对所有广告商都应一视同仁，不应存歧视。这并非是说，特殊版面位置或特殊类型版面及长期合作的广告商不应该享有特殊的付费比率，否则就是不合伦理。它仅仅只是意味着，对于同一行业内的两个广告商，如果他们所用的广告版面大小以及登报的广告数量都相同，那么在广告的版面位置或者价格方面不应该存有偏见。这正是"一口价原则"（one-price principle）的运用和推广。这一原则曾把美国商业从讨价还价的局面中解脱出来。

广告的审查问题或许比出版业的其他商业伦理问题存在更多的争议。如同公布发行量需恪守诚信一样，广告也要讲求诚信，这体现了现代社会的进步。但是，广告商的表现远不如报纸出版商那么诚实。事实上，广告中诚信的不断提升，很大程度上是由报纸出版商促成的。广告的标准，尤其对那些大型广告商而言，从未像今天这么严格，而且在当下社会，美国的广告标准显然要高于其他国家。

但是，仍然有一些广告商故意不讲求诚信，还有一些广告商因为过于热情，或粗心，或员工的疏漏，导致广告中出现误导性信息。针对虚假广告，国家法律从未发挥过实质性作用。普通大众不懂得商品买卖中的玄机，要保护他们免受虚假广告的蒙骗，最有效的方法就是借助于刊登广告的各种报刊发行物的力量。尽管如此，不同的报纸在刊登广告的执行标准方面有天壤之别。一种极端的情况是，某些发行商对于那些通过邮件取得联系，抑或是连邮件往来都没有的广告商的广告，也愿意予以刊登。当然，这种现象现在已经较少出现。总体而言，在美国，目前具有这一倾向的臭名昭著的例子，正是那些外语报纸。[①] 而与此截然相反的情况是，有些人对于广告栏实行严格的审查，他们整批整批地拒绝特定类型的广告，例如专利药品、投机性股票等，并对所有的广告都予以细致审查。

某些情况下，报纸对广告真实性有特殊的担保。相较于杂志而言，报纸较少遇到这种情况，但是，一旦报纸作出了担保，便会比杂志期刊

---

① 具体统计资料可参见帕克的《移民报刊及其控制》，369—373页。

牢靠得多。担保广告真实性的实践起源于 1880 年的《农场杂志》(*The Farm Journal*, 费城)。在报纸领域，这种做法于 1914 年《纽约论坛报》(*The New York Tribune*) 发起激进运动之后，开始变得司空见惯。有时，我们会听闻由于财务原因而反对担保计划的言论，其实并无事实依据。一份报纸按照这一计划返钱给顾客，由此产生的开销不会超过广告收入的 0.2%。这一计划在一些小城镇和中型城市里都已得到成功实行。

人们通常认为，保证广告真实性的做法仅仅只是出于保护读者的利益而被保留下来。实则不然。诚信、细致的广告商有充分的理由相信，如果在同一份报纸中存在其他不讲信誉或者劣迹斑斑的商家的广告，那么，其自身广告的价值也会被削弱。一个特定的保证可以提升报纸中所有广告的价值。如果广告商提前知晓——并且也理应被告知——报纸上所有广告的类型，随后也插入自己的广告，他也就没什么正当的理由抱怨广告的质量。服务是商业之本，从这个立场出发，报纸发行商考虑到广告商的利益，对所登广告进行严格审查并予以保证，即便没有主动考虑公众的利益，这种做法也值得推荐。

一方面，如果即将刊登的某个广告和报纸上现有的其他广告是竞争对手，或者某个广告因某种原因不能为其他的广告商所接受，抑或是报纸出版商个人反感某个广告商，从伦理的角度讲，这些都不是报纸出版商拒绝刊登某则广告的理由。例如，某个出版商出售版面，给一个五金店打广告，而不允许其他五金店染指，这是不合理的行为。有些出版商拒绝为塞缪尔·霍普金斯·亚当斯 (Samuel Hopkins Adams) 的小说《号角》(*The Clarion*) 做广告，显然是因为其广告收入中有一大笔是来自亚当斯先生口诛笔伐的对象——专利药品生产商，这种行为无疑是不符合商业伦理准则的。出版商理应拒绝的是那些攻击竞争对手的广告商，倘若其广告中含有诽谤信息，为保险起见，出版商须严词拒绝。另一方面，如果在某个有争议的问题上存在对立的双方，出版商的报纸上刊载其中一方的所谓的宣传广告，而拒绝刊登另一方类似性质的广告，亦非合理行为。把东西卖给一切有需要的人，这种商人的伦理责任已经被写进许多地方的法律之中。类似的许多责任，尽管没有形成法律条文，但依然存在于报纸和广告领域。

虽然如前文所言，服务原则是现代商业之基，但报纸却没有义务给广告商提供任何特殊的服务，比如进行市场调查，或者帮助广告商在该报发行的区域推广其商品。尽管这些推广活动很适合报纸去做，但是，不像卖布匹的商家要为女性客户预留一个洗手间，报纸无须尽到类似的伦理责任。

此外，报纸不能因为某个广告不能盈利就拒绝刊登它，这种特殊伦理并不存在。以《芝加哥论坛报》（*The Chicago Tribune*）为代表的极少数报纸，采取了这种做法，目的是为了通过使广告盈利来提升整个广告行业。

出售广告版面是一种商业交易行为，广告商通过支付一笔合理的费用，换取在规定版面内向报纸读者传达信息的权利，现在人们对于这一点的认识仍然不够充分。出版商给广告商任何额外的版面或者特权，都是不合法、不道德的。

出版，作为一种商业行为，现在还处于起步阶段，其发展之初步履维艰的状态如今依然存在。须知，作为一种广告度量单位的玛瑙行①，是在三十多年前才开始采用的，即便在规模最大的报纸上亦是如此。因此，在公众（包括广告商）的心目中，这种收费标准与传统不同。此外，更糟糕的是，还有传统观念认为，广告是向入不敷出的印刷工人献爱心的一种形式，或者说是避免敲诈的一种做法，在报纸的专栏中寻求支持，或者顶多只是帮助报社维持其社会机构的形象。在一些小地方，民众对这些看法毫不掩饰，如出一辙的观念甚至在一些大都市也较为普遍。

与此相呼应的是，有些小城镇里的商人但凡在买入季度股票时，都会要求报纸为其作免费报道；或者有些银行家会要求报纸刊发他为某个

---

① 表示报纸上广告大小的度量单位，指报纸上一栏宽、1/14 英寸长的广告面积。——译者注

政治党派撰写的文章,并要求将其包装成报纸社论的模样。一家售卖纪念品的公司,在投放招聘销售员的广告时,写道:"如果我们把这个广告投放在贵报,希望贵报在地方新闻版块中发出公告,助我们一臂之力,努力争取到我们想招聘的人。"剧院和影院都坚持要求报纸为其免费宣传,以至于许多出版商会向他们收取更高的广告费。虽然高收费给所谓的免费发行留下余地,但是,这显然不是一种理想的商业行为,即使我们认为——也不见得总是正确的——读者能识别出免费的"宣传广告",并将其和真正的硬新闻区分开来。在大一些的城市,涉及大型商店或其老板的新闻,有时会在广告商的要求下被撤下来,有时甚至他们没有提出要求报社也会主动撤下来。现在,这种情况比想象中要少,且比以前也少多了。

十几年前,专利药品的广告商在与发行商的合同中增添了一个条款,即在任何限制专利药品销售的法律通过时,或者任何有损于药品制造商利益的事情出现在报纸上时,都可以撤销合同。为了适应广告商的需求,美国多地的报纸要求立法机关驳回公开专利药品配方的法案,并且,有一个州的报业协会因此通过一项决议,反对这一法案,还指派一个委员会专门与之斗争。[①]许多报纸读者在1904年和1905年就已知晓这一情况,并知道相关的争斗至今依然存在。

在这些问题上,报纸开始倾向于拒绝广告商的不合理要求,一部分原因是出于伦理的考量,确实应该如此;另一部分则是纯粹的商业原因。一方面,令广告商产生一种"能够操纵报纸"的错觉是一种糟糕的策略,因为满足了一个广告商的要求,会导致更多的广告商提出类似要求。另外,刊登对于某个广告商不利的内容,会有利于其竞争对手。从伦理的角度讲,满足了广告商要求的出版商,是在欺骗报纸读者,这一点后文将会详述,同时,这对那些只是以商业交易方式购买报纸版面的广告商而言并不公平。在这种情况下,无论享受了多少免费的宣传和服务,广告商都难以确定,自己花相同的钱是否能和其他广告商获取同样

---

① 亚当斯:《美国大骗局》,163—164页。

的收益和价值。

  称职、诚实的报纸从业者面对这种要求时，会礼貌而坚决地回绝，并解释报纸的立场，不断劝服广告商。当广告商提出撤回自己的广告时，报纸专栏公开对此做出解释，既符合伦理要求，又有所裨益。伊尼德（属于俄克拉何马州）的《鹰报》（*The Eagle*），是一份读者不足两万的小镇日报，早在1922年，当电影院撤回广告时，它就勇敢地做出应对。刊登在《鹰报》上的解释如下：

> 根据周一早上的声明，剧院所有者于周日在伊尼德召开会议，并达成从《鹰报》上撤掉所有广告赞助的决定。
>
> 这一决定的原因，据说是因为《鹰报》刊登了关于电影人士不道德行为的新闻，还刊登了当地周日要求关闭电影院的集会活动的新闻。另据剧院所有者称，在周日早晨的报纸上，有一篇关于著名喜剧演员"Fat Arbuckle"的新闻[①]，他们对此非常不满。
>
> 剧院所有者有权撤销他们对《鹰报》的赞助。然而，《鹰报》也从不允许电影经营者在公共道德问题上恣意妄为，更不允许他们对《鹰报》的新闻内容进行审查。
>
> 本地的影业，对广告商的权利存有误解，凡是会影响到电影和歌舞表演行业的《鹰报》报道，这些广告商都想干预和操控。从报纸撤回他们的赞助只怕是在所难免。

《鹰报》同时还发表一份罗列了剧院赞助商要求的详细清单：

> 压制那些关于抵制剧院周日开门的集会活动的报道。
> 不要刊登顾客针对舞台剧中侮辱性语言的投诉。

---

① Fat Arbuckle，与卓别林同时期的美国喜剧演员，原名 Roscoe Arbuckle，因眉毛较低、身材肥胖而获此艺名。1921年11月至1922年4月间，他被控强奸并杀害一位名为 Virginia Rappe 的女演员。——译者注

利用你们个人和报社与市长的关系来阻止电影立法。

压制为城市审查委员会发声的报道。

压制"家长—教师协会"因反对剧中不良信息而举行集会活动的消息。

拒绝所有可能不利于剧院的消息或言论。

支持被剧院所有者所认同的市政候选人。

撰写反对增发剧院执照的社论。

压制传染病的相关报道,以免影响剧院的票房。

印刷免费的头版文字广告,并且每一则广告都削减费用。

定期印刷一部分由电影明星的经纪人发出的宣传材料,这些材料即使无实际内容,依然可以在潜移默化中起到广告效果。

招揽其他商家一起"合作"广告,通过有特殊吸引力的免费广告为付费广告增值。

压制类似于顾客观影时被老鼠咬伤或皮衣被老鼠咬破的新闻。

在一个类似性质的事件中,广告商甚至对报纸提出更为琐碎的要求,《芝加哥论坛报》则巧妙地解决了这一问题。一位广告商的代理人,期望通过报纸施展政治影响力,于是给报纸编辑部写了一封信。这封信被刊登在报纸的通讯版块,同一版上还刊发了报纸编辑给这封信的回复。信件内容如下:

芝加哥,9月2日讯——过去的几年间,贵报和其他一些报纸一样,一直受到国家 Kellastone 公司的恩惠,也就是美国最大的菱镁矿商品制造商的广告津贴。

毫无疑问,贵报将此广告视为一笔非常理想的业务,因此,我们认为贵报一定想知道以下情况:华盛顿的委员会会议正在讨论菱镁矿商品关税规定。一旦规定实施,你们的这笔广告收入也将受到严重影响。

换句话说，一旦这项菱镁矿关税规定被正式采纳，国家Kellastone公司以及其他所有涉足国内菱镁矿和相关商品的公司，都会遭受严重损失。因为这些公司在价格方面将无法与国外的菱镁矿公司竞争，根据新的关税规定，国外的菱镁矿可以运送到美国的海港，其数量之多，美国本土公司无法企及。

如果你们了解关税会议的来龙去脉，肯定会意识到，依据原来的福德尼关税法案，外国进口的菱镁矿原石和煅烧过的菱镁矿分别被征收每吨10美元和15美元的关税。这一规定令美国的利益方十分满意，而且该法案已经议会通过，并被送往了参议院表决。

但与此同时，进口国外菱镁矿的商家以及外国出口商，也通过强大的影响力向参议院施压，诸多代表显示出了强大的干预能力，以至于参议院竟把原定的菱镁矿原石的关税削减至每吨6.25美元，煅烧的菱镁石的进口税率定为每吨12.50美元。

很快，美国生产商的代表找到了参议院委员会，通过事实和数据证明原定关税的合理性。但是，他们的申诉无效，关税较低的新法案已经被移交给会议委员会，等待最后的裁决。

现在，正如我们所指出的，如果新的关税规定通过了，就意味着美国本土的许多菱镁矿相关公司将倒闭或垮台。事实上，在这个行业内，来自国外的竞争始终是许多企业的心头之痛。这已经导致了美国许多菱镁矿开采作业不得不中止，因为矿老板们支付不起美国标准的薪资和运费，而该关税协定却成功地满足了国外产品的定价要求。

美国菱镁矿行业的员工在国内属于高收入人群，并且工作环境优越。但是，进入美国通商口岸的国外菱镁矿，却是最低廉劳动力的生产成果，而且工作环境恶劣。这些菱镁矿工人的工资仅相当于每天1美分的水平。

如果是来自国外资源的公平竞争，美国同行没有异议。他们非常愿意参与竞争，只是竞争需建立在公平公正的基础之上，而不是以牺牲美国国内产业为代价，这一行业代表着百万级的投资，还有雇用的成千上万薪资优渥的美国工人。

因此，美国菱镁矿生产商仅为寻求公平竞争的机会，以保生存，而贵报对美国国内思想能产生重大影响，在倡导公平竞争方面大有可为。我们写这封信，是为呼吁你们支持上述这些观点，表明你们的合作意愿，并且声援我们争取原福德尼关税法案所作的努力。

我们非常希望，贵报能代表我们的客户国家 Kellastone 公司，以及整个行业，给参议员和众议员写一封信，请求通过原法案。如此，即使这个行业还处于起步阶段，也会起到良好效果，维护我们双方的利益。

Simmonds and Simmonds，
佩尔·西蒙兹

以下是编辑的回复：

一份威胁和一份答复

来自广告代理公司 Simmonds and Simmonds 的一封长信，出现在今日的"人民之声"版块，以一种报纸或多或少都已习惯的方式，为自己说话。不过，其语气相比之下并不是那么官方客套，语句也较往常更为直接。事实上，这封信对我们构成了威胁，如果我们拒绝为其争取较高的保护性关税，他们将会撤销刊登在鄙报上的广告。

来信中说，鄙报一直受到这笔广告经费的"恩惠"。我们会坦诚相告，与其说《论坛报》将广告呈现在读者面前以获得广告费，是一种"受惠"，还不如说《论坛报》认可并刊登广告是一种"施惠"。广告，对于广告商而言才是一种"恩惠"。这是一种保证双方利益的普通商业命题。不过，这并非我们要

讨论的重点。

重点问题是，我们是否应该仅仅为了自身利益而在胁迫下"讨好"一个行业，而对国家的整体利益坐视不管。这其实是一种为达成关税计划而采取"互投赞成票"的政治交易，遗憾的是，我们并不支持这项计划。菱镁矿的关税到底应该是每吨 10 美元还是每吨 6.25 美元，较低的关税是否会让美国菱镁矿行业无利可图，外国公司的竞争到底会给整个国家带来积极的影响还是消极的影响……这些问题应该由合适的权威机构进行研究和解答。不过，它们应该是基于各自价值的优劣而被裁定，而不是依据短期的利益回报或产生的特殊影响而被评判。

一份受这类特殊影响而改变既定方针（或有此动机）的报纸，对于其支持者而言，所犯下的错误，就好比一位众议员为收受钱财而投票一样。鄙报的广告部门和编辑部门都不会以此方式行事。

就广告而言，报纸到底发挥着怎样的作用，我们很难给出最贴切的答案。

从伦理层面讲，事件中，报纸发行商的立场，能让广大的读者和广告商感到公平。或许，报纸没有义务针对此类争议事件发表看法或撰写文章。一个人对此的判断，还取决于他对新闻的定义。但在文章作者看来，这类事件亦是有价值的新闻。而且，这场探讨对广告商和读者都有教益，毕竟很多人从来没有遇到过这样的问题。

无论是否有公开的数据佐证，一个不争的事实就是，广告商几乎须臾不能离开为其谋利的广告媒介。1920 年夏天，当时的波士顿有数不清的报纸，一群鞋商却单单对《波士顿晚报》（*The Boston Evening Transcript*）发起抵制活动，因为该报曝光了有关制鞋市场的一些事实。这次抵制活动持续了七周才逐渐平息。很多时候，读者会告诉商家，如果其广告没有登在他们最喜欢的报纸上，他们便不再支持其商品。一旦报纸无法承受广告商的攻击，随之而来的将是遭受来自财务支援和编辑声誉方面的双重打击。

如果读者对某则广告持有疑义，报纸便拒绝刊登，不仅合乎情理，而且有时也是职业伦理所需，除非涉及严格的商业交易问题。这方面的一个例子可追溯到1897年。彼时，报纸的行业水准整体上还不能与今时今日相提并论。《纽约时报》（*The New York Times*）的埃尔默·戴维斯[①]（Elmer Davis）如是写道：

> 几个月后，市政府的所有常规广告都出人意料地交给了《时报》（*The Times*）（《纽约时报》的简称）。这相当于每年大约150,000美元的广告费用，对于那个时期的《时报》而言，这是一笔相当可观的收入。有一位绅士，既是出版商的朋友，也是坦慕尼派（译者注：纽约市彼时的当权派）领导的朋友，曾向《时报》管理部门保证，这次的广告交易没有任何附加条件。坦慕尼派并不期望（也不喜欢）《时报》因此在某种层面上受到影响。这也可以理解为，广告资源的分配不是为了、也不会消除《时报》对当地政治体系中坦慕尼派的敌意。根据这位绅士的说法，获得这笔意外之财的唯一原因，就是因为坦慕尼派的领导坚信，对于民主党的一般利益而言，纽约城有一家保守的民主党派报纸，并不是一桩坏事。而该报对坦慕尼派的倾向和态度，则不在他们的考虑范围之列。
>
> 《时报》的发行商相信这位绅士做出的保证，并且认为没有必要去质疑坦慕尼派领导的诚意。但是，不管其用意是否高尚，他们的提议还是不能被接受。因为根据人性的特点，我们可以预料到，《时报》有理由批判坦慕尼派时，肯定会发生这样的情况（不久之后就曝光其庇护赌场的贪污行径），《时报》的工作人员即便不是有意的，潜意识中也会受到这150,000美元的影响。而到那时，报纸或许已经习惯了这笔资金带来的更

[①] 《〈纽约时报〉的历史》，221—223页。

大发展，并且不愿舍弃。此外，与竞争对手相比，《时报》的发行量还远远落后。如果这笔巨额费用像天上掉馅饼一般，突然落到当时纽约的晨报系列中发行量最小的报纸头上，那么，无论该组织或报纸管理部门的动机多么纯良，所有人都会认为，坦慕尼派买下了《时报》。在这种情况下，这件事的影响会和其本质一样恶劣。从任何角度分析，《时报》都不该接受这笔金钱的馈赠。

报纸评论家有时会认为，自由派和激进派高级报纸的广告营收相对较少，是因为广告商自身对自由派和激进派观点的反对。他们认为，保守派报纸得到广告，是因为保守派遵从广告商的观点。于是，他们得出这么一个结论：在出版业，营收上的成功，归功于屈从广告商的要求。

事实上，问题并没那么复杂。广告媒介成功的因素众多，不只是取决于读者的购买力，还取决于其购买意向。在广告商看来，许多激进刊物的读者并不具有足够的购买力，因而刊物难以收取较高的广告费率。虽然自由派报刊的读者具有较强的购买力，广告商却认为，除了购买某些特定的商品，比如书籍之外，这些读者的购买意向会因为报纸内容而大打折扣。换句话说，读者的情绪并不利于他们购买商品。广告商感兴趣的是金钱回报，而非抽象的方针政策等。激进或自由派刊物很少受到广告商中保守派方针政策的影响，此类报刊通常不依赖于广告的支持。

总之，我们可以推断，报纸虽无法全然摆脱广告的操控，却倾向于争取更多的自由，尤其是那些在财务上较为稳定，并且毫不掩饰自身处境的报纸。整个过程中，读者都扮演了重要角色，他们能够辨别是非正义。遇到纷争时，报纸如果能在广告商面前明辨是非，事情的结局就鲜有争议。和其他行业一样，出版业若要保持一份伦理操守，不仅需要较高的从业准则，更需要将其应用于实践。

补充阅读

亚当斯：《号角》。

亚当斯：《美国大骗局》，133—185页。

罗威尔：《美国报纸名录》，1879年，序言。

发行审计局：《版面的科学选择》，70—90页。

帕克：《移民报刊及其控制》，359—411页。

戴维斯：《〈纽约时报〉的历史》，219—223页，315—322页。

摩西：《庸人阅读须知》。(《纽约晚报》小册子)

《如何建立自信》。(《农场杂志》(费城)小册子)

《如何开展工作》。(《纽约论坛报》小册子)

路易斯，保证广告，见于《华盛顿大学的公告栏》中，总集 No. 101，46—51页。

鲍威尔：《扩大发行量》，密苏里大学公告，第15卷，第6期，10—23页。

史密斯：《广告》，见《美国文明》，381—395页。

第二章　作为一种职业的新闻

　　报纸从业者与广大读者之间存在一种共识,即新闻业不只是出版生意这么简单,它不仅仅是销售一种商品。自报纸诞生伊始,或者说,自报纸的前身——新闻书(newsbooks)和类似出版物问世以后,报纸的从业人员,以及社会其他阶层的人们,也都或多或少意识到这一点。在那个无需出版执照或者办理执照的要求不那么严格的年代,管理新闻界的出版特许法令就出台了。这表明新闻一直被视为拥有某种公共或准公共的功能。

　　后来,有少数人仅把报纸出版当作一门生意看待,因为他们并不了解其历史或公认的功能。这些人的一个共同点是,首先在其他行业发展,然后转行做新闻,这与他们转行卖干货、不动产,或其他任何商业性质很强的职业没什么两样。不过,尽管其数量在逐渐增多,相对而言这类人仍是少数。一般而言,他们只在大型都市日报工作,而这类报纸所需的雄厚资本,除了资本家以外,其他人都无力担负。相对较大的发行量以及在人口密集的区域发行,使得这些报纸拥有了相当大的影响力,但是,这些大型日报在美国众多的新闻报纸中仍然只占少数。

　　对于占绝大部分的小型报纸,其所有者要么是专业的新闻从业者,要么是印刷从业人员。这两类人都秉持着一种担负公共责任以及为公众服务的传统理念。同样的,大型日报采编岗位上的工作人员也强烈地认为,报社并不只是一个商业化的企业,而是一个准公共机构。政府赋予报纸和期刊较便宜的二等邮资(The second class mail rates),体现了一种普遍观念,即,报纸是为了服务公众而存在。几年前,这一费率被上调,毫无疑问,一部分原因是,公众觉得报纸不能做到这一点。这无疑是一种错觉。当下报纸为公共利益做出的服务,比二十年前、五十年前甚至一百年前要好得多。但是,公众的良知以及对报纸的要求在迅速提升,而报纸公共服务的提升却相对迟缓。

事实上,杂志、书籍和公共演说中所有关于报纸的讨论,都是基于这一假设,即报纸的存在是为了满足准公共性质的功能。对报业的监管比对其他任何行业的管理都影响深远,这种预判亦是基于这一前提。

当我们探讨人们期望报纸能够实现哪些特定的公共或准公共功能时,观点则见仁见智。一些人要求报纸无所畏惧或毫无偏袒地陈述所有事实;而另外一些人则要求报纸隐去所有可能产生诱导作用的犯罪行为,隐去可能引诱精神病人的反常行为,或隐去向孩子展示错误行为的新闻。有评论者指出,报纸的职责是为支持的自由派或激进派观点发表社论,也有人认为,报纸的责任是支持国家安全联盟及其他类似组织对宪法做出的阐释。还有人想利用报纸出售鱼、煤或其他东西,只是为了打破当地的垄断。当然,也有人想让报纸专注于挑选好人一起工作,而把坏人挡在门外。

这些关于报纸应承载何种公共功能的异议,不能说全部,但在大体上,是由于思想不一致造成的。直到最近几年,才有人意识到报道事实的重要性,却仍然只是少数。在古典时代,即使证据的标准已经被制定出来,人们仍然没有办法确认证据的可信度。例如,有谁质疑过希罗多德[①]?或者,有谁挑战过盖乌斯·尤利乌斯·恺撒[②]?尽管后者习惯于

---

① 希罗多德(Herodotus,约公元前480年—前425年),古希腊历史学家,史学名著《历史》一书的作者,西方文学的奠基人之一。——译者注
② 即恺撒大帝(公元前102年7月12日—公元前44年3月15日),罗马共和国(今地中海沿岸等地区)末期杰出的军事统帅、政治家。——译者注

一字一顿地表达意见，似乎是其诚信的有力证明。事实上，只有在某些精密的学科中，例如几何学，才会尝试建立一种无可争辩的事实。而其他的学科，建立的都是一套抽象的哲学体系。这点直到最近仍影响着我们每一个人的思想，在中世纪，它被阐述为"深刻的、荒谬的极端"。基于观察和事实，我们有可能构想出一个形而上学体系，但这样的体系从不存在。形而上学体系通常是建立在传统、假想的上帝箴言、民间信仰的基础之上，或者完全出自一些理论思想家的精打细算。依据这些体系，人类通过直接或间接由造物者植入其体内的一些神秘能力，触及真理或是美德。圣·保罗①依据他的构想对耶稣的神力深信不疑。在托马斯·杰斐逊②看来，农民在公共事务方面是睿智的，因为上帝暗中赋予了他们政治智慧。

随着人类发现和实证能力的显著提升，以及科学研究方法的不断发展，谨慎的思想家们已经意识到，在生活中，经过证实的事实是得出可靠结论的唯一确凿路径。科学研究中所采用的方法，同样适用于经济学、社会学、政治学、日常对话以及报纸新闻中可能涉及的各个学科的研究，这一点已经成为人们的共识。据此可以推断，没有经过事实调查而得出的结论，错误的可能性为 50%，而在现实生活中，这个概率可能会更高，因为现实生活中存在许多本身就不合理的种族偏见和禁忌，它们会扭曲、粉饰一些事实。

只有少数人通过实践才意识到注重事实的重要性，并将其应用于生活中的其他问题。另外一小部分人在理论层面上支持注重事实，而在生活实践中，只有面对那些没有固定立场的问题时，他们才会实践这一理念。而绝大多数人根本没有意识到这一点，他们执着于固有的观念和偏见，就像几个世纪以前他们的祖先一样。

---

① 圣·保罗，原名扫禄·大数（公元约 5 年－67 年），早期基督教领袖之一，其著作构成《圣经·新约》的重要组成部分。——译者注
② 托马斯·杰斐逊（Thomas Jefferson，1743 年－1826 年），美利坚合众国第三任总统（1801 年—1809 年），同时也是《美国独立宣言》主要起草人，美国开国元勋中最具影响力人物之一。——译者注

因此，过去人们忽视了许多事实，前面提及的第二类少数群体对这些事实所表现出的态度，与 60 年前的人们无异，从进化论的角度看，这种无知的循环如今依然存在。反过来，这仅仅只是培根、伽利略和其他科学家们经历的一种重现，当时，这些科学家用事实挑战同辈人的固有观念。那些理应聪慧的资本家、社会学家、单一税制主张者（single-taxer），可能会在理论上承认事实的重要性，却谴责所有不符合其利益的事实，并将之贴上"不道德的""破坏性的""不受欢迎的"或是"不可信的"标签。

当然，芸芸众生依然不够智慧。在美国，大众对一些观念坚信不疑，譬如美国的绝对优越，法国人的风流倜傥，俄国人的野蛮暴戾，以及其他一些沾沾自喜的臆想。在其他国家，大众的臆想也很奇特，但由于文化普及率较低，他们并没有清晰地表达出来。

特罗特①对于这一情况的表述既合理又充分：

> 对于真正感兴趣的事情，人们无法接受结论的不确定性，科学领域更是如此。人们太急于去确认，以至于没时间去了解。所以，在科学领域，数学是第一个出现的，然后是天文学，接着是物理学、化学、生物、心理学、社会学。但是，新的领域总是排斥新的方法，并且，人们仍然不承认社会学是一门科学。如今，国防、政治、宗教领域的事情对于人类知识而言仍然非常重要，并且依然存在亟待弄清的问题。也就是说，对于这些问题，我们习惯于偏好本能的信仰，原因是目前的知识水平还不足以使我们重视预测的能力。
>
> 另外一个直观事实是，人类的大部分观念是不理性的，这种不理性程度之深，无需额外审视，常识便足以证实。如果我们审视一个普通人的思维构成，我们会发现，它是由很多关于大量极其复杂事物的精确判断组成的。对于宇宙的起源和性

---

① 即威尔弗雷德·特罗特，《和平与战争时期的群体本能》一书的作者。

质，以及那些说得出意义的事物，他会有相当明确的观点。至于死后会发生什么，行为的基础是什么以及应该是什么等问题，他都有自己的结论。他也知道应该如何治理国家，为什么这条立法是好的而那条是不好的。关于陆军和海军的战略、税收原则、酒精和疫苗的使用、流行性感冒的诊治、狂犬病的预防、市政交易、希腊语的教学方法以及什么是艺术中允许的、什么是文学中令人满意的、什么是科学领域里有希望的……他都持有明确的观点。

这些观点大部分都没有合理的根基，因为其中许多是专家都承认还有待解决的难题，而对于其余的那些，我们很清楚，没有哪个普通人所受的训练和经历的事情让他有能力提出任何见地。大量理性方法的运用已经证实，对于大多数的这些问题及其悬而未决的判断，普通人能有的仅是一种态度。

依据上述观点，我们必须把这种对不理性观点的全盘接受看作是一种正常现象。影响它的机制需要一些考察，因为，不可否认的是，事实在意见形成中所发挥的作用，与当今盛行的看法有很大的冲突。

一开始就很清楚的是，一些拥护者会认为，这些观点始终都是合理的，并一直为之辩护，而持对立观点的人的立场显然是不合理的。宗教人士批评无神论者肤浅而荒谬，而无神论者对宗教人士也有类似的指责。对于保守党而言，自由党最令人吃惊的地方是，他们无法明白并接受解决公共问题的唯一可行办法。考察揭示的事实是，区别并不在于简单机械的逻辑谬误，因为即使对政客们而言，这也很容易避免，并且我们没有理由认为，在这样的争论中，某一党派会比另一方更没有逻辑。相反，区别源自一种认为对方持敌对态度的基础假设，而这些假设来自群体意见。对自由党而言，一些基本概念已经成为一种直觉性的真相，已经成了"一个超前的集合体"，因为周遭充斥着大量的这种意见。关于无神论者、基督徒和保守党的看法,也可以做出类似解释。要记住,最终,各方都坚信其立场合理无瑕,那些在对手看来非常明显的谬误,他们完全察觉不出。对于对手而言,他们的一系列假设并不被群体意见所认可。①

政治争议一次又一次地揭示出,人们习惯于罔顾事实的重要性,即使是涉及重大事件亦是如此。这一点在探讨新闻界的功能时显得尤为重要,因为在很大程度上,报纸要和那些充满了政治意味的事务打交道。此外,一般来说,日报的主要受众是普罗大众,而政客相对而言拥有更高的受教育程度,广大读者对于事实的态度,不会比参议员、众议员或其他有志于参与公共事务的学生的态度好到哪儿去。

最近,在国会发生的一件事情上,政客的态度得到了充分的体现,沃尔特·李普曼②转述如下:

> 在1919年9月29日的早餐上,一些参议员在《华盛顿邮报》上读到一则关于美军登陆达尔马提亚海岸的新闻。新闻如是说:
> ### 事实已得到确认
> 以下这些重要的事实已经得到确认:在亚得里亚海指挥美国海军部队的海军少将安德鲁斯,接到了英国战争委员会和海军少将克内普斯(Knapps)从伦敦发来的命令。该命令的发布没有经由美国海军同意或是反对……
> ### 丹尼尔斯并不知情
> "丹尼尔斯先生自认为对作战军队拥有唯一控制权,但是,

---

① 威尔弗雷德·特罗特. 和平与战争时期的群体本能 [M]. 伦敦:麦克米伦出版社,1917:35—37.
② 沃尔特·李普曼(Walter Lippmann,1889年—1974年),美国著名政论家、专栏作家,传播史上具有重要影响的学者之一,在宣传分析和舆论研究方面享有很高声誉。其《舆论学》被公认为传播领域的奠基之作。

他收到电报时,上面却显示军队在他毫不知情的情况下参与了海上战争。诚然,此时丹尼尔斯处境非常尴尬。这让人充分意识到,英国海军可能希望下令,让海军少将安德鲁斯代表大英帝国及其盟友来展开行动,因为在当前的情况下,如果邓南遮(D'Annunzio)的追随者受到牵制,就需要牺牲部分国家(的利益)。

"这让人进一步意识到,在新的国际同盟计划中,外国人在紧急情况下可以直接指挥美国海军力量,而不管美国海军司令部是否同意……"等(斜体为作者所添加)。

"第一个发表意见的参议员是宾夕法尼亚州的诺克斯(Knox)先生。他愤怒地要求调查。当接下来康涅狄格州的布兰德基(Brandegee)先生发言时,愤怒已经导致了盲从。诺克斯先生愤怒地希望知道这份报告是否属实,而半分钟后布兰德基议员却想知道如果海军灭亡之后会发生什么。诺克斯议员对这个问题很感兴趣,以至于忘记了自己的询问和期盼的答复。如果这支美国海军失败,势必会引发战争。这时,辩论继续,语气仍然是假定性的。伊利诺伊州的议员麦考密克(McCormick)先生提醒参议员们,威尔逊政府倾向于发动小规模未经允许的战争。他重复了西奥多·罗斯福对'缔结和平'论调的讽刺。布兰德基议员提醒道,海军是在'位于某处的最高委员会的命令下'行事的,但他记不起那个组织里谁是代表美国的。美国宪法中没有关于'最高委员会'的表述。因此,印第安纳州的议员纽恩(New)提议调查到底有没有。"

直到这时,参议员们还没意识到他们在讨论一个流言。如果是作为律师,他们还会记得证据的某些形式。但是,作为血气方刚的男人,他们已经表现出全部的愤怒。美国海军在没有经过国会同意的情况下被外国政府命令参加战争,他们的愤怒可想而知。从感情上来说,他们想要去"相信它",因为他们是反对国际同盟的共和党人。这激起了民主党领袖、内布拉斯加州的希契科克（Hitchcock）先生的不满。他为"最高委员会"辩护，认为它是按照战时权力在行事。而正是由于共和党人的拖延才导致和平迟迟没有到来，因此，这个行动是必要且合法的。现在，双方都假定报告的内容是真实的，并且假定他们的结论就是其党派的结论。然而，这个离奇的假定恰恰还处于决心调查该假定是否属实的争论之中。这说明，即便是训练有素的律师们也很难在弄清事实之前保持克制，而不妄加回应。于是争论一触即发，因为他们把想象当作事实。事实上，他们太需要这种想象了。

几天后，一份官方报告表明，海军并没有应英国政府或最高委员会的命令登陆。他们没有和意大利人打仗。他们是应意大利政府的请求而登陆的，为的是保护意大利人。并且，美国指挥官已经受到意大利当局的正式感谢。美国海军没有和意大利开战。他们依据一条现存的国际准则做出决定，而该准则与国际同盟一点关系也没有。

行动的现场位于亚得里亚海沿岸。在华盛顿的参议员们的脑海中，行动在该事件中可能带有欺骗的意味，他们似乎看到了一个完全不关心亚得里亚海只关心如何挫败联盟的人。针对这幅脑海中的画面，参议员们从强化各党派对联盟态度的分歧角度做出了回应。①

关于报纸是否具有准公共功能的观点，在很大程度上，是心理状态有意或无意地导致了意见的分歧。有一些政治家，希望报纸为其党派观点或利益服务。也有一些牧师和其他人，认为报纸应当秉持诸如维护道德等他们认可的理念，方才算得上"公正"。还有其他数不清的团体有着类似的观点。他们认为，报纸首先是"舆论的铸造者"，并且，铸造的过程不一定必须基于调查证实了的确切事实，而是基于未经调查的假

---

① 沃尔特·李普曼：《舆论学》，17—20页，Harcourt, Brace & Co. 授权出版。

定事实，并包含着伦理、政治和其他同样未经任何严格检验的教义层面的训导。

纽约著名牧师戴维·詹姆斯·伯勒尔（Rev. David James Burrell）在最近的一次布道中，阐述了他的观点，其中使用了这样的比喻："有好消息从远方传来，就如同把凉水送给口渴的灵魂。"演讲中，伯勒尔博士说道：

> 我们希望有一份报纸将刊登新闻。刊登所有新闻？很难……
>
> 我们希望有一份报纸不仅仅反映公众舆论，而且能够塑造舆论，塑造正确的舆论。没有人质疑新闻的力量。塔尔梅奇（Talmadge）博士将编辑定义为"用笔尖输出思想并将之投掷到地球最远方的人"，这并没有夸大。但是，这种表达却不完整，除非配合约翰·福斯特的话，"最后一个原子的力量是责任"。一位才思敏捷的作家手中拉弯的弓，不是射出安慰的信息，就是射出穿透围城墙壁的毒箭……
>
> 一份基督教的报纸吗？嗯，为什么不呢？如果我将一把铁粉抛到空中，它们落下时就像蓟绒一样无害，但若将铁粉填进炮弹，它们足以让军舰沉没。在社区中，有很多基督徒希望获得对信仰的某种尊重；但是，千万不要企盼从作家手里获得这种尊重，因为他们对法治和一般道德吹毛求疵，却披着救世主的外衣坐在十字架下占卜吉凶。期待这样的人为了取得进步的潜在力量而作理性演讲不过是种奢侈。对我们来说，耶稣的到来是"宇宙万物中至神至圣的事件"；而对他们来说，却什么都不是。如果今天耶稣出现在天空的云彩间，明天的晨报将会是什么样的呢？司空见惯的头条又将去哪儿呢？①

---

① 《马布尔学院讲坛》，第32卷，第13期，第2页和第8页。

这一立场甚至超越了公元 4 世纪圣·安布罗斯（St. Ambrose）①的看法，他认为"讨论地球的本质和位置，并不能让我们期待的生活快快到来。知道圣经上说'耶稣在地球上被绞死'就足够了。"②后一作者的进步仅在于没有直截了当地否认事实的重要性。

直到最近，这种观点在报纸中还相当普遍。在美国及其他国家的早期报纸中，事实总是带着观点的色彩。报道客观事实的信条虽然得到了一些口头上的支持，却常常又在报纸的实践或编辑的表达中打了折扣。

与提及的批评家相反的另一个极端例子是，有些支持"报纸应当是客观事实的唯一传播者"的人，甚至到了要求省略所有社论、特写及其他非严格意义新闻的程度。当然，新闻工作者极少持这种观点，他们知道公众不仅需要特写，也需要重要事实；他们也知道，一份报刊少了公众支持便不能运营下去。但是，新闻工作者至少在理论上要坚持这样的信条：传播客观事实即便不是报刊的唯一功能，却也是一切的根基，并且其他可能的功能都服从于此。

这种信条是基于民选政府的现代理论。正如前文指出的那样，托马斯·杰斐逊注意到民主在农村地区运行效果最好。他本性厌恶城市，认为民主在农村社区的成功是因为造物主给农村人植入了优良品质。现在，我们知道，杰斐逊的观察是正确的，结论却是错误的。民主通常在农村或小城镇社区中运行较好，因为个体投票者对当地状况和当地名人较为熟悉，这些情况在城镇会议、学校会议及其他人人能发声的集会上被详细地讨论过。人们获取了客观事实，并在很大程度上以此为基础得出自己的结论，从而产生自己的投票。

随着更多的人口迁入城市，以及政府的问题变得愈加复杂，选民越来越难以通过个人观察和调查获取客观事实，以指导投票。人们对事实的依赖，须依赖于新闻界，因为它可能是唯一令人满意的以发掘事实为

---

① 圣·安布罗斯（公元 340 年－397 年），罗马圣人，古代基督教拉丁教父，米兰大主教。出生于罗马皇帝近卫队队长家庭，在罗马成长。约 370 年任列古里亚和以米里亚的总督。四年后，他战胜一名阿利乌斯派的候选人，成为米兰市的主教。——译者注
② 《论〈创世六日〉》，见米恩的《父亲》一书，第 14 卷。

目的的机构。成功的民选政府依赖于客观事实，因而也依赖于新闻界。此外，其他所有非严格意义上的大众问题，都有同样的双重依赖性。因此，我们得出一个不容否认的结论，报纸的基本功能是传播公众关心问题的客观事实。

尽管不被多数人所接受，但报纸的这一理念正在迅速积聚力量。在大众眼中，这是一个无意识的标准，然而也是一个实际标准。诸如"你不能相信报纸文章""这只是个新闻故事"此类话语的频率，见证了一个公共理念的发展，即报纸应当呈现事实，虽然它同时也见证了许多违反这一理念的现存信念。

补充阅读

特罗特：《和平与战争时期的群体本能》，1－41 页。

鲁滨逊：《决策中的思维》，14－48 页。

埃德曼：《人类特征》，368－410 页。

伯勒尔：《要犯：一份报纸》，《马布尔学院讲坛》，第 32 卷.

李普曼：《舆论学》，1－32 页，253－314 页。

李普曼：《自由与新闻》。

第三章　公众对报纸的指控

正如前文所述，公众作为一个整体，有意识或无意识地认为报纸首先应充当客观事实传播者的角色，并且这种事实需具有公共意义。公众是否真正欢迎报纸完全履行这项职能，则是另外一个问题，后文将重点讨论。

显而易见的是，公众认为媒体没能履行该职能。他们指控报纸没有告知真相，或者更确切地说，报纸没有以公正的方式刊发客观事实。更细致的观察家，包括作家和演说家，指控报纸传播客观事实时具有某种特定的不足之处。

最主要的一项指控是报纸虚构新闻。一个公认的事实，当公众看到社会系统中任何一个子部分变糟时，他们就会将问题归咎于过去的某种状况。该项指控便就是这一事实的明证。虚构新闻曾一度成为惯例。在《新闻的主要内容》(The Staple of News) 一书中，本·琼森 (Ben Jonson) 指控 17 世纪公然造假的记者。《纽约太阳报》(The New York Sun) 的市场影响力开始于 1835 年著名的月球骗局 (Moon Hoax)。骗局由理查德·亚当斯·洛克 (Richard Adams Locke) 一手炮制，却声称是著名科学家约翰·赫歇尔爵士 (Sir John Herschel) 的重大天文发现。而《太阳报》坚称，这个假新闻"没伤害任何人"，埃德加·爱伦·坡 (Edgar

Allan Poe)① 写道:"从骗局的新纪元开始,《太阳报》闪烁着耀眼的光芒。它成功地在全国范围内建立起坚定的'便士体系',(通过《太阳报》)我们感谢天才的洛克先生,他迈出了人类发展史上最重要的一步。"

当该骗局家喻户晓时,洛克不仅没有被报纸解职,反而承担了更多职责,后来成为《布鲁克林之鹰》(*The Brooklyn Eagle*)的编辑。直到1917年,《太阳报》出身的历史学家弗兰克·M·奥布莱恩(Frank M. O'Brien)还在著作中声称这是个"华丽的"骗局。②

1844年,"中伤性谣言"一词因虚构事件被添加至美国语言中。一位作者借名为罗尔贝克(Roorback)的旅行者之口,描述了一段奴隶制的恐怖事件,其中包含关于时任总统候选人詹姆斯·K·波尔克(James K. Polk)给43个奴隶打上其姓氏首字母烙印的虚假陈述。文章刊发在纽约的一些全国性期刊上,后被《阿尔巴尼看守人报》(*The Albany Argus*)揭开真相,变成一种"中伤性谣言",使得波尔克的政敌信誉扫地,并帮助波尔克成功当选总统③。

1864年,两个年轻记者伪造了一个声称是亚伯拉罕·林肯(Abraham Lincoln)草拟的公告,并成功地在两份报纸上发表,企图操纵股票市场。结果,其报社被临时关停,但是,当政府确信这不能责怪报社时,便允许报社重新营业。

1899年夏季发生了一个臭名昭著的伪造案例。据某报载,当地突然出现了大量的广为人知的昆虫,其中包括最著名的吸血锥鼻虫,许多人还遭到了叮咬。当事实尚不确凿时,该报就推出了一组"'接吻虫'致人伤亡"的误导性报道,称伤亡的原因只是遭到蚊子或马蝇的叮咬。当天的新闻通过散播无耻的谎言,在美国的许多城镇都造成了恐慌,从而

---

① 译者注:埃德加·爱伦·坡(Edgar Allan Poe)(1809年—1849年),十九世纪美国诗人、小说家和文学评论家,美国浪漫主义思潮时期的重要成员。在世时长期担任报刊编辑工作。
② 关于骗局的更多细节,参见奥布莱恩《〈太阳报〉的故事》一书,64—102页。
③ 美国第11任总统。

在情绪激动的人群中形成了真正的疾病。①

最近,在哈里·K·肖(Harry K. Thaw)②因精神疾病住院时,记者关于他和其他病友之间的访谈纯属虚构。另一则虚假新闻讲述了肖是如何被任命为马塔瓦医院养鸡场的负责人的,还引述了他经营养鸡场的法则。关于肖的大量其他报道同样毫无依据。就在最近,那些对明眼慧心的读者而言明显是假新闻的可笑报道,从纽约和新泽西的小城镇传出,之后满天飞。记者坚称这些报道并没有欺骗公众,只是显得太过荒谬而不被公众所接受。但是,一些读者可能误认为这些假新闻是事实,另一些读者则会因此对新闻机构产生偏见。

19世纪末,随着黄色新闻的发展,报纸开始在头条新闻中作歪曲报道。新闻故事本身确实存在,但一则两到三人轻微受伤的火灾新闻见报后,标题就变成了多人死亡。这样做,无疑是为了促进街头的销量。

在这一时期,报纸还产生了虚假配图的假新闻。耸人听闻的新闻往往需要图片,但图片并不像今日这般容易获得。如果一位重要人物去世,但报社缺乏图片,常见的做法是从档案中选取一位与去世要人相似的照片,作为逝者的肖像印行。某些情况下,想象的画作和半色调的图纸都会被当作真实的照片发行。

直到1903年,《芝加哥记录先驱报》(*The Chicago Record-Herald*)的文学编辑埃德温·L·舒曼(Edwin L. Shuman)解释了新闻从业者对事实的态度:

> 报社经常收到缺乏必要细节支撑的重要新闻。闭门造车以补充缺失材料就变得十分必要。有时,敏锐的报纸办公室所保存的"资料档案"或传记以及讣告材料,可以用作新闻的补充材料;有时,参考书籍能提供大部分所需信息。但是,在许多

---

① 关于实际情况的讨论,参见如下新闻报道,L. O. 霍华德. 1899年夏季"接吻虫"开始流行[J]. 美国农业部昆虫学系,公告22,新系列:24—30;也见L. O. 霍华德. 蜘蛛叮咬与"接吻虫"[J]. 大众科学月刊(56):31—42。
② Harry K. Thaw,匹兹堡富商之子,从小患有严重精神障碍。——译者注

情况下，凭记忆或想象等意识活动补充缺失材料，成为记者和编辑的职责。只要记者的想象针对的是非重要细节，这种方法似乎是被允许的。

这种许可在报道事件的写作中必不可少，一旦见报，这些事件就会成为新的材料，但是，这点必须在发生前就加以说明。很久以前，抢发最新消息的激烈竞争促使编辑在这类新闻中发挥"新闻工作者的想象力"。以这种方式编辑的新闻事件，其数量之多，可能会令普通读者大吃一惊，晚报新闻尤其如此。这一事实可以解释新闻误差产生的原因，但是，令人不解的是，从整体上看，新闻足以像事件本身一样准确。这一行为的伦理问题有待读者去评判。我只是记录这一事实，而每一种乐于探索的报纸某种程度上都有此做法。①

如今，以上这种做法在大部分报纸中都不会出现。即便有，也可能是零星的。通常，不诚实的记者或通讯员所犯的错误在于，他们要么自发为之，要么因为编辑明示或暗示自己只是个下属，就不管新闻特征而肆意抄写。某些摄影人员也习惯了造假。如果没有构成实际的犯罪，报纸只需承担从不可靠信源购买照片带来的风险。

此外，报纸偶尔会使用明显被处理过的照片，这种行为相当于虚构新闻。一家耸人听闻的都市日报，刊登了墨西哥儿童站在水中的图片，以证明他们为躲避强盗的侵扰而沦为难民。而先前刊登出来的同一幅图片仅仅表现的是一群墨西哥儿童在洗澡。值得注意的是，这份报纸曾努力劝说美国向墨西哥开战。

不去评判事件的伦理问题，报纸的这类做法必定会让读者疏远，并让他们相信新闻界不够诚实。《纽约世界报》（*The New York World*）误把泰恩河畔纽卡斯尔的图片当作哈特尔浦刊发后，一位读者写信说明他认出这幅图片，并附加了下面一段话：

---

① 《应用新闻学》，103—104 页。

你不可能**一直**愚弄**所有**民众。当你手边恰巧没有图片匹配新闻稿件时,千万不要给读者一些与之相似的东西。"和原图一样好,他们不会看出有任何差异",是对报纸鼓吹的公平竞争不利的一种策略。要知道,我已经追随贵报很多年。

这个案例的最后,报纸侥幸地让这位读者相信其错误完全是无心之举。①

即使记者知道报纸反对编造新闻,但依然存在一些引诱他们以身犯险的因素。记者唯一能遵从的原则是:虚假新闻皆有害。这是唯一适合于现状的表述。拉尔夫·普利策(Ralph Pulitzer)解释了所谓的"无害虚假"给社会造成的巨大伤害。他的《纽约世界报》是逐步朝着准确和公平竞争迈进的先锋:

造假的哲学值得警惕。造假的趋势通常始于滑稽的琐碎新闻,作者采用夸张手法,利用想象力加以编造,加入一些滑稽的情景。你不能指责这则新闻完全错误,因为它如实地呈现了事实,并坦白有编造之处,没人会因此上当受骗。

唯一的错误在于,它迈出了糟糕的第一步。对作者而言,为第一个这类报道庆幸将可能下一次写出同样滑稽的报道,虽然坦承其中存在细节的编造和滑稽的幻想,但是新闻中的事实和虚构却紧密结合在一起,导致了读者分不清孰是孰非。这样的报道混淆了愉悦身心和胡作非为的界限。但是,他们坚称新闻"没给任何人带来伤害"并且极其有趣,而幽默感很强的总编辑急切地想出版新颖的报纸,于是报纸慢慢走上这条不归路。

现在,作者的下一部作品是写出幽默细节构成的新闻。剔除少量事实,新闻变成幽默小说,读者自然不买账。对此,作者会反问:"这样的故事并没有伤害到任何人啊?"一开始,你

---

① 事件讨论参见《〈世界报〉准确与公平竞争局双年度报告》,1915年,16—17页。

不能明确指出新闻伤害到了某人。但经过短暂的思考后，你会发现，即便没有伤害到读者，却伤害到了其他人和一个机构。这样做伤害到了写新闻的记者、新闻编辑、文案编辑、新闻主编以及报纸本身，他们判断力的准确性和灵敏度不知不觉地变迟钝，进而报纸也受到了损害。对记者而言，以同样的方式采写重要人物和重要事件的重要报道的时机已经成熟，无需再靠想象力来增强幽默感，我们会发现，其想象力还增强了悲剧效果、加深了痛苦感、强化了戏剧性。在某些报纸上，你仍会发现类似这些新闻"没有伤害任何人"的借口。制造这个借口的人似乎并没有意识到，公众使用"新闻故事"一词所带来的伤害，它本应是"事实"的同义词，却变成了"谎言"的委婉表达。

这种"虚假进步"逐步推进，从严肃事实背景点缀谎言，到毫无事实根据地编织故事，而人物角色却使用真实姓名。与此相类似的是讽刺性的"噱头"，几乎没有报纸鼓励这种行为，但一些报纸却有意纵容，如果记者找不到好的新闻线索，他们就会雇人制造新闻，比如发生群殴时在公共场所枪击，或在罢工中悬挂雇主肖像，正如我在前文提到的一样。

现在，不负责任、不讲道德和冷嘲热讽的记者已经无可救药，最后一步将是诋毁正直男人的人格，破坏清白女人的名誉，摧毁纯洁无瑕的生命，致使无辜的人自杀。堕落到这种程度的记者无疑成了谋杀犯，甚至不配给许多正直的杀人犯提鞋。幸运的是，此时，早已生效的诽谤法开始介入这个游戏。尽管我们现在的诽谤法很难送报社的恶人进监狱，但是，犯罪的报纸可能会赔偿一大笔钱，当报纸的财务神经开始疼痛时，报纸就会逼迫相关记者辞职。至此，全部过程结束，从幽默而无害的短暂想象力开始，到罪恶作品伤害无辜生命，最后失去了恣意妄为所赚取的罪恶利润，同时将一个堕落的记者推向最后的毁灭。

正如虚假新闻的恶意有所不同，报纸所负的责任也有程度上的不同。看似可信的新闻从远方通讯员那里发回报社，其准确性没有理由遭到质疑，也无法得到证实。因刊登虚假新闻而责备报纸有失公允。在此类事件中，唯一能做的是立即辞退犯错的记者，却又显得冷酷无情。幸运的是，那些被指控新闻造假中的大多数案例属于此类。那些已经刊登的假新闻，报社和其他记者都不用负责任。从快速交通系统到歌舞团女演员，都成了捏造事实的对象，行为不端的新闻代理通过持续的策划，慢慢混入一份报纸。有经验的编辑通常有察觉新闻代理编造的第六感，即便如此，这些令人生厌的混合物频繁渗入新闻，致使整份报纸受到责备。

也有这样的案例：报社无辜地刊登了记者或通讯员的假新闻，后来因善良本性、同情怜悯或迟钝的判断力，没有辞退假新闻的作者。在此，报社对虚假新闻承担了大部分责任。这不仅会鼓励个别记者对某个专栏新闻深入造假，以获取额外稿费，还会引诱其他记者做出类似的事情。

最极端的例子是报纸故意激励记者造假。好在这极为罕见。具有讽刺意味的是，有些报纸称其格言是："事实只会令人尴尬！"你可以掰着手指数出所有的这类报纸。它们或许有短暂的繁荣，如跳梁小丑般表演一番，但最终都会逐渐没落。它们建立在淤泥而非岩石之上。任何在谎言帮助下实现病态繁荣的机构，即便能取得一时的成功，但绝不会长久，乃至其生命亦是如此。

我可能在最后勾勒出一幅黑暗的图景，但幸运的是，这只适用于少部分报纸。这些报纸的数量逐年变少。我相信，任何知晓自己报纸历史的人都不会质疑这一事实，即，对准确性的追求变得更强烈、更广泛。报纸在核实新闻上花费的金钱和精力越来越多。一份负责任的报纸，花 4 美元获取一则新闻，却会花 6 美元去核实它。①

虚假新闻逐渐消失，一部分原因是报纸和报刊协会的增多使得新闻更易获取和核实，另一部分原因是新闻价值得到更广泛的认可，以及新闻工作者的职业尊严和荣誉感不断增强。公众对虚假新闻的非难和蔑视，已对那些不够小心谨慎的记者产生了影响。

但是，过去泛滥的虚假新闻已经促成一种"共识"，即弄虚作假依然是报纸的惯常做法。不仅是普罗大众，连经验丰富的观察家也认为这类现象很普遍。例如，圣路易斯华盛顿大学的历史学教授罗兰德·G·亚瑟（Roland G. Usher）最近宣称："你所读到的电缆新闻也是这样写成的，当然极少数情况除外。因为发送冗长新闻电报的成本高昂，所以，新闻以 8 至 10 行的电讯发送，报馆收到后，改写员将之扩展为两个专栏。"对此，美联社总经理弗雷德里克·罗伊·马丁（Frederick Roy Martin）做出了答复。他指出，在电讯发送中"唯一会遗漏的是一些类似 the、and、etc. 等虚词，其含义简单，但我们绝不会缩略语意清晰的整句或整行。"马丁先生出示的日常有线报道包含约一万词。②

《纽约时报》（*The New York Times*）总编辑范·安达（C. V. Van Anda）提供的数据表明，《时报》通讯员通过有线或无线电报，日发送量超过九千词。

在虚假新闻大范围甚至完全消失后，长期以来公众的指控促使报纸尽可能地对公众保持公正，这点变得极其重要。因此，今时今日的不诚实或不公正，会使新闻界在之后的 25 年内在法学家和普通公众面前抬不起头。

在对报纸的所有指控中，没有哪一个指控像虚假新闻那样完全被变化中的新闻实践所摈弃。尽管没能有效应对所有指控，但新闻实践依然在逐步改善。

---

① 普利策，《新闻职业：新闻的准确性》，12—15 页。
② 《编辑与出版商》，1923 年 2 月 17 日。

例如，虽然新闻实践中已不存在完全的虚构，但是，新闻中引入"噱头"（hokum）的行为仍然存在。"噱头"是一种"一点就着"的元素。每个国家都有自己的独特之处，这是由大众的品位和人情味来决定的。"噱头"在电影和小说中的流行，可能刺激了它在报纸中的运用。

美国的"噱头"是感性的，包含某种模糊的理想主义，同时促成了金融和商业的成功。从《小木屋里走出的伟大总统》到哈罗德·贝尔·赖特①（Harold Bell Wright），占主流的中产阶级对"噱头"的爱好只有轻微的摇摆。富人变得正义而虔诚，以及诸如真爱等其他主题，要优于金融算计。还有，伟人总会对无助的动物非常友善等，都是牢牢嵌入中产阶级思想中的"噱头"。

新闻工作者了解到公众对于"噱头"的爱好，于是频繁地将其加入到新闻报道中，目的是让事实看起来更符合公众的想法。例如，不久以前，一位继承了亲戚留下的百万财产的女士，与她青梅竹马的发小结婚了。事实是，两位年轻人曾在同一城镇中长大，女方的父母即便是依据当地标准也并不富有，而男方的家人却坐拥大量财产，在当地和其他一些城镇拥有商店。结婚时，他每年所享有的利息可能已达25万美元。他是一个讨人喜欢的商人，是当地的社交名人。结婚后，他们住在男士的乡间别墅。别墅坐落在一个大庄园之中，约有20间房。

该案例中的事实真相，几乎不能引起中产阶级读者情感上的共鸣。机灵的记者将之改写成一个完全不同的故事。年轻男士变身一个穷小子，且代表了理想主义。记者们发现，他在绘画方面有些天赋，几年前，他为家乡的一份小报创作了一系列政治卡通画，并用手中的画笔做了一些其他零散的工作。根据记者笔下的故事，这位挣扎谋生的年轻艺术家放弃了通过经商谋出路，而去追逐他的艺术理想。此外，当发现自

---

① 哈罗德·贝尔·赖特（1872年—1944年），20世纪上半叶美国畅销书作家，是第一个卖出一百万本书的美国作家，也是第一个写小说赚得一百万美元的作家。多部电影以赖特的故事为原型，包括加里·库珀的 *The Winning of Barbara Worth*（《芭芭拉·沃斯的胜利》），亨利·哈撒韦的 *The Shepherd of the Hills*（《山岗上的牧羊人》）。——译者注

己的爱人成为百万财产的继承人时，他表示不愿意向她求婚。但是，宽宏大量的爱人知道他的爱夹杂着对艺术理想的追求，决定和他结婚。于是，他们住在河边的一个小木屋，当然同样拥有前文提及的约有20个房间的别墅。因此，公众再次看到了感人的印证，金钱不能也不可能阻止真爱的脚步，真爱和艺术将在简陋的小木屋中愉快地结合在一起。

一个更险恶的"噱头"，几乎完全出自编造，被《纽约世界报》记者艾萨克·D·怀特（Isaac D. White）报道出来：

> 在邻州的一个工厂区，一位年轻女士与一个磨坊工人夜间划船，结果女士溺水身亡。男士浑身湿透，非常害怕，第一个报告了悲剧消息。他解释说，两人换座位时，船在离岸约100码的地方突然翻了。黑暗中，他尝试接近女士，却没有成功。由于泳技糟糕，他挣扎着勉强自救。第二天早上，船和桨漂浮在湖面，在男士指认位置附近的水底，女士的尸体被打捞出来。尸体上没有标记和伤痕，死亡原因鉴定为溺水。
>
> 这位不幸的意外遇难者是个妓女，她的外貌非常不讨人喜欢。她长着兔唇，讲话结巴，自出生起就很愚笨。她是小镇中某位声名狼藉女人的好友。纽约几乎所有的报社都派出记者，匆忙赶到事发地点，当地警方很快向记者道出了溺水事件始末和年轻女士名声等。但是，一份报纸的报道是"一位年轻貌美的女士"在"维护自己的清白"时溺水身亡；当地民众群情激愤，对当局没能抓住她的男伴而愤愤不平，他们认为，那名男伴受到某股未知而神秘势力的庇护，他的所作所为是公开抵抗法律和正义。但是，社区愤怒的矛头很快转向故意对民众和政府撒谎的记者。这个伪造新闻的记者持续一周发布骗人的新闻报道，诱使一位不明真相的逝者亲属向州政府递交请愿书，谴责当地政府包庇凶犯，请求州长能够干预调解此事，从而维护正义。事件至此达到高潮。在请愿书邮寄给州长之前，这个记

者还将其刊载于报。"①

另一种"噱头"因为难度不大，所以现实中更为常见，即制作关于新闻中人物的某种刻板印象式的标题，以吸引公众注意力。一个在被抓捕时恰巧穿着晚礼服的男士，可能被冠以"花花公子"或"小镇名流"的称呼。那些被指控为不道德的女人，不管其实际长相如何，常常被形容为"漂亮"或"美丽"。

新闻工作者对这种"噱头"既宽容隐忍又冷嘲热讽的态度，在1917年《芝加哥先驱报》（*The Chicago Herald*）刊登的幽默故事中有所阐述。其"资深记者"向申请记者许可证的新人提了以下一些问题：

> 城市的夜生活中，一位花花公子需要喝下多少杯高球鸡尾酒，才能成为众所周知的名人？
> 一个名媛变成女王，需要参加多少次午后茶会？
> 名门望族的子弟与富人家的儿孙有何不同？
> 一位父亲去世时需要留下多少钱财，他的女儿方能被称之为女继承人？42岁的她还会年轻貌美多久？
> 以"据说"开头写一句话，让读者相信这个表述准确无误。
> 请描述一位富有的卡车司机和一位年轻貌美的女继承人在鹅岛的浪漫婚礼。
> 失火新闻被刊登在报纸的哪一版才能称之为火灾？
> 一个女人入店行窃被捕后多久变成了一位前女演员？
> 你会形容已故政客的已故父母"贫穷但正直"吗？或者最好不称呼他们为"漂洋过海来到金色陆地，在新大陆披荆斩棘的移民"吗？
> 你认为校园美女怎么样？她们是美貌的女学生，或者只是

---

① 怀特：《新闻的公平性与准确性》，《纽约世界报》，1912年12月22日。

拉拉队女孩?①

参与制作"噱头"的记者们认为,在大多数情况下对其他人无害。年轻夫妇的新闻取悦了一大波读者,使他们对自己的感情生活更加坚定。这种"噱头"大概娱乐了那些关注新闻主角是谁的人,因为新闻将他们置于半主人公的光环下,而只有极少数人厌恶成为主人公。这则新闻只是"基于事实"进行编造,正如我们在孩童时期所听闻的那些故事一样。

但是,对于那些生活在这对夫妻所在城镇的人们而言,这则新闻意味着什么?他们会认为,报纸上刊登的消息都不可靠。每一个类似的故事都会产生这样的影响,无疑是为人们的偏见增添佐证。他们会进一步怀疑国际关系或其他与公众利益相关新闻的真实性。

在很大程度上,人们将进一步认为,新闻与公众见面之前,都会被篡改、歪曲或操纵。任何公正的观察者都能发现这类证据,正如对俄国革命之中和之后新闻的处理那样。当报纸刊登讽刺"死亡""监禁"等主题的漫画,以及列宁总理的人生沉浮时,人们可能没有质疑俄国现状的虚构程度。此外,梅塞尔·李普曼与梅尔茨(Messrs. Lippmann and Merz)在《对新闻的检验》(*A Test of the News*)中指出,其中有相当多的歪曲,例如报纸头条曾宣称,布尔什维克军被"粉碎",彼得格勒被焚毁,以及随后彼得格勒被尤得尼奇(Yudenitch)的军队占领!②

不过,虚假新闻远不如普通读者想象的那么普遍。如今,记录切实发生的合理事实,都不太可能被伪造。即便不参与报道事实的竞争,报纸也不会丝毫歪曲选举结果、证券交易行情或陪审团裁决。伪造通常发

---

① 引自《文学摘要》,第 54 卷,1021—1022 页。
② 《对新闻的检验》,第 30 页和第 33 页。这项发表于 1920 年 8 月 4 日《新共和》的研究,分析了著名的《纽约时报》1917 年 3 月至 1920 年 3 月间关于俄罗斯的所有新闻报道。

生在事实很难被获取而谣言极易被接受的场合。① 当然，更简单而更正直的做法是，当编辑没有可信赖的消息时不发布新闻。报纸拒绝采取这种做法，因为竞争迫使他们刊登一定数量的关于既定或预期事件的新闻。他们束缚良知，试图通过"据谣传""据说""高层坚称"等类似表达，规避读者的抱怨，防止被控诽谤。这些行为不受法院禁止，当然也不会超越公共道德。如果被贴上了"据谣传"这些标签，报纸的言论即使没有诽谤任何人，或者只是轻微伤及个人，也一定会被有见地的公共舆论认为是危险的。报刊应提供关于人类事务的明晰观点，成为公民的行动范本。

另一项针对报纸的普遍指控是新闻压制。在小城镇，说服编辑压制可能给广告商、朋友或订户造成不愉快的新闻，这并非是件难事。在大城市，这类压制就不那么常见。② 特定报纸也会压制不利观点。例如，在一次会议上，纽约贸易联盟的成员为支持钢铁工人罢工，捐助了数百万美元，纽约的报纸以此为头版头条，而匹兹堡（译者注：当时的匹兹堡是世界钢铁之都）的报纸则没有提及此次捐助或相关会议。③

新闻压制的问题较为复杂，因为报纸没有足够的版面刊载所有收到的新闻。这其中必然存在一个选择的取舍。有些新闻一定会被压制。报

---

① 但是，李普曼在新闻的不确定性和有据可查两者之间的讨论（《舆论学》，342－345页）中走得太远。他对记者或编辑的粗心、懒惰或其他一些心理特质的强调并不充分。例如，1917年9月20日，在关于参议院拉福莱特（La Follette）著名演讲的报道中，美联社插入单词"no"，以至于把"我们有抱怨"变成"我们没有抱怨"。对于这篇报道的编辑而言，很明显这个错误是无心之失，美联社也为其疏忽大意而道歉。但是，作者会提出这样的问题：这是不是由现代心理学认为的个体无意识造成错误的案例之一？编辑反对拉福莱特先生，自然对演讲者产生不好的印象，因此无心地多加入一个单词。新闻学研究更应多关注此类问题。

② 经常被引用的例子是关于许多年前费城的报纸，它们一致压制一位著名费城广告商在纽约自杀的新闻。当时，广告商正陷入不光彩境地。参见罗斯的文章，《新闻职业》一书中《要闻的压制》，第84页；另见辛克莱，《无耻收买》，也译《财团给报界的贿赂》，第227页。

③ 教派联合世界运动、调查委员会：《公众舆论与钢铁工人罢工》，150－151页。

纸的批评家认为,当新闻被报社压制时,涉及公共意义的新闻当然也会被压制。这在某种程度上是判断的问题,不幸的是,不公正的偏见往往紧随而至。报纸希望为自己或报社保留尊重,通常会努力压制那些可能涉及自身利益的新闻。

此外,新闻的倾向性受报纸政策左右,亦是公众对报纸的指控之一。这种现象的例子可以从报纸头条,或新闻故事本身中发现。尽管记者会因个人偏见或新闻中人对记者的态度而让新闻带有某种倾向,这种倾向通常在为维护报纸利益或记者和编辑预设立场时产生。大量有倾向性的新闻,可以在代表不同产业立场的报纸争论中找到。保守报纸中出现倾向性新闻的频率更高,因为其数量居多。但是,对激进报纸的调查显示,在有争议的问题上,出现了相似数量的倾向性新闻。例如,自称"客观报道"的联邦通讯社,以如下口吻结束一则关于厄普顿·辛克莱(Upton Sinclair)[①]的批评者的报道:

> 除了服从他人的命令,卡特(Carter)[②]没有其他理由要急于维护这些农业学院,因为他自己甚至连大学都没上过。[③]

为了达到煽情的目的,这则新闻的倾向性很强,一部分原因是出自

---

① 美国现实主义小说家、"社会丑事揭发派"(muckraker)作家。1906 年发表《屠宰场》(*The Jungle*),描写大企业对工人的压榨和芝加哥屠宰场的不卫生情况,引起人们对肉类加工质量的愤怒,导致《纯净食品药品法案 1906》的诞生。后以反法西斯英雄兰尼·巴德为主人公写了 11 本系列小说,反映 1914 年以来的重大事件,其中《龙齿》(1942)获得普利策小说奖。他一生共著有小说和社会研究著作 80 余部。——译者注
② Carter(卡特),原名 Jerrod Carter,是《纯净食品药品法案 1906》争议中商业方的一名代表。由于厄普顿·辛克莱的一本著作的流行导致该法案的诞生,卡特作为肉类加工厂等商业方的发言人,猛烈批评厄普顿·辛克莱。而肉类加工厂的领导者都是农业学院的毕业生,但卡特只接受过初级教育。因此,激进报纸《联邦通讯社公告》(*Federated Press Bulletin*)嘲笑卡特仅是肉类加工行业领导层——农业学院毕业生的傀儡,因其自身连大学的门都没踏进过。——译者注
③ 《联邦通讯社公告》第 5 卷,第 9 期,第 4 页。

报社政策，一部分是由记者自己的判断力决定的。《大急流城新闻报》（The Grand Rapids Press）的主编埃德温·W·布斯（Edwin W. Booth）讨论最近刊登的一桩离婚诉讼案时，提及芝加哥和底特律一些报纸对这个案件的处理："如果将庭审报告一字不差地报道给公众，公众可能会公正地评价案件的是非曲直。但事实上，针对特罗特（Trotter）的指控被大肆宣扬，他的辩护却显得不那么重要。虽然法庭判他无罪，但在公众舆论的旋涡中，特罗特的声望受到极大的损害，以至于我特地去询问他的工作是否还如以前一样。不仅在本地，在其他地方也会产生不公正新闻。"①

新闻标题显示出倾向性亦是激烈批判的对象。许多人仅浏览标题就能读出新闻的态度，即使新闻内容毫无偏袒，那种印象也挥之不去。在标题中表明态度的做法不断增多，从而损害了报纸应作为客观事实传播者的价值观。例如，以下是关于哈定总统②写给新泽西中央铁路联邦办事处秘书史蒂芬·E·康纳（Stephen E. Connor）的同一封信的11个新闻标题：

哈定指责铁路部门未能解决罢工
——固执少数派宣称对煤炭短缺和货船拥挤负责
——《纽约世界报》

哈定责备铁路罢工者佯装痛苦
——他致信新泽西中央铁路领导，称后悔拒绝少数派回归工作，唯恐情况变更糟，并批评他们阻碍煤炭交易、挫败行业信心
——《纽约论坛报》

哈定要求结束铁路罢工

---

① 《密歇根州大学出版社俱乐部第四次年会演讲与会议记录》，第101页。
② 沃伦·甘梅利尔·哈定为美国第29位总统（任期1921年3月4日—1923年8月2日），生于俄亥俄州，卒于任期内。哈定在农村长大，先当一个小报记者。他与弗洛伦斯·克林·德沃尔夫人于1891年结婚，婚后，弗洛伦斯即经营报纸来支持哈定投身政界。——译者注

——他的关于铁路罢工的信激起新泽西中央铁路方面否认,并宣称维护总统公告;哈定帮助解决劳动救济金,让少数派为未能解决罢工负责

——《纽约先驱报》

总统指责铁路工人,哈定称去年罢工不应拖延至今

——《布法罗快报》

哈定表示铁路罢工不正当,少数人因交通状况而罢工

——《辛辛那提询问者报》

哈定欲终止铁路罢工,称工人没有理由闹下去

——《芝加哥论坛报》

哈定阻拦铁路工人罢工

——总统因煤炭短缺责备不妥协的铁路工人,称罢工无任何正当理由,在写给新泽西领导的信中,他认为少数路段应服从于大型线路

——《纽约时报》

哈定建议铁路工人让步

——工会官方认为没有理由延期解决罢工问题

——《费城公共基石报》

哈定着手解决铁路罢工

——总统称少数人没有任何理由影响秩序,他批评中断的煤炭交易,并将之归咎于没能终止罢工

——《巴尔的摩太阳报》

哈定严厉批评罢工者

总统称铁路工人应回到工作岗位,责怪那些中断煤炭交易的工人

——《芝加哥每日新闻》

哈定要求铁路工人停止罢工

——总统看不出有什么理由宣扬铁路工会冲突

——《罗切斯特民主党人编年史》

可以看出，这 11 份报纸中，有一些认为总统责备铁路部门未能解决罢工问题，还有一些责备罢工者无故制造难题，其他报纸也表现出这样或那样的偏见。只有《辛辛那提问者报》（Cincinnati Enquirer）和《巴尔的摩太阳报》（Baltimore Sun）以严肃客观的方式报道了这则新闻。正如利益相关方对公正报道新闻的态度一样，美国劳工联合会（该机构因国际劳动新闻社而闻名）的新闻稿贬损《辛辛那提问者报》的标题，认为其"毫无意义"，而《巴尔的摩太阳报》"与《辛辛那提问者报》一样毫无意义"。

考虑到对公共生活的直接影响，美国报纸专栏的不准确性显得没那么重要，却备受关注。每一位报纸读者都能发现报纸的错误。他们发现朋友的名字或自己的名字被拼错，或者《决策中的思维》（The Mind in the Making）与《爱德华·波克的美国化》（The Americanization of Edward Bok）被称为"最流行的科幻作品"，甚至可以在美国编辑质量最高的报纸之一中，看到将埃德娜·圣文森特·米莱（Edna St. Vincent Millay）称为"埃德娜·史蒂文森特·希拉里"（Edna Stevincent Hillay）。

在作者熟人的一份报纸中，第一版出现了如下标题：参议院以 50∶23 拒绝雅浦条约。① 新闻的导语如下：

> 华盛顿 2 月 28 日报道——尽管政党路线存在分歧，参议院今日在裁军会议上拒绝修改雅浦条约。这项决定在针对影响国际契约协商的第一轮较量中达成，投票比例为 50∶23。

在这个案例中，编辑表现得极其不称职和懈怠，记者本来也可以表现得不那么无知。

不仅是准确性，报刊其他较为迫切的地方也遭受批评，对于没有偏见的学生而言，新闻显然比事件中平庸的观察者要做得更好。听到公正

---

① 《莱文沃思时报》，1922 年 3 月 1 日。

且细心的证人的证词，任何人都会因新闻故事各执一词而遭受打击。同样，在日常会话中，一般人都会改变事实细节来佐证自己的观点，并自觉或不自觉地沉溺其中。

另一方面，虽然新闻实践经常如此，但不能充分证明当下这种实践的合法性，只能为减轻处罚而狡辩。作为一种狡辩，它远不如一位称职理发师的坚持更有价值，因为理发师比普通门外汉更善于修剪头发。报纸需由受过专业训练和实践的人主办，从而实现新闻的功能。在专业能力领域，记者不应和普通公众作比较，而要以其他更好的记者为标杆。

补充阅读

李普曼：《舆论学》，338－357页。

梅西：《新闻业》，《美国的文明》，35－51页。

罗斯：《新闻职业》一书中的《要闻的压制》，79－96页。

辛克莱：《无耻收买》，228－313页。

李和辛克莱：《〈无耻收买〉的讨论》，《纽约环球与商业广告》，1921年6月和7月。

霍尔特：《商业主义与新闻》，1－49页。

沙利文：《国家洪水遗迹》，160－166页。

教派联合世界运动、调查委员会：《公众舆论与钢铁工人罢工》，87－162页。

萨蒙：《报纸与历史学家》，138－157页，412－467页。

格拉登：《被污染的新闻业》；索普《未来报业》一书中的《好与坏》，27－50页。

李普曼与梅尔茨：《对新闻的检验》，《新共和》，1920年8月4日。

第四章　报业的缺陷：唯物主义的控告

但凡指控报业的人都振振有词，且各种解释与公众思维趋向一致，这表明了公众对这些指控的态度。

首先，大众思维中存在"习惯的暴行"。似乎每一种问题的产生都是违背民主政府、道德、文明等重大准则的结果。或者说，问题本身即暴行。与之密切相关的是思维习惯的反叛，即一个群体持续密谋毁坏公众最高利益的感觉。暴行、反叛——这两种元素将公众从昏睡中唤醒。

这在美国历史上并非新现象。波士顿倾茶事件①是暴行情结的结果。许多年来，反共济会党一直存在着暴行与反叛的双重情结。根据史学家的观点，他们在佛蒙特州影响力巨大，以致共济会的每一个集会地都不得不交出其特许执照。在内战期间，暴行情结在北方占主导，而反叛情结在南方占优势。每一个参与战争的南方人都是野蛮的奴隶监工，而每一个北方人则是密谋破坏南北分治下各州资源的诡计多端的北方佬。美国人民党对老党派施以暴行，其辩护者之一认为，有必要"少种玉米，

---

① 波士顿倾茶事件是发生在 1773 年 12 月 16 日的政治示威，因北美民众不满英国殖民者的统治，当地居民塞缪尔·亚当斯率领 60 名"自由之子"化装成印第安人潜入商船，把船上价值约 1.5 万英镑的 342 箱（约为 18,000 磅）茶叶全部倒入大海，来对抗英国国会，最终引发美国独立战争。——译者注

多种仇恨"。美国进步党则将自己的起落沉浮归咎于这两个思维习惯,他们破坏信任和监禁官员使得群情激奋。两种情结互为狼狈,当进步党头目气数已尽,被处决示众时,人们开始追逐其他的暴行和反叛,于是其他的人又开始谴责他们。

美国民众的欲望刺激了暴行和反叛,无怪乎他们在最近的战争中,一方面通过极端的爱国者,另一方面通过激进分子(只要行政机构有机可乘),迅速积蓄力量。暴行仍在继续。共产党、世界产业工人联盟、社会主义者、工人联盟以及大量其他机构,被认为犯下暴行的反抗"美国主义"。从激进分子的角度看,资本家有组织、有支援的反叛,压制了所有关于改变现状的建议。

公众对报纸的态度是接纳了其暴行和反叛理论,这在普通对话和印刷文字中得到了体现。很少有人提出拘捕报纸经营者的建议,不过也有相关文章建议出台法律来管理新闻业。对报刊缺陷的解释通常会引出这种观点。报纸未能准确而公正地报道新闻的原因之一,在于报纸为了发行量而制造轰动性新闻。一些报纸凭借耸人听闻的办报方针极大地提升了发行量,并反过来以此为办报方针辩护。在某些情况下,他们会采用故作惊人之举的方式促进报纸的发行。轰动性新闻中最著名的例子出自赫斯特报业集团,他们成功地向从未读过报纸的人群发行自己的报纸。促进报纸发行的成本通常高昂,尤其是为了促销而赠送绿玻璃黄油碟,或一幅《丹尼尔在狮群中》的画作,而最便宜的方法是说服不买报的人购买某份报纸,这比说服别人放弃手头的报纸、选择别的报纸更加容易。在后面的论证中,一定会加入耗费光阴、成本高昂以及黄油碟和画作等理由。在赫斯特报业组织大规模营销时,那些非报纸读者的知识相对欠缺,一桩有趣的离婚案比严肃的国际问题更能引起他们的兴趣。他们能读懂离婚案,却不能理解国际关系。为了吸引他们的注意,报纸推出了耸人听闻的报道。这就引出一个问题,报纸到底是为了吸引读者而变得耸人听闻,还是变得耸人听闻后才有了天然的吸引力。

美国报纸变得耸人听闻只是为了吸引读者,这种理论总体上是站不住脚的。发行量审计局的一项发行数据表明,在拥有一份或多份"黄色"报纸、保守报纸（新闻处理保守而非政治理论保守）和介于二者之间报刊的中等城市，发行量最大的是温和派报纸，"黄色"报纸位居次席，保守派报纸排在最末。

但是，对任何一种有一定规模的报纸而言，发行量仅仅是促进广告刊发的手段之一。正如前文所言，一份大报很少能从订阅者和报摊主那里获得足够多的资金，以支付报社开支。发行量极其巨大，意味着报纸注重发行数量，凭借发行规模来吸引广告商；发行量小却瞄准富裕人群的报纸，注重的是发行质量。广告费率通常在每广告单位或每英寸发行单位的基础上进行比较。注重发行数量的报纸其广告费率总是很低，而注重发行质量的广告费率则很高。大城市中日报的最低广告费率为每百万发行量单行 1.08 美元（重发行数量的报纸）到 7.31 美元（重发行质量的报纸）。[①] 于是，出现了报纸可能在发行量极小时盈利的结果。

许多人指出报业的另一个缺陷，报纸运营需要一定的现金流，因此会谋取某些企业、政治家甚至罪犯的赞助。当报纸支持有违公共福祉的事情时，通常会被认为是存在商业交易。

毫无疑问，直接受贿的案例也时有发生。在《我自己的故事》[②] 中，弗里蒙特·奥尔德（Fremont Older）道出了这类交易的细节。作者认识的一位出版商（现已去世），认为金钱可以为他换取任何支持。尽管他拥有所在城市唯一的一份报纸，他利用各种不诚信手段，大力支持特许经销权，却被 1：5 的投票结果挫败。他的每一位员工都对特许经销权投了反对票。这是长久以来背叛公众信任的后果。这位出版商出售了他的报纸，离开这个城市之后，公众才彻底明白了一切。资深的新闻工作者会亲自罢免接受了贿赂的记者。

作者相信，直接受贿的报纸或新闻工作者现在很少了；但过去是否很普遍仍值得怀疑。这种现象与大选中公职人员和个体选民的受贿一起逐渐消失。原本漠不关心的和长期忍受的公众，最后都会反感所有形式

---

① Milline Rate 指百万发行量的单位广告费率，更多具体报纸的数据参见《标准价格和数据服务》。

② 23—30 页。

第四章 报业的缺陷：唯物主义的控告

的受贿。随着公众警惕性的提高以及对受贿的强烈反对，那些贿赂官员、选民或媒体的人逐渐发现，即便能找到适合的受贿者，也难以达成期待的结果。

还有些人认为，即使报纸不直接接受贿赂，也可通过承诺刊登或威胁撤回广告而间接受贿。如同直接受贿一样，这种现象也不像过去那么普遍。多年前，当自行车流行起来时，所有的自行车广告都从纽约同一家日报撤出，因为该报指出自行车售价为制造成本的五到六倍。此外，同一城市的百货商场，因为报纸对关税的态度而撤回其广告，甚至关停了在争论中那些站在报纸一方的顾客的信用账户。① 最近，正如本书前文所述，《波士顿晚报》（*The Boston Evening Transcript*）因为曝光了马萨诸塞州制鞋工厂的真相，结果失去了大量的鞋业广告。不过，以上提到的每一个案例中，广告商最终都回归了报纸。

还有，报纸同意广告商提出的要求压制新闻的例子也很多。每一个案例中，广告商的要求都在逐步加码。压制或出版某些声明的要求，有些来自广告商，还有些来自非广告商，他们大多数可能没有意识到其要求的无耻以及反社会本质。

整体而言，大报不像小报那样易受广告商诱惑或威胁的影响。倘若让广告商认为他们可以控制报业，将是一件非常糟糕的事情。无论如何，广告商都不能长久地置身于优秀的广告媒介之外。但即便是大报也存在这样一种趋势，即在影响广告商的新闻事件中，通过主动顺应广告商的心意，传递出一种感激态度。对于那些发生过意外、入店抢劫和其他不愉快事件的百货商店，报纸通常的做法是省略其名称。感激广告商，对于一份大报而言，显然是一种非常荒谬的动机。刊登广告纯粹是一种商业交易，广告商期待从购买的版面中获取利益回报。感激广告商是一种落后的遗风，彼时报纸发行量还很小，广告费率尚未完全标准化，刊登广告对出版商而言是一种慈善。如今，出版物没有必要再视广告为慈善。

---

① 这两起事件及其他更多事件请参见霍尔特《商业主义与新闻》一书，66—68页。

在报纸没有强大的财政支撑时，取悦广告商是一种巨大的诱惑。报纸从发行量中获取的平均收益仅为35%，这个比例远远低于都市类报纸。不仅收入甚微，而且发行收益的浮动还很大。除了那些按年收取订户费用的小乡村周报，读者没有义务周复一周甚至日复一日地阅读报纸。报纸每一期都必须努力符合读者的利益。除了给报纸提供大部分的收入外，广告商比读者更频繁地赞助报纸的各种活动。

对于任何一个熟悉出版业的人而言，财务问题非常现实。十年前的一项调查表明，堪萨斯州82%的报纸印刷厂都靠抵押贷款运营。① 消息灵通的塔尔科特·威廉姆斯博士（Dr. Talcott Williams）声称，考虑到报纸的年度盈亏账目，过去的50年中很少有美国日报没触及"红色"警戒线。② 经营报纸是一种高风险的商业行为。

人们难以清楚地描述广告商对报纸新闻的影响程度，但是，这种影响无疑比想象中要小很多。通常被忽视的一个现实因素是，广告商之间存在着竞争关系，这强烈影响着广告商的特殊喜好。报纸取悦某个广告商，就可能得罪其他人，反之亦然。此外，广告商很少对大量新闻感兴趣，但广告商的确有其影响力。广告不应被视为报刊缺陷的主要原因。

当然，广告在左右报纸这方面的影响力也不容忽视，报纸应增强其商业基础。有影响力的报纸正努力实现这一目标。一家知名报纸努力坚持新闻的真实性标准，并在社论专栏中明确其方针，即便这些不受欢迎。多年来，该报对这个国家的偏远地区进行储备投资，确保资金充裕，以防报纸的态度屈服于财务问题。对于任何一个从私人资本获取收益却对公共利益负责任的机构而言，财务独立对伦理独立而言十分必要，这一点很重要。

此外，报业缺陷的另一种解释是，报纸受商业关系的强烈影响，例如，资本的所有权，或者报纸与其他公共服务企业（如铁路、知名农业企业）间建立的互锁董事会，再或者土地投机计划。事实上，具有这类

---

① 索普，《未来报业》，第13页。
② 《新闻人》，第146页。

关系的报纸并不多，但确实存在，也有证据表明其影响。银行家通过收放贷款来影响弱小报纸，正是一种体现。出版商在政治、社会生活或商业领域的个人野心同样会导致报纸误入歧途。现有的解释表明，美国报业缺陷的根源在于未能坚持客观事实报道的高标准。这类解释涉及暴行与反叛，实质上代表了唯物主义的新闻观。这种观点内化为一种普遍的感觉，即认为报纸本质上已沦为妓女，并以妓女的方式与其他阴险的利益相关者媾合。很多人都认同厄普顿·辛克莱的以下说法：

"财团给报界的贿赂是什么？对于编写、印刷、发行报刊的人而言，答案可以在你每周的工资信封里找到。当你取走事实的公正躯壳，转卖给市场，背叛人类圣洁的希望，进入令人作呕的大财团的妓院时，贿赂就是你羞耻心的价格。账房下面坐着一位受益于你羞耻心的'女士'。偶尔，她会离开妓院，来到棕榈滩或新港滩，炫耀她的珠宝和翎羽。"①

很自然，这种观点广为传颂。前文中还能找到一些支撑它的证据，它与思维习惯的暴行和反叛一样被广泛传播。

但是，如果这种解释很充分，则应当体现在激进报纸中。激进报纸强烈反对资本主义，声称其他报纸中准确、公平及公正的缺失正是资本主义的阴谋所致。而事实上，激进派报纸与保守派报纸一样也存在这些缺陷。唯物主义理论无法对报业的缺陷做出解释。

补充阅读

辛克莱：《无耻收买》，32—38页，221—249页，258—310页。

霍尔特：《商业主义和新闻》。

贝洛克：《自由的新闻业》。

威廉姆斯：《新闻人》，145—151页。

奥尔德：《我自己的故事》

亚当斯：《成功》

亚当斯：《号角》

---

① 《无耻收买》，第436页。

索普:《未来报业》,1—26页。
安吉尔:《新闻与社会组织》,11—75页。
安德森:《蓝色铅笔》,《新共和》,1918年12月14日,192—194页。

第五章 报业的缺陷：现实主义的解释

有人指出，关于当下报业的唯物主义解释，只有一小部分是正确的。美国的报纸之所以未能实现其基本功能，主要原因并非人们普遍认为的那样，其原因深深植根于美式生活之中。那些原因很微妙，潜移默化，且与我们文化中的许多其他特征交织在一起。

浸染美式生活的不是腐败，而是无知、惰性和恐惧。同样也是这种无知、惰性和恐惧，导致美国报纸未能向大众报道事实。

熟悉欧洲报界的人来到美国后，发现美国记者和编辑会无视最基本的事实，这让他们都大吃一惊。不过，当他们看到高中生和大学生也都无视事实时，就不再大惊小怪了。一般的地理和历史常识、名人姓名，都会被记者荒唐地弄错，更不用说经济、政治或美术术语，编辑们也根本不注重这些细节的错误。

这种无知虽然可悲，但还没有让人警惕。如果实际情况是，一般的记者都没有意识到这一点或者根本不想改变，那就不一样了。他们都被惰性所羁绊，不给选民分析政治问题，甚至阻止其投票。当接触一个自己不熟悉的专题时，记者们太过武断，甚至不查看相关书籍，也没想过向前辈请教，撰写报道时甚至不查字典。有一次，一个记者被派去采访约翰·巴勒斯（John Burroughs，美国博物学家），记者一心认定约翰是计算器的发明者,但是,采访了几分钟后,记者显然对被采访者的机械知识产生一些疑问,终于脱口问道:"对不起,巴勒斯先生,请问您从事的是哪个行业?"

笔者熟悉的一个记者,平时只做日常的报道。某次在写作中对一个宗教故事产生了疑惑,只好求助于之前不屑一顾的工具书,他竟然试图在《美国名人录》中找到(宗教人物)玛丽亚(Mary Magdalene)的介绍。

这种情况就让人觉得美国报纸在技术报道方面很不可靠,在普通新闻方面也好不到哪里。在很多情况下,错误并不会直接影响公众对重要问题的判断,但很明显这样会让美国新闻业蒙羞。

另外,当记者在报道一则重要的国际新闻时,他的无知会带来可怕的后果。美国人对于欧洲战争及战后情况的误解是因为美国记者在历史、地理和经济方面的无知造成的。在华沙的记者之所以报道称,维尔纳(译者注:又名维尔纽斯)在历史上就属于波兰,这不仅是因为无知,而且是因为过于懒惰而不愿意去查证确认事实。这也可以解释美国的编辑为何不加确认就进行报道了。

美国新闻人的无知在经济类报道中尤为明显。再强调一下,他们只是反映出美国大众的无知,事实上,他们的大多数读者更加无知。英国工党以及法国工会的成员对美国经济史和当下经济问题的熟悉程度,甚至令美国的大学毕业生相形见绌。欧洲、澳大利亚以及世界上的其他地方正在进行着各种经济变革,很多美国记者对于一些现代经济学中广泛运用的术语并不了解或者一知半解。所以,他们错误地使用"布尔什维克的""激进的""社会主义的"或"无政府主义"等概念就一点也不令人惊讶。他们不重视这些术语的本意,使用它们只是为了改变现状,或是试图以此混淆新闻事实。

还有一个同样严肃的问题是,一些美国记者对于什么样的事实能作为证据一无所知。事实上,证据并不能随意被确定,法院事务就很好地证明了这一点,其中有一些是记者应该了解的基本法则。比如说,大家都明白,无论何事,未经证实的陈述不足以构成事实。更重要的一点是,即便是在持客观态度的专业人员参与的科学调查中,一般惯例是,个人记录由自己保存。但是,记者或新闻编辑更愿意接受的是未经证实的事实,甚至是谣传。

在美国或其他国家,新闻记者们普遍接受高官们发表的言论,或者接受那些外行人士对于某个专业领域发表的言论。一部分原因是记者们易受误导,另一部分原因是出于惰性。没有比从某些个体来源获得新闻更简单的方法了。同样的,不加核实地接受一个"事实",不加核实地接受某种"专业"言论,抑或不假思索地相信某人出于政治或个人偏见发表的自由言论,这些都是再简单不过的新闻处理方法,正因为如此,记者们在报道时有意或无意地歪曲了事实。

美国人对于俄国自改革以来发生的各种情况的误解,很大程度上是由于美国记者的无知和轻信。尽管我们对俄国的真实情况并不了解,但还是能轻易地看出美国记者们对那段时期(特别是俄国抵制革命运动时期)的描述非常不可信。李普曼和梅茨先生对于美国记者不实报道的评论发人深省:

> 分析显示,《纽约时报》由于太过相信官方新闻来源而被严重地误导。事实表明,从政府或官员的圈子,或是从政治运动领导者那里传出的消息,不足以成为判断事实的依据,独立报刊不应轻易地采用。这些消息多有倾向性,具有某种特殊的目的性,因而是不可信的。假设俄国战争部长宣称俄军实力之高前所未有,新闻人不应该接受这个言论而报道称俄军实力空前强大,正确的表述是,俄国战争部长声称其军队实力更强。以新闻报道的高标准来看,这位战争部长的言论如果涉及特别重要的事实,那么对独立调查来说则是一种挑战。
>
> 分析显示,比官方言论更具误导性的事实是半官方或半权威人士的匿名言论。这类新闻常与以下短语并列出现:
> "美国国务院官员"
> "政府或外交人士"
> "惊人报道"

"最高权力机构声称"

这些报道可能来自一位小官员，一段餐桌边的谈话，宾馆大厅里的流言，一个有过一面之交的人或者是雇来的消息人士。这种敷衍了事的报道让编辑们感到轻松闲适，读者们也不假思索地相信，因为他们无法查证事实，也没有想过要求报道者们充分核实信息来源。记者无需知道个体信源的名字，只需给他安上某种"名号"即可。①

分析还指出，即使是《纽约时报》这样有财力又有影响力的报纸，也没有认真充分地发掘记者的才能。在非常时期进行非常的报道，报纸需要的不仅仅是普通的记者。新闻报道是最复杂的专业之一，需要报道者有相当的专业知识和严谨学识。旧的观念认为训练有素的人缺乏"新闻敏感"，但该观点无法驳倒"没有经过良好训练的人可能会误导整个国家"这一事实。读者习惯于接受记者的报道，所以，记者的价值与占星师或炼金术士齐平。出版业有必要向工人、雇员和政客们传递一些知识，但是，出版者自己学习这些知识也同样重要。报纸的影响并非由意志坚定的人创造，而是取决于其责任和抱负。

谈及美国新闻工作者，特别是记者们的无知时，结论通常是记者不太可能有很广的知识面。如果将1920年美国日报上关于俄国消息的文章与英国《曼彻斯特卫报》（*Manchester Guardian*）上亚瑟·兰塞姆（Arthur Ransome）先生所写的文章相比，以上结论的错误之处便一目了然了。这位英国记者熟知总体状况，并随时准备投身缜密的调查中以获取具体数据。例如，兰塞姆先生给出了如下中肯而切实的报道：革命前，俄国各种进口工业制成品的比例；从1914年起，该国每年可使用的火车头数量；彼尔姆政府为生产木材使用的马匹数量；每个煤矿里每名工人月均产煤量；国有金属厂实行法定工作时间的比例；共产党成员

---

① 《对新闻的检验》，41—42页。

的准确数量；共产党的机构组成、各分部党员数量及其权利分配。

这些数据，还有很多其他的资料，一同给人勾画出了一幅清晰的俄国经济状况图。尽管兰塞姆先生的很多信息并非新闻报道，但他还是对新近发生的情况做出了迅速的反应，形成了围绕一个主题的客观事实，从而让人们透过这些事实更好地了解新闻事件。①

再举一个本土的例子。美国报纸经常夸大、嘲弄甚至因无知而误报关于科学集会的消息。但是，在1922年，《纽约时报》派阿尔瓦·约翰斯顿（Alva Johnston），一位气质出众而又训练有素的记者，去报道美国科学促进会的年度大会。面对纷繁复杂的各类科学主题，约翰斯顿先生凭借广泛的知识积累和追求精确事实的严谨态度，在大会期间写出了一系列新闻报道，无论从准确性、清晰度还是从把握读者兴趣方面都无可挑剔。这些报道获得了普利策奖，成为人们越来越关注记者可靠能力的最好例证。②

这些例子清晰地表明，记者同时具备发掘事实所需的心理素质和身体能力并非不可能。报业之所以存在惰性和无知，仅仅是因为没有人要求记者们具备专业知识。"一个好的新闻故事"是许多报纸编辑室里常用的表达。但是，故事的真实性却很少受到质疑。报社里流行的观点是，公众要求的是"好故事"，而对故事的真实性并不十分关心。文笔优美的故事，会有一部分基于事实，有一个风趣幽默的开头，再加上一个吸引人的大标题（这确实已经发展成报纸的重要组成部分），这样的组合足以让人忽视故事本身的真实性。普通记者更愿意思考，如何将一个为争奶油蛋糕而大打出手的虚假街头故事写得风趣幽默、吸引眼球，而不是去扩充自己的现代经济学知识。编辑则称，公众对奶油蛋糕事件比经济学更感兴趣。

报纸未能报道完整、公正又真实的新闻，除了因为无知和惰性外，更重要的是因为恐惧。恐惧不仅是美国报纸的特点，更是美国公众的特

---

① 兰塞姆先生的很多材料见于其著作《俄国危机》。这些材料极为珍贵，很多是《卫报》中没有的素材。

② 该文见于1922年12月28—30日的《纽约时报》。

点。这种恐惧不是生理上的，美国人已经无数次地展现了他们的勇气和毅力，而是更偏向于智力和精神方面，有些虚幻，无法解释。几乎所有的美国人都有这种恐惧，他们倾向于顺从群体。保护自己的族群在历史上显得很有必要，在今天看来却是异类。

必须承认的是，群居本性使人类有种天生的欲望——尽管这种欲望正不断消退——个体想通过信念和观点获得群体的认同。或许一个人没这种强烈的欲望，甚至主动放弃获得大多数人的认同，却也会设法获得小团体的认可，并认同这个小团体的观点，即所谓"大群体里的小群体"。① 另外，对群体的顺从与恐惧阻止了个体在认知及其他方面的进步，长久以来被视为民主政体的威胁之一。

在约翰·斯图尔特·密尔（John Stuart Mill）的论文《论自由》②（*On Liberty*）中，他指出，如果两种意见中"有一个比另一个较占优势，那么，我们应予以宽容并且鼓励的应是在特定时间和特定地点居于弱势地位的那一个。"接下来，密尔称既有观点的统治地位会慢慢变成"品味、观点以及生活方式的一致僵化，最终导致比中国式停滞更为严重的情况发生"。在美国，对群体的过分顺从不仅缘于民主的自然趋势，而且缘于这个国家在早期的团结统一，这种团结是基于共同的憎恶而非共同的同情。

恐惧显然毫无意义。正如弗洛伊德博士所说："凡事只要不受恐惧的影响都可以尽善尽美。"③ 人们认识到恐惧毫无意义可能是因为它总是伪装成合理的事物。没人愿意承认自己是懦夫。恐惧情结会被心理潜意识压抑，而通过间接的方式表现出来。受恐惧刺激而产生的行为，个体会以虚假的理由进行解释。

因而，恐惧虽然没有背负上堕落的污名，却更具破坏力。堕落关乎是非对错、诚实与否，即便是恶棍也总有机会明辨是非并改邪归正。但是，恐惧却不涉及这些问题。即使是受恐惧驱使，也没有人会承认自己

---

① 对该现象的详细讨论，请参见特罗特的《和平与战争时期的群体本能》，23—41页。
② 第二章。
③ 《精神分析引论》，第341页。

丧失了所有理智、伦理或是情感上的抗争。

新闻业的恐惧起源于记者，并很快地渗透到了新闻业的各个部门，一直延伸至出版商。通过与大量记者交谈，笔者相信大部分人非常诚实，而且他们要么是自由主义者，要么是激进分子。但是，只要随便拿起这些人写的一篇新闻，你就会发现，他们对保守、反动政策以及自由、激进政策都存有偏见。

那些批评报纸却不熟悉新闻实践的人认为，问题出在出版商要求记者务必带着某种偏见撰写新闻。确实存在这样的情况，但是，这些出版商往往不是专业的新闻工作者，而是把报纸当作工厂经营的商人看待。在多数情况下，即便是商人也不会这样要求记者。在多数报纸的员工工作须知里都强调准确和公正的重要性。[①]

一位新上任的总编辑把员工召集在一起，对他们说：

"伙伴们，我对大家的要求是获得新闻。我们要获得所有的新闻，并确保准确无误。我们不在乎新闻涉及什么，也不管它关乎谁。只要我在任一天，就没有什么新闻是不能碰的。如果发现有不对的苗头，我会在它蔓延之前扼制住。"

伙伴们都听进去了，他们微笑着奔赴采访现场，但还是以旧的偏见写着旧式文章。那么，问题出在哪儿呢？

归根结底，原因在于记者们及其上一层工作人员的恐惧。几乎所有的报纸，在处理新闻时都持有保守的偏见。记者相信出版商需要的是保守的新闻故事，如果他采写了一个客观公正的或者表达出激进或自由主义观点的政治、经济类新闻报道，是不会被刊登出来的，他自己也会被开除；即便没有被开除，他的文章也会被编辑部门改得面目全非。而那位总编辑的话并没有消除记者的这种恐惧。在记者看来，总编辑不过是在"发泄精力""自我欺骗"或是"例行发言"而已。记者可能受到了新闻编辑的影响，这些编辑要么在报社里慢慢变老，越发愤世嫉俗，要么出了报社很难找到工作。年轻的新闻从业者慢慢发觉，既然出版商活

---

① 在本书附录 A 部分可以查阅更多实例，211—238 页。

跃于各种资本主义行业，其商业和社会关系广泛，那么，他出版报纸也一定是为了资本主义的利益。

这就形成了恶性循环。一名年轻的新闻记者经过耳濡目染，也开始带着偏见采写新闻。下一批年轻记者可能看过他的文章，听过他的演讲，从而如法炮制，步其后尘。

即便是美联社这样的机构亦是如此。一位曾与美联社关系密切的评论家厄普顿·辛克莱[①]先生表示，美联社迎合了资本的兴趣，在本质上是堕落的。情况是这样的：每个城镇的美联社报纸——政治上几乎都持保守态度——凭借会员身份，成为美联社驻当地的通讯部。真正处理新闻事务的通常是报社里某个聪明的年轻人。年轻人深知报社还有其他人垂涎这份工作，因而不愿冒任何风险，唯恐丢掉饭碗。他在采写新闻时，会延续一贯的保守风格，然后发给美联社。其实，只要报道内容清楚明白，同样也可以通过。问题就在于他不相信这一点，而且理由很充分：害怕失去工作。

有些情况会进一步消磨记者们的士气，比如"黄色新闻"报纸经常让记者卷入不光彩事件——盗取图片、恐吓证人，甚至是行贿受贿等。这类人通常是轻度伤残者、酒鬼、瘾君子或是放荡体虚者。尽管理智上记者觉得应该保有新闻伦理，但他们耳濡目染这些人的习性，认为为新闻伦理的理想而努力并不值得。

在这种情况下，记者自然会形成一种玩世不恭的态度，认为报纸仅仅是商业机构，它不会因为你诚实就付给你钱。在他们看来，报社与卖百货、五金的杂货店并无二致。报纸售卖的是人们想要的东西，或是经营者认为人们想要的东西，或是出于某种原因，经营者决定要卖的东西。记者中渐渐出现意识分离的心理现象。在他们脑海中，一方面想要报道真相，表达自由、创新的观点，另一方面又想遵守新闻界的商业规则。尽管记者和执事都不一定是伪君子，但他们的态度就像教会执事一样，到了工作日就对来访者说公事公办。

[①] 《无耻收买》，353—376页。

这种情况也不能完全归咎于记者。有时，记者认为报纸需要带有偏见的新闻也许并非听命于出版商。但是，出版商面对记者的这种态度时，或保持沉默，或敷衍塞责，公众认为记者出于恐惧就说得通了。出版商本可以明确表示，其报纸只需要客观公正的报道。必要时，他完全可以开除所有坚持传达相反意见的编辑。

在很多情况下，出版商从未面对过这个问题。一方面，身处大城市，他不可能是一名专业的新闻工作者，而更多的是一名商人，一名要在广告部门穿梭、称自己为"报纸生产者"而不是报纸工作者（编辑或是记者）的商人。他视报纸为商业企业，力求取悦或吸引大众的注意力，扩大其发行量以保证广告收益。如果有人直截了当地问他，他会说希望自己的报纸诚实公正，而且将努力保证这一点。他将报社的编辑工作交给能干的下属，不会多加指导，他相信他们能做得让他满意，因而没有必要去干涉他们的工作。他每天阅读自己的报纸，觉得这是一份诚实公正的报纸，他的朋友也说他的报纸诚实公正。新闻中带有特定的偏见，让人曲解新闻本意并视其不诚实，似乎从来都不是出版商的授意。

如果某份报纸是合伙经营，由董事会共同管理，那么新闻的真实性就更成问题了。因为共同经营的一群人通常会更加谨慎，只要一切看似顺利运行，他们更不愿去干涉报纸的经营。

报纸合并后所有权归一，不论是归一个人还是一个团体，结果都是一样糟糕。

一个商或多个出版商，对群体产生理智和精神上的恐惧，并顺从之。而报纸工作人员最大的恐惧来自出版商。于是，对群体的恐惧会在报社中蔓延开来，上至出版商，下至刚入职的新人。

现在，报纸实质上是群体机构；而与其他国家相比，美国报纸的这种群体更具规模，由坚定的信仰结合在一起，其坚定程度仅次于神圣无比的教堂。美国信仰中有一长串的禁忌，性、政治、经济以及社会等方面。正如教堂的教条神圣不可侵犯一样，美国信仰的教条也不容置疑。有信仰的人对其信仰的解释无外乎因信称义或因行称义。如果你质疑教条，信徒们就会认为你即便不是个异教徒，也是个俗人。即使是那些宣称要检验自己信仰的人，在实行时也会偏爱之，或者他们的尝试仅是浅尝辄止——为了继续相信这些教条而找到说辞，根本没有真正地自我怀疑。

忠于事实，不管是因为本身的缘故，还是作为唯一的行为准则，都不是教条主义所推崇的。的确，美国人由于对真理的"鸵鸟心态"而恶名远播，从不愿抬头正视事实。最近，一个电影审查委员会将一部名电影中的台词"男孩更好"改成"是个男孩"，从而使人们在面对孩子出生的事实时保持克制。就像电影中的小女孩对待男孩的态度一样，美国人喜欢的不是事实，而是"美好的"事实。

群体教条是美国人信仰的一部分，已从经营者自上而下深深地渗透进了新闻传统。当代报纸对大众抱有怜悯之心，强调的"人情味"给报纸带来一种大众视角。教条主义追求的不是忠于事实，现在的趋势是，在没有任何既定方针的情况下，排斥报纸上所有与群体信仰相冲突的内容，即使它是正确的，也不例外。

多年来，女性和女性组织的新闻一直不受报纸重视，一些相关的重要事实基本被排除在外或被曲解误传。幸好现在的情况有所改观。一些人将这种改变归因于女性不仅能建议甚至能决定家庭订什么报纸。这个解释较为肤浅，而真正的原因是：群体对女性的态度发生了转变，大部分人开始意识到女性也是群体的一部分，新闻工作者的态度也在不知不觉中发生了改变。

正如前文指出的那样，关于俄国的新闻因无知和缺乏常识而带有偏见，并非缘于新闻业的腐败，而是因为新闻界认为群体有反苏联的传统，事实也确实如此。这种群体传统很大程度上是受报纸的引导，同样的，报纸也受到了官方和半官方信源的宣传影响。这种宣传巧妙地营造出一种假象，即苏联传统与美国信仰相冲突，例如，婚姻忠诚、民主政府及私人财产拥有权等。再一次引用李普曼和梅茨先生的研究，即：

> 总体而言，新闻是由新闻机构组成人员的意愿主导的。刚开始时，新闻记者像是一场盛大战役中斗志激昂的游击队员，仿佛背负着国家的未来。直至各方休战，他们才开始攻击德

国。而此前他们一直袖手旁观，直到俄国筋疲力尽。当看到俄国已无力再战时，他们才开始干预调停，反对德国。与德国的战争结束后，他们又找到了继续干预德国的理由。"德国威胁"曾是干预的理由，但停战协议已经消除了这个威胁。"红色威胁"立刻填补了这个空缺。很快，"红色威胁"又不及"白色将军"带来的希望和喜悦。这些希望破灭后，"红色威胁"又复苏。在很大程度上，美国报业关于俄国的新闻报道不是事实，只是人们希望看到的事实。

在作者看来，这种推论最为重要。在记者和编辑的心中，首席审查员和首席宣传员是其希望所在，也是恐惧之源。他们想赢得战争，也想避开布尔什维克主义。这些阻碍新闻工作者追求客观事实的主观障碍，可以解释进取心强的他们为何向新闻审查和宣传屈服。出于主观原因，他们接受并相信了大部分来自美国国务院、俄国驻华盛顿大使馆、俄国驻纽约情报局，俄国委员会驻巴黎分会以及遍布欧洲的特工和相关人士的消息。出于同样的原因，他们赢得了赫尔辛基、鄂木斯克、海参崴、斯德哥尔摩、哥本哈根、伦敦和巴黎等重要地方官员的重视。同样的，他们还接受了政府控制的海外新闻报道，接受了与情报机关、俄国旧贵族相交甚密的记者的报道。①

这些事件中，新闻工作者自己受到群体思维的影响，因为他们本质上也是群体的一部分，同时又出于恐惧，他们刻意写出了自己认为大众想要的报道。正如他们所说，他们提供了"大众想要的事实"。

除了美国传统的群体心理，不同收入阶层中也存在特殊的群体心理。富人、中产阶级、无产阶级和其他工薪阶层都有自己不同的群体本能。从遗传、传统、教育和社会关系来看，男女新闻记者通常属于中产阶级，也就是商业贸易阶层，所以，大部分人也对商业事务感兴趣。报

---

① 《对新闻的检验》，第3页。

纸的所有者，只有少数几个是富人，很可能持有中产阶级的标准、本能和理想。

在美国，最常见的现象就是高级阶层轻视其他低级阶层，而低级阶层的人又都在拼命地巴结高级阶层。这种情况在中产阶级身上体现得最明显。即使别人只是开玩笑，新闻工作者——不论是出版商还是记者——都讨厌被称为"布尔什维克分子"或"激进分子"，这是中产阶级的观念使然。他可能会宣称自己相信激进主义，但是，潜意识里他还是想与同阶级的理智者站在一起，从来不否认和反抗他们的群体意识。

更甚者，即使他偶尔摆脱对同阶级和上层阶级的顺从，内心还是会产生一丝恐惧。无产阶级也有从众本能，但是，他们解释不清。报纸不需要惧怕群体心理。追求事实不是任何一个阶层（包括富人、中产阶级或穷人）的群体心理，至多只能算是人类从众本能的一部分。

群体越小，群体心理的作用就越发明显。而大城市能给个体提供安全感，因为它规模够大又缺乏好奇心。美国大多数的报纸都是在小城镇里印制的，与都市报相比，这些报纸更易被仔细品读，在读者群中更具影响力。同时，他们对群体的依赖度也更强。一个简单的例子就可解释清楚。小城镇的报纸通常会隐去普通或轻微罪犯的姓名，尽管在小城镇里这些行为无疑是新闻。报纸解释说，隐去姓名是为了避免给无辜的罪犯亲属带来伤痛。从心理学角度分析，这种逻辑显然不合理，不能解释什么才是群体恐惧的真正产物。

对群体的恐惧是一种难以察觉的现象，普通的新闻工作者不仅看不见它，甚至感觉不到它的存在。如果告诉一个人，他其实受制于对群体的顺从心理，他一定会否认，并列举各种各样的理由进行反驳，证明其行为是出于自我判断。

有时候，当报纸报道了与群体教条相悖的事实时，整个群体或是群体的一部分会因恐惧和反感而震惊。经常有读者取消订阅或者广告商撤销广告，因为报纸报道了他们不喜欢却无可否认的事实。那些未与报纸斩断经济关系的人通常会写信谴责。随后，那些自称爱国者的暴徒就会声称报纸的报道有误，出于私人利益而宣传炒作。在小城镇，个人或组织向报纸施压，好点儿的只是发表针锋相对的评论，不好的则直指报纸误报事实。我们可以看出，在所有情况下，压力都是来自群体中清晰发声的人。这些事件引发争论，通常是由愤世嫉俗的记者发起，称美国公众偏爱美好的谎言，不愿接受不幸的事实。有人进一步总结为，事实冷酷客观的一面是那些习惯看到温馨轻松谎言的人们所不想看到的。

然而，尽管大多数的群体成员还保有从众本能，对群体心理显示出恐惧和顺从，但很多报纸出版商自认为可以凌驾于群体之上。有时，他们的言论中透露出一种深意，即自己天生就是来控制公众舆论的或是群体的领导者。同时，他们对群体又有一种明显的不信任和生理上的恐惧感，与其他人对群体无意识的恐惧和顺从大不相同。

他们对公众的不信任和恐惧，表示他们不愿给大众提供事实。这种不情愿当然也不是什么新鲜事。很多年前，政府打压报纸就是因为政府不想告诉公众事实，特别是关于政府的真相。在英格兰，有段时间只允许报道外国新闻，政府认为，公众阅读这样的新闻才相对安全。后来，管理政策放松了，英格兰报纸终于可以报道国内新闻，那些隐藏的不为人知的事实才被揭发出来。那些管理政策一部分是以法令的形式出现，一部分是通过法庭判决的形式出现，即事实愈重大，诽谤罪就愈严重。这一条法庭诡辩被解释为：若不掩盖事实，将会扰乱和平。那时，反对报道事实的压力来自国王、土地贵族和富有财团——他们中的少数人意识到现在的权力巨大，但是害怕以后在面对多数人时无法保持影响力。于是，报纸出版商冒着被判刑的风险站了出来，为的是争取报道事实的权利。

那时，统治者的这种态度有一定的理由。人们不愿相信民选政府，除了少数可以忽略不计的狂热分子，没有人愿意相信。那个政府不是大众的政府，而且也无意改变，那么大众为何还要在意它呢？

如今，虽然新闻工作者严谨地保留着隐瞒事实的权利，就像多年以前被征服的君主、贵族和富商一样，他们却没有旧时代统治者隐瞒事实的理由。他们选择相信民选政府。他们喜欢提及独立宣言、宪法和民主政治。同时，他们又做好隐瞒事实的准备，而这些事实正是公众做出诚实可靠判断的唯一基础。

各种因素共同促成了这种发展。其中一个很重要的原因是，美国政治、公民和商业生活渐渐默许并接受了一个理念，即只要目的正当，可以不择手段。这也不是新的教条，但是，共和国早期的民主党人对此并不赞成。还有一条华而不实的座右铭也广泛流传："我们的祖国……愿她永远正确；但是，无论对错，她永远是我们的祖国。"在它变得极端荒谬之前，热烈的拥护者们在发言中不断解读："不管对错，她永远是我们的城镇"，或者"不管对错，她永远是我们的俱乐部"。

报纸促进了这种情绪的滋生和发展。每个人都知道，城镇里出现的严重疾病的消息通常会被压制，或被淡化以保护当地的声誉。一旦予以报道，当地商会精心打造的"方圆500公里以内的最健康城市"将被毁于一旦。公众依然记得，加利福尼亚州的报纸对旧金山火灾和地震的报道态度。本书还会提到很多其他的例子。

在（第一次）世界大战期间，人们因相互不信任而隐瞒事实的行为不断出现。1916年秋天，当局开始禁止报道事实，以营造总统"正努力让我们免于战争"的假象。整个世界大战时期一直如此。当权者认为，这样有助于赢得战争或是造福于美国外交。所谓的"自愿审查制度"是一方面，另一方面是反间谍法，明确了政府对于报道事实的态度。没人会质疑这些阻止战时秘密外泄的手段，但是，隐藏所有不容乐观的事实，是否有助于增强民主的氛围却非常值得怀疑。但可以肯定的是，这种行为将对未来的民主社会造成不可估量的损害。

这是修正报纸隐瞒事实行为的绝佳时机。战争时期，只要没有特殊原因，几乎所有的报纸都服从于群体，都表现得像十足的爱国者、政府百分百的支持者。当政府以政策相逼，规定人们只能知道哪些事实，报纸自然会遵从。很多人对此似曾相识。这种行为逐渐变成很多报社的传统，战后也延续了下来。一个傲慢而缺乏经验的年轻记者在报道前反复问自己："告诉公众所有事实是否安全呢？"更值得注意的是，那些被隐瞒的事实通常不是犯罪活动的细节，而是政治、经济和社会领域的重大事实。

在美国，在所有对民选政府构成威胁的现象中，没有什么比报纸不愿给大众报道事实更为严重了；在所有对报纸公共性或准公共性的控诉中,没有什么比质疑其提供事实的能力更为严厉了。有人可能会说,公众缺乏智慧,才会被偏见和非理性所左右。他们只有获知事实,才会理性地思考并理智地行动;或者说,报纸人员——编辑或记者——认为这样才是他们理智思考和行动的方式。但是,如果不是因为报纸采取这一方针才使得大众缺乏判断的智慧,那又是因为什么呢?谁又能说,如果大众获知了所有事实,他们的判断能力还会比美国报纸工作人员差?

推崇这种行为的另一种解释甚至让人嗤之以鼻。他们说,某些报纸会隐瞒一些事实,而另一些报纸会隐瞒另一些事实,这样一来,公众获知的就是全部事实。这就好比是说,新闻工作者期望读者像法庭审讯目击证人一样去发掘公共事务的事实。民选政府得以实现的唯一机会是,将所有的事实清楚、客观地传达给公众。人们不可能永远那么聪明,但是,没有获知全部事实的经验,他们就不可能积累智慧。任何人或者机构,只要试图隐瞒事实,就表明他并非发自内心地相信民选政府。否则,他要么是一个骗子,要么是在自欺欺人。

补充阅读

兰塞姆:《俄国危机》。

科学服务社发布的新闻稿与复制件。

美国科学促进协会大会稿件:《纽约时报》1922年12月28—30日。

特罗特:《和平与战争时期的群体本能》,23—41页。

弗洛伊德:《精神分析引论》,340—355页。

密尔:《论自由》

萨蒙:《报刊和史学家》,114—137页,195—248页。

哈克特:《看不见的审查员》,1—10页。

李普曼和梅尔茨:《对新闻的检验》,《新共和》,1920年8月4日。

根特:《错误的新闻检验者》,《书评》第4期:488—489页,509—511页。

哈普古德:《新闻业》,载于《每日伦理》,1—15页。

布利文:《新闻道德》,载于《新共和》,第35期,17—19页。

第六章　客观性原则的应用：平衡与比例

前面的章节中提到过一种明确的新闻哲学，即客观地传播事实是新闻报道的首要任务。现在，假设所有人都认同这一理念，并对它的实践应用也喜闻乐见，那么，究竟该如何实现呢？当遇到难以判断的情况时，我们是否有明确的实际操作准则呢？

必须要承认的是，这种新闻哲学的实践会遇到重重困难。任何哲学都如此。报纸是由人运行的机构，因而不可能一直准确地遵守某种伦理或哲学观念。毫无疑问，大多数报纸正朝着这个目标慢慢迈进。同样毫无疑问的是，为了新闻客观性的理想，记者还需要取得更快、更大的进步。自然科学界正是放弃了主观臆测的方式，采用调查研究的方法后才取得长足的进步。关于人类各种机构如何解决最棘手的问题，这是一个很好的范例。

在所有确定的困难中，新闻界必须要面对和解决的是平衡与比例问题。你不会一次性碰上所有的问题，却会在一天的工作中不停地遇到问题。这个问题还涉及门外汉通常所说的"新闻压制"。在很大程度上，这还涉及煽情新闻——坚持某种伦理标准的人经常对新闻报道的一种指控。

在小镇上，比例和平衡的问题并不引人注目。镇上的报纸足以涵盖当地所有的新闻，版面很充裕。如果有一条新闻没有被刊登出来，基本上可以判定是出版商的故意隐瞒。同样的，关于某一特定地方事件的新闻价值问题也很少受到质疑。这个问题相对简单。

报纸规模越大，这个问题就越复杂。这种说法也不成立。都市日报的记者充分利用了版面以刊载尽可能多的新闻。另外，如果报道更加细致，发行量还会更大。显然，许多具有新闻价值的素材还是没出现在报纸中。很多新闻会被"压制"——简而言之就是不见报。这里的"压制"当然不是报纸批评家通常所指的重大公共事件被故意隐瞒，秘而不发。

大报的编辑都需要解决一个难题。新闻被压制的现象不仅真实存在，而且比人们想象中的还要严重。此外，编辑必须考虑所有事件的真实新闻价值，以及读者对这些事件的兴趣，尽管大多数报纸都过分强调后者。编辑在考虑日常新闻的平衡时，每则新闻的版面大小、某些新闻是否需要精简或直接删去等，所有这些问题都会扑面而来。

无论一个人多么努力地确保客观性，他（或她）都会在关键时刻受到自身生活理念或兴趣爱好的影响，除非有一个明确的标准在指引他。所以，为了在处理和平衡新闻时确保公平，一些报纸对于必须刊载哪些新闻都有具体的规定，或许所有的报纸都应如此。在大城市，某种级别的法院规定，所有入档的案件都要刊载在新闻专栏里。城市越小，需要将审判过程记录在案的法院级别就越低。但是，在小城镇，很多编辑都倾向于压制不光彩的新闻，理由是避免伤及新闻中提到的个人及其家人，而实际上，这不过是出于恐惧罢了。

威廉·艾伦·怀特（William Allen White）以一个醉汉的案例对这种态度做出了合理化的解释："一个喝多了威士忌的人出尽了洋相，妨害了公共安宁，如果放任不管，就会成为公共威胁。公众对这件事很感兴趣，这种关注是保证他今后不再犯错的因素之一。当地报纸没有理会他的第一次犯错。但是，当他被捕时，报纸记录了他的第二次犯错，无论他职位的高低，都会曝光他的名字。我们不断地提醒并警告过这些醉汉，所以，当他们质问为何不考虑他们的妻子儿女、患病的母亲和穷困年迈的父亲时，我们提醒他回忆之前的警告，如果他们犯罪前都没有考虑过自己的父母妻儿,那么他们犯罪后,我们也没有必要再予以考虑。"

另一种对压制犯罪新闻的常用解释是,避免破坏该城镇对外的声誉,不仅如此,还会激起该镇居民的反感。但是,如果按照这种逻辑,牧师应当放弃反对邪恶,甚至法院也无须惩治犯罪。这种解释自觉或不自觉地都基于一个理念,即无论压制什么新闻都是为了不造成危害。而且,赌徒、暴徒和其他惯犯的朋友和声援者都极力推崇这种说法,其目的无非是阻止这个城市清除犯罪行为。认同这种解释的报纸被罪犯和社会的堕落分子玩弄于股掌之间。

正如怀特先生指出的,对犯罪和不法行为的报道是一件公共事务,公开罪行是对邪恶力量的一种威慑。

而且,新闻报道还可以保护犯罪者的权利,防止犯罪事实被无限夸大,在小城镇尤其如此。如果有些事实没有被报道,流言会将其无限夸大。事实确凿的报道能让公众了解实情,从而做出公正的判断①。

在某些小城镇,甚至是大城市,新闻压制有时是因为涉及名人。但是,在大城市里,报纸间的竞争基本消除了这种可能性,多数都市日报都会报道名人所犯的小罪,如果是普通人犯了同样的事,反而不会关注。原因就在于公众对于名人的一举一动很感兴趣,而且,他们的举动确实可能造成一定的社会影响。当然,人们对于这个观点一直还存有争议,有待更合理的解释。

任何人的知名度都是由社会赋予的。一个人可能因为财富、家族地位或是自身的能力而出名,但这些都来自社会,都得益于生活在社会之中。同样的,社会也对知名度高的人有更浓厚的兴趣。

关于何种新闻可以被剔除,许多报纸都有相关的规定。这类新闻通常分为两类:(1)出于对事件涉及人员的考虑;(2)出于对社会整体利益的考虑。

第一种多涉及女性和孩子的过错。很多报纸都规定,不可报道法庭审判少年的过程,也不可提及涉案人员的姓名,除非当事人被判到改造

---

① 引自 J. S. 迈尔斯的《新闻道德规范》,第 30 页。

学校或类似机构。很多州都有相关的法令规定，例如，少年法庭既是特别法庭，又有权代替父母给予少年忠告和建议，甚至对他们进行体罚。因此，法令规定，少年法庭的听证会不对外公开，而为了保证诚信和司法声誉的公共法庭则不在此讨论范围。若未判刑，少年犯就不会受到玩伴的嘲弄，也不会被奉为英雄。童年总是特别敏感的，所以，对少年犯的判决不应公之于众。

涉及女性的案件与上面提及的观点相似。尽管明智者意识到似乎不应如此，但是，从当下文明的角度来说，女性失贞后很难挽回名声。即便女性自己并不十分重视贞洁，但是，她经常因卷入不幸状况而给自身造成不良的影响，就像马斯特斯的《匙河诗集》中那个女孩的遭遇一样。因此，城市里所谓道德法庭的审判往往不对外公开。几乎所有的报纸在涉及女性声誉方面都更加谨慎，很多都明确规定报道中不能涉及女性姓名以保全其声誉，除非涉案者是妓女或涉及其他重要领域。但是，所有其他犯罪案件中，新闻报道对待男女的态度应无二致。一般记者也有可能对涉及女性的新闻更加慎重——有些是应报纸要求。这当然不尽合理，对待所有人的新闻都应该尽最大努力保持谨慎。

通常，报道中删除的细节包括自杀者使用的毒药、盗贼作案的特殊手段，以及变态犯罪的猥亵细节。删除这些的主要原因是防止精神变态者或罪犯模仿。我们发现，很多自杀者采用了自杀案新闻报道中提及的某种毒药。犯罪行为的证据也不宜明示。

可以肯定的是，并非所有的报纸都删去这类细节。比如，一份都市日报报道了一个年轻盗贼第一次是如何得手，又是如何逃脱追捕的。① 也许，报道这则新闻的年轻记者只是为了显示自己对偷盗技术的丰富想象力，或者只是为了给读者提供消遣，而编辑部却忽略了对新闻作修改。

有些报纸强调，语言的使用是个伦理问题。笔者知道的一份报纸，有时会带着偏见报道新闻，有时会完全歪曲事实，但明确禁止使用一切

---

① 详见1920年2月25日《堪萨斯城星报》，《抢劫大叔的家》。

侮辱性的语言，例如"该死的"。很多报纸为了体现出道德感，会使用一些在中产阶级看来具有更高伦理标准的语言。比如，他们通常形容一个女子"未着寸缕"而非"一丝不挂"，尽管两个词的意思没有差别。这种行为只能表现出他们对道德和习俗的困惑。

对于前文提及的内容，报纸完全可以设定明确的规则。只要在不断地进步，这些其实都不是那么重要，在新闻报道中仅是鸡毛蒜皮的琐事。

对于新闻报道中更重要的部分，我们无法设定规则。随着事实被更为有效地记录下来，新闻压制的问题会随之减少。现在，报纸可以遵循的一个有效伦理标准是：不要因为涉及个人利益，不要因为编辑的爱憎喜好，不要因为质疑有无必要向公众公开，就压制新闻，除非你坚信其他的新闻比该新闻更加重要。保持新闻平衡是对一个记者是否具有客观性视角的重大考验。特别要指出的是，如果一个记者将观点高高凌驾于事实之上，他就可能在不知不觉中背叛了公众。倘若如此，没人能拯救他，因为他已经沦为一个背离客观事实的人。

补充阅读

班尼特：《公众所需》。

专题论文：《提供公众之所需》，索普的《未来的新闻人》，223－247页。

威廉·罗克希尔·纳尔逊：《人、报纸和城市的故事》，115－133页。

李普曼：《舆论学》，338－357页。

第七章　客观性原则的应用：煽情主义

和上一章谈到的新闻的平衡与比例一样，煽情新闻亦是编辑必须面对的一个尖锐的现实问题，对日报而言尤其如此。从某种程度上讲，煽情是新闻比例问题的一个方面，即便没有其他作用，至少它强调了新闻事实的某些方面，而排除或削弱了其他方面。煽情主义关乎报纸的商业利益，其影响比新闻压制更为直接。许多读者渐渐变得只关注煽情新闻，而对好的东西兴趣不大。煽情主义倾向于"夸大"生活中罪恶、邪恶和污秽的一面，因而也涉及伦理问题。

煽情主义产生的因素相对简单。虚构新闻、歪曲事实或带有偏见都应遭到谴责。仅仅为了吸引读者而故意煽情，与为了某种目的而传递有关重大事件的假信息一样，都应受到谴责。仅仅为了吸引读者而捏造离婚事件，与为了保护个人利益而捏造罢工事件一样，都有违新闻伦理。为了煽情而歪曲事实的行为虽比以往减少了很多，但仍然普遍存在。

在很大程度上，1898 年美西战争也因报纸的煽情报道所致。他们之所以挑起战争，不是因为美国确有发动战争的正当理由，也不是为了提升美国的声望或经济利益。他们的动机似乎主要是为了获得好的故事题材，而一场战争恰好能够提供这些。根据芝加哥种族关系委员会提供的资料，1919 年 7 月，《先驱考察家报》（*The Herald-Examiner*）报道了这样一则新闻：数千人冲进第八团军械库抢走枪支弹药，当局出动了警察，该事件造成了人员伤亡。委员会称，第八团军械库中根本没有武器，虽然窗户确实破了，但人们并没有强行冲进去，也没有与警察发生冲突[①]。该委员会也批评了其他芝加哥报纸，称其发布了不实的煽情新闻：1919年夏天黑人和白人之间发生暴乱[②]。众所周知，在当时获得真实的新闻并不容易。时局不好时，报刊不断提升责任是一件有压力的事。

记者撰写煽情新闻的情况时有发生，有时是报纸没有规定，有时是故意违反规定，他们还辩称，这样做是希望提升报纸的价值。这些记者没有荣誉感，而他们的老板一边为自己开脱，将责任全推向记者，一边又刊登了记者的煽情新闻。

为了煽情而侵犯隐私是另一种不可宽恕的行为。当然，我们有必要仔细思考一下什么是隐私。年轻记者总是不愿报道一些入情入理的新闻，因为一些前辈名人劝他们说这些与报纸无关。关乎公共福祉的事情就是公众的事，记者有权以任何正当的途径获得这些新闻。记者没有义务等到有人利用这些事实为个人谋取私利时，方才发布给公众。的确，记者没有等待的义务，只要能通过正当的途径获得可靠的新闻事实，就不用承担责任。当许多公众关心的事实直接涉及个人时，这些人就不愿公开或者只愿部分公开事件内容。没人会反对公布真相，除了一些别有用心的人，企图将本该公之于众的事实掩盖起来。

具有是非观念的人都反对侵犯隐私，侵犯隐私的问题也备受公众关注。尤其是女性，即使她们可能与煽情新闻没有直接的关联，她们也反对侵犯隐私。例如，一位声誉不佳的年轻女性被杀，当局宣称将审问一位知名的已婚富豪，该男子曾与被害者关系甚密。迫于报刊舆论压力，当局公布了该男子的姓名。此案中，报纸扮演了一个特殊的角色。公众有权知道该男子是谁，当局则被迫扮演公众代表，而不是私人侦探，没

[①] 《芝加哥的黑人》，第29页。

[②] 同上，25—33页。

有因为这些人拥有财富和地位而庇护他们。但是，紧接着，一些报社找到该男子的妻子，试图问她一些观众并不关心的问题，甚至监视她的家，以至于她必须请保安来保护自己的隐私。报纸公开了获取到的所有关于该妻子的信息，包括她的照片。报纸这样做的目的，仅仅是为了引起某个读者群体的病态好奇心罢了，却丢掉了报纸应提供新闻事实的职能，变成了一个廉价的流言蜚语传播者。令人振奋的是，这种行为最近受到了代表这个国家最高新闻标准①的《编辑与出版商》的批评。

但是，这些受批判的行为依旧普遍存在，甚至在那些不喜煽情的报纸中亦是屡见不鲜。每天的报纸中都有一些类似的做法，例如，发布罪犯亲人的照片，采用与新闻没有直接关联者的访谈……

没有哪种观点为这些煽情主义的把戏正名，甚至那些发布煽情新闻的人也认为其不正当。

煽情主义问题的解决，需要消除各种歪曲事实和侵犯隐私的行为，这在很大程度上是一个平衡的问题。如前文所言，为了隐瞒涉及公众利益的事实，而在报纸的整个版面或是部分个人故事中进行的新闻选择，都是不公正的。但是，即使不是为了隐瞒，一份报纸也可能在选择新闻方面采取各种方针。

如果一份报纸的目标读者是高知人群，其新闻选择便主要考虑新闻的重要性。极度煽情的报纸是另一种极端，这类报纸对新闻的选择，建立在读者兴趣的基础上，普遍使用的术语是"人情味"，这也是人们的兴趣转向流行小说和舞台音乐剧的原因。伴随着大城市中煽情报纸发行量的飙升，尤其是早期赫斯特旗下的报纸，"人情味"理论作为新闻选择的一个标准不断发展。煽情报纸最大的销量源自那些以前从未读过任何报纸的群体。这些人属于工人阶层，多来自欧洲，初到美国还不超过两代人。他们对美国的政治、经济和社会问题知之甚少，感兴趣的事情还局限于自己的家庭、周遭的小店和一些熟悉的栖息地，与一桩轰动性的刑事审判、日俄战争或宾夕法尼亚州钢铁工人罢工相比，前者更能引

---

① 《新闻业、编辑与出版商》，1923年3月31日，第34页。

起他们的兴趣。报纸出版商发号施令：要给这些读者提供他们想看的。于是"人情味"报纸便蓬勃发展起来。

有人说，煽情报纸也有功劳，就是让那些相对没什么文化的群体能在阅读报纸时学到一些知识。而且，煽情新闻确实影响了美国新闻业的方方面面。《堪萨斯城星报》（The Kansas City Star）的资深出版商W·R·纳尔逊（W. R. Nelson）曾指出，困扰大多数编辑的问题在于，他们为赫斯特先生经营的报纸工作。

煽情报纸带来的其他的方面影响主要有两点。其中，浮夸的大字号新闻标题已受到评论界的强烈批评。这不一定涉及伦理，却可能是品位问题。从伦理的立场看，大字标题唯一可能的危害在于它挤掉了那些本该刊登的新闻。煽情报纸发明大号标题以吸引读者，时至如今还有许多报纸这样做。这对于街边卖报和报亭销量具有一定的商业价值，却不是煽情主义的标志。一些报纸在新闻调查和撰写的过程中十分保守，却也使用大号标题。另一些报纸虽然主张在新闻故事中引入煽情，却使用小号标题。他们这么做的目的，可能是为了迎合思想保守但知识欠缺的读者，因为以前"黄色新闻"常常使用夸张的大号标题，以至于让这些读者认为标题越小，新闻故事越真实。新闻故事的重要性尺度与标题的相对大小有关，而与实际采用的字号无关。暗示新闻的相对重要性是否有必要，也颇受质疑，因为这种暗示实质上是编辑的个人想法，也阻止了读者对客观严肃事实的进一步探索。当代读者花在报纸上的时间很少[①]，对将要发生的变化，他们无疑还没有做好准备。

煽情新闻对美国报业的另一种影响显得更为重要，虽然评论界对此没有给予足够的关注。即，倡导在检验新闻方面强调读者兴趣而非事件本身的重要性。这样，煽情报纸便满足了人的一种强烈的原始本能需求。正如约翰·梅西所言，"人人都爱看故事，只有极少数人会在吃早餐时渴求时事信息。"[②]这种情况的缺点在于，煽情报纸及其效仿报刊，

---

① 根据沃尔特·迪尔·斯科特的一项调查，典型的芝加哥商人或职场人士每天花一刻钟阅读当地报纸。参见斯科特的《广告心理学》，375－394页。
② 《美国的文明》，第45页。

在很大程度上只关注那些唾手可得的、琐碎的、纯娱乐的、肤浅的故事。1923年夏天，美国报刊对拳击手登普西和吉本斯的决斗以及美国教育协会召开大会的报道情况，就可窥见一斑。7月5日，美国主要城市的报纸这两事件时使用的版面英寸数分别如下：①

（单位：英寸）

	登普西和吉本斯的决斗	教育协会大会
纽约	1425.75	93.5
芝加哥	1353.5	1.75
华盛顿	405	8

美国报纸过去做过并在以后可能继续做的是，保持重要信息言简意赅，且饶有趣味。科学服务社的经验很好地体现了这一点，让乏味的科学材料变得生动有趣，以吸引普通读者。让重要信息明白易懂并非易事，而煽情主义采取了最简单的方式迎合了读者的兴趣，这或许是其主要的害处。如果这种给重要信息增加趣味性的做法持续下去，煽情新闻最终的影响将十分可喜，因为对于那些只是为了兴趣和消遣的读者而言，阅读内容的重要性增强了。

对煽情新闻进行客观评价时，我们应承认它在促进新闻报道发展方面确实有一定的贡献：让调查成为记者工作的一部分。虽然煽情报纸的调查并非总是正面的，但它至少表明了报刊有机会、有责任成为一种社会调查力量，而记者亦不仅仅是一个倾听者。

需进一步思考的是，煽情主义对伦理标准和读者行为的影响。如何处理犯罪和负面新闻，可以检验报刊报道煽情新闻时采取的各种方针和实践标准。有一种极端是，当报刊认为刊登负面新闻对读者丝毫无益

---

① 数据引自1923年7月6日波士顿的《基督教科学箴言报》。《箴言报》没有报道登普西和吉本斯的决斗，却用227英寸的版面报道了教育协会的大会；《波士顿晚报》则用了25.5英寸的版面报道了登普西和吉本斯的决斗，用40英寸的版面报道了教育协会的大会。《波士顿邮报》《波士顿全球报》《波士顿先驱报》都没有报道教育协会的大会，它们合计用了942.5英寸的篇幅报道了登普西和吉本斯的决斗。

时，它们会放弃所有此类新闻。在新闻界，职业新闻工作者很少有人支持这种观点。美国的《基督教科学箴言报》（*The Christian Science Monitor*）是此类报纸中的典型，但它绝非排斥所有关于犯罪的新闻。而且，该报的特别之处在于，它并非地方报纸，而是国际报纸。《基督教科学箴言报》虽在波士顿出版发行，但它的多数销量是在波士顿范围之外，这与一般报纸的情况完全不同。即使是最为知名的美国报纸，其销量也往往局限于各自的城市。

还有数量较少的一类报纸，以《波士顿晚报》为代表，对犯罪新闻的处理总是很简单。《波士顿晚报》报道某个轰动一时的谋杀案时，使用了两英寸的版面和一个双行标题。与之相比，波士顿的其他煽情报纸对此的报道往往覆盖三个以上新闻专栏，使用通栏标题，还会配上两幅图片。从《波士顿晚报》处理犯罪新闻的方式可知，公众有权知晓这类新闻，同时，报纸也要捍卫社会团体的伦理观，以及公开犯罪事实确保正义执法，而大量地曝光犯罪细节则是败坏道德和自贬身价的行为。

美国多数大型报纸则属于另外两类：一类包含翔实的犯罪新闻，同时有丰富多彩的其他内容与之平衡；另一类则用煽情性、暗示性的细节包装犯罪新闻。对于这两类报纸采取的策略（尤其是后者），比较流行的辩解是，既然阻止和惩治犯罪是公众的责任，那么他们就应该对犯罪现象感到震惊。恐怕多数情况下，这种观点只是文过饰非，为过分渲染犯罪新闻的行为做了辩护，为的是迎合读者或作者或双方病态的情感。

报纸发布细节丰盈的犯罪新闻，迎合了大众的心理和需求，却普遍削弱了新闻原有的效果。例如，一般而言，报纸和读者对性犯罪的直接反应是"魔鬼""堕落"等。他们对这些违反社会习俗的行为普遍感到反感，将性犯罪视为一种故意违反道德的罪行。事实上，性犯罪通常被认为是精神变态的结果。

令人吃惊的是，涉及哈里·K·肖的案件中，某些报纸刊登了一些令人厌恶的细节，以至于面临刑事诉讼。然而，据笔者了解，没有哪家报纸刊物，对折磨肖的性心理变态事实，发表过任何合理、中肯的解释，也没有就如何避免这种威胁进行过任何讨论。

1921 年，堪萨斯城所有的报纸对"卖淫团伙"的报道都有一些性暗示内容，这很容易引起一个未成年男孩或女孩去深究。同时，没有哪家报纸对事件中主犯饱受折磨的同性恋心理做过合理的说明，也没有哪家报纸从精神病理的角度予以分析。没有这些解释说明，新闻就是不完整的。

煽情新闻是否大力助长了犯罪行为，这是一个有争议的话题，直接的证据大多是消极的。一方面，道德家认为，煽情新闻削弱了道德观，降低了伦理标准。另外，相反的观点认为，如果道德观的削弱和道德水平的下降确实存在，那么它应该与煽情主义互为因果。事实上，对煽情主义的反对大多基于审美角度，而非伦理角度，尽管反对者并不这么认为。

很明显，煽情新闻排挤掉了内容更重要的其他新闻。煽情新闻的特点是，强调犯罪和社会阴暗面，关注鸡毛蒜皮的琐事，这意味着留给重要新闻的版面更少了。如果某份报纸将一个专栏都用于报道某个音乐喜剧明星的 47 卡车衣服，或者消防员如何花半个小时营救一只困在电线杆上的猫，那么国内、国际新闻都将遭殃。无疑，要想吸引读者，新闻必须有趣。如果不能吸引读者，新闻就毫无社会价值可言。另外，若想具有公共价值，新闻就要传递重要的新闻事实。公众对琐碎和煽情新闻感兴趣的程度，以及报纸在这方面的努力程度，是一个公开的问题，这就好比是问：如果报纸不报道琐碎事件，它还能在吸引广大读者的道路上走多远？试想在某个特别的城市，有大量受过良好教育、具有文化修养的读者，支持一份纯粹提供信息的报纸。这明显与美国城市或城镇的一般情况格格不入。很少有报纸能像《波士顿晚报》那样，即使没有煽情新闻，也能成功地经营下去，有着 30,000 份以上的期发行量，其广告费率是每玛瑙行 20 美分。

另外，报纸也没有必要为了与其他煽情报纸竞争而保留煽情新闻。保留煽情新闻或许是最简单易行的方法。公众更喜欢煽情题材的新闻，因为易于理解，因为有"人情味"，从而为人们提供一种情感宣泄的途径。但是，重大新闻中也可以注入"人情味"，增加感情因素，而重要事情与日常生活的关系又是显而易见的。这点在现实中却难以实现,因为重大事件涉及的当局都是糟糕的发言者或写作者,很少有记者或编辑能将这些题材转换过来,并在智力和情感上吸引普通大众。《堪萨斯城星报》的快速增长在美国新闻界是有名的案例之一,其成功在于主办者制定的政策,即从其他出版物中遴选兼具重要性和趣味性的内容。在这种政策指引下,该报纸摒弃了煽情主义的主张,与一些高度煽情的出版物相匹敌,保持着较大的订阅量和良好的广告运营。

在小镇上,煽情主义的问题并没有那么严重。小城镇的电报服务并不繁荣,其报纸只在当地发行。想看煽情新闻的读者,可以在附近的城市购买都市日报。在小城镇,煽情新闻少得多。即便有,一般也不会做煽情化处理,一部分是因为当地新闻工作者在撰写煽情新闻方面缺乏训练,另一部分是因为公众对此缺乏需求。而且,小镇居民更希望看到的是关乎自己切身利益的新闻。对这些报纸而言,公众关注的就是重要的事情。而且,在一些大城市的煽情日报中占有一席之地的谣言故事,在小城镇靠口口相传。增加这些内容并不会改善小镇报纸的质量,除非增加的是一些看似与社会结构相关的重要内容。

毫无疑问,煽情主义的潮流正在退去。一份明智的报纸需要在新闻工作者和读者两方面下工夫。例如,1923年初,洛杉矶女性发起了一项要求减少南加州报纸对犯罪和丑闻报道的运动。① 1922年,俄勒冈州编辑协会采取的解决之道,或许用来表达编辑和出版商的态度:

> 我们认为,报纸职业是最荣耀、最重要、最具影响力的职业之一。因而,在追求最优服务、积极考虑公德与私德方面应该最为谨慎。
>
> 我们坚信,过分注重丑闻、犯罪和不道德新闻会对公众的思想意识造成不良影响,尤其对可塑性强的年轻人影响更甚。

---

① 参见新闻故事《300,000加州民众呼吁内容更干净的报纸》和社论文章《呼吁内容干净的新闻业》,《基督教科学箴言报》,1923年1月6日。

既然我们已对此深信不疑，意识到报纸在发布新闻时的责任，那么我们奉劝同行不要过分强调淫秽内容，尤其奉劝各类报刊协会对此进行监督。

补充阅读

《芝加哥的黑人》，芝加哥种族关系委员会，436－594页。

斯特里特：《报纸真相》，《芝加哥论坛报》，1919年7月25日。

芬顿：《报纸报道社会犯罪和社会阴暗面所带来的影响》，美国社会学期刊第16期，342－371页，538－564页。

阿尔杰：《轰动性新闻和法律》，布莱耶的《新闻职业》，167－180页。

劳埃德：《报业的良知——关于半真半假报道的研究》.《美国社会学期刊》第27期，197－210页。

格拉登：《被污染的新闻业：好与坏》，索普的《未来报业》，27－50页。

《新闻业、编辑与出版商》，1923年3月31日，第34页。

斯科特：《广告心理学》，375－394页。

《呼吁内容干净的新闻业》和《300,000加州民众呼吁内容更干净的报纸》，《基督教科学箴言报》，1923年1月6日。

威廉姆斯：《主席演讲》，夏威夷世界媒体大会，70－77页。

第八章　客观性原则的应用：社论引导

当客观性受到重视，并成为报纸追求的首要目标时，问题自然就来了：当代新闻界难道没有社论引导的容身之地了吗？

如今，鲜有记者或者舆论专业的学生会认为，报纸有责任发表社论以引导读者。他们坚称，引导舆论的理想很大程度上已经被传播客观事实的理想所取代。或许，一些人会带着遗憾回顾过往，尤其是那些年长者。其他持现实主义观点的人则质疑：在一个民选政府的国家，引导公众舆论还有必要吗？

大多数人虽然认为社论引导不是报刊最重要的功能，但仍然承认它是必要的功能之一。很少有报纸会放弃社论引导。但是，许多农村周刊都没有社论文章，除非编辑偶尔觉得有必要对社区说点什么时，才会刊登一两篇；而大城市的报纸几乎都有社论文章。

报刊社论的影响力在逐渐减弱。观察者指出，在纽约市的选举中，候选人虽遭到几乎所有报纸的反对却仍然竞选成功。类似的情况在堪萨斯城也出现过。他们还提到，尽管俄克拉荷马和堪萨斯两个州新当选的州长此前在报纸上的负面新闻很多，但这并未妨碍他们竞选成功。考虑到这些实际发生的情况,人们很难相信,报刊社论的影响力与其发行量一样大。

社论影响力下降的原因之一在于,公众认为,涉及争议性问题尤其是党派政治问题时,报刊上的新闻并不可信。公众的逻辑是,如果新闻专栏中有假,那么,报刊社论专栏的推理便不可靠。从这个角度考虑,报刊社论不会影响政党选举中的大多数选民,因为他们对政党产生的依赖和惯性难以克服;但还是会影响到独立选民,这些虽属于少数派,数量上却足以左右选举的结果。

报刊在选举中的影响力不够以及公众对报刊信心不足,原因还在于,报刊仅在选举期间发表大量批判性言论。因此,公众会认为,报刊只对赢得选举感兴趣,而不是倡导涉及公众利益的政策。倘若报纸支持自己认可的政策,并时刻监督官员们对这些政策的履行情况,报纸就能在美国选民中获得良好的影响力。

有人断言,报纸社论文章的阅读量不如从前。如果只考虑社论读者在总读者中的比例,这种论断确实成立;如果考虑这些读者的实际数量,则不成立。早期,报纸的阅读人群属于小众。1812年战争(译者注:美国第二次独立战争)结束时,纽约所有报纸的发行量都未超过2,000。① 那时,这些订阅者几乎阅读报纸上的所有内容。报纸版面也很少,读者有足够的时间读完。虽然那时的读者只占选民的一小部分,却可能比现在相同数量的读者群拥有更大的影响力。今天,任何一个识字的公民在任何地方都能轻松地获得一份报纸。大部分读者对社论文章很少关注,或根本不关注。一般而言,都市日报的读者中有20%的人阅读社论文章,就报纸整体而言稍多于这个比例。大部分读者可能关注幽默专栏、读者来信或社论专题。知识分子和有影响力的人倾向于阅读社论,尽管他们更愿意接受学术周刊的观点而非报纸的观点。与100年或50年前相比,这类读者在总人口中比例变得更大了。对于那些思想独立的人来说,报纸的社论专栏跟过去一样,是一个取经的好地方。

---

① 李:《美国新闻史》,第142页。

为了扩大社论文章的阅读群,很多报纸采取在头版刊登社论的策略,常见的如赫斯特报业集团,为记者亚瑟·布里斯班(Arthur Brisbane)设有社论专栏。还有《堪萨斯城星报》,当记者发现某个合适的新闻适合写社论文章时,就付诸行动。

许多报纸设有署名专栏,用于发表个人评论观点。署名的社论比非署名的社论是否更有影响力,还不得而知。使用署名社论版面的,读者都知道这些专栏是某些个人所有。受专栏署名影响的读者都知道,赫斯特集团报纸代表赫斯特先生本人的个性和观点。读者即使不知道这一事实也无妨,署名专栏对其影响也不会大过报纸上的其他内容,除非专栏作者在国内有很高的知名度。的确,如果报纸编辑给自己的社论署名,他们会有更高的知名度,这对报纸的发展也有利。无论是读者还是报纸自身,都期待社论文章有署名。观点型杂志采取这种署名做法,因而大大提升知名度。

但是,报纸作为一个社会机构发声有某些优势。大型都市日报的社论委员会每天都有会晤,讨论所有可能作为社论主旨的选题,并最后确定方向。经过充分的讨论之后,除了一些技术性问题外,社论文章的大致主题也会被敲定。决议可能通过投票产生,更可能是由报纸主管人员确定。而社论的撰写任务则被分派给不同的作者,在这个过程中,通常会参考作者的信仰问题,即是否与主题一致。如果某位作者在内心里觉得不能按照社论委员会的决定写作,撰写任务则会被分配给另一位作者。这种情况极少发生,社论委员会的观点通常较为一致;报纸在聘请员工时也会优先考虑那些认同自身方针的人。保守型报纸,其社论委员会成员同样保守;开明型杂志,其社论委员会成员也较为自由开明。有什么样的社论委员会就会出现什么样的社论文章,尽管文章由个人撰写,观点却不代表个人,而是受到委员会其他成员的影响。

对于小型报纸,几乎所有的社论文章均出自一人之手,而这个人可能常与报纸出版商发生争执,除非他们对公共政策持相似的观点。英国报纸中，编辑的地位最高。① 美国报纸却不同，社论作者宁可辞职也不愿撰写任何他认为是错的东西。如果必须得写，他可能会写出不符合报纸规定的文章，以对抗上司，如果歪曲自己的观点，会被认为是背弃公众。

对于更小型的报纸，出版商往往自己撰写社论文章，作为一名服务公众者，他只对自己的良知负责。多数情况下，这些小型报纸的出版商在谈论国内或国际大事时表现欠佳，但在有效处理社区事务时则得心应手。与大型都市日报相比，一份小镇日报或周报在其社区中的影响力最大，因而既有责任又有特权。

任何一份报纸的社论作者都有一种主要职责，即澄清事实，帮助读者透过事实得出可靠的结论。人们越来越深刻地意识到，社论更多的是解释而非倡导，集公诉人、公诉辩护人和法官的身份于一体。因为负有责任，所以社论不可对新闻事实有任何解释，总结时也不可使用任何似是而非的论据。然而，编辑常常使用这类论据，并且是无意识地。作者会被自己的偏见、恐惧、希望所误导，或者他在合理的逻辑推理方面能力有限，许多优秀作者亦如此。

很多情况下，报纸社论的影响体现在所谓的"社论运动"中。这些活动反复出现，产生的效果比社论文章更为明显，至少现在是如此。1899年7月4日，詹姆斯·基利（James Keeley）在《芝加哥论坛报》发起的改革运动就是一个例子，近几年，该报在禁止私人燃放烟花方面也斩获一些成果②。另一个例子是《纽约论坛报》发起的取缔欺骗性广告的运动，但由于执行时间和力度不够，以至于没有达到理想效果③。这些运动和其他社论引导一样，并非报刊的伦理责任，一份报纸可以依据自己的意愿，选择参加或不参加改革运动。

有人认为，报纸运动并非严格意义上的新闻，基于伦理的考量，报

---

① 这种做法有着悠久历史。若看对比性内容，请参见贝洛克的《自由的新闻业》。
② 详情请参见 W. G. N.，第60页。
③ 《芝加哥论坛报》在其宣传册中就新闻活动方式进行了讨论：《如何工作》，案例取自1914年至1916年《芝加哥论坛报》的"建言"栏目。

纸的义务是向读者报道事实。而现实并非如此。以《纽约时报》为例，该报并非真正意义上的"改革报纸"，却在1870年到1871年曝光了特威德集团的丑闻。1922年，《底特律新闻报》(*The Detroit News*) 曝光了赛马博彩造假事件，虽类似于新闻，但终究还不是新闻。记者的新闻观比一些评论家，例如著名的沃尔特·李普曼先生，更为宽泛。他认为，"新闻的（唯一）功能在于让人们关注某事件"①，新闻是事实的代名词，而报刊却要满足不太可能的需求。该观点有很强的合理性，但经验丰富的记者却很少像他那样局限于新闻本身的定义。他们意识到，有时没有做某事，与事件本身一样，是同等重要的新闻。在特威德集团丑闻事件中，《纽约时报》曝光了城市的财务账目一直处于隐瞒状态，尽管法律规定其为公共财产。在记者看来，市政官员没有公布财政的使用情况，就是一则有价值的新闻。与李普曼先生持相同观点的评论者认为，如果民众采取法律程序要求城市的公共账目公之于众，则是新闻，其他的则不是。不让报刊曝光某些明显是新闻的事件，让记者放弃必要的调查职能，都是不切实际的。若是那样的话，报刊上的新闻将会越来越不重要。

与改革运动有关的事件与新闻都密切相关，因而存在一种触犯伦理准则的风险。

当一个组织（例如报刊）或个人为了公众的利益而发起某种运动时，他们会强调与该运动目的相符的事实，而忽视与之相悖的事实，甚至捏造与事实不相符的内容。如今，报刊在反对禁酒令以及倡导禁酒措施时，这种倾向很明显。当报纸对某种运动感兴趣，尤其是自己发起某种运动时，会更加小心翼翼，以免被谴责是只重结果不重过程的教条主义者。

除了新闻事实，一个人在报纸运动中的伦理立场在很大程度上取决于他对社会机构的态度。一位记者很可能认为，报纸运动对新闻的至高地位是一种威胁。他注意到，过分关注改革运动的报纸，留给新闻的空

---

① 《舆论学》，第358页。

间和关注就会减少。即使报纸运动不会干涉新闻，记者也会认为运动可能会以投票表决或其他形式分散民众对客观事实的注意力，从而损害记者本人在新闻报道中的表现。

在报纸圈内和圈外，坚定或不坚定的理想主义者更倾向于大量发起各种运动和特别服务。"只要是对公众有利的事，报纸都应去做。"这代表一种缺乏判断力的态度。煽情报纸强调各种运动以及对读者的特别服务，一方面无疑是为了商业目的，另一方面是给报纸增添"人情味"。用一个著名的新闻业观点来形容，就是"报纸应该有灵魂"。无可否认，报纸提供的特别服务确实能感染读者。社论引导的目的亦是如此。这种情况的发展对出版业而言有一定的好处，一方面增加了社论文章的分量，另一方面加强了新闻的可信度。人们喜欢从仰慕对象那里获得观点或"事实"。正如西格蒙德·弗洛伊德博士（Dr. Sigmund Freud）所说：

> 信仰会不断重复上演，它是爱的延伸，而首先需要消除争议。如果论点是由所爱之人提出的，最终都会被接受，且之后的论点也会和它一致。没有得到支持的论点毫无用处，对多数人而言一无是处。人若能抵御性欲控制，终将才华横溢。[1]

需指出的是，如果某份报纸通过特别服务或其他方式获得了公众的信任和喜爱，那么它需要很小心，不可发布虚假新闻或社论影响到这种信任。

报纸与社论引导的关系密切，我们很容易从报纸上看到代表舆论的表达，而非引导舆论的言论。因为通信专栏给我们提供了这种机会。这些专栏并没有想象中那么重要，因为观点只是来自大众中的少数人，多数情况下，对于涉及个人利益的事件，这些人的观点常常因脱离事实而变味。

诚实的编辑在处理读者来信时会十分小心。他没有必须刊登某封来

---

[1] 《精神分析引论》，第385页。

信的责任，而有自己的判断权。但是，他有义务对自己造成的或读者指出的错误进行校正。在刊登读者来信时，编辑如果没有保持各种观点的平衡，就是对读者的不公平。如果他只选择那些赞扬的信件，忽视不同观点的信件，也是有违伦理的。

如果编辑给某封读者的来信拟了一个违背作者本意（甚至完全相反）的标题，就更加有违伦理了。人们对此颇有微词。例如，阿尔弗雷德·H·劳埃德教授（Prof. Alfred H. Lloyd）曾以切身经历作为例子呼吁大家对此有所关注：

> 不久前，我向某家与我持不同政见的报纸投了一封信。该信件仅是一个实验。信中，我提到某位公众人物的投机行为，引用其不同时间的演讲，以指出其内容前后矛盾的问题。我好奇该报会不会刊登这封信，并予以曝光。结果是，信件被发表了，标题却作了删减，文中也省略了一些重要的语句，于是，一位表里不一的政客看起来像一位爱国者！我感到很无助。如果报纸并非为公众服务的，至少它有权不发表这封信，但是，它无权篡改作者的标题或内容。①

当然，有时报纸想要发表的信件太长，在压缩内容时就存在风险。以细心和诚实为基础的删减相对安全一些。没有哪家报纸不作说明就删减，最后还能言之有理。忠实于原文的编辑，可能无意中省略了某个重要部分而违背伦理，也可能删掉了确实不重要但作者却认为重要的内容，导致作者觉得编辑的行为有违伦理。这和做了有违伦理之事一样，都对报纸的立场有害。有一种建议是，编辑将他认为要删减的信件退回，并说明需要删减之处，让作者自行决定是否愿意按意见修改。由于可操作性不强，这种方法也饱受诟病。

报纸为了扩大发行量，增加利润，可以通过发表华丽的社论文章、

---

① 《美国社会学杂志》第 27 卷，第 3 页。

迎合舆论等途径来实现。仅从财务角度考虑，我们不能推断说："除非记者提供受人欢迎或符合道德的内容，否则他不会成功。"[①]《波士顿报》和《纽约时报》近期的发展恰好证明了相反的情况。即使采取这些方法能提升报纸的利润，但如果这与报纸传播客观事实的功能相冲突，代价则显得太大。

补充阅读

维拉德：《一些报纸和报人》。

戴维斯：《〈纽约时报〉的历史》，81—116页。

奥·布莱恩：《〈太阳报〉的故事》，304—312页。

希顿：《一个新闻版面的故事》。

《W. G. N.》，53—79页。

斯科特：《〈曼彻斯特卫报〉：一个世纪的历史》。

《赛马场贪污》，底特律新闻报宣传册。

李普曼：《舆论学》，358—365页。

莱普：《报刊力量的衰弱》，布莱尔的《新闻职业》，30—51页。

---

① 佩恩，《美国媒体的历史》，第326页。

第九章　建立专业标准：法律措施

当涉及政府、文明的丑闻甚或不快曝光在美国民众面前时，他们会立即将注意力聚焦于他们认为负有责任的个人或团队，并愤慨地说："应该把这些人送进监视。"当民众意识到没有法律能将肇事者送进监狱时，他们便开始议论："应该制定这样的法律。"

相比于记者，美国民众的法律信仰应是心理学家关注的问题。无可否认，这是美国社会的一个既成事实，也是每个公共机构或准公共机构必须要面对的事实。

随着公众对法律的依赖的加深，为了提升报刊规范而提议出台一些法律也就不足为奇了。现存的法律中主要有关于诽谤罪、禁止色情描写的，还有关于禁止某些类型广告的。① 一般而言，法律规定对报纸和公众都是公平的。但是，禁止色情描写却是个例外，虽然已经扩展到了许多文学领域，但对杂志和书籍的影响更深，而非报纸。敏感法官对于报纸工作者藐视法庭的指控，于直接当事人而言并不公平，对报纸履行正当的职能也是不利的。

从法律上限制新闻业的其他提议，旨在凭借法律手段确保新闻报道

---

① 更多关于法律对报刊约束的讨论，请参见黑尔斯《报刊的法律》。

准确、公正。其中，最强烈的一项建议是，要求报纸履行"强制性真实"。爱德华·保罗（Edward Paul）提议时，是这样表述的：

> 报纸的强制性真实和对食物要求强制性安全一样，都不是对民主权利的侵犯。新闻报刊暗示我们，纯粹的新闻法律将与新闻"自由"相冲突，民主更关注健康的身体而非健康的思想。只有当民主维护那些本不该享受特权的少数人时，健康的思想才与民主相抵触。当包装工人内部意见发生分歧，或管理铁路事务的各利益方争执不下时，思想更健康的民众才会将更多具有民主思想的人送上华盛顿政坛。而获得选票的人，最后的特权才是欺骗选民，就像去年11月发生的那样。社会进程已经发展到需要我们擦亮眼睛的阶段了。
>
> 重要的是，报纸在实现强制性真实的目标之前，还有很长的路要走。任何时候，经济形势的压力都会使民众意识到，他们不能再信任某些机构发布的新闻了。当民众意识到这些时，他们会质问，究竟是怎样的政府，竟然允许大多数民众遭受蒙骗，而大多数的人们继续埋头苦干，对此视而不见。①

为了实现绝对准确，人们提出的法律建议是："任何人肆意在报纸或者期刊中发表不实言论，故意或大意地发布不实、错误言论，都属违法行为"。

除此之外，每份报纸都应该保留一个专栏，留给具有文学修养的公共辩护人。辩护人"由民众选举产生，能够对被埋没的新闻给予足够的重视，能补充一些常被遗漏的观点"。

报纸《仲裁员》负责执行这一计划，该报编辑认为，"该体系一旦流行起来，将可能维护新闻自由。如果正确的观点在同一份报纸上受到同等的重视，一些看似令人吃惊的观点也就会被接受了。如果报纸的方

---

① 该处引自1919年7月《仲裁员》（第二卷，第2期）

针是反对征兵和敛财,那么报纸就需要经常解释为何这些在政府官员眼中站不住脚的观点对民众却是负责任的。"

他还说道,"另一种做法是,将对报刊的所有不满都提交给当地的各种委员会。这些委员会要做的就是通过罚金或暂停营业的方式对报刊的虚假言论进行惩罚,或者强令肇事者在专栏的显著位置澄清事实。这样的委员会不仅能减轻法院的负担,还可以安排相关部门和人员维护公共正义。"虽然对经验丰富的记者和严谨的新闻专业学生而言,这些提议显得有些荒谬,但对于那些不了解报纸现状、希望靠法律解决所有问题的人来说,这些提议很有吸引力。按照提议,歪曲事实属于违法行为。如果记者罔顾事实、捏造新闻,被提议的法律便适用于此。除非记者粗心,这种情况很少发生。法庭上的案例报告、市政事务的报告、法律和执法程序报告,都应有理有据、准确反映事实。倘若一位记者出于大意或故意且习惯性地歪曲事实,他便不可能在任何重要的报纸中再有一席之地。

还有其他情况,比如,对事实进行认真彻底的调查之前,允许对真相持不同的观点。有时,呈现的相互冲突的例证太多,法官都难下判决。起诉记者因粗心而犯错的案例即属于此列。熟悉法庭的人都知道,陪审团很乐意原谅这种情有可原的错误,在许多法律程序中,报纸工作者无意识犯错的案例也会被原谅。

某些州的现有法律对散布虚假信息或不实新闻的知法犯法者制定了惩罚规定。纽约州《刑法》第1,353条就是这样一条法规,但很少被用到,以至于许多新闻人都不知道它的存在。最近,明尼苏达州出台了类似的法律,纽约州的一些报纸称其为一部新型法规。1922年,马萨诸塞州通过的一项法规中规定,发布关于政府职务候选人虚假新闻的行为将被处以罚款或监禁。① 假定确保新闻真实的途径是通过法律,那么,这些被提议的法律明显作用不大。这无疑会带来很多诉讼,而焦点却是鸡毛蒜皮的琐事,而且诉讼还得花费一段时间。之后,除了一些明显的违

---

① 《马萨诸塞州基本法》,第55章,第34a条。

法行为（如诽谤等）会被追责外，法规形同虚设。

关于设立公共辩护人的提议显得更荒谬。任何一位与官员打交道的新闻人都知道，一旦涉及这些官员的个人或所在党派的利益时，无论是乡镇议员，还是国家高官，都很难保持公正客观。有人会说，公共辩护人在有争议的问题上能代表大多数人的观点。但是，美国有争议的问题太多，没有哪个官员会在所有问题上都代表大多数人的观点。这些官员竞选成功的因素有很多，一些选民看重这个问题，而另一些则看重另一个问题。而且，发布客观事实是报纸的最大职能，公众一般不会或者从来不去寻求全部真相。设立公共辩护人的提议者幼稚地认为这是"正确的想法"，显然他也属于粗心的思考者，认为正确的想法应该靠多数人投票产生。若真是这样的话，那么试问：当年苏格拉底、伽利略和达尔文的观点也是他们那个时代大多数人的观点吗？

科利尔[①]（W. T. Colyer）提出了更为严厉的法律建议。他主张每份报纸每期至少保留半个专栏，用于回答一些关于报纸持有者、报纸员工以及作者的问题。他还建议，每份报纸在发布读者来信时，都应将其他未发表的来信也罗列出来。科利尔的这些建议，旨在引入报纸编辑或所有者的个人偏见问题，或企图将报纸变成公众论坛，反而混淆了对新闻准确性的理解。众所周知，报纸的社会功能并不在此。演讲厅的主人不必为每个演讲者提供讲台，同样的，报纸没有义务刊登所有读者的来信。当然，读者来信指出稿件的错误时，报纸有义务校正。

厄普顿·辛克莱建议出台专门管理报纸的法律。他在《无耻收买》[②]（又译作《财团给报界的贿金》）一书中提出建立法律约束机制，规定报纸不可以发表未经审批的采访稿件，也不可以发表未经被采访者同意的稿件。事实上，一些报纸在重大事件上会提出这样的要求。很多情况下，被采访者提前知道自己要接受采访，因而会提前准备发言材料，以表达自己的观点。1910年实行的《堪萨斯报纸伦理准则》提出了和辛克

---

① 《义务性答复》，《仲裁员》，第二卷，第2期，12—13页。
② 第404页。

莱相同的要求。①

一般而言，现代报纸工作周期的限制导致这些建议没有可行性。假设一位记者要在纽约的布鲁克区采访某位当事人，然后再回到纽约市中心开始撰写新闻故事，或打电话将故事报告给编辑部，由他们撰写。无论是哪种情况，在纽约市中心和布鲁克区之间进行信息沟通并获得上级批准，在这个过程中，一些新闻故事的内容必定会丢失，而且会产生与事件本身不相匹配的昂贵费用。有时甚至会遇到获得采访对象同意的情况，比如，碰上犯罪事件、被采访者失踪等。

此外，采访获得批准的要求会歪曲或更改一些原本正确的采访文章，被采访者读过这些文字后，会认为那些原本属实的内容与其个人利益相冲突。确实，采访有时会造假或部分造假，但是，每个新闻人都清楚，在这些受到造假指责的报道中，有相当大一部分代表了被采访者真实的想法。一些被采访者否认采访内容，往往只是因为发表的采访不受其欢迎或者与其利益有冲突。某些高官给报纸记者留下了极其糟糕的印象，因为他们常常否认那些原本真实的采访。

辛克莱还建议："法律应规定，如果哪份报纸对某个人进行了虚假陈述，并由此引起了公众注意，该报应在下一期同一版面，以相同的呈现方式对虚假陈述进行澄清。"②

关于错误更正或回应指责，法国报纸的做法③很有意思。法国法律规定，如果报纸对官员的行为进行了不实或歪曲报道，该报需要在头版以不超过原报道两倍的篇幅对事件进行澄清。回应需置于头版，后面需附上利益相关方的公告。当澄清文字超过原文的两倍时，报纸可以按照发表法律文书的价格标准对超过的部分收费。

如果不实新闻中涉及私人姓名或者指名道姓，报纸需在收到法律回馈后的三日内，发表篇幅相当于原文两倍的文章进行澄清。澄清文字应

---

① 参见本书附录A，第206页。
② 《无耻收买》，第405页。
③ 作者非常感谢哥伦比亚大学保罗·德·巴科特（P. de Bacourt）教授提供的法国法律条款和执行方面的权威数据。

置于原文发表的同一版面,且排版字体相同。

现实中,该法律却很少发挥作用,报纸一般在没有接到法律通知前,就已将反馈内容刊登出来。

辛克莱还建议,法律应规定美国各报纸的新闻分配应受公众的监控。辛克莱认为美联社一直处于垄断地位,他希望任何城市的任何想办报的个人或组织都可以享受美联社提供的服务,而不需要历经复杂的程序,当然提交申请表和缴纳服务费还是必要的。① 辛克莱相信,美联社使得美国的舆论"在源头上被玷污"②,鉴于此,他关于扩展该社服务范围的想法有些不合常理。事实上,辛克莱主张的这些法律在堪萨斯州和肯塔基州都已存在,却从未被执行过。新闻的处理已成为跨越州界的问题。当然,新闻界都知道美联社并非处于垄断地位,合众国际社和国际新闻社都是其强劲的竞争对手,而且在某些领域还有其他的竞争者。

上述建议无法代表新闻从业者的真实想法。唯一能在某种程度上代表专业记者观点的法案是,成立一个新闻理事会,有权向记者授予执业证书,也可撤销执业证书,以维持新闻的专业性。此法案旨在为新闻界建立与法律、医疗等行业相似的专业主义标准。最早提出这一建议的是经验丰富的新闻人巴勒特·奥哈拉(Barratt O'Hara),美国伊利诺伊州前任副州长。1913年,奥哈拉先生的提议包括以下几点:

发放执业证书的要求如下:

1. 申请人已达到法定年龄;
2. 完成高中及以上教育;
3. 在正规新闻学院就读两年,或在新闻机构当过两年的实习记者;
4. 证明自己道德品质良好;
5. 顺利通过州委员会定期举行的书面考试。

"新人应做好充分准备,向委员会提出申请,提供良好道德品质证明,以及普通高中学历和实习证明。申请者需有能力完成一个新手记者

---

① 《无耻收买》,第406页。
② 《无耻收买》,362—376页。

的基础性工作，但无资格通过自己或他人稿件的终审。也就是说，新人可以开始写稿，但在印刷发表之前，稿件需由持证记者审阅和修改。经过两年的培训和限制，以及为考试进行充分准备，新人基本能写出高质量的新闻作品，成长为一名出色的新闻人。或者在有资质的实践型新闻学院学习两年，也符合条件。

"撤销执业证书的情况如下：

1. 有重大犯罪行为；

2. 故意歪曲事实，误导读者，恶意诽谤，有偿报道或收受行贿，挑起偏见，或有其他不专业、不负责、不诚实的行为。①"

1923年，美国俄克拉何马州立法机构提出一个类似的法案，但遭到该州报纸的强烈反对。报纸普遍认为，这种提案是出于复仇心理，而不是为了改善新闻业现状。法案未获通过。该法案提议，新闻理事会应包括州立大学校长和州立大学新闻学院院长，以及由州长挑选的另外三名成员。由理事会授予执业证书的成员，需在俄克拉何马州有五年以上的记者从业经验。出现以下任一情形时，新闻记者执业证书将被撤销：

1. 申请人在申请从业资格证时弄虚作假；

2. 已取得执业证书，但违反俄克拉何马州法律，包括道德败坏者；

3. 已取得执业证书，但习惯性酗酒者；

4. 已取得执业证书，但出版或造成出版或允许出版有关本州或本国公民的不实文章或报道的；

5. 已取得执业证书，但出版或造成出版或允许出版通过商业或社会行为直接或间接向公民收取费用，损害公民名誉的新闻、报道或社论；

6. 出版或造成出版或允许出版任何不道德或有辱人格的新闻、报道或社论。②

类似的法案已在美国康涅狄格以及其他一些州出台。

新闻职业将来可能会提高准入门槛，这是基于内部新闻从业者的需

---

① 索普，《未来报业》，154—156页。
② 《编辑与出版商》，1923年3月17—18页。

求考虑的,而非受外界因素影响。依据各行各业的经验,组成审查委员会的应是行业内部人士。除非建立比现今更专业的伦理准则,委员会的考查和其他行为仅是为了维护新闻业现状,而阻碍其朝着更高标准发展。在能够改善新闻业现状的法律出台之前,新闻工作者的专业意识、伦理观念和社会影响亦至关重要。

补充阅读

黑尔:《报刊的法律》

安吉尔:《新闻与社会组织》,76－89页。

辛克莱:《无耻收买》,403－407页。

《仲裁员》,1919年7月,第2卷,第2期。

奥哈拉:《本州新闻工作者执照》,索普,《未来报业》,148－161页。

《编辑与出版商》,《俄克拉何马州新闻法案势在必得》,1923年3月17日,第18页。

第十章　建立专业标准：记者组织

　　从普通记者成长为专业记者的最好标志之一是，其专业精神逐渐提升，渴望加入记者组织。新闻教育、经济因素，以及新闻业并不理想的现实情况，都对此有所影响。然而，仍有很多新闻工作者并不把新闻看作是一种职业，而仅仅把它当成一份工作，并以此为跳板谋求其他出路，跳槽做广告代理人或股票销售员的都有。鉴于新闻业薪资太低，记者明明受到轻视却又不得不和商业、社会和政治生活保持直接接触的矛盾现状，新闻工作者跳槽的现象就见怪不怪了。

　　在记者组织方面，其他国家比美国做得较好。尤其是英国，几乎每位记者和助理编辑都加入了三大新闻记者组织之一。①

　　其中，最古老的组织是记者协会，经1889年的《皇家宪章》批准建立。另一个较小的进步青年组织是全国新闻记者协会，虽仅限于地方性报纸，却体现了理想主义青年的愿望，在许多方面都取得显著进步，例如，提供长达13周的失业基金援助，建立辩护基金以提供法律咨询、解决新闻纠纷，资助记者遗孤，提供低收入保险等。所有会员免费进行

---

① 申请相关信息时涉及的组织机构办公室的地址如下：记者协会，伦敦都铎街，E. C. 4. 英国记者联盟，伦敦舰队街180号，E. C. 4。

就业登记。

记者协会没有针对准会员的考试和一些其他的特殊测试,但有一套属于自己的计划。这也是协会章程中的规定,能为今后各项工作做好准备,包括那些尚未启动却已在计划之中的项目。规划具体内容如下:

> 对候选人进行理论和实践测试或其他实际考察,以确定其是否有资格成为协会专业会员。
> 尽一切可能提升新闻工作者的地位和素质。
> 遵守与新闻职业相关的法律法规,监督协会会员的职业活动和使命。
> 为会员收集、编校、发布服务信息或趣味内容。
> 关注与新闻职业相关的法律变化,努力推进那些影响记者及其职责、兴趣的法律修正案。
> 充当会员间沟通的平台,发展业务关系,寻找雇主。
> 促进会员间的友好交流,举办专业研讨会、兴趣交流会和业务分享会。实时更新并发布会员名单,记录会员的兴趣爱好。
> 图书馆和资料室对所有会员开放。
> 为新闻工作者创办专业期刊。
> 为老、病、死、灾难事件提供完善而成熟的应对、援助措施。
> 修建协会会堂、固定会议室以及其他场所。
> 努力促进新闻业各方面的发展进步,提高新闻工作者的职业地位。
> 采用一切合理手段保障新闻业和新闻工作者的利益。

在大英帝国时期,记者协会的附属机构遍地开花。有些分支专门研究特定的新闻类型,例如,贸易新闻。协会的工作职能不仅是制定伦理准则,还有为记者间的交流创造有利条件。在培养英国报人的专业意识方面，协会已成为一股强大的力量。

另外一支具有领导力的记者行业组织是英国记者联盟（The National Union of Journalists），于1906年作为一个工会组织而成立，之后迅速发展壮大，到1923年已有成员4,200人，是当时英国其他任何一家记者组织的三倍之多。

英国记者联盟仅由职业记者组成，不包括报纸所有者、主管或经理人，当然，持有报纸股份的优秀记者并不一定被排除在外。此外，联盟还吸纳自由撰稿人，例如，H·G·威尔斯（H.G. Wells）就是其中一员。

英国记者联盟修正后的工作职能如下：

1. 保障和促进新闻职业旨趣，保障成员的薪资待遇、就业条件和职位任期。

2. 建立失业保险、慈善基金和退休福利制度。

3. 处理一些影响成员职业表现的问题。

4. 遵循国家健康保险法案，并以此为准绳开展业务，处理事务，满足卫生部的标准要求，塑造一个被法律、政府都认可的协会。

5. 监督1920年失业保险法案在新闻界的实施。

薪资问题向来颇受关注。英国报业人员的工资低得惊人，这涉及多方面因素，其中一点是，依赖职业收入的记者数量庞大。战争造成物价攀升，因此许多记者面临饥饿问题。这时的英国记者联盟已经足够强大，能采取措施改善局面。这不仅是出于满足记者的经济需求，更是因为在保障生活收入的前提下，记者才能拥有更多专业自主性。

英国记者联盟与伦敦的报纸所有者签订了相关协议，因而，与战前相比，各地区的记者工资增加了一到两倍。战前，许多能力较强的记者在伦敦的舰队街从事新闻工作，工资每周仅为3英镑。而现在（1923年），伦敦记者每周最低工资已有6.6英镑，商业报刊记者甚至能达到9.9英镑。地方性周报和日报的最低工资也分别为每周4.7英镑和5.3英镑。伦敦还规定了每周最长工作时限：助理编辑（sub-editors，美国称"技术编辑"）为38.5小时，文字记者与摄影记者为44小时，图片印刷员（在英国该工种也属于记者）为 48 小时。联盟还为伦敦记者争取到每年三周的假期。

英国记者联盟通过工会行动取得上述成就，大多离不开印刷行业中机械工人的支持。

记者联盟中常设名誉顾问，为记者维权提供咨询服务，需要处理的问题有著作权、版权、非法解雇、病期工资等。截至目前，联盟负责的每一个案件都取得了胜利，为会员讨回大量资金。

记者联盟有会员登记表，对于失业成员会给予一定补贴。第一个 13 周之内，每周补助 2 英镑，接下来的 13 周，每周补助 1 英镑。会员享有英国国民健康保险，这一规定由伦敦大学新闻委员会和联合工业委员会为报业颁布。

另外一个英国记者组织是女记者协会。当然，女记者也可加入其他组织，不过，她们大多选择由女记者协会来处理具体问题。

澳大利亚、新西兰和南非的记者都有自己的组织。事实上，英国记者组织与其殖民地的记者组织达成了协议。在澳大利亚和新西兰，雇主和记者间的协议受到殖民地工会法律的保护。协议规定了工作时限和工资，包括记者给新闻材料润色的最低费用，以及其他一些细节问题。

美国现有的记者协会没有一个能与其他英语国家的组织相提并论。美国有许多报纸出版商的组织，以处理商业问题为主。1922 年成立的报纸编辑协会，主要关注新闻伦理问题，采用了一套受人推崇的新闻业伦理准则。[①] 然而，该协会几乎全部由报纸中职位较高者组成，仅 124 人，尽管这些报纸多属于都市群，意义重大。各州的报业协会多关注商业和专业问题，同样仅由报纸所有者组成。很明显，这些组织并不能代表整个新闻业，因为报纸的所有者只是一小部分人。广大新闻工作者才能代表新闻业的根本利益。

美国已在尝试建立更多全国性的记者组织，却没有取得显著进展。究其原因，主要有以下三点：（1）资金缺乏；（2）新闻工作者的个人主

---

① 《编辑与出版商》，1923 年 4 月 28 日，第 15 页。

义；(3) 报纸出版商的敌意。某些出版商，甚至是那些标榜为自由主义者，一直都反对员工加入记者组织，阻挠这些社会机构（如报刊俱乐部）发挥职能。他们这样做的理由很明显。另一方面，这种反对收效甚微，报人越来越倾向于集体协作。

目前，该领域只对一定的新闻工作者组织开放，而最具影响力的记者组织是美国职业新闻记者协会（Sigma Delta Chi）和职业女性新闻工作者协会（Theta Sigma Phi），分属男性和女性的职业新闻联谊会。尽管这些组织在成员数量和影响力方面都迅速增长，但其规模仍然很小。他们一般只接收具有大学学历的人员，有些经验丰富的记者也能成为准会员，但这个国家绝大多数新闻工作者都被排除在外。另外，协会成员都是在小范围或小团队内投票选举产生的，一些有突出能力和特征的记者反而未被选上。当然，美国职业新闻记者协会正朝着更具包容性的方向迈进。其他一些组织，如美国记者协会等，规模更小，成员也更少。

美国各地的记者经常参加工会运动，[①] 成为国际印刷工会的一员。他们也在努力获取美国劳工联合会的认可。

一方面，在多数人眼中，工会性质的记者组织并不受重视，或许因为它在某种程度上表明新闻是一种商业活动，而非一种职业。另一方面，工会组织也不会真正阻止专业人士加入。人们认为，新闻工作者不该附属于工人组织，否则就会损害新闻的公正性。但是，他们忽略了一个事实，那些加入了商会、扶轮社和其他类似组织的新闻人，都不曾视工会组织为畏途。

在澳大利亚和新西兰，这场运动开启之初，也出现了同样的反对声音。沃尔特·威廉姆斯博士（Dr. Walter Williams）对此进行了一项态度调查，说道：

> 尽管人们反对甚至是怨恨新闻业引入薪酬委员会和工会制度，但是，对于大多数雇主和部分新闻业雇员而言，这显然是

---

① 《新共和》杂志新闻记者地方版，《新闻作者》，8—9页。

大有裨益的。人们反对的理由是,这种做法会有损新闻业尊严,减少优秀记者的机遇,拉低薪资水平,削弱专业性奖励给记者带来的激励作用。反对的理由似乎站不住脚。澳大利亚的报纸出版商和总编辑在是否谴责这些制度方面未能达成一致意见。某些人做出了谴责,但大部分人声称,目前的制度尚未经受长时间的检验,无法判断其是好是坏。而少数人表示,这将实现各方利益最大化。另一方面,澳大利亚记者协会的成员表示,他们的工资有所增加,假期更多,工作状况有所改善,专业精神也并未受到影响,同时,财务独立和终生雇佣关系对新闻业和记者个人发展都有益处。①

英国的情况有些许不同,工会运动远远超过美国,活跃的反对派也较少。此外,年轻的高校毕业生对工人运动更具包容性,许多还是英国劳动党的活跃分子。所以,英国记者组织受到诺思克利夫勋爵和知名出版商的嘉许,也就不足为奇了。

美国和英国新闻业薪资的较大差异,使得薪资问题十分引人注目。英国报纸主编无论是否拥有公司股权,都能掌控报纸。这是英国的古老传统。因此,记者和出版商之间的矛盾难以避免,不管是有意还是无意,都会歪曲新闻内容。这在英国并不鲜见。不过,情况有好转的迹象,现存的新闻记者组织可能改善这一状况。

不久的将来,在美国,区分男性记者和女性记者的专业组织可能才是最有前景的,并在很大程度上会学习英国记者组织的做法。

记者组织的成员若全是实践经验丰富的专业人士,就能提高行业的准入标准,建立切实可行的新闻业伦理准则,同时确保较高的薪资水平。当然,这离不开公众的理解与支持。记者组织最终或许能制定审查规章,发放记者执照。新闻业最为不幸的特征之一,即某些没有经过专业训练的人控制了报纸的编辑业务,仅把新闻当作买卖,但这种现象也

---

① 《世界新闻业》,第29页。

有逐渐被根除的趋势。

补充阅读

记者协会,英国记者联盟,女记者协会的宪法规章。

威廉姆斯:《世界新闻业》,密苏里堪萨斯大学公告,新闻系列9,20—29页。

安吉尔:《新闻与社会组织》,76—123页。

劳工党研究部:《新闻业》,35—43页。

辛克莱:《无耻收买》,415—428页。

布伦:《英国执业证书计划的替代品》;索普,《未来报业》,162—170页。

《新共和》杂志,新闻记者联盟地方版第一期,8—9页。

美国律师协会:《职业伦理准则》。

美国医学协会:《医学伦理准则》。

第十一章 建立专业标准：报纸职责

151 那些坚持认为新闻界是从本质上且有意识腐败的人，不会从行业内部寻求改善新闻界的办法。如果他们认为法律途径也无法消除新闻界的弊端，那么他们会倾向于从其他行业寻求补救措施。这种传统并非意味着所有的建议都是不明智的，而应该客观谨慎地看待，因为鲜有机构完全不愿或不能自我改善。

除了用法律管理私人报纸，呼声最高的建议则是，受资助的报纸和政府、联邦、州或市所有的机关报也分别受法律约束。

152 反对受资助报纸和政府所有报纸的人中就包括职业记者，理由是这些报纸实在是太枯燥，以至于无法吸引公众。但凡阅读过政府出版物的人都会认同这点。除了专门人士，很少有人会对政府出版物感兴趣。美国政府在战争期间创办了一份名为《官方公告》（*The Official Bulletin*）的报纸，尽管它由专业的报纸工作者负责编务，但仍然是当时最枯燥乏味的出版物之一。严格来说，美国还没有受资助的报纸，因此，无法判定其是否具有吸引力。不过，有几家观点型杂志是受资助创办的，尽管对于一些知识分子读者而言它们既有趣又刺激，但是，如此少的发行量说明它们无法吸引普通公众。如果报纸受政府或私人的资助，员工则不会很重视能否吸引大量读者阅读。尽管这对消除轰动性煽情新闻有益处，但与此同时，也会降低出版物的传播价值。

反对受资助报纸的理由还有另外一个。资助者的目的可能是推进某项特殊事业，而非单纯地传播客观事实。此外，无论如何都无法阻止的一个趋势是，不管资助者是怎么说的，资助活动都在一定程度上代表了其意图。事实上，教育机构对类似的情况抱怨颇多，我们无法否认受资助的报纸会遭受相同的诟病。一旦抱怨产生，无论其是否有理有据，报纸的影响力都会大大受损。

政府所有报纸的一个重要功能是宣传，因此也更易遭到公众反对。确实，如果那些熟悉政治甚至是抱怨当前政治的人拥护政府所有的报纸，那才是不可思议的。政府官员向报纸提供的所谓事实是不可靠的，这一点已被反复强调。任何一个读过《国会议事录》(The Congressional Record) 的人，或者听过行政长官在发布会上声明的记者，都很清楚：他们的话中，事实与结论之间毫无逻辑可言，且基本观点纯粹是先入为主的想法。

政客不会利用政府所有的报纸来谋求自身、团队及其党派的利益，这是不可能的。政客试图影响私人报纸，歪曲或压制事实，当他们控制了政府报纸的财务时，同样的情况必定也会发生。即使政客们认为自己是为了给国家谋求最大利益，其行为方式也可以通过加拿大和美国卷入第一次世界大战时发布的通告来说明。

通告 No. C. P. C. 57a.

给加拿大编辑的机密通告

(不供出版)

加拿大农业劳动力的短缺，导致军队中的成年男性严重不足。鉴于确保农作物产量最大化至关重要，政府正尽可能地将美国劳动力引入加拿大西部省份。记者编辑不得报道此事，以免公开宣传对计划造成妨碍。

欧内斯特·J·钱伯斯（Ernest J. Chambers）

加拿大首席新闻检察官

加拿大首席新闻检察官办公室，

国务秘书处，

渥太华，1918年1月19日。

当涉及某个政客个人或其党派利益，而非国家利益时，他会采取隐秘但更阴险的方式来处理。

此外，除非政府报纸拥有独家新闻权，否则它们难免会遭遇失败。最好的记者仍在私营报纸工作，公众也更偏爱后者。尽管19世纪上半叶，华盛顿特区已有半官方报纸存在。[①] 如果将独家报道权留给政府报纸，这无异于重现17世纪英国统治时期的职权滥用，彼时，殖民地政府努力控制所有新闻的传播和对公共事务所有的言论。当然，那时也有地下出版社出现，就像1914—1918年间处于德国统治下的比利时一样，最终，政府还是被迫取消了管制。毫无疑问，美国政府也曾试图接管报纸。

政府在许多重大问题上可以做到有案可查，例如，记录法庭审理、立法机关行为及其他事件等，尤其是记录那些可能成为社会和经济问题的事件，以此促进新闻界发展。李普曼先生认为，情报部门虽然能提供事实，但既不做决定也不采取行动，如果能够迅速有效地采取应对措施，那么，报纸传播客观事实的能力将取得决定性的进步。情报系统必须脱离直接的政治控制，反过来，它也不能控制政治和新闻界，而应成为专业的真相调查机构，与事实传播、政策宣传或执行的机构等区分开来。[②]

目前，政府采取的其他措施，大都是有害无益的。政府掌控的新闻报刊本质上变成了宣传部门，而报纸希望取得的主要成就之一则是远离宣传。

这是个严重的问题：从专利药贸易到政府重大事件，各类机构都存在宣传行为。战争期间，政府高薪聘请最有经验的思想家、作家以及大

---

① 西伊·佩恩，《美国新闻史》，238—239页。
② 每位新闻专业的学生都应该阅读李普曼先生的《舆论学》，369—410页。

量记者出身的人，对敌方采取宣传攻势，而效果却颇受怀疑。几年前，仅纽约市就有 1,200 名专业的新闻代理和宣传专家。如今这个数目无疑更大，一家大型报社每天能从各种各样的宣传机构收到近 15 万字的文件。

宣传的目的是让己方获得更多的支持。为了实现这一目的，人们可能采取不正当的手段。虚构新闻、策划新闻、歪曲事实、压制新闻——所有的一切都是为了取得想要的结果。这些非记者所为的恶习，最终都会让报纸付出代价。另一方面，宣传人员所采取的方式或许是值得尊敬的，例如，他出于自己的考量，将可能被人们忽视的新闻事实呈现了出来，正式而公开地做了每个人都在做的事，但他仅算得上是一个宣传员。

宣传员对新闻界的危害，部分体现在日常新闻活动中，部分反映在宣传员这一身份上。一个专业的宣传员很难以记者的身份公正、准确地把握新闻。同样的道理，新闻代理人或宣传专家经常阻止调查记者接触新闻当事人，以免记者获得足够多的信息。这种情况下，报道只能接受模式化声明，而这些声明往往是尽力掩盖真相，而非澄清事实。

新闻代理人不能忽视的是，报纸至少在两个方面刺激了宣传的专业化发展。第一，记者经常错误引用发言词或歪曲个人观点，个人出于自我保护会转向宣传机构，借宣传之口传达准确的观点。第二，若记者缺少新闻源，就很有可能采用宣传员已准备好的演讲稿、采访稿和其他类似材料。

尽管报纸通常极力对抗宣传趋势，尤其是在影响舆论方面，却仍显示出这方面的倾向。当报纸受到批评时，习惯把责任推给新闻事件相关的人或组织，从而导致宣传的进一步发展。例如，当有人指责报刊报道美国教育协会会议的力度不如拳击手登普西－吉本斯的决斗时，《编辑与出版商》（*The Editor and Publisher*）对外宣称，教育协会的"主题只能吸引本地的家庭，无法在报道中体现足够的'人情味'，而蒙大拿州平原上的专业决斗就不一样了"[①]。观点很明确：教育非常重要，但记者无法将教育新闻也写得很有趣，从而引发读者的兴趣。记者要让报道

[①] 社论，《公众利益》，《编辑与出版商》，1923 年 7 月 14 日，第 38 页。

富有人情味，显然，最简单的办法是通过新闻代理人。这一观点已得到《基督教科学箴言报》的认可。该报有一篇名为《新闻代理人的广阔领域》的社论，称其能唤醒记者激情，从而改变"教育推广者的冷漠"。[1]

在报纸的压力下，宣传代理所能发挥的作用很快就会消失，与前文所述不同，他们的一些做法纯粹是出于自己的利益考量。除非记者处理新闻更专业、调查技巧更高明，并且做了更充分的准备，否则宣传代理很难获得一席之地。报纸远离宣传的办法是，只有在宣传代理提供的是明确事实、使用通俗语言阐述专业问题时，才接受其协助。报纸也会明智地拒绝与无职业伦理的宣传代理人开展任何形式的合作。多数报纸秉承此法，无论受到多少盲目的攻击，从本质上记者应认识到，自由的报刊才是有价值的报刊。

除了减少宣传稿的数量，新闻业还应怎样做才能提升行业标准呢？第一步，需认识到一个行业不可能十全十美。新闻业存在这样一种趋势：专业新闻人努力提升自己，不与门外汉为伍，以维护专业优势。新闻行业刊物甚至报纸本身刊登大量关于新闻界缺点的社论文章，以此证明一个明智的编辑绝不会洋洋自得。太多非编辑出身的出版商显得非常傲慢，但他们不可能长此以往。

第二步是自我分析。这并非易事。最好的办法显然是，推选出一个客观、公正并熟悉新闻实践的委员会，由他们对美国新闻界的典型案例进行分析。这种分析应包含全国各地区、各种不同类型的报纸，从都市日报到乡村周报。目前仅有的研究多集中于大城市的日报，而实际上，美国大多数报纸是由小城镇发行，可能它们对新闻界的影响更大。此外，某些强烈反对或强烈支持新闻界的报道，通常更容易吸引公众注意力，但证据的信度不高。多数情况下，报道中缺乏足以推出结论的证据。委员会的调查分析项目需要大量资助，但调查结果将证明这是值得的。这些结果是关于美国新闻界不容置疑的客观事实的，出版之后将进入公众讨论，如此一来，必然会促进新闻业的快速发展。倘若有公德心

---

[1] 《基督教科学箴言报》，1923年7月24日。

的出版商愿意资助此类调查,这将会对新闻业产生难以估量的推动作用。

上述调查分析完成后,每家报纸都应进行自我分析。目前有几份报纸这么做了。《底特律新闻报》聘请编辑秘书,负责核查报纸言论的准确性。1913年,拉尔夫·普利策(Ralph Pulitzer)为《纽约世界报》建立了专门负责准确与公平竞争的内部机构,目的是"促进报纸的准确与公平竞争,校正粗心大意的错误,甄别虚构内容和虚构者"。《纽约世界报》收到的每一条投诉都会被仔细地核查。如果投诉合乎情理,就会刊登修正公告,并确定责任人。凡投诉者都会收到调查结果。任何弄虚作假或有重大疏忽的记者和通讯员都会被解雇。[①] 其他一些报纸也有类似的做法,只是没有这么严格和详细。越好的报纸越是经常校正错误,有些在"致歉启事"专栏处理此事,有些则刊登在常规新闻版。相比于报纸不愿公开承认错误的旧传统而言,这是一个标志性进步。拒不改正的情况也同样存在,除非涉及报纸认定的"重要"事件。这种做法只会让公众对报纸的诚信产生怀疑。

乍看之下,报纸只有一个消极的自我分析方法,无法调查所有刊登的故事,因为报道数量过于庞大,无论报道是否准确,每篇报道还需追踪数条线索。报纸可以每周选择性地调查一些由不同记者写的报道,也可以在报刊显著位置邀请读者指出新闻中的不准确之处。的确,很多失误都会被忽略,但报纸需要明白的是,在提升报道准确性方面,读者有参与合作的意愿。

第三步,报纸可以尝试消除自我分析时发现的错误,正如前文提及的《纽约世界报》一样。记者在大多数情况下都应尽力做到准确、公正,尤其是当他们知道一旦犯错就会受罚时。许多报纸都为员工制定了伦理准则,从中可以看出改善新闻业现状的强烈意愿。各州的报刊协会等也有伦理准则。[②] 除非这些准则能被切实地执行,记者及员工能真切

---

① 参见两年一度的《纽约世界报》准确与公平竞争局的报道。
② 详见本书附录A中两类规章实例。

地体会到职业伦理的重要性,否则规章制度将成为一纸空谈。伦理准则更多的是代表一种理想,而非当前现实,但我们可以朝着理想不懈努力。

报纸能做的只有这么些。报纸工人、记者、文字编辑或社评作者,是否能为保持良好的标准而不懈努力呢?作为个体,他们虽比不过强有力的记者组织,但依然能有所作为。他们能在实际新闻活动中遵守伦理准则,例如,绝不故意歪曲事实,杜绝不公正报道,不为抢发新闻而不择手段,不辜负公众信任,不接受贿赂,不做有偿报道,绝不故意给受众制造错觉。只有设置伦理规章,新闻工作者才会有被解雇的危机感,而不去触犯它。

实际上,记者不太可能因为虚假报道而被报纸解雇,但这并非导致问题出现的主要原因。有些情况可通过个别方法得以改善,例如,偶然的新闻失实、粗心大意,以及所谓"无害的"欺骗等。这些缓解式的治标办法难以解决深层次的问题,但是,新闻界可通过与记者组织、教育机构合作的方式,慢慢清除之。

补充阅读

佩恩:《美国新闻史》,230-239页。

威廉姆斯:《作为英国新闻业基础的公报史》。

马萨特:《比利时的秘密报刊》。

李普曼:《舆论学》,369-410页。

辛克莱:《无耻收买》,408-414页,438-443页。

布朗:《新闻界威胁》,《北美评论》,214:610-618.

布劳内尔:《宣传与伦理》,《北美评论》,215:188-196.

布朗:《评论》,北美评论,215:197-199.

查菲:《言论自由》,1-228页。

布莱斯:《公益宣传》,《星期六晚邮报》,1923年8月4日,20-21页。

《纽约世界报》的《准确与公平竞争管理局双年度报告》。

《官方公告》文件。

第十二章　建立专业标准：教育机构

　　社会的进步在很大程度上取决于由创造性智慧的人所领导的教育事业。新闻业的进步亦如此。研究发现，无知、惰性和恐惧等心理，是造成美国报纸未能实现向公众传递客观事实这一基本功能的主要原因。作为普罗大众中的一员，消除、净化或控制这些心理因素的唯一方式就是接受教育。同样，影响报刊实现其功能的意识因素也应被消除，正确的教育是对抗反社会行为的最好保障。

　　实现这些目标的必要教育，不限于学校教育，目的也不是给学生灌输现成的理论和结论。但是，我们必须以学校教育制度为基础，同时辅以尽可能多的其他方式。学校教育制度拥有公众的支持，即便有时这种支持并不强烈，但也能改善新闻实践活动。那么，为了实现这一目标，美国学校需要做些什么呢？

　　学校如何处理报刊中有意识的反社会趋势？更重要的是，如何消除无知、惰性和恐惧等因素？

　　关于教育与新闻的讨论，新闻学院必须占据重要席位。美国只有20个新闻学院开设了新闻学位课程，另外有200多个高等院校提供专业指导。高校中，准备在新闻学院接受更高水平教育的学生超过2,500人，准备从事记者职业的学生接近6万人。四十年前，高校新闻专业学生中从事记者职业的比例，要低于法律专业中从事律师职业的比例，也低于医药专业中从事医生职业的比例。现在，年轻人选择新闻学院的一个重要因素，也许也是最重要的因素——希望几年后进入美国新闻界工作。

新闻学院的教学、目标和理念成为公众关注的焦点。新闻学院有两种截然不同的理念，每一种都有学校支持。一种理念认为：新闻学院的作用是培养出能写"好报道"的记者。此理念认为报纸想要的只是记者，而学校培养出的记者能在报社学到其他一切关于新闻界的"游戏规则"。这是商业学校的模式，重视培养学生能力，强调新闻技能高于一切。学生们灵活、自信、办事效率高，毕业第一年便以记者的身份在美国报业发光发热。

这类学校就是在为美国报业培养记者——同种类型的记者，也许会有细微差别，或机智或温和，跟美国新闻界现状有几分相似。文字编辑、地方编辑甚至出版商因为学校提供的实践教学而称赞之："不需要关于权利、责任和伦理的这类理论知识。"一个出版商强调说："上帝！记者所需的全部伦理就是忠于他的报纸。我需要像忠于国旗一样忠于报纸的人。"出版商希望雇用的是商业学校中能为忠诚宣誓的毕业生。

新闻学院的另一种理念认为：新闻是一个专业，新闻学院是一个专业学院，学校应当提供新闻写作的技术训练，但是，安排一些简短课程就足够了。学校的主要功能是向学生提供知识和伦理教育，从而使他们通过报刊能更好地为公众服务。

像商业学校一样，新闻专业学院旨在培养记者，有才华、讲诚信的记者是建立可信赖的新闻界的基石。但此种理念认为好记者并不一定就是能写出"好报道"的人，而是努力探寻客观事实的新闻调查者。

如果学校想做到理论与实践相结合，就必须鼓励有资质的青年人为新闻职业生涯而学习，并劝诫那些缺乏相关品质者离开这个行业。真诚、智慧和追求客观公正是最重要的品质。同时，也要具备机智圆滑（有助于与人打交道）、人道主义以及其他一些素质，但这些并非是最重要的。倘若缺乏智慧，记者所做的基本是无用功。也许，他接受过各种专业培训，却从未意识到自己在做什么，为何要这样做；倘若缺乏公正客观，报刊必然会背离其主要功能；记者需要真诚也是毋庸置疑的，如果他脑海中的观点多过事实，这对他的职业有百害而无一利。

学校若想保持专业理想，就必须设置某些课程进一步培养学生的职业素养，消除高校学生的无知。这就意味着需要给学生开设特殊课程，训练他们灵活、自由地处理新闻事实的能力。学校需开设政治、经济、社会等课程，而非仅探讨理论问题、不涉及实际新闻业务的学术课程。学校应为学生理解当代人类文明中的巨大技术进步提供科学依据，训练学生追寻事实证据的能力，以避免在将来的记者生涯中被他人误导。学校的宗旨也在于培养学生的思辨能力，不盲目地接受群体的教条，不迷信报纸的公开声明，而是笃信经过独立思考所获知的真相。

专业新闻学院目前的趋势是，鼓励学生专门研究现代生活中的具体领域——国际事务、商业、劳工、农业、政治及其他重要领域，以便在今后的新闻工作中更好地为人类文明服务。公众依靠报纸了解当代生活现状，而当代生活又十分复杂，一个人不可能精通其多个领域。记者假装无所不知的旧观念已然消失，越来越多的公众要求新闻人不仅能写出"好报道"，而且要对其报道的领域非常熟悉。

新闻学院要培养合格的记者，保持这些理念和标准并非易事，却又不是遥不可及。大多数新闻学院都在朝这个方向努力，克服重重困难，不断取得进步。

首先，他们有时会遭到出版商的反对。出版商会优先选择与自身利益最相关的学校。他们可能专门为医生、商人、工程师、农民等特定群体提供信息服务，把学校视为他们财产的一部分。出版商常把新闻学院看作是为自己服务的机构，认为新闻院应培养出他们想要的人才。然而，专业新闻学院则反对称，每个教育机构的目的都是追求客观真理，从而造福全人类，新闻业尤其如此。年轻记者的主要服务对象并非某张报纸，而是公众。如果某人以牺牲公众利益为代价，服务于出版商的利益，并因此得到出版商的褒奖，他便是人类文明的叛徒。专业的新闻学院希望得到新闻工作者的建议和忠告，但更希望他们能懂得，最重要的是怎么为公众谋求利益，而不是如何维持新闻业现状。

专业新闻学院不但时常违背出版商的意愿，而且也要承受来自富人、政客、牧师和其他阶层的压力，不接受未经调查的群体教条。学校努力为公众谋求福利，公众却往往并不领情，尤其是学校将不受欢迎的事实真相摆在公众面前时。

新闻的主要功能是传递客观事实，意识到这一点的人，可能会明智地选择专业新闻学院，在与无知和恐惧作斗争的过程中，看到未来的希望。另一方面，商业新闻学院难以得到公众的支持，除了那些想要雇用其毕业生的报社。

商业新闻学院需废除所有把新闻当作一种职业来讲授的课程。1920年，此提议被全美英语教师委员会一致通过。这类课程一般都与英语相关，除非学校管理者太过愚昧，或是屈于报纸的压力，才会选择保留这些课程。这些课程只提供廉价的新闻技巧，而不教授学生未来职业生涯所必需的知识和伦理储备。这些储备使得报纸员工会因出版的失信与不公行为而离职，而那些既无能力也无勇气反抗出版商的学生便成为他们青睐的对象。职业高校的新闻课程当然会有所局限，仅仅把新闻写作当作是提升学生英语写作水平的手段。

在笔者看来，无论大学崇尚的是何种新闻教学理念，只要学生论文需送交导师或其他报人审查的传统被废除，都会对民主、文明有所帮助。笔者提出这个建议是经过深思熟虑的，它源自笔者在新闻界和教育界工作多年的经验及对美国大学新闻教育状况的深入了解。大学审查制度并不是为了剔除荒谬的论文错误，而只是向大学评委会提供一个幌子，以压制不同意见者的批判言论。

现行审查制度的主要目的是欺瞒公众，审查机构的权威们认为公众不该知道某些事实。简言之，这是一种压制真相的伎俩。近来，笔者从一个退休的审查机构主席口中了解到，尽管机构中的大多数教会成员都反对大学生跳舞，但学生仍被允许举办舞会。身为一个教堂牧师，该主席禁止大学校报提到"跳舞"二字，若涉及则用其他字眼代替。在与一个学生编辑谈论此事时，他很坦白地说，如果不隐瞒自己支持跳舞的事实，学校会给他制造很多麻烦。不必为这些偏见感到惋惜，它们只是为了迎合大学主席所设置的伦理观。

支持高校审查制度的人给出两个理由：第一，学生缺乏判断；第二，压制事实以获得"更好的结果"。第一点完全正确。但是，学生需从实践中学会判断，任何一个编辑、学生或其他人都会因为肩负的责任而变得清醒。此外，审查制度的负面影响，远远超过因学生判断力不足带来的尴尬局面。对于第二个理由，没有哪所大学能坦然接受。在所有诚实的教育领域中，没有什么是比发现和传播真相"更好的结果"。

这种诡辩的结果是，学生不再相信真相是最好的结果，而可以通过适当隐瞒或歪曲客观事实，以实现他们认为满意的结果。观察者发现，导致新闻工作者决定对公众隐瞒真相的深层次原因是人们的生理恐惧和不信任。不只是大学报刊的成员，所有熟知该制度的学生都会受到影响。他们带着满腔热情加入新闻业，却见识到对真相的压制和对公众的欺瞒。在不知不觉中，通过其他人的言传身教，他们已经对民治政府产生了深刻怀疑，并坚持认为政府脱离了人民。

说到教育，一定不能忽略的是，美国报纸的缺陷不仅体现在新闻界本身，相反，它们已渗透到美国生活的方方面面。因此，改善新闻界现状的教育，不能只针对未来记者或者普通大学生，而必须制订出一个更彻底、精细的教育计划。

在美国出版物中，报纸的阅读最为广泛。在大多数学校，甚至是大多数高中与大学，从9月到次年6月都不提及报纸，这难道不算是一种异常情况吗？学校从不提及政府司法和立法机构，难道不奇怪吗？目前，人们若想了解司法和立法机关的举动，还必须依赖报纸。他们从报纸上了解信息，以便选出理想的法官和代表。一个小孩从有阅读能力开始，到大学毕业，报纸应当吸引其注意力，并将这作为一种社会现象来研究。报纸应让孩子懂得，若没有一个真实的新闻界，就不可能有成功的民选政府；若没有公众的合作，就不可能有真实的新闻界。他也该知道，任何个人或团体意图压制真相、歪曲事实、引起偏见、恶意引导舆论的行为，都是对真实新闻界和民选政府的打击。如果让那些努力推进新闻界发展、传播客观事实的正义人士受到年轻人的尊重，那么背叛民选政府的行为便会愈来愈少。

如果通识教育的作用是让报刊在民主社会中发挥更大作用,我们也必须清晰地认识到李普曼先生指出的一个事实,即人类生活在两个环境中,一个是现实环境,一个是拟态环境,我们通常以为后者才是真正的环境,并据此行动。我们想要真实、全面地反映客观世界是不可能的,而只能尽力减少这两个环境之间的冲突,复杂的文明中必定存在某些刻板印象和笼统表述。学校必须认清现状,强调虔诚信仰的重要性,具备识别刻板印象的能力,并能在发掘真相过程中快速修正或摈弃刻板印象。①

这方面的教育会让公众的恐慌情绪逐渐消退,新闻界的恐慌亦然。特别是人们对群体的无意识恐惧也会消失,只要能认识到观点仅仅是观点,无论它多么普遍与流行,也总会有些特例,经不起某些事实的检验。同样,任何时候都不应对事实感到恐惧。事实不会夸大先入为主的成见,但会检验所有的观点,从而得出新结论。

这当然不是一个一蹴而就的过程,对于那些相信在新法律或新社会经济体制的支持下正义能迅速取得胜利的人而言,这个过程会变得出乎意料地漫长。然而,既然自然科学能克服重重困难,在相对短时间内取得巨大进步,那么,新闻界是否也能提早取得相似的成果呢?无论前进的步伐是快是慢,无疑都是竭力而为的结果。为改善新闻界所做的每一分努力,都是对无知、惰性和恐惧的反抗。同样,为了让美国民众摆脱绝望的奴役所做的每一个努力,也都推动着美国新闻界的解放。无知、惰性和恐惧是真理永恒的敌人,而没有真理,报纸便不能发挥作用,也不可能有真正的民选政府。

补充阅读

美国教师新闻协会会刊,1921,1922 年。

霍纳迪:《美国新闻教育》;威廉姆斯,《夏威夷世界报界大会会议

---

① 详情参见李普曼《舆论学》,3—32 页,79—156 页。

录》，115－155页。

李：《高等教育机构的新闻教育》。

阿林顿：《成为高校教育之一的新闻》，67号会议：476－484页。

哈格：《以新闻工作为职业》；布莱尔，《新闻职业》，264－277页。

威廉姆斯：《新闻人》，114－144页。

李普曼：《自由与新闻》，69－104页。

李普曼：《舆论学》，3－32页，79－156页。

附录 A　记者组织、报纸杂志所遵循的新闻伦理准则与规范

记者组织所遵循的新闻伦理准则

新闻规约[①]

报纸的首要功能是传播人类的行为、感觉和思想。因此，新闻从业者应具备最深入的理解力、最广泛的知识和经验，以及与生俱来或训练有素的观察、推理能力。作为历史的记录者，新闻业承担着"社会民众的教师"和"社会信息的诠释者"的双重角色。

为了将美国新闻业的良好业务实践和社会宏愿编撰成文，我们设立了以下从业规范：

一

职责。报纸享有吸引读者注意力的权利，但同时也受制于公共利益的考量。报纸肩负的责任取决于它如何利用"赚到"的公众注意力。这

---

① 由美国报纸编辑协会的新闻伦理委员会主席哈利·赖特所撰写，并于1923年被该协会采用。

种责任应由所有员工共同承担。如果记者为一己私利而滥用权利，那就是对公众信任的背叛。

二

新闻自由。新闻自由应被视为人类的一种重要权利加以捍卫。没有被法律明文禁止的事物都在其探讨之列，还有那些限制性法规里所蕴含的理念。

三

独立。除了忠于公共利益，新闻业没有其他义务。这一点至关重要。

1. 不管出于何种原因，所有损公肥私的行为都与诚实的新闻业格格不入。那些来自私人信源的所谓的"新闻信息"，如果没有公示其信源，或不能在形式及内容方面证明其新闻价值的，都不应被刊载出来。

2. 众所周知，社论应以事实为准绳，否则就违背了美国新闻业的最佳精神，破坏了新闻职业的根本原则。

四

真诚、真实、准确。忠于读者是新闻业名副其实的基石。

1. 无论从哪种角度考虑，报纸都应该确保真实。如果是可控的因素导致了完整或准确性的缺失，或者没有保证新闻本应具有的根本特征，任何理由都是借口。

2. 标题应与新闻内容完全相符，而不宜夸大其辞。

五

不偏不倚。公正的报道应将新闻报道和意见表达明确地分开，不受任何意见或偏见的影响。

此准则并不适用于所谓的"特殊文章"。"特殊文章"或旗帜鲜明地倡导某种观点，或署名表达自己的观点和意见。

六

平等性。如果不能给予对方平等的辩解机会，报纸不应刊发影响他人声誉或品性的非正式控诉。对于司法程序外的所有控诉，报纸正确的做法是，给予对方平等的辩解机会。

1. 如果不是为了公众利益（不同于公众好奇心），报纸不得侵犯私权或私事。

2. 如果报纸所载事实或观点存在严重错误，它应该及时全面地纠正，无论错误的源头在哪。这是报纸享有的特权，也是应当承担的责任。

七

正直。如果报纸一面标榜追求高尚的道德目标，另一面却刊载犯罪和恶习的细节，且明显不是出于公共利益，那么，报纸难辞其咎。伦理规范的执行如果缺乏权威，就会沦为一纸空文。故意迎合人的邪恶本能，会遭到公众的抵制，或受到职业领域的普遍谴责。

华盛顿州新闻伦理准则[①]

I will be 我将（做到）

Truthful in News 新闻真实

Truthful in Editorials 社论真实

Truthful in Advertising 广告真实

True to all my Obligations 履行所有责任

Honest with my Competitors 诚实对待对手

True to the Ideals of Journalism 践行新闻理想

Mindful to the Value of Sincerity 铭记诚信价值

Faithful to Community, State, Nation 忠于社区，忠于国家，忠于民族

Firm in Publication of Clean News 确保报道透明

Honorable in all of my Dealings 保证业务信誉

Thorough in all of my Studies 调查力求彻底

Unselfish in all my Services 无私奉献

Faithful to all my Friends 忠于朋友

Fair to all my Critics 直面批评

---

① 查宾·福斯特（Chapin D. Foster）等人撰写，华盛顿州新闻协会于 1923 年采用。

俄勒冈州新闻伦理准则[①]

"不仅是每种技艺与研究,而且人的每种实践与选择,都以某种善为目的。"

——亚里士多德,《尼各马可伦理学》,第一卷(1)

前 言

我们深信伦理学家的教诲:尘世间快乐与幸福的一般状态都可实现,而且,这样的状态也是人类社会追求的终极目标。

我们发现,每位善者身上都有一种本能,即言行一致地为实现这种终极状态而努力;尽管这种状态看似遥远,但我们的信念坚定,毫不动摇。

我们认为,处于群体之中的人们也应遵循指导个人行为的伦理准则。不管是什么将人们联系在一起,为了将有德之士与普通大众区分开来,人们付出了持续的努力。但是,个人或群体所采用的"媒介"以及"工具",都应以该时期人们的最高伦理标准为基础,从而加速实现社会的终极发展目标。

所有的媒介中,印刷文字传播最为广泛,影响力最为深远。而印刷文字又是报刊行业使用的唯一工具,对于塑造人们的思想和行为有着不可估量的作用。因此,我们一再强调,新闻业肩负着所有职业责任中最为重要的伦理责任;在现在及以后的工作中,我们渴望在公正合理的范围内,能够最大限度地承担起这种责任。

因此,我们将采取以下规范作为行为指导,名为《俄勒冈州新闻伦理准则》。

一、诚实、真实

诚实是新闻伦理的基石。一位诚实的记者在采访和写作过程中,都应该诚实如一。他应竭力保证真实,呈现真相。对待真实的态度是区分

[①] 科林·迪蒙(Colin V. Dyment)院长撰写,俄勒冈大学,俄勒冈州编辑协会于1922年采用。

记者有德无德的标准。当然，要保证所有写作不出一点差错，显然不可能；但在写作中不出现故意的"差错"，却是可行的。伪君子、歪曲事实者、撒谎者、隐瞒事实者或者不诚实者都将难以在新闻业寻得一席之地。

因此，本规范的第一部分认为，我们应该坚持不懈地以真诚的态度开展业务，而作为新闻从业者，真诚意味着有许多方面的要求，例如：

1. 在写作中，不管是社论、广告、文章或新闻故事，准确性是第一要义。

2. 准确性不仅意味着在写作中不出现错误的陈述，还意味着写作应呈现所有必要的事实要素，以防读者做出错误的推断。

3. 为了以真诚的态度对待事实，我们将开放地对待所有信念，无畏且坚定，但永远不会冥顽不化；因此，我们不会拒绝倾听，也不会拒绝新出现的事实证据。

4. 如果新出现的证据证明了不同的观点，我们将以表达旧观点时的开放态度来接受新观点。

5. 我们将敦促他人以相同的态度对待事实，不要求或不允许员工撰写不真诚、不真实的内容。

二、关怀、能力、深度

通常，新闻业出现的不准确现象并非记者态度低劣所致，更多的是由其能力不足引起。一个知识储备不足的人不足以胜任记者一职，正如他不足以胜任医生或工程师的工作一样。假定每位记者的伦理道德水平相当，那么，他们对自己的社区或社会所做的贡献大小几乎与其能力成正比。我们认为，新闻业是一种需要精确知识和博学修养的行业。因此，本准则的第二部分如下：

6. 通过学习、探索和观察，我们要不断地提升自己；唯有如此，我们的写作才能更加可信，更有见地，更有利于社会福祉。

7. 对于我们所雇用的员工，他们不仅应坚持伦理观，而且应该具有将理想化作现实的能力。这一点是必需的。

8. 我们将以忠诚的态度陈述事实、表达观点。

9. 我们将在各自的团队倡导深度的挖掘、充分的准备、出色的技能，这些也是我们对自己、员工以及同事的要求。

10. 肤浅和虚伪是我们积极对抗的敌人。

三、公正、仁慈、善意

从宪法、法规、文化传统来看，美国比世界其他地方享有更多的出版自由。出版自由的存在，为全体民众的其他权利提供了保障。但是，有时出版自由的行使也会成为侵犯群体和个人其他权利的"通行证"：因为传统习俗与法律为出版自由提供了豁免权，使出版自由凌驾于其他权利之上，由于轻率或狂热或恶意或冷漠，个人会受到不公正的待遇。然而，出版自由仍然应该按照宪法制定者和公众所预设的宽容方式来实施。只是，人的声誉生而圣洁，不容丝毫诋毁。因此，在新闻规范中强调以下内容恰如其分：

11. 我们不会将"话语特权"当作幌子进行不公正的攻击，或用以掩盖新闻调查中的疏忽，为政党或个人辩解。

12. 我们旨在合理范围内保护官方文件中提及的各种个人权利，不管其对"好故事"或社论方针有何影响。

13. 我们将在力所能及的范围内平等地对待所有人，不会因个体的财富、影响力或个体处境而背离本规范中的任何程序规定，但以下情况除外。

14. 在任何环节，新闻操作对仁慈和善良的考量都应合理合法，这是我们的重要准则之一。如果不披露事实能更好地保护社会公共利益，我们将压制事实，但动机永远应该是顾及公共利益，而不是出于个人或商业利益的考虑。

15. 我们将以此来规范我们的新闻出版，或指导我们的新闻写作，从而使我们的作品浸润着公正、善意和仁慈。

四、中庸、保守、均衡

鉴于公众从记者的报道中获知事实从而形成自己的观点，因此，记者所报道的事实应该是高标准的。如果记者诉诸公众情感而非理智，他便不是一个好的事实传播者，因为这样的事实有失偏颇。通过片面的强调,或技巧性的谋篇布局,或特殊的字体编排,或修辞手法的运用,记者的报道可能导致读者产生不合理的观点。我们希望借此伦理准则表明立场,反对煽情式职业行径,建立以下行为标准:

16. 我们将竭力规避在社论述评、新闻报道、解释说明中草率地下结论,以免造成不公正。

17. 我们不会为了轰动效应而炒作新闻或社论,那样会误导读者的推断。

18. 我们将把新闻报道的准确性和完整性置于时效性之上。

19. 我们将尽力维持各种新闻报道的适当比例,以防无足轻重的事件优先于具有重大公共意义的新闻。

20. 我们将竭力在新闻写作与出版中全面遵循适度和稳健的原则。

21. 万花筒式不断变化的新闻易让公众的思考停留在肤浅层面上,基于此,我们将竭力贯彻"持续而长远地影响社会思想"的方针。

五、党派、宣传

我们相信,公众对新闻报道的信任源自对记者业务能力和动机的信任。公众对我们的动机失去信任,是因为他们怀疑记者的报道迎合了其他非公共利益性质的目的,或怀疑我们为了宣传而设立专栏,或两者兼而有之。因此,我们应该遵循以下职业规范:

22. 知识自由贯穿于新闻工作的所有阶段,我们将抵制所有来自外部的控制。

23. 我们的新闻写作和出版应该超越任何的党派偏见和纷争;只有当党派的观点符合公众利益时,我们方可表达对相关党派及问题的支持。

24. 除非特殊情况,我们不允许刊载任何非自己员工所提供的新闻和社论;我们坚信,原创作品是克服宣传弊病的最佳方法。

六、公共服务和社会政策

我们常听人说,就公共道德和政策问题而言,报纸应该迎合而不是引导大众。对此,我们持不同的观点。尽管我们不奢望远远走在时代前列,那样一来,我们的各种方针将变得不切实际;但我们还是希望能够与这个时代最先进的思想并驾齐驱,而且,如果可能的话,希望能够成为其向导。报纸从业者的道德水准与其读者的平均水准持平就够了,这种说法并不正确。只有道德水准高于社区平均水平的人,才有资格涉足新闻职业。因此,我们宣布以下准则:

25. 我们将确保作品与出版物远离粗俗,除非我们确信披露污秽细节有利于社会公共利益。

26. 我们所写和所载的作品将会成为社会公共消费品,因此,我们将评估其对社会政策的影响;如果确信作品的材料于社会有害,我们会竭力避免之。

27. 我们将把所享有的特权,即为出版而写作或作为公共消费品而出版,当作兼具社会性和商业性的事业;因此,我们将时刻警惕任何有悖于社会利益的行为。

28. 我们相信,此方针的核心在于,我们不应该成为徇私枉法之人。

七、广告与发行

我们反对"购者自慎"原则。尽管不能保证广告内容绝对真实,但我们能把握自身在创作、招揽或刊载广告时的态度。我们认为,应用于新闻和社论的真实性、公正性等原则同样适用于广告与发行。因此,我们认同以下商业准则:

29. 我们将努力与其他社会机构协作,以提高广告业伦理标准。

30. 我们将阻止或禁止在专栏上刊登广告,因为这样的广告意在欺骗读者,使读者对广告内容做出错误评估。(该条款涉及欺诈、不公平竞争,以及广告文章有害于消费者道德水准或健康等问题。)

31. 我们不会刊登广告以吹嘘自己的报纸或发行,或与本伦理准则条款不符的其他事项。(本条款涉及对公众或广告商具有误导性的观点陈述、实际印刷总数、订阅数量、零售数量,以及本地发行比例等问题。)

32. 我们不会向有害于社会或有欺诈意图的广告提供印刷设备。

对于以上伦理准则,我们诚心实意地将其视为社会责任的一部分。我们坚信,只有当伦理观念趋于完善且实用,并被全世界的人们所接受和践行时，我们的世界才能更加美好。

南达科他州新闻准则[①]

作为新闻从业人员，尤其是从事报纸出版发行部门的人员，我们认为制定新闻伦理规范十分必要，这体现了新闻业的服务理念、分寸感和荣誉感，能激发从业人员的积极性，并为即将踏入该行业的所有人员提供行为指南。

该伦理准则的制定是基于真实和公正两大基本原则，在追求人类理想的过程中，我们应尽可能遵循"己所不欲，勿施于人"（whatsoever ye would that they do unto you, do ye so unto them）的黄金行为原则。

服务

新闻业与公众是服务与被服务的关系。它与读者之间潜在的契约关系为其赢取了公众的信任，也保持了独立性。报纸受益于这样的互惠关系，因此，必须坚持不懈地以高标准要求自己，忠于这些广受认可的动机、情感和行为理念。

真实与诚实

真实是新闻业的基石。毫不动摇地坚持"一切皆真，一切皆诚"的理念，这应该成为所有新闻从业人员的永恒目标。

新闻报道应该是所有重要事实的客观报道和准确陈述，在目前的情况下，我们能够做到这一点。

社论应该是基于事实的真诚讨论，并且通过逻辑推理的形式进行论证。

广告传播应该有诚实和得体的销售意图，不能误导受众或传播不实内容。

公正性与准确性

新闻业必须以公正的方式与公众打交道。社会的存在和法律的制定

[①] 由 J. H. 麦基佛（J. H. Mckeever）、H. A. 斯特奇斯（H. A. Sturges）、保罗·W. 基泽（Paul W. Kieaer）和 J. A. 怀特（J. A. Wight）等撰写，南达科他州出版协会于 1922 年采用。

是基于一个权力来自公众的政府。

为了维持这种机制,首要的问题就是保证全体公众能够充分、全面地获知信息。

印刷文字是传播和使用最为广泛的媒介,与人类思想有着密切的联系,而报纸是信息传播最有力的工具。因此,新闻从业人员肩负着神圣的职责,保证人类强大的传播手段具有纯净的信息来源、纯洁的传播意图,且不受各种偏见的影响。

新闻业具有影响人类判断的强大力量。因此,公正地呈现并准确地陈述所有事实后再做出判断,最为重要。这里的准确性不仅要求在报道中不出现错误的事实陈述,而且要求能够有序地呈现所有相关事实。

准确性原则还意味着,党派偏见或宣传污点都不应出现在公正的新闻业中。

真诚与得体

目的真诚和写作诚实是每位遵守职业伦理的新闻工作者所应具备的品质。诚实的理念影响其遣词造句,支撑着他们的真诚愿望,激励着所有崇高理想的实现。

充分理解这一点之后,南达科他州报刊协会的成员应该肩负起报道事实、引领思想和塑造社会行为的重任。我们承诺在各自的社区竭诚努力,最大限度地实现这一目标。

新闻业享有出版自由,但自由权绝不是万能的"通行证"。是否享有该权利取决于新闻业能否对出版内容做出正确的抉择。

这样规定的目的在于保护出版内容免于粗俗,在合理范围内保护个人权利和名誉,保护报纸免于污秽,除非我们确信出版这些粗俗污秽的内容有益于社会。

我们认为,如果基于高尚目的,为了公共利益而非自私意图,压制、删除不适宜的内容,这是符合新闻伦理规范的正当行为。

如果广告用词不当或动机不纯,或带有欺诈意图,或于正确用途无益,那么,它在真诚的新闻出版行业中将找不到一席之地。

荣誉

受可耻动机驱动而发表不真实的内容,或为了个人或政党利益对半真半假的事实展开带有偏见的讨论，鉴于新闻业荣誉，这些都应摈弃。

个人性格和行为能折射出一个行业的好坏，理解这一点的人会更加珍惜和维护职业荣誉。人人如此，行业的荣誉也将得到保护而不受玷污。

报酬与尊重

正如佣人理应拿到相应的工钱一样，新闻从业人员有权获得与其付出相称的报酬。而新闻从业人员的付出必须通过社会需求来衡量，因为新闻作品的刊载发表是通过完善的商业方式进行的，所以，只有足够的社会需求才能推动出版内容发挥其作用。

这是最重要的一点，原因在于：如果出版物能够通过辛勤的努力而获得成功，与任何经济政治利益无牵连，其服务覆盖范围将会更宽广，对各种观点的接纳更自由，同时也将有更多的机会为社会做出贡献。成功地为公众服务是新闻业的终极追求。然而，只有清楚地认识到新闻从业者的职能，诚实经营、勤奋工作，才能获得成功。

新闻业要求从业人员诚实、公正、平等地对待所有人，反过来，他们也有权要求从服务对象那里获得公平的待遇、评价和尊重。

密苏里州新闻实践原则与规范宣言[①]

前　言

在美国，公众的支持是政府稳固的基础。因此，作为公众获取信息的媒介，报纸的工作效率、稳定性、客观性以及诚实的品质等都至关重要。在很大程度上，合众国的未来依赖于一支拥有高标准的新闻从业者队伍；新闻从业者的职业动机和行为须值得认可和信任，否则这样的高标准难以为继。

新闻业具有与其他知识行业并肩前进的权利和责任，同时，又比其他任何一种行业都能更深入地参与到公共事务中。因此，如果新闻工作者没有认识到自己对公众的重大责任，那么他们就不能正确地对待新闻

---

① 威廉·萨瑟恩（William Southern）撰写，密苏里州出版协会于1921年采用。

职业。报纸并不完全属于其所有者,如果它仅被用于牟取私利,就没有发挥其崇高作用。因此,密苏里州出版协会提出以下原则作为新闻业的总体指导,尽管这并不是一套全面细致的行为准则。

社 论

我们声明,"事实是全部新闻事业的基石",这是我们奉行的基本原则。如果事实理应被公之于众,而报刊却予以压制,那就是对公众信仰的背叛。

社论应该始终如一地秉持公正、公平原则,而不应受到任何商业或政治利益的操纵。如果作者的真实身份未被公开,社论就不应被发表。

如果是出于商业利益考虑而控制新闻或评论,那么这份报纸就配不上"报纸"称号。新闻应始终以公共利益为标尺来衡量新闻的报道、写作和诠释。同时,广告商无权享受报纸的任何优待,除非他们以读者和社区成员的身份竭尽所能为社会或公众服务。

掌控报纸编辑方针的人不应同时掌控其他权力,或加入其他机构,因为这些机构的多重职责有可能与报纸肩负的公共服务职责相矛盾。

广 告

招揽不真实、欺骗性或误导性的广告业务既不符合行业伦理,也非精明的商业行为。那些企图利用报纸专栏来倾销问题存货或其他商品,或指望以小投资换取大回报的相关企业或个人都应被仔细调查。我们的读者应该受到保护,免受虚假广告的欺骗。新闻与广告的比例应该固定为一个数值,保证盈利即可,永远不要削减新闻版面。读者和广告主都应受到公正的对待。

伪装成新闻或评论的广告不应被接受。尤其是政治性广告,须让人能一眼看出它是广告。接受政治赞助的贿赂与收受政治献金的受贿并无不同,都糟糕透顶。

为了反衬自己强大而诋毁竞争对手,既不是明智的商业行为,也不合乎伦理。报纸之间的"争议"永远不应出现在报纸专栏里。人们期望竞争对手如何对待自己,就应该以同样的方式对待竞争对手,这是商业伦理的要求。我们应该创造新的商业机会,而不是惦记着从别人那里抢走生意。

永远不要因为广告商曾把广告给了其他报纸,而向客户索要业务。考虑接受某一广告业务时,企业的价值、产品和服务都应符合标准。

订阅

为了保证更高的广告价格而虚报订户数,且虚报数目远远超过实际的付费订阅者数,这种弄虚作假的赚钱方式是错误的。广告商有权知道自己支付的钱买到了什么,报纸卖给了他什么。我们应努力避免以虚价编造订阅名单,或通过奖赏、争夺的方式获得订阅量。

我们的行为准则

在新闻工作的每一环节,我们都坚持并声明对公众负责,对事实负责;同时,我们将以公正处事为己任,以无私服务为信条,谦卑前行。

堪萨斯新闻出版商伦理准则[①]

广告活动准则

定义——广告是以一个商业交易或一家专业企业为主要内容的新闻报道或观点评述,这些报道或观点能够直接促进其利润或业务的增长。

然而,如果新闻仅是报道了一家企业的产业或商业的发展情况,没有涉及产品质量的优劣,则不属于广告。

除了能够带来利润的新闻报道,在非新闻版面刊载的通讯、专题、感谢信等也属于广告的范畴。报纸会对后者收费,这带有罚金的性质,从而限制其无限刊发。

责任——合同或广告的末尾应该明确标明作者身份,从而引起读者的注意。

如果新闻专栏里出现未署名的广告内容,广告上方或下方应该标示"广告"一词或其缩写。

版面自由——我们享有作为出版商的权利,即通过广告专栏充当土

---

① 威利斯·E·米勒(Willis E. Miller)撰写,堪萨斯编辑协会于1910年采用,最早的伦理准则,并被记者组织所广泛采用。

地、贷款、租赁和商业交易的经纪人，我们谴责任何限制出版商行使该权利的行为，因其阻碍了出版商以联系买家和卖家为目的而进行的版面销售。

该条款并不能成为出版商处理交易细节、合同条款等内容的依据，而仅是对出版商所享有的版面出售自由的捍卫，其他谈判细节则交由相关负责人处理；出版商出售版面是为了联系买家和卖家。

我们的广告只负责联系买家和卖家，而卖家、买家或中间人是否付费、是否订货等其他事宜则与我们无关。

如果报纸屈服于交易者的其他过分要求，都会对广告业的根基——版面自由造成冲击。我们认为，版面自由（即能够付费交换的版面）仅受广告业伦理规范的约束。

我们认为，版面自由并没有赋予我们与企业任意签署合同的权利。如果企业的合同里包含对版面措辞的限制，而这些措辞也会出现在我们与其他公司签署的合同里，或者限制我们提及其他公司商品的名字，我们恕不签署。

报酬——我们拒不签署发行一定数量免费读物的合同。

我们不接受任何交换性条款，例如，通过业务交换或人情交换来偿付广告费用，所有广告费用都应该以现款的方式支付。

我们谴责针对广告费率给予的任何秘密回扣的行为。

价格——任何广告都是以一千发行量为单位计价的，因此，所有广告商有权全面了解报纸的发行情况，不仅包括发行数量，还包括人群的分布情况。发行情况说明里应该明确显示真实订阅者数、交换订阅者数、赠阅者数，以及卖给报纸经销商的数量；如有可能，应尽量说明订阅者的地域分布情况。

广告版面位置——签署广告版面位置合约应该收取固定比例的费用，该费用并不包含在报纸广告费之内。如果合约规定"不能给予相应的广告版面位置，那么就大幅削减报纸广告费，甚至超过版面位置佣金，或索取的赔偿金额超过版面位置佣金"，恕不签署。

比较——我们认为，如果出版商在其专栏文章里将竞争对手的广告业务数量或报纸发行情况拿来和自己进行不公正的比较，则有失身份、尊严。

新闻代理人与无偿广告——某特定商品的商标名，或某商人、制造商的名字，或与其货物、产品或服务名称有关的专业人士等，都不应出现在纯粹的新闻报道里。

我们谴责任何违反道德规范、导致伤风败俗的广告，例如，涉及私人医疗隐私、情色按摩室、私人婚姻、治疗私密疾病的医生或医院的广告，以及任何包含此类暗示的广告。

发行准则

定义——发行量是报刊所拥有的直接读者数量，由付费读者、赠阅读者、交换读者和广告读者组成。

报酬——只有以现金付费方式提交的报纸订阅的请求才会被接受，报纸和付款是此交易中仅有的两要素。

报刊经销人——大批量采购报纸的交易是一次性完成的，不允许退还未售出的出版物。

投机——我们谴责通过降价销售和奖券赠送的方式促进刊物的订阅。

赠阅——赠阅刊物不应赠给医生、律师、牧师、邮局人员、警察或法庭官员来换取新闻线索或邮递特权。

预算准则

定义——预算是计算各种成本的科学。预算的结果用以确定价格。

基本原则——我们不赞同在出版商之间达成一个统一的最低广告收费标准，我们更倾向于深刻地理解成本的内涵，并向我们的成员推荐最近在芝加哥召开的第一届国际成本大会暨美国印刷成本会议的成果。深刻地理解成本之后，我们根据自己的投资、生产成本等情况建立一个价目表，而不用顾虑广告商的相对支付能力或广告活动的半新闻性质。

批量折扣——我们认为，如果允许广告价格折扣超过初始价格的10％是不明智的。

新闻准则

定义——新闻是对思维、人物以及事物活动进行的不偏不倚的报道，前提是这些活动不会违背人们的道德情感。

谎言——我们谴责任何违背事实的行为：

1. 刊载任何吸引眼球的虚假人物或事件。不管报道看似有多真实，只要报道中没有标明事件或人物照片并非真实，就应受到谴责。

2. 刊载虚假采访，在被采访人不知情或不同意的情况下，为被采访人编造观点。

3. 除非使用被采访者认可的原话，否则刊载引文也是违背事实报道的行为。

4. 发布虚假新闻报道，不管它们是否有着相同的目标，如影响股市行情、选举，或影响证券、商品的销售等。其实，世界上效果最佳的广告往往是那些从无耻新闻机构偷用新闻专栏，并以新闻报道形式出现的广告。股市行情受到虚假报道的影响而起起伏伏，别有用心的报道者赚取了大量不义之财。

不公正——我们谴责任何违背公正原则的行径：

1. 记者通过伪装成侦探和间谍的方式调查嫌疑人的罪恶事实或证明其清白。

在审判罪犯的过程中，记者不应介入司法领域。他们不应为了迎合读者的猎奇心理而化身为侦探或添油加醋的中间人。

在公众的巨大偏见下，犯罪嫌疑人很难得到公正的审判，而公众的这种偏见正来源于报刊对嫌疑人所做的新闻报道。这类报道甚至会出现在嫌疑人被逮捕之前。

我们不应该含沙射影地将事实解读为结论，除非我们能为这些结论负责。阐释、解释和解读等都应该留给该领域的行家或专家。

2. 在相关嫌疑人的批捕或审判情况悬而未决的情况下，不应该刊载与其批捕或最终审判相关的谣言、流言或记者个人的假设。记者不是侦查人员，记者的捕风捉影，或传播毫无根据的谣言，侵犯了嫌疑人被公平、公正审判的权利。

粗鄙丑行——分类：为了做到清晰、条理，我们将相关犯罪划分为以下几类：违背公众信任类（例如，受贿、挪用公款或政府官员的贪污）；侵犯私人机构或雇主权利类（同样包括挪用公款和泄露机密）以及违背个人道德类，通常情况下，此类犯罪大部分都围绕着家庭关系。

1. 在处理政府官员或受托人的嫌疑情况时，我们要求在新闻报道中只能使用与其相关的真实关系和记录等事实。

记者个人的假设或结论不应出现在新闻报道中，即便其中包含了正确结论所具备的所有因素。

采访报道得出的结论和假设部分，应该标明作者的身份。

如果编辑想对案件下结论，请让他署上名字。不要将个人意见隐藏在报纸的客观性之中。

2. 对待具有嫌疑的私人机构经理人时，必须将事实关系理清。

但是，在这种类型的新闻故事中，所有的怀疑和推论都仅限于直接利益相关的当事人。不应该只刊载一方陈述的事实，而不刊载被指控方所做的事实陈述。

在正式逮捕或审判前，没有直接关联的评论都不应被发表。

3. 在报道违背私人道德的案例时，不管事件的记录多么真实，在法院正式下达审判结果或嫌犯被正式逮捕前，我们都不能刊载该事件的任何记录。即使是正式下达了审判结果或做出了逮捕，新闻也只应该报道原告控诉的概要和被告的回复，例如，从原告、被告各自的代理律师处所获得的材料。

关于这类案件的社会流言或丑闻，不管多么真实，我们都不应该予以报道和刊载。

无论涉事主体知名度有多高，违背私人道德的报道永远不应放在头版，而且尽可能不要披露相关细节。

几种违背私人道德的行为，如果只是违背了我们的美德标准，就应该被忽视；然而，如果演化为公共事件，危害性被放大，那么，我们可以做一个关于基本事实的报道，其中应尽量少用暗示语言。

嫌疑人的无耻行为绝不能被吹捧。

4. 除非嫌疑人处于潜逃状态，否则绝不刊登其照片。

编辑行为准则

评 论

评论——评论是报纸上所刊载的对人或事物的印象、信念或观点，包括出自报纸评论员、外来投稿者或采访报道的评论。

区别说明——我们认为，无论何时，如果出版物将其评论局限于特定类型的思想、观点，或一个毫无意义的问题，那么，它就变成了某种特定类型的出版物，而不再是真正意义上的报纸。

解释——你会发现，我们对新闻的定义，即新闻是对思维、人物以及事物活动进行的不偏不倚的报道，同样适用于那些具有特定倾向的出版物，只要把定义中的"不偏不倚"一词替换为"带有偏见"即可。

在该部分，我们将以报纸的编辑方针或观点为指导，不偏不倚地呈现社会的思想活动。

责任——鉴于观点或结论是思想或思维活动的产物，且一个观点的价值和意义大小取决于作者的认知水平；因此，读者有权获知作者的个人身份，不管是以署名的方式，还是在采访、文章里以记者陈述的方式，都可以予以告知，即便是那些我们并不提倡的特殊类型的文章也应如此。

影响（社论）——如果真实地报道新闻或自由地表达观点将严重影响大型机构或巨头个人的利益，我们就应该避免他们持有我们出版业务的股票或成为我们的债主。

影响（报道）——不应雇用那些接受人情礼物、不寻常优待或自谋私利的记者，或如果客观地报道新闻会影响其利益关系，这样的记者也不应雇用。

欺骗——新闻工作者的身份不足以让我们在没有取得被采访人同意的情况下，就直接引用他们接受采访时所说的话。这样的认识和行为是不被允许的。但是，一旦我们获得了被采访人的许可，我们将坚持行使刊载这些观点的权利，除非被明确禁止。

忠于采访——未经作者同意，采访内容或观点陈述不应在发表前就公之于众。

公开限制——个人的姓名与肖像属于其私人财产，我们协会应该对隐私和公开的边界作出界定。

新闻准则与建议摘录
员工职业行为指南[①]
《布鲁克林之鹰》

编辑方针

1.《布鲁克林之鹰》（以下简称《鹰》）属于家庭类报纸。它刊载所有类型的新闻，但主要目标仍然是强调有益而非有害的事实。它有强烈的进取心，但绝不追求煽情主义。作为一份标价三美分的报纸，它必须坚持新闻业的最高标准。尤为重要的是，它自始至终都必须真实、准确、公正。

2."布鲁克林优先"是编辑方针的首要原则。这份报纸是布鲁克林人的组织，同时也是一个公共服务机构。凡有益于布鲁克林的皆有助于《鹰》。越是了解布鲁克林和《鹰》，越能够为这两者服务。

3.《鹰》是世界上最好的报纸之一，全世界都属其关注范围。它的兴趣点遍布人类的一切活动。作为最具广泛代表意义的报纸之一，只有那些具有自由理念和世界眼光的人，才能为《鹰》的声誉贡献一己之力。

一般准则

好的新闻工作最基本的原则是准确，《鹰》遵循此原则，且在工作中坚持此道。核查你的事实，不要依赖别人的说法，去参考书籍材料。

写对人名：对于一份报纸而言，没有什么比拼错别人的名字更糟糕的事了。本手册里列出了《鹰》常用的人名。在这本手册之外，补充你自己的人名清单。

公正：《鹰》意在交友而非树敌。不要因担心损害一个好故事而隐藏任何部分的事实。摆出双方的观点。不要让《鹰》成为任何人发泄仇恨的地方。给予受到攻击的个人或机构澄清事实的机会。

---

① 许多报纸虽无此类明文规定，但它们有着自己的编辑传统和口头指导。

当一个人被控告有罪或做过什么不道德、不光彩之事时，不要在报道中提及与此事无关的亲戚的姓名。此外，讣告中不要强调好声誉者一生中经历的不幸事件。

警惕那些寻求免费宣传的人。请铭记《鹰》版面的每一行都值25美分，放弃多余的内容。不要帮助广告代理欺骗广告部门。

不要涉及任何可能冒犯种族或宗派禁忌的内容。也许你用的一个词就冒犯了《鹰》的20,000多名读者。不要提及被逮捕者的国籍或宗教信仰，除非这是必不可少或不可避免的内容。在关于火灾或盗窃类新闻或报道时，不要强调事件的具体地点，这会给特定区域带来不好的名声。

仔细通读《鹰》，从第一页到最后一页。只有这样，你才能够熟悉其风格、方针和特殊偏好。如果阅读时发现了错误，请及时报告；如果你有好的建议，请及时提出来。再阅读当地其他报纸，留意它们是如何处理相同故事的。如果你发现它们在事实、长度或者重点上有很大不同，请报告给城市版编辑，让他留心。成为一个知名且上进的人，才符合晋升的标准。

警惕自己的偏见。你个人的喜好不应该流露在新闻写作中。如果你想对某个主题表达强烈的意见，尝试撰写评论或给论坛版面写信。但不要让你的新闻报道带有社论评述的痕迹。

永远不要压制新闻报道。当你作为《鹰》的员工时，你所采写的新闻报道属于《鹰》的财产，你的上司才有权决定什么可用、什么不可用。如果收到要求，让你压制或删除某则新闻报道，一定要上报，并要求给出理由，但你对该要求的回应只能是"你会传播它"。

以感激的态度接收外部人士提供的新闻线索或建议，有些线索或建议也许无用，但感激的态度最终会赢得别人的帮助。这些帮助对你个人和《鹰》都是无价之宝。

《基督教科学箴言报》

1. 规范使用语言——《基督教科学箴言报》的一大特征是：广泛

的报道范围和多种多样的部门设置，因此，其专栏版面非常珍贵——每一个词都应该切中关键，寓意丰富。

2. 简洁、明晰的写作同样可以令文章生动别致，而且更加有影响力。一言以蔽之——"浓缩"。

3. 旨在简单明了，清晰地表达你的想法，措词通俗易懂。错误的句法、冗长的句式，使主谓语与一长串修饰短语、从句搅在一起，而代词用法又不知所云——所有的这些都是需要避免的错误。尽量使用单音节词，而非多音节词。尽管使用多音节词会显得你有学问，但我们的大多数读者不会随身携带一本字典，或有闲工夫去查字典。

4. 你是为英语读者写新闻，但读者中只有少数人上过大学——不要忽略了大多数的读者。有些情况时有发生，即意义上的精细差别只能使用源语言——如果它确实是你"报道"的精髓，那就尽可能地使用它；但一般而言，只有那些长时间被使用且为人们所熟悉的外来单词和词语，才能够在日报专栏里使用。

5. 令人作呕的词语——永远不要使用那些表达恶心想法的单词和短语，例如"烧焦""取出内脏"等。

6. 避免累赘的表达方式，如"结婚婚礼""丧事葬礼""窒息致死"等。

7. 俚语使用——俚语无疑是口语中常用的表达，但必须从《基督教科学箴言报》里清除它。除非得到总编辑的批准，否则，即便是在采访中也不能使用。当内容简单易懂时，禁止使用俚语。

8. 新闻或评论——新闻专栏只刊载新闻，不发表评论，但以新闻形式报道的观点除外。记者或通讯员试图越权行使编辑职能，不经编辑的评判而直接使用文章，一经发现就予以压制，不管删除该部分内容会给新闻报道造成多大的漏洞。

9. 警惕对离奇消失的人或事作污名化报道。除非涉及公共利益，否则对该类事件的评论属于不正当。同时，报纸的任何评论都要有可靠的依据。

10. 传闻永远不能用于报道失败事件或其他影响商业信誉事件。

11. 准确——编辑和记者在准备复印"样刊"时，必须将正确的名称写清楚，确保不会弄错。同样，在排版等流程中，也应尽可能地使用印刷品，以免出错。对《基督教科学箴言报》而言，工作人员履行职责时最重要的一点就是做到准确，以使得各部门可能完成出色的报道和评论工作。应写下个人姓和名的全称，以及中间名的首字母。

12. 只要时间允许，核实所有引文，尤其是出自《圣经》的语录。

13. 标题——用数字标示标题的风格。计数时请仔细，从而保证记录下的数字与风格相匹配。大标题应该是报道的内容提示，而不是其特征描述。标题应该是描述性的，而不应具有倾向；是具体的而不是抽象的。同时，标题禁止带有头韵、煽情色彩或空洞无物。一般的标题，像"告上法庭""被判入狱""被起诉赔偿"等，是不被接受的。同时，像"杀死自己的孩子""疯狂母亲的恐怖行为""轮船在风暴中失踪""巨浪导致（海洋生物）大面积死亡"等标题则应该避免。

14. 请记住，最重要的是，你是在为《基督教科学箴言报》准备新闻报道，其标准是真实，不容一丝煽情。

《斯普林菲尔德共和报》

采访准则

在没有遵循以下规则的情况下，不要擅自引用被采访者的言论：

第一，告知被采访者，他们在采访中所说的内容将被引用。

第二，让被采访者知道你对采访内容的处理，并与其确认发言内容。

特别是被采访者具有争议性或涉及私事或个人利益时，以上两点为必须遵循的准则。

当引用被采访者所说的话时，报纸应确保被引用的段落是原话。引用语不准确是不可原谅的。

除非获准直接引用采访内容，一般情况下，以间接引语代替直接引语。例如，你可以这样写：史密斯先生在讨论该主题时说道，实际上……

公共演讲的报道不要将演讲内容直接放进引号内，除非是复述演讲者的原话。

在采访一个人前,准备好你要问的相关问题。如果被采访者侃侃而谈,那你就跟着他的节奏继续采访。如果被采访者不是那么想说,那你就紧跟自己准备好的采访问题。如果采访任务困难重重,在你自己尝试解决前,向城市版编辑咨询是否能够找到解决问题的最佳办法,并尽可能地熟悉采访谈论的主题。

讣告准则

讣告写作时需加倍小心。尽可能准确地采写各种事实。除非特殊情况,否则不要提及死者的某些生平,那样会令其亲戚和朋友悲痛。采写讣告时,褒奖死者生前的良好品质和成就,会给报纸带来善意的回应。

其他准则

通读自己的文章,确保读者读到的内容与你头脑中的内容相符。

不要依赖编辑修改你的错误;需自己修改。

永远不要以动物的痛苦或死亡为主题撰写幽默类文章,同理,人类的痛苦或死亡也不应该这样写,因为这些痛苦或死亡会给他们自己或亲朋好友带去耻辱、羞愧或悲伤。

仔细地评估你采写的每一条新闻。确保重要新闻有足够的版面;非重要新闻尽可能简单地处理。

每个社区都会有人时不时地做出错误的事情或陷入不好的境地。无惧且无偏好地刊载所有新闻是一家诚实报纸的职责。曝光的确会让人们改正错误。但如果新闻报道被这样解读——为了记者个人或报纸的利益而曝光细小的错误,并将这些错误行为归咎于某个人,这说明新闻的写法出现了差错。《斯普林菲尔德共和报》在斯普林菲尔德地区的发行已经有近百年的历史,我们可以自豪地说,尽管该地区有着较高的新闻标准,但《斯普林菲尔德共和报》以无畏的新闻方针为这些高标准的保持贡献了一份力量。然而,《斯普林菲尔德共和报》不会为了迎合仇恨情绪而"招惹"他人,它想广交朋友,而非四面树敌。

《斯普林菲尔德联合报》

1.《斯普林菲尔德联合报》(以下简称《联合报》)旨在成为一份有

价值的报纸,让你感到有一种为公众服务的自豪感。

2. 致力于准确、公正地表达,《联合报》只刊载无偏见的事实。

3. 记者应该像绅士一样去写作。

4. 竭力采写与公共利益相关的新闻,并给予匹配的版面,在标题中指出其重要性。

5. 记住,这是一个繁忙的世界,不管事件多么重要,很少有人有时间或动力去阅读冗长的事件叙述。

6. 用清晰、准确的语言讲述你必须讲述的故事,措辞需传达真实意义。

7. 不要强调人性的弱点,或试图给一般事件制造耸人听闻的效果。如果没有狼的时候你喊狼来了,当狼真的来了的时候,你喊也没有用,因为公众不会再相信你了。公众信任是报纸拥有的最大资产,同时也是你拥有的最大资产。

8. 新闻业应该避免黄色内容,但可以学习黄色新闻记者所具有的进取精神。

9. 关于世界艺术和科学新发现、新进展的重要新闻,能够带来重大变革的新发明的新闻,劳动力感兴趣的企业新闻,金融机构和大型企业的新闻,关乎铁路和其他公共设施的新闻,房地产交易新闻,关于公共事业进步的新闻,室内外运动和消遣性活动的新闻,知名人士的新闻,与教育、宗教等话题相关的新闻,政治性质的新闻等,都可以被视为有特殊价值的新闻——简言之,即对思维健全者具有天然吸引力的所有新闻。因为思维健全者都渴望知晓周遭世界正在发生的事情,以及与自己有关的信息。

10. 站在读者的立场思考问题,并问自己"这则新闻是否能够引起一般读者的兴趣?如果能,有多少人会感兴趣?"你对读者的判断将会反映在你的写作方式上,反映在你的版面安排和标题处理上。

11. 为慎重起见,尽力为《联合报》找到众多不同的新闻选题,请记住,《联合报》有着大量口味各异的读者。

准确与公正

准确性!《联合报》要求记者遵循准确性原则,且在工作中坚持此道。每位通讯员、记者、样刊校对者、编辑都应遵循准确性原则。而且，仅仅做到准确还不够，公正原则也同等重要。不公正的事实甚至比谎言更糟糕。讲真话，完整无缺的真话，而且只讲真话。

不要听从任何人的一面之词，应关照所有的主体，全面呈现各方观点。一些事情看起来是如此，也可能的确如此，但只有你亲自验证清楚之后才知道它是否真的如此。不要用想象来填补细节。

世界上最有趣的莫过于事实了。如果你写的是事实，且公正地写，你就可以笑对诽谤诉讼。

《联合报》对错误留有一定的余地，知道错误偶尔会发生，但希望每位员工能从错误中吸取教训，不重复犯错。长期粗心大意者会被解聘。如果你不能正确地做事，《联合报》就不会再聘用你了。

不准确的新闻报道会严重伤害无辜的个人，会影响你的晋升，将摧毁公众对报纸的信任。《联合报》希望读者相信它所刊登的一切信息。

准确。

公正。

事实。

《联合报》的部分编辑方针

1.《联合报》旨在成为一份具有建设性而非破坏性的报纸。采写新闻时，要保持和善。

2. 在政治上，《联合报》偏向共和党，但并不狭隘地局限于此。它相信广泛意义上的共和党的基本原则，并非支持共和党的所有主张，也不会无条件地支持共和党阵营的每一位候选人。它认为，公共利益高于政党或其他利益。它旨在公正地对待所有政治党派，不带有自身观点地报道新闻，并以开放的态度主持专栏。它是一份完全摆脱了各种同盟纠缠关系的报纸。

3.《联合报》不刊载陷入警务事件的孩子的姓名，亦不会在未成年人法庭审讯前曝光此类案件，除非有足够理由这样做。

4.《联合报》不报道因醉酒而被捕的人员的姓名，亦不会曝光因醉酒被法庭判处罚金的人员的姓名，除非其逮捕和出庭应诉是在特殊情形下进行的。应该给他们一个改过自新的机会。

5.《联合报》的报道不提及犯罪人员或其他可耻行为人的国籍，除非其国籍信息构成事件的核心细节。在通常情况下，姓名已经传达了足够的信息，而其同种族或同国籍的人会极其厌恨提及犯罪人员的国籍。

6.《联合报》的编辑方针规定，尽可能简洁地报道自杀事件，除非情况非常特殊或自杀者具有极端显著特征。如果是服毒身亡，请不要在报道中提及毒药的名字。如果自杀事件中使用了手枪，请不要说明子弹穿过的地方。如果是自缢死亡，请不要描述自缢方式。因为这些会让那些正在考虑自杀的人效仿。

7. 在机动车辆事故的报道中，不要提及车辆品牌，而枪击案的报道则不要提及武器的配置。

8. 不要在新闻专栏里做任何广告。对免费供给刊载的文章应持怀疑的态度。一般说来，这些人非常狡诈，总是试图免费做广告。不要帮助广告代理欺骗我们的广告部门。

《底特律新闻报》

本报应该是：

风格犀利但无恶意。

有趣但不煽情。

无畏却公正。

竭尽全力确保准确。

永远致力于采写与传播信息。

尽量做到通俗易懂，但永远不要以牺牲可靠的信息为代价。

探寻振奋人心而非腐朽堕落之生活。

我们应努力确保报纸每一页的用词都准确可靠。

以上目标的实现需从员工开始：首先，招聘具有良好品格的人从事新闻采写与编辑，随后，以我们的思考模式、新闻处理方式等对他们进行培训。

这并不是批评我们现在的员工或反思我们一直发行的报纸，我们已经有了一支训练有素的员工队伍和一份令人满意的报纸。我们的目的是尽可能地促进二者的进步。

如果你犯了错，你需要履行两项责任：一是对被错误报道者的责任，另一个是对受众的责任。永远不要向《新闻报》的读者误传信息。如果你错误地推断一个人做了某事，而事实上他没有做过；或推断他说了某些话，而事实上他没有说过，那么，他就受到了不公正的报道。这是一方面。同时，这对成千上万的读者也是不公正的，因为你传达了关于那个人的错误信息，使读者对他形成了错误的印象和判断。永远都要及时更正错误。如果你所更正的错误与原刊载内容存在差异，请用更大号的字体标示出来，使之醒目、完整。

如果一个记者喝得酩酊大醉，人们不会说，"那是某某人"——叫他的名字，而会说，"那是《新闻报》的记者"。个人行为是对员工整体情况的反映，上述行为在某种程度上会损毁报纸的声望和形象。对于一个醉汉，没人会对他的工作有信心。任何编辑部的成员，如果被发现酩酊大醉一次，或有意刊载虚假报道，将会立即被解雇。

美国公众想要知悉社会、了解现状、获取信息，引用一位作家的话，即"信息比意见更重要"。给予受众充足的信息，让他们自己下结论。任何评论，不仅要向读者传达完整而全面的事实，还要告诉他们今天发生的事与昨天的事之间有何联系，从而启迪读者。同时，尽可能地让读者自己得出结论。

如果一个问题经不起所有事实的检验，反对的观点就会很容易推翻它。每个问题的正反两面信息都应涉及。

善意、有益的建议常常能够正确地指引官员，而纠缠不休的唠叨则会使之固执地坚持错误的方向。但这并不意味着我们不需勤于监督、反对图谋不轨的骗子。

只有每一位员工都很强大时，队伍才会强大。显然，一个人，不管是受环境的影响，还是因为自己性格的原因，不符合我们组织的要求时，无论是出于善良还是出于对报纸负责的态度，都应让他知晓这一点，让他去从事能够取得成功的职业，而不是仍由其占据这个职位，阻挡能够胜任该工作的人。

将报纸的每一版都尽力做到最好，这样一来，如果记者的报道没有被刊载在头版，他也不会感到失望，反而会觉到只有那些有价值的报道才能够登报。这就避免了报纸沦为"头版报"。

故事应尽量简洁，但简洁并不意味着粗劣。尽量以最少的话把故事讲述完整。

事实的性质决定了其趣味性，这超出了任何记者的想象。每个新闻故事都具备有趣的一面，你要做的是将其挖掘出来。如果还是不够有趣，那是因为你挖得不够深。

任何报纸，最珍贵的资产是讲述事实的信誉。而取得这种信誉的唯一方法就是说实话。记者粗心所导致的不真实报道，对报纸信誉所造成的伤害，不亚于故意编造事实所带来的伤害。

任何抱怨的人都应受到尊重，且给予其善意的倾听；尤其是贫穷或地位低下者，与条件优越的人相比，他们缺乏表达生活苦楚的途径，因此，应该给予他们特殊的关照。一位受过良好教育且优秀的人，知道怎样找到领导办公室去倾诉委屈。洗衣女工则不同，也许她们会来到门口，羞怯、迟疑，几乎不知该怎么办。而她们受到的委屈甚至比其他申诉人更多。因此，她们应该受到礼貌的接待，由此助其倾吐心声。

简单易懂的语言最有力，也是最好的。这样一来，读书不多的人也能够读懂；而受过良好教育的人通常在结束工作后的夜晚读报，简单易懂的语言使之饶有兴致。永远不要使用晦涩的词语来炫耀学问。新闻或评论的目的在于提供信息，或劝服读者相信，如果读者不得不研习晦涩的词语或长难句式，这就很难达到目的。必须一直坚持使用通俗易懂的语言。也许有少数人能够理解和欣赏拉丁语或法语，或其他外语引言，但我们读者中的大多数只是一般人，大都很难做到这一点。

公正性。诽谤法条款不应成为权衡新闻报道是否被刊载的判断标准，而公正性才是。如果你做到了公正，就不用担心任何诽谤诉讼。

给其他同事一个倾诉的机会。他也许是错的，即使只是小问题，也要给他一个倾诉的机会。如果问题有缓和的余地，将错误全部归咎于他，则有失公允。

210　没有必要告诉人们我们是诚实的，或明智的，或谨慎的，或报纸上的新闻是独家报道。如果确实如此，公众自然会发现。一位诚实的人不会到处宣扬其诚实。

时间可治愈一切，但一个女人一旦声誉扫地，却很难自动修复。因此，在处理关乎任何一个人的声誉的事情时，必须小心、谨慎、公正、得体；尤其是涉及女性姓名时，更应该加倍小心。如果能避免，尽量不要在新闻报道中讲述笑话、举例说明或提出问题时直接提到女性姓名；通常情况下，这是可以避免的。即使一位女性犯错了，我们应该大度一点。这可能是她人生的一大危机。刊载她的故事会把她逼到绝望的深渊，而友善的处理则会带给她希望。没有任何新闻报道有权毁掉一位女性的人生。毁掉一位男性的人生也同样不行。

保持报纸用语文明和思想高洁，猥亵或暗示性的语言是没有必要的。当你怀疑这一点时，想一想，一位13岁的小姑娘正在读你写的新闻，会是什么情形？

不要把报纸工作当作是一种冷酷的印刷"游戏"——报纸上刊载的内容你也半知半解，纯粹为了打败另外的报纸；相反，应该将其看作是一种严肃且富有建设性的工作，投入你所有的精力，让读者尽早获取有价值的可靠信息。

在没有致谢原作者或原刊物的情况下，不应该转载其任何内容。仅仅通过致谢文章原作者或原刊物来"交换"转载内容亦是不公平的。

如果大选即将在下周二来临，不允许任何候选人或政党晚于本周五刊登其新的竞选宣言或声明。如果不给予别人充足的时间回应，报纸就不应刊登任何人的任何信息。

对记者来说，最难做到的是学会保持客观。他必须清晰准确地写下所见所闻，不带一丝偏见。他自己的观点，个人的感受，以及朋友的关系等不应对其采写的新闻故事产生任何影响。

211　最理想的记者应该是，向公众告知自己不共戴天的仇敌的信息时，依然据实以报，即便这些信息会让仇敌在公众面前显得像一个英雄。

《赫斯特新闻报》[①]

广告准则

我们报纸的广告部门应该像新闻和评论部门一样,在员工中牢固树立起管理方针和原则,且使这些方针和原则为每一位员工所熟知。

新闻和社论的品质只能建立在可靠事实的基础之上。广告亦如此。我们的报纸团队中不允许出现歪曲事实的人。诚实是一种常识。

我们将雇用有智慧、有教养的饱学之士。除此之外,胜任广告工作最需要的是正直品格。

我们的报纸只会根据广告费率卡来销售广告。如果广告费率卡出错,那就改正;如果没错,那就遵守广告费率卡的标准。不应对广告买家和卖家施行双重道德标准。削减广告费率、特殊优惠以及秘密回扣等就像"回飞镖"一样,会在人们不经意时,反弹回来从而破坏正常的广告业务。制定"君子协定"的人不受待见。

拒绝接受任何可能危害公众利益的广告业务。颇有嫌疑的金融广告、招人讨厌的医疗广告、宣扬特异功能的广告、唯心论广告、算命占卜广告以及各种虚假广告等,全都不能出现在赫斯特集团的报纸上。既然读者信任我们,我们就不能在新闻或社论专栏欺骗他们。同理,我们也绝不允许他人利用我们的广告专栏来欺骗读者。

新闻准则

确保报纸内容准确可信。

对比我们和其他人的报纸,看看哪个更准确。

剔除信息总是不准确的记者、编辑。奖励提供可信消息的人,就像奖励其他领域有价值的人一样。

杜绝夸大。对于真正有趣的内容而言,这是廉价、无效的替代品。对能将事实写得有趣的记者表示敬意,并将不能做到的人剔除。

[①] 该部分摘自威廉姆·伦道夫·赫斯特(William Randolph Hearst)对该报纸的个人指导。

在新闻专栏中，保持公平、公正是最基本的要求。你的报纸不是民主党、共和党或独立团体所办，因而，将它打造成一个全民所有——无论信仰和党派——提供不偏不倚新闻的报纸。

将新闻适当压缩。大部分新闻经过适当压缩后会变得更好。

完善你的组织结构，使之值得信赖。那么，读者会发现，他们首先能获得更全面的新闻，其次能获取更准确可靠的新闻。

深入挖掘报道，刊登所有新闻。不仅仅要将新闻采访后进行编辑，还应将之付梓。

选择最佳的报道，置于醒目处，即，突出优秀报道，使之富有生机，同时让报纸特点鲜明。

如果你的特点足够瞩目，就要不顾一切地展示出来，但仅仅显示出来还不够。

不要用独占一版的方式突出一篇报道。整版特写往往看起来过于沉重。一篇报道要通过内容新颖有趣、排版以及措辞等加以突出。将特写置于一个专栏中看起来会比较有趣，而铺满整个版面则可能显得乏味。

为精英打造报纸。读者比报纸工作者所想象的要更加优秀、聪明。

不要发表大量讨正派人士喜欢的内容，同时将那些会得罪正派人士的内容剔除。

避免脏话、俚语、低俗用语。如果写作得体，最煽情的新闻也能见诸报端。

避免使用以下一些带有冒犯性的词语："谋杀""丑闻""离婚""犯罪"等。我们并非因其犯罪属性而报道谋杀等犯罪故事，而是因其神秘、浪漫或富有戏剧性。因此，报道时应挖掘神秘、浪漫或戏剧性的特质，同时避免冒犯性的内容。

让报纸内容有用、友善和赏心悦目。

在新闻专栏中避免责备、埋怨和攻击。

如果遵守规则，偶尔进行有理有据的审判和曝光也并无不可。

日常会议中，总结每天的报纸，找出相对于其他报纸的显著优势，如果找不到，那就是失败的一天，应立刻制订出计划，让明天的报纸有更好的表现。

《萨克拉门托蜜蜂报》

《萨克拉门托蜜蜂报》（以下简称《蜜蜂报》）将准确性置于首位。宁可失去一篇报道，也不要浪费第二天的时间去更正它。

《蜜蜂报》要求绝对公平地对待新闻。报道不得谄媚友方，或污蔑敌方。

不要在新闻专栏发表评论。一篇准确的报道本身就是最完美的社论。

不要夸大其词。夸大其词的害处不可估量，将远远超过其试图产生的益处。

如果犯了错误，必须立刻更正。对于《蜜蜂报》的记者而言，纠正错误的责任如同预防错误一样重大。

谨慎对待女性的名字和名誉。即便是在处理悲剧新闻时，也要谨记，只要她没有犯下失去贞洁的罪刑，就应该获得同情。

杜绝种族、宗教、残疾歧视。不要使用"Dago（对意大利人、西班牙人、葡萄牙人的蔑称）""Mick（爱尔兰人的蔑称）""Sheeny（犹太人）""Chink（中国人的蔑称）""Jap（日本人）"等词。这一准则意为在任何情况下都要照顾他人的感受。

新闻亦庄亦谐，视具体场合而定。《蜜蜂报》绝不允许在严肃主题中出现任何轻佻之语。

项目赞助商始终拥有知情权，而非冠名权。如果后者确有必要，编辑部将采取相应的措施。

受访人应报纸要求接受采访时，应免于被嘲笑或批评。

对政府官员或普通公民的控诉，必须明确提出证据。

当指控消息并非出自法庭或来自公共信源时，与其犯错，不如不报。《蜜蜂报》总是像法庭一样公平公正，贫富一视同仁。

《西雅图时报》

以下正式规章适用于任何情况：

1. 记住,年轻女孩儿也读《西雅图时报》(以下简称《时报》)。
2. 《时报》不讨论怀孕、分娩及其所有相关的问题。
3. 除非主管部门下达相反指令,否则任何诽谤内容都要剔除。
4. 若必须提及男女之间的不正当关系,《时报》允许的陈述如下:"这对夫妇已离婚"或"夫妻分居",抑或"发生了许多不便在《时报》上刊登的变化"。
5. "强奸""通奸""不雅裸露""乱伦""强暴"等词汇、短语或句子,及其他类似的表达,都是禁止的。
6. 最大限度地避免性犯罪事件见报。当一个人因侵犯妇女、儿童而获私刑,其私刑缘由通常会被隐瞒,其判决处理会采用如下陈述"暴徒被指控伤害了一名女性"。
7. 考虑到母亲的感受,内科医生出具的确认性犯罪中女性清白的证明,或其他高度相似的话题,也将被最大限度地省略。
8. 被害人事故地点等所有引人不快的受害细节也需省略。禁止使用"碾压"一词,同理,在处理其他类似细节时也需谨慎。

《堪萨斯城市邮报》

每个故事都有两面,报道时缺一不可。

最好的故事需形式简单且内容简洁。

确保真实。

用事实说话。

《堪萨斯城市邮报》会将政治评论置于社论版,因而政治报道需不偏不倚。

虔诚地对待宗教问题。

避免让无辜的男人、女人、孩子蒙羞。

《堪萨斯城市邮报》的理念是真实、宽容、公平、正直和清白。

人名必须核实。

《马里恩星报》[①]

记住：每个问题都有两面，缺一不可。

确保真实。

用事实说话。错误在所难免，但务必尽力追求准确。我宁愿要1个完全正确的报道，也不要100个半真半假的故事。

正直、公平、宽容。

以鼓励代替批评。每个人都有好的一面，发掘其善而不要对任何人的感情造成不必要的伤害。

报道政治集会时，获取事实：据实以报，而非按照你的意愿报道。

平等对待所有党派。若要玩弄政治权术，我们社论专栏见。

虔诚地对待所有宗教问题。

若能避免，报道恶行或不幸时尽量不要让无辜的人蒙羞。不要等到被责问才执行本条。

最重要的是清白。不要在报道中使用脏话或影射性报道。

我希望这份报纸进入每个家庭，而不会破坏任何一个孩子的纯真。

报人守则

沃尔特·威廉姆斯

我坚信新闻业的专业性。

我坚信，大众报刊为大众所信赖。与之紧密相连的是，记者需全面衡量肩负的责任和大众的信任，宁可让对得起这份信任的服务少一些，也绝不能容忍背叛这一信任的行为。

我坚信，冷静的思考、清晰的陈述、准确性和公平是好记者的基本要求。

我坚信，记者只有在调查清楚事实真相之后才能开始撰稿。

我坚信，社会福祉从来都高于新闻压制。

[①] 美国前总统沃伦·G·哈定（Warren G. Harding）在编辑《星报》时撰写。

我坚信，每个记者都应该文雅地撰写新闻；管不住自己的贪念与奢想别人口袋的钱一样可耻；个人的责任不能因他人的命令和贿赂而转移。

我坚信，广告、新闻和社论专栏都应为读者提供他们最感兴趣的内容；坚持事实和明晰的标准无往而不胜；公共服务是检验新闻业成败的至高标准。

我坚信，最成功的新闻业和最应取得成功的新闻业包含以下要素：敬天畏人；保持独立；不因观点的傲慢或权力的贪婪而动摇；保持建设性、宽容，但绝不敷衍；自持、耐心、永远尊重读者、永远无所畏惧；怒视不公；不因特权和舆论压力而摇摆；在法律和道德范围内，赋予每个人平等的机会、公平的报酬；认可人类博爱；深刻的爱国情怀，并真诚地推进国际友好，巩固世界和平；符合当今世界的人道主义精神。

附录 B 参考文献选辑

书籍和书籍的部分章节

[1] 塞缪尔·霍普金斯·亚当斯：《号角》，波士顿：霍顿米夫林公司，1914年。一本关于报纸和专利药品业务关系的小说

[2] 塞缪尔·霍普金斯·亚当斯：《美国大骗局》，芝加哥：美国医学会，1906年。关于专利药品业务及其对新闻的影响。

[3] 塞缪尔·霍普金斯·亚当斯：《成功》，波士顿：霍顿米夫林公司，1921年。一本涉及报纸及其伦理问题的小说。

[4] 美国律师协会：《职业伦理准则》，巴尔的摩：美国职业律师协会，1917年。美国律师的道德标准。

[5] 美国医学会：《医学伦理原则》，芝加哥：美国医学会，1914年。美国医学会伦理原则的陈述。

[6] 诺曼·安吉尔：《新闻与社会组织》，伦敦：劳动出版公司，1922年。关于报刊与社会组织关系的研究——知识劳动的视角。

[7] 发行审计局：《版面的科学选择》，芝加哥：发行审计局，1921年。基于数据演变得出的广告版位基本原则。

[8] 希莱尔·贝洛克：《自由的新闻业》，伦敦：乔治艾伦出版社，1918

年。商业主义对英国新闻业的影响——兼论"新闻自由"作为传播真相的手段。

[9] 阿诺德·班尼特：《公众所需》，纽约：乔治·H·多伦公司，1911年。一家只满足于取悦公众的英国报业。

[10] 威拉德·格罗夫纳·布莱尔，编辑：《新闻职业》，波士顿：大西洋月刊出版社，1918年。不同作者关于不同发展阶段新闻业的论文，最初发表在《大西洋月刊》上。

[11] 小撒迦利亚·查菲：《言论自由》，纽约：哈考特出版社，1920年。一位著名法学教授关于言论自由的历史意涵以及最近背离表现的讨论。

[12] 芝加哥种族关系委员会：《芝加哥的黑人》，芝加哥：芝加哥大学出版社，1922年。新闻界处理种族暴乱新闻的数据和关于黑人问题的舆论。

[13] E·T·库克：《战争时期的报刊》，纽约：麦克米兰公司，1920年。一位英国作家关于战时报刊处境的详细讨论。

[14] 查尔斯·戴纳：《报纸制作艺术》，纽约：阿普尔顿公司，1895年。19世纪杰出编辑关于新闻伦理及其他问题的三次演讲。

[15] 埃尔默·戴维斯：《〈纽约时报〉的历史：1851－1921》，纽约：纽约时报社，1921年。由其编辑成员撰写的一家美国杰出报纸的历史。

[16] 马克斯·伊士曼：《新闻与艺术》，纽约：Alfred A. Knopf 出版社，1916年。关于新闻对艺术影响之批评。

[17] 欧文·埃德曼：《人类特征及其社会意义》，波士顿：霍顿米夫林公司，1920年。当代社会环境中的人类特征。

[18] 《每日伦理》，纽黑文：耶鲁大学出版社，1910年。一封关于新闻伦理问题的通信，通信者谢菲尔德科学学校的诺曼·海古德。

[19] 西格蒙德·弗洛伊德：《精神分析引论》，纽约：麦克米兰公司，1922年。关注信仰形成过程中情感的重要地位。

[20] 菲利普·吉布斯爵士：《此时真像可大白于天下》，纽约：哈珀兄弟出版公司，1920年。揭露战时虚假宣传的大量事实。

[21] 弗兰西斯·哈克特：《看不见的的审查员》，纽约：B.W.许比希公司，1921年。一本关于特殊指向新闻和舆论的论文集。

[22] 黑尔·威廉姆·G：《报刊的法律》，圣保罗：西方出版公司，1923年。论美国报纸的各种法律问题。

[23] 伯纳德·哈特：《精神病心理学》，英国：剑桥大学出版社，1916年。关于恐惧和精神分裂等诸如此类的精神问题。

[24] 约翰·L·希顿：《一个新闻版面的故事》，纽约：哈珀兄弟出版社，1913年。约瑟夫·普利策的《纽约世界报》中社论的影响史。

[25] 汉密尔顿·霍尔特：《商业主义和新闻》，波士顿：霍顿米夫林公司，1909年。在加利福尼亚大学的一次演说。

[26] 教会世界运动，调查委员会：《公众舆论与钢铁工人罢工》，纽约：哈考特公司，1921年。通过报纸和其他手段完成的关于1919年钢铁工人罢工的民意调查。

[27] 劳动研究部：《新闻业》，伦敦：劳动出版公司，1922年。关于英国经济一部分之报纸行业的调查。

[28] 詹姆斯·梅尔文·李：《美国新闻史》，波士顿：霍顿米夫林公司，1917年。1923年第二次修订版。来自报纸和其他有价值参考资料的引述。

[29] 沃尔特·李普曼：《自由与新闻》，纽约：哈考特公司，1920年。三篇分析现代自由的本质及其与新闻关系的文章。

[30] 沃尔特·李普曼：《舆论学》，纽约：哈考特公司，1922年。舆论的最佳和最现代的表现。

[31] 埃德蒙·罗卡：《刑事侦查的科学方法》，巴黎：艾内斯特·弗拉马利翁，1920年1期。展现如何观察到难以观察到的事物客观特征。

[32] A·劳伦斯·洛维尔：《战争与和平时期的舆论》，剑桥：哈佛大学出版社，1923年。哈佛大学校长关于影响意见的因素和意见之间相互影响的讨论。

[33] 琼·马萨尔：《比利时的秘密报纸》，纽约：E·P·达顿公司，

1919年。一家遭到德国军队镇压却顽强坚守的比利时报纸的历史。

[34] 埃德加·李·马斯特斯：《匙河诗集》，纽约：麦克米兰公司，1914年。一本有助于理解美国村庄的报纸与舆论的诗集。

[35] 雅克·保罗·米涅，编辑：《元老拉蒂尼（十四卷）》，巴黎：卡尼尔兄弟出版公司。圣·安波罗修的《论〈创始六日〉》被大量引用，展现了人们对客观事实的传统态度。

[36] 约翰·斯图尔特·密尔：《论自由》，纽约：亨利霍尔特公司，1882年。一位伟大经济学家关于自由的最好的英文讨论。

[37] 威廉·哈姆拉斯·米尔斯：《〈曼彻斯特卫报〉：一个世纪的历史》，纽约：亨利霍尔特公司，1922年。英国伟大的自由报纸的历史详述。

[38] 艾伦·内文斯：《晚邮报：一个世纪的新闻业》，纽约：博尼利弗赖特出版社，1922年。美国最古老和最受尊重的报纸之一的历史。

[39] 弗兰克·迈克尔·奥布莱恩：《〈太阳报〉的故事》，纽约：乔治H. 多伦公司，1918年。一家最与众不同的美国报纸的历史。

[40] 弗里蒙特·奥尔德：《我自己的故事》，旧金山：The San Francisco Call出版社，1919年。旧金山报纸太平洋海岸记者的经历。

[41] 罗伯特·E·帕克：《移民报刊及其控制》，纽约：哈珀兄弟出版社，1922年。关于大部分获得资助的外文报纸的调查。

[42] 乔治·亨利·佩恩：《美国新闻史》，纽约：阿普尔顿公司，1920年。以政治事件为视角切入的美国报业阐释史。

[43] 亚瑟·兰塞姆：《俄罗斯危机》，纽约：B·W·许比希公司，1921年。《曼彻斯特卫报》艰难报道的完整案例。

[44] 詹姆斯·哈威·鲁滨逊：《决策中的思维》，纽约：哈珀兄弟出版社，1921年。人类思维发展的现实考量。

[45] J·E·罗杰斯：《美国报业》，芝加哥：芝加哥大学出版社，1909年。十五年前不同类型新闻在报纸版面上的分布情况研究。

[46] 乔治·P·罗威尔：《美国报纸名录》，波士顿：乔治·P·罗威尔出版社，1879年。提供报纸出版索引的持续出版物。

[47] 露西·梅纳德·萨蒙:《报纸与历史学家》,纽约:牛津大学出版社,1923年。报纸作为历史资料来源的优势与不足。

[48] 瓦尔特·迪尔·斯科特:《广告心理学》,波士顿:斯莫尔·梅纳德公司,1908年。报纸阅读时间的问卷调查。

[49] R·G·斯科特—詹姆斯:《报纸的影响》,伦敦:帕特里奇公司,1913年。关于英国本土也兼指美国报纸发展影响的讨论。

[50] 埃德文·L·舒曼:《新闻实务》,纽约:阿普尔顿公司,1903年。关于早期新闻实践和报业发展趋势。

[51] 厄普顿·辛克莱:《无耻收买》,加利福尼亚州帕萨迪纳:作家出版社,1919年。对美国报业的抨击,认为报业已卖身资本主义。

[52] 哈罗德·E·斯特恩斯,编辑:《美国的文明》,纽约:哈考特公司,1922年。由约翰·梅西和史密斯·索恩撰写的关于新闻与广告内化于美国人生活的文章。

[53] 马克·T·沙利文:《国家洪水遗迹》,纽约:乔治·H·多伦公司,1915年。克里德斯·韦尔兹关于新闻业病症的社论。

[54] W. G. N. 芝加哥:论坛报公司,1922年。《〈芝加哥论坛报〉的历史》,为纪念其创刊七十五周年而出版。

[55] 梅尔·索普,编辑:《未来报业》,纽约:亨利霍尔特公司,1915年。刊登于1914年新闻周刊上的堪萨斯大学的通信。

[56] W·特罗特:《和平与战争时期的群体本能》,纽约:麦克米兰公司,1916年。从众本能与当代文明的关系。

[57] 奥斯瓦尔德·加尔森·韦尔德:《报纸与新闻人》,纽约:Alfred A. Knopf,1923年。美国杰出编辑记者的讨论。

[58] 亨利·沃特森:《"亨利主人":一本自传》,纽约:乔治·H·多伦公司,1919年。《路易斯韦尔信使日报》的杰出编辑的新闻经验。

[59] 李·A·怀特:《〈底特律新闻报〉:1873—1917》,底特律:晚报协会,1918年。一家优秀的中西部报纸的历史。

[60] 罗克希尔·纳尔逊·威廉:《人、报纸和城市的故事》,剑桥:河边新闻出版社,1915年。堪萨斯城市星报的杰出编辑的故事。

［61］J·B·威廉姆斯：《作为英国新闻业基础的公报史》，牛津：牛津大学出版社，1908年。展现了十七世纪新闻业遭遇的诸多限制。

［62］塔尔科特·威廉姆斯：《新闻人》，纽约：斯克里布纳父子公司，1922年。呈现新闻职业的机遇与缺陷。

［63］沃尔特·威廉姆斯，编辑：《夏威夷世界报刊大会论文集》，密苏里州哥伦比亚：斯蒂芬斯出版公司，1922年。此为国际新闻业的论文集合，其中包括几篇关于新闻伦理的文章。

大学公告与报纸宣传册

［64］密歇根大学新闻社第四届年会的议程及发言，密歇根大学安娜堡分校，1922年。

［65］双年度报告，精确与公平竞争管理局，《纽约世界报》。

［66］宪法和法规，记者协会，伦敦E.C.4区都铎街。

［67］宪法与法规，全国新闻记者协会，伦敦E.C.4区舰队街180号。

［68］宪法与法规，妇女新闻社，伦敦W.C.2区南安普顿街，Sentinel House。

［69］瓦尔多·C·库克，报纸上的人物，爱荷华大学延期公告62号，爱荷华城，1920年。

［70］《新闻业的伦理问题》，华盛顿大学公告，普通系列101号，西雅图，1916年。

［71］《如何建立自信》，费城：《农场杂志》。

［72］《如何开展工作》，《纽约论坛报》。

［73］詹姆斯·梅尔文·李：《高等教育机构的新闻教育》，华盛顿：美国教育局，1918年。

［74］伯特·摩西：《庸人阅读通知》，纽约：《晚邮报》。

［75］约瑟·S·梅尔斯：《新闻伦理准则》，俄亥俄州立大学公告，26卷第8期，俄亥俄州哥伦布，1922年。

［76］J·B·鲍威尔：《扩大发行量》，密苏里大学公告，15卷第6期，密苏里哥州伦比亚，1914年。

[77]《美国新闻协会教师协会会议论文集》,1921—1922年。明尼阿波利斯市:R·R·巴洛,明尼苏达大学。
[78]《华盛顿州的某些报纸问题》,华盛顿大学公告,普通系列111号,西雅图,1917年。
[79]《新闻专业补充讲座》,华盛顿大学公告,普通系列103号,西雅图,1916年。
[80]《更好的报纸》,华盛顿大学公告,普通系列81号,西雅图,1914年。
[82]《赛马场贪污》,底特律:新闻报出版社,1922年。
[83] 瓦尔特·威廉姆斯:《世界新闻业》,密苏里大学公告,新闻系列9号,密苏里哥伦比亚。

附录 C　新闻伦理学词汇索引

A

Absence of Malice《并无恶意》

Accuracy 准确（性）

Advertising 广告

advertorials 社论式广告

boycotts 抵制

criticisms of 批评

defenses of 保卫

    sincerity in 真诚

    target-marketing 目标市场营销

    deception 欺骗

Advocacy 拥护，提倡

Aesthetics 美学

Akron Beacon Journal《阿克伦灯塔新闻报》

Albany Times Union《奥尔巴尼联合时报》

America's Most Wanted《美国头号通缉犯》

Amnesty International 大赦国际

Aristotle 亚里士多德

ASNE 美国报纸主编协会

Associated Press 美联社

Atlanta Journal Constitution《亚特兰大宪法报》

Authenticity 真实性

B

Bacon, Sir Francis 培根，弗兰西斯爵士

Bakersfield Californian《贝克斯菲尔德加利福尼亚人报》

Balance Theory 平衡理论

Beavis and Butthead《比维斯和巴特黑德》

Beneficence 仁慈

Bill of Rights 人权法案

Blair Witch《女巫布莱尔》

Blockbuster 流行佳作

"Bonding" announcements "成亲"告示

Book banning 禁书

Boston Herald《波士顿先驱报》

C

Cape Cod Times《科德角时报》

Capital punishment 死刑

Care, ethics of 关怀，伦理学

Case study method 案例研究方法

Categorical imperative 绝对命令 See also Kant 参见"康德"

Caveat emptor 购者自慎

CBS 哥伦比亚广播公司

Celebrity 名流，要人

Censorship 审查制度

Channel One《第 1 频道》

Charlotte Observer《夏洛特观察家报》

Chicago Tribune《芝加哥论坛报》

Christians，Clifford 克里斯琴斯，克利福德

Circles of intimacy 亲密圈

Citizenship 公民身份

Civic Journalism 公民新闻事业

Clear Channel Communications 清晰频道传播公司

CNN 有线新闻电视网

Cognitive dissonance 认知失调

Collective responsibility 集体责任

Columbia Journalism Review《哥伦比亚新闻学评论》

Columbine High School 哥伦拜恩高中

Comic Relief《喜剧桥段》

Communitarianism 社群主义

Community 社群，社区

Compassion 同情

Conflict of interest 利益冲突

Conscience 良心

Consequences 后果　See also Utilitarianism 参见"功利主义"

Constitution，U. S. 美国宪法

Consumers Reports《消费者报道》

Consumerism 消费主义

Cops《美国警察》

Copyright 版权　See Cyberspace 见"赛博空间"

Crisis communication 危机传播

Cross ownership 交叉所有权　See also Media economics 参见"媒介经济"

　　access issues in 途径问题

anonymity in 匿名性
copyright in 版权
    mores 道德观念
    pornography and 色情描写和

D
Daily Me《每日我报》
Dallas Morning News《达拉斯晨报》
Dateline《日界线》
Day One《一日》
Deep Cough "深咳"
Deep Throat "深喉"
Detroit Free Press《底特律自由新闻报》
Dewey. John 杜威，约翰
Dignity 尊严
Distributive justice 分配正义
Diversity 多样性 See also Minorities 参见"少数族裔"
Duty 责任 See also Kant, Ross 参见"康德""罗斯"
E

Elections 选举
Eminem 痞子阿姆
Enlightenment 启蒙运动
Entertainment 娱乐
    disguised as news 假扮成新闻
prosocial benefits of 亲社会作用
stereotyping 刻板印象
    See also Aesthetics 亦见"美学"
EPA 环境保护局

Epistemology 认识论

Ethical dialogue 伦理对话　See also Test of publicity 参见"公开性测试"

Ethics defined 伦理学定义

Eugene Register-Guard《尤金纪事导报》

Everett The Herald 埃弗雷特《先驱报》

F

Fairness 公正

Farm Aid 援助农场行动

FBI 联邦调查局

FCC 联邦通讯委员会

FDA 联邦食品与药品管理局

Federalist Papers《联邦党人文集》

Fidelity 忠实

First Amendment 宪法《第一修正案》

Flourishing 繁荣

Fox Network 福克斯电视网

Freelance writing 自由撰稿写作

Freud，Sigmund 弗洛伊德，西格蒙德

G

Golden mean 中庸之道

Good 善

Grapes of Wrath《愤怒的葡萄》

Gratitude 感激

H

Harm 伤害
Harper's Bazaar《时尚芭莎》
Harvard Law Review《哈佛法学评论》
Hate speech 仇恨言论
HBO 家庭影院
Hegel 黑格尔
Hemlock Society 赫姆洛克协会
Hill and Knowlton 伟达公关公司
Hoffa《霍法》
Huckleberry Finn《哈克贝利·芬历险记》
Hutchins Commission 哈钦斯委员会

I

Insider《惊爆内幕》（又译《知情者》）
International news 国际新闻
Investigative reporting 调查性报道

J

Jefferson, Thomas 杰斐逊，托马斯
Journalism education 新闻教育
Justice 正义
Justification model 正当模式

K

Kant, Immanuel 康德，伊曼纽尔
Knight－Ridder 奈特－里德报团
KMGH－TV KMGH－TV 电视台
KUSA－TV KUSA－TV 电视台

L

Leaks 泄露

Leviathan《利维坦》

Lexington Herald-Leader《莱克星顿先驱导报》

Libertarian Theory 自由主义理论

Lippmann, Walter 李普曼,沃尔特

Los Angeles Times《洛杉矶时报》

Loyalty 忠诚

    articulation of 精确表达

    conflicting 相互冲突

    defined 定义

    layers of 层次

    problems with 存在问题 See also Roles 参见"角色"

Lying 撒谎

M

Magic bullet 魔弹

Marketplace of ideas 观点的自由市场

Marxism 马克思主义

Matrix《黑客帝国》

McCarthyism 麦卡锡主义

McLuhan, Marshall 麦克卢汉,马歇尔

Media Economics 媒介经济学

    boycotts 抵制

    impact of content on 对内容的影响

    impact on news 对新闻的影响

    mergers 合并

    public service 公共服务

Mediated reality 介导现实 See Reality television 参见"真人秀"

Merchant of Venice《威尼斯商人》
Miami Herald《迈阿密先驱报》
Mill, John S 密尔,约翰. S.
Mills, C. right 米尔斯,C·赖特
Milton, John 弥尔顿,约翰
Minorities 少数族裔
Moral Development 道德发展
   ethics of care 关怀伦理
   stages of 阶段
Morally relevant facts 道德相关因素
Morals 道德
Mother Jones《琼斯妈妈》
Ms《女士》
MSNBC 微软/全国广播公司
MTV 音乐电视频道
Muckrakers 扒粪者（黑幕揭发者）
Munsey, Frank (*Munsey's Magazine*) 芒西,弗兰克（《芒西杂志》）

N
NAACP 全国有色人种协进会
National Enquirer《国民问询报》
National security 国家安全
NBC 全国广播公司（ABC 美国广播公司；CBS 哥伦比亚广播公司）
NEA 全国编辑协会
Need to know 知情需要
New England Journal of Medicine《新英格兰医学杂志》
New Orleans Times-Picayune《新奥尔良花絮报》
New York Daily New《纽约每日新闻》
New York Sun《纽约太阳报》

New York Times《纽约时报》
New Yorker《纽约客》
   defining and constructing 定义和构建
preservation of 保存
Newsweek《新闻周刊》
Nickelodeon 尼克国际儿童频道
NPPA 美国新闻摄影记者协会
NRA 美国步枪协会
NRDC 自然资源保护委员会
Nurture 教育

O
Objectivity 客观性
Of Mice and Men《人鼠之间》
Off the record 不供发表
Olympic Park bombing 奥林匹克公园爆炸案
Ownership of information 信息所有权

P
Pack journalism 一揽子新闻事业
Parade《行列》
Paramount 派拉蒙
Partisan press 党派新闻
PBS 公共广播公司
Penny Press《便士报》
Penthouse magazine《阁楼》杂志
Persian Gulf War 波斯湾战争
Persuasion 劝服
Phaedo《斐多篇》

Philadelphia Inquirer《费城问询报》
Philip Morris 菲利普·莫里斯公司
Philosophical anthropology 哲学人类学
Photojournalism 摄影新闻学
 electronic manipulation 电子操控
epistemology of 认识论
 staging 导演
Police Gazette《警察公报》
political advertising 政治广告
political character 政治个性
political reporting 政治报道
 See also Democracy, elections 亦见"民主政治,选举"
Pool coverage 记者团报道
Popular culture 流行文化,大众文化
Pornography 色情描写
Post modernism 后现代主义
Potter Box 波特方格
Practical wisdom 实践智慧
Pragmatism 实用主义
Principles 原则
Privacy 隐私
invasion of 侵犯
 need for 对……的需要
 right to 对……的权利
 victims of tragedy and 悲剧中的受害者
Professionalism 专业主义
Promise keeping 守信
Propaganda 宣传
PRSA 美国公共关系协会

Pseudo events 假事件

Public health 公共健康

Public meetings 公开会议

Public officials 公职人员

Public relations 公共关系

Pulitzer, Joseph 普利策，约瑟夫

Pulitzer prize 普利策奖

R

Race 种族

Ratings 收视率

Rationality 理性

Rawls, John 罗尔斯，约翰

Reality television 真人秀

Reciprocity 互利

Reflective equilibrium 反思均衡

Reformation 宗教改革（Protestant Reformation）

Reparation 赔偿

Reporting, event centered 报道，以事件为中心的

Republic《理想国》See also Plato 亦见"柏拉图"

Rescue 911 救援 911

Right to know 知情权

Riverside Press Enterprise《加州河滨企业新闻报》

Rock Against Drugs 摇滚反对毒品

Rocky Mountain News《落基山新闻报》

RTNDA 广播电视新闻主任协会

S

San Francisco Chronicle《旧金山纪事报》

San Jose Mercury News《圣何塞信使新闻报》

Schindler's List《辛德勒的名单》

Science reporting 科学报道

Seattle Times《西雅图时报》

Self－improvement 自我改进

Self-interest 利己主义

Simon & Schuster 西蒙与舒斯特公司

Situational ethics 情景伦理学

60 Minutes《60 分钟》

Sleeper effect 睡眠者效应

Social responsibility theory 社会责任理论

Socrates 苏格拉底

Sources 消息源

Spin 编造

SPJ 职业新闻工作者协会

St. Paul Pioneer Press《圣保罗先锋报》

St. Petersburg Times《圣彼得堡时报》

Stimulus－response model 刺激－反应模式

Sufficiency 足量

Suicide 自杀

Survivor《幸存者》

Symbol formation 象征形成

Syracuse Post Standard《锡拉丘兹旗帜邮报》

T

Talmud《塔木德》

TARES test TARES 测试

Telecommunications Act of 1996 1996 年《电讯法》

Tenacity 坚韧

Time magazine《时代》杂志
Time Warner 时代－华纳公司
Tobacco ads 烟草广告
Truth 真相；真理
　changing views of 变化的观念
　enlightenment and 启蒙运动和
　objectivity and 客观性和
　oral tradition of 口语传统
　pragmatism and 实用主义和
　rationality 理性
Turner Broadcasting System 特纳广播公司
Turning Point《转折点》

U
UNICEF 联合国儿童基金会
United Church of Christ 联合基督教会
United Way 联合劝募协会
Universality 普适性
U. S. *News and World Report*《美国新闻与世界报道》
USA for Africa 美国援非行动
USA Today《今日美国》
Utilitarianism 功利主义

V
Valuational hedonism 算计的享乐主义者
Veil of Ignorance 无知之幕
Veracity 真实
Viacom 维亚康姆公司
Video news release 视频新闻稿

Vietnam War 越南战争
Virtue 美德
Voyeurism 窥阴癖

W
Wall Street Journal《华尔街日报》
Want to know 知情欲望
Washington Post《华盛顿邮报》
　watchdog 看门狗
Watergate 水门事件
Whistle-blowing 告发
Wilmington News Journal《威尔明顿新闻报》
Women's Sports Foundation 妇女体育基金会

Y
Yellow journalism 黄色新闻

译者跋

任何事业都需有一定的规约和限制。限制并非负担，相反能激发创新。新闻业亦如此。20世纪初，美国报刊业经历了便士报时期的野蛮生长和西进运动时的东西弥合之后，到达一个发展的巅峰期，同时也进入了瓶颈期。激烈的内部（报刊之间）和外部（广播电台）竞争使得报业的黄色新闻和煽情主义大行其道。在这种背景下，有责任感的新闻组织和报刊，如堪萨斯编辑协会、美国报纸编辑协会和《基督教科学箴言报》等，开始意识到自律的必要性，只有自我规约和限制才能维系长远的发展，于是纷纷制定自己的新闻伦理准则和行为规范。基于相当数量的实践和积累之后，世界上第一部新闻伦理学专著——《新闻伦理学》于1924年在美国诞生。

该书作者纳尔逊·安特宁·克劳福德（1888—1963）一生富有远见且兴趣广泛，身兼教师、作者、演讲者、编辑和记者等多重职务。职业生涯中，他曾任美国大学编辑协

会主席、新闻教师协会主席、大学羽毛球协会主席、国家出版俱乐部的官员,还曾是美国农业部的第一位信息总监。1914年至1925年间,他任教于堪萨斯农业学院,先后担任工业新闻系教师、主任,印刷系主任和学院新闻服务部主任,他在敏锐地发现和研究问题的基础上,撰写了美国第一部关于新闻伦理学的大学教材,即《新闻伦理学》。

《新闻伦理学》的出版,标志着系统研究新闻伦理的开始。90余年过去了,现今美国关于新闻伦理、新闻客观性和专业性、新闻教育的著述依然反复引用该书的材料和观点。

学者理查德·斯特克福(Richard Streckfuss,1990)以"客观"(objective)和"客观性"(objectivity)为主题,进行了细致的文献搜索后发现,正是克劳福德的《新闻伦理学》首次对"客观报道"(report objectively)作了详细定义,并称其为时代的产物,文化的结晶[①]。的确,克劳福德在文中约25次提到"客观事实"(objective facts),坚信客观报道一定能带来社会变革,只是过程不会一蹴而就;3次提到"客观态度"(objective mindedness),并视之为新闻工作者必备的品质。更为重要的是,他在目录框架中就提出了客观性原则的实践应用:平衡与比例、防止煽情主义、运用社论引导。

再说新闻专业性。作为一种职业,新闻的主要功能是传播客观事实。由于黄色新闻和煽情主义盛行,新闻业未能很好地履行该职能,因而受到公众的各种指控,比如虚构新闻,比如追求"噱头",比如带有偏见等。克劳福德从唯物主义和现实主义两个层面分析其原因,指出报业的这些缺陷是对商业伦理、社会伦理的戕害,反思"报纸即商品"的商业主义思潮,明确了报业不同于其他行业的"准公共性质"。而践行这种"准公共性"的标准即"新闻伦理"。为了应对报业缺陷,建立专业标准,作者还从法律措施、记者组织、报纸职责和教育机构四个方面给出了参考对策。

---

① Streckfuss, Richard. Objectivity in journalism: A search and a reassessment [J]. Journalism & Mass Communication Quarterly, 1990, 67 (4): 973-983.

在这部分当中，克劳福德对"噱头"（hokum）的例证亦是一大亮点。无论今昔，"噱头"都是种"一点就着"的元素，并且某些"噱头"已嵌入中产阶级的思维中。"噱头"在西方的电影和流行小说中被广泛地使用，甚至促进了金融和商业的成功。为了迎合公众口味和读者愿望，各种"噱头"被报人频繁地使用于新闻作品中，制造了许多半真半假的"新闻"。这种现象至今未有多大改观，甚至在以转发量、点赞数、点击率论英雄的网络时代大有愈演愈烈之势，借古喻今，饶有启发，值得深思。

说到例证，旁征博引是本书一大特色。作者 7 次引用沃尔特·李普曼的著作，另加多个推荐阅读片段，由此可见他对李普曼的推崇，可谓李的忠实布道者。这也为读者了解李普曼及其作品打开了另一扇窗。此外，大量的史料和翔实的案例，例如对美英早期小型报纸和知名大报纸（《纽约时报》《纽约论坛报》《芝加哥论坛报》等）早期情况的分析，以及英语国家（尤其是英国）记者组织的详细记述，为外国新闻史研究开辟了新领地，更加突显了该书的新闻史学价值。

当然，最具史学价值的当属作者收集自美国各州记者组织或知名报纸的 17 套伦理守则，其中包括世界新闻史上第一条新闻伦理准则——1910 年的《堪萨斯新闻出版商伦理准则》。该准则为广告、发行和新闻部门设置了实践标准，后来被其他一些组织所采用。不过，影响最大、采用率最高的当属美国报纸编辑协会于 1923 年采纳的《新闻规约》，不仅其第一句被广为引用："报纸的首要功能是传播人类的行为、感觉和思想"，而且，其精髓后来还被 6 家著名的组织或报纸所采用，分别是：美国报纸编辑协会（ASNE）、广播电台—电视台新闻主任协会（RTNDA）、专业记者协会（SPJ）、美联社编辑主任协会（APME）、纽约时报公司、甘尼特公司报业部。

通过词云（Word Cloud）对这 17 套伦理准则进行分析，可得以下可视化图像（见图 1）。直观可见，排在第一位的是 public，即 public interest，指的是"公共利益"，意为多数伦理准则都在强调新闻应当为公共利益服务。这与克劳福德从头至尾的大声疾呼不谋而合：报纸的功能是传播客观事实，最终目的是为公众谋求利益。按此思路，我们对全书（不包括参考文献以后部分）进行词云可视化分析，则可看出（见图2），排在第一位、占据绝对优势的是 newspaper（663 次），其次是 news（460 次）、public（383 次）、fact（310 次）等。由此可见，新闻伦理最初研究的是"报纸伦理"，其属性是围绕新闻报道（news）的实用主义伦理观（pragmatic ethics），其精髓是"传播客观事实（fact），为公众（public）谋利益"。后来，随着社会文明的进步以及科技水平的发展，传播手段变得多样化，媒介伦理也呈现出"泛化"特征。但是，万变不离其宗，只要有新闻报道、社论引导的实践，就离不开实用主义新闻伦理观。这正是克劳福德《新闻伦理学》的恒久价值所在。

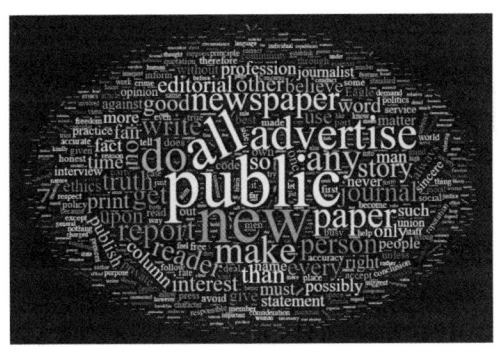

图1　17套新闻伦理准则的词云可视化图像

"一名之立，旬月踟蹰"，翻译之难，可见一斑。面对具有恒久价值的经典之作时，尤其如此。所幸，从筹备翻译到翻译完成的过程中，我们获得许多人的鼎力相助。首先是陈力丹教授的惠识与指点。2013年秋，力丹教授来武汉讲学，课余在与华中师范大学新闻传播学院师生交谈时，提起美国早期三部有影响的新闻理论著作中，已被译介到我国的有两部，即李普曼的《舆论学》和约斯特的《新闻学原理》，而克劳福德的《新闻伦理学》迄今尚未在我国翻译出版，殊为可惜。嗣后，在华中师范大学的资助下，译者即着手启动这项翻译工作。然因年代久远，国内遍寻不得原书踪迹，好在经中国传媒大学出版社司马兰女士的帮

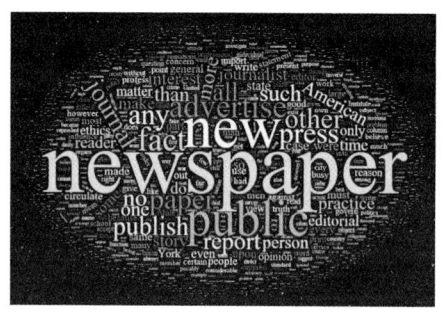

图 2　*The Ethics of Journalism* 的词云可视化分析图像

助,终于在遥远的美国的一个旧书市场淘得这部近百年前的旧著。随后,译者在对华中师大文化传播学博士生的教学中,将此书分段译出用作教材。其间,译者之一王敏由国家公派至美国伊利诺伊大学香槟分校联合培养,得到了享誉世界的媒介伦理学者克利福德·克里斯琴斯(Clifford Christians)教授的大力帮助,对本书一些疑义做出了独具价值的解读。例如,第三章论及新闻偏见时,引用了《联邦通讯社公告》(*The Federated Press Bulletin*)上一则新闻的结尾部分,却未交代事件、人物、时间和背景,亦无其他线索可循。当我们向克里斯琴斯先生求教后,他不仅通过各种渠道找到了这则 90 年前的新闻,还翻阅多本书籍,写出了长篇文章对此进行补充解释。

尤其要感谢的是,克里斯琴斯先生和陈力丹先生分别拨冗为本书赐写了序言,尽显美中两位学术大家张扬学术之卓见,令译者感念在心。中国人民大学博士生廖金英副教授为参考文献的翻译做出了贡献,华中师范大学博士研究生刘文军、武汉大学博士研究生晋艺菡作为译事助理做了很多工作,武汉大学硕士研究生彭雨蒙、汪艳、肖璐凝、甘荣荣、龚灿、欧维维、钟新星等在文本电子化和资料搜集整理等方面也提供了帮助,在此一并表示感谢。限于译者水平,文中错讹之处在所难免,敬请读者朋友不吝斧正。

江作苏　王敏

2017 年 5 月

武汉—芝加哥

The Ethics of Journalism

Preface

It is a truism that no human institution is more potent, for the good or the evil of society, than the press. It is of the utmost importance, therefore, not alone to journalists, but to the general public as well, that its standards of practice shall be such as to further the best interests of society.

This book is an attempt to stimulate the formation, development, and acceptance of such standards. It seeks to present the contemporary status of the press and the reasons therefor, not theoretically but realistically. While the writer nowhere hesitates to state his own views or the views of others, he does not offer them as the final word on the subjects under discussion, but rather as stimuli to independent thinking on the part of the reader. The function of the volume is not to lay down a series of rules for the guidance of the young journalist, but rather to aid him in formulating for himself an ethical philosophy of his profession that will be realistic, discerning, intellectually honest, and applicable to the press as a social institution. When a sufficient proportion of the members of any profession hold and act upon such philosophies, that profession has, potentially at least, achieved its social salvation.

Throughout the book, as will be observed, extensive reference is made to other writings on journalism and to specific practices of newspapers. In some instances, passages of considerable length are quoted for the benefit of those to whom the sources are not easily accessible. The book may thus be read rapidly as a unit, by individuals or by classes in which a limited time is devoted to the ethical problems of journalism; or it may be used as the basic text for a term or semester course in the subject, the several subtopics being elaborated through use of the reference material indicated.

The writer is grateful for the innumerable suggestions, from sources known and unknown, which have aided him in the preparation of the book. In particular, he is indebted to many practicing journalists and teachers of journalism. The suggestions of Dr. J. W. Cunliffe, Director of the School of Journalism, Columbia University, and of Dr. M. L. Spencer, Director of the School of Journalism, University of Washington, have been of special value. He acknowledges with thanks the courtesy of the several authors and publishers who have given him the privilege of quotation, and of *The Nation*, *The Washington Newspaper*, and *Mental Hygiene*, which have kindly permitted the use of portions of articles originally written by him for these publications.

Nelson Antrim Crawford.

I The Business Ethics of Publishing

A newspaper, obviously, is a commodity. Copies of newspapers are bought and sold. Advertisers pay, reluctantly or gladly, large sum of money for the privilege of publishing advertising in them.

The newspaper, if soundly and legitimately run, has no substantial sources of income other than its circulation and its advertising. Here and there are country newspapers which are unsoundly run in that the job printing done by the publisher serves to cover a deficit run up through the operation of the newspaper. Here and there are newspapers, still fewer in number, which accept or even solicit contributions from individuals, corporations, or political parties as compensation for assistance which the publisher gives. The great majority of American newspapers, however, are outside these small categories. The typical American newspaper derives its income from circulation and from advertising, except for the relatively insignificant sums obtained through the sale of waste newsprint and similar items.

So far, the newspaper is a commercial enterprise. Persons who look at the press from this point of view refer to publishing as "the newspaper business," just as the colt-like young reporter refers to it as the "newspaper game." Regarded as a commercial enterprise, the newspaper owes to the persons directly concerned, the advertisers and the subscribers or buyers, the same obligations that are owed by any other commercial enterprise, modified only by the inherent differences between the newspaper and other such enterprises.

The subscriber, when he takes the paper, is entitled to know what he is getting. No solicitor or other person connected with a newspaper has any right to make any misrepresentations concerning the paper, concerning a premium offered by it, or concerning any other factor involved in the transaction. If the newspaper is to maintain the standards of ordinary business, it cannot follow the old legal motto, ***Caveat emptor***, any more than the enlightened merchant can follow this motto with reference to goods sold in his establishment. It is too much to expect that the solicitor or newsdealer shall be able to discuss with nicety the fine points of the news, the features, and the editorial policy of the paper. He can, however, in a general way, present the paper as it is. Few papers intentionally misrepresent to prospective subscribers the quality of their product. Where misrepresentation in solicitation takes place, it is commonly due to the ignorance or dishonesty of the solicitor.

Once the subscription has been obtained, the newspaper is under obligation to see that the publication reaches the subscriber promptly and regularly, and to furnish the edition which is most satisfactory as to news contained, time of delivery, and other factors. All substantial newspapers make an effort to fulfill these obligations. They are a part not only of ethics but of ordinary business policy.

In the case of the large metropolitan dailies, which are in a small minority among American newspapers although they have the largest circulations, subscriptions are frequently a minor factor. The newspaper is sold from day to day and persons become the equivalent of subscribers by their habit of constant buying rather than by the fact of having their names enrolled on the books of the paper. The obligation of the newspaper to these persons is nevertheless the same.

Some large newspapers refuse to sell extra copies which they suspect are to be used for propaganda purposes. In at least one office, there is a rule that a request for twenty or more copies must be referred to the general manager, who investigates the reason for the request. The basis of such rules goes back to the time when certain newspapers and magazines were subsidized by corporations or individuals, the method being the purchase of great numbers of extra copies containing material laudatory of the subsidizers. Many persons today believe that newspapers are extensively subsidized; and their belief is strengthened if, for example, they receive from a railroad company a marked copy of a newspaper containing an editorial defending the railroads. The public would be unable to believe that the editorial was sincere and published with no expectation of reward. For this reason, the newspaper would be wholly justified in refusing to sell any copies to the railroad company. It would thus avoid even the appearance of evil. While it is sometimes argued in opposition to this point of view that the company could reprint the editorial and circulate it, this would not be true if the newspaper were copyrighted, as is the case with a large proportion of metropolitan dailies.

In building its circulation a newspaper has also certain obligations to the advertiser, because, from a financial standpoint, its primary purpose in building circulation is to obtain a higher rate for advertising. To the metropolitan daily, deriving at least eighty per cent of its revenue from advertising, and receiving from circulation less than enough money to pay its white paper bills, additional circulation means actual financial loss unless the advertising rate can be increased. Smaller newspapers, which are able to make a profit on subscriptions, nevertheless reckon the advertising revenue added by increase in circulation as the more important factor.

Obviously, the manner in which the circulation has been built will be of significance to the advertiser. The subscriber who is taking the paper because a young woman friend has asked him to subscribe in order that she may win votes toward an automobile or a piano, will not have the same interest in it that will be manifested by a subscriber who takes the paper only because lie likes to read it. The housewife who subscribes for a newspaper in order to secure a set of silverware offered as a premium does not, by reason of that fact, become an interested reader. Her interest in the paper, it may be assumed, varies inversely with the value of the premium. If, as sometimes happens, the premium proves to have been misrepresented, the silverware, for instance, turning out to be brass, there is introduced into the transaction a factor calculated to make the subscriber not merely indifferent but perhaps actually hostile to the paper.

While, except in case of actual misrepresentation, neither the contest nor the premium plan can be condemned as contrary to sound ethics, the fact remains that the publication which abstains from both plays somewhat more fairly with its advertisers. This is true even though the advertisers, under modern methods of circulation statements and audits, know in just what way circulation is obtained.

The fundamental ethical obligation of the newspaper to the advertiser is, of course, not to misrepresent its circulation. It cannot be emphasized too often that the advertiser buys space not simply as space but as an opportunity to address the readers of the paper.

Honest circulation figures are a development of recent years. Not long ago publishers expressed resentment at the suggestion on the part of advertisers or advertising agents that dependable circulation figures should be presented and that these should be subject to verification, by disinterested parties. The first attempt to give circulation figures at all was made by George P. Rowell, who published the first issue of his *American Newspaper Directory* in 1870. The newspaper situation of the day is shown by the fact that nine years later he was forced to resort to a key in giving circulation ratings. In some cases the key allowed for a variation of 50,000 in circulation, although Mr. Rowell expressed the hope that it would "work more entirely to the satisfaction of all persons interested" than the former plan of publishing actual figures. In his 1879 directory, he made the following statement:

"In 1870, when it was first decided to give information on this subject, the editor applied to proprietors of newspapers for statements, and inserted before the figures so obtained the word, 'claims'. After a time objections were urged against this word, and to avoid its use, publishers offered to prove reports, by affidavits and otherwise. Many, however, were satisfied with the word as used, and arguing that one "claim was as good as another, set up pretensions which could not be substantiated. It became evident that if the book was to become an authority the 'claimed' circulations would have to be excluded- Thenceforth, those newspapers whose proprietors offered proof had their circulation figures given positively, without any preliminary word; in all other cases the figures were followed by the word 'estimated.'

"In the course of a year or two the word 'estimated' became as objectionable as the other, and newspaper publishers frequently asked that it be omitted. To this request, the response was uniformly made that the word could only be omitted in those cases where an offer to prove correctness accompanied the circulation statement when given.

"This position gave offense to many. It was a system introduced for the protection of honest publishers against their more unscrupulous neighbors. It seemed a good one when it was adopted. It doubtless answered an excellent purpose in its time, but it finally gave rise to so much dissatisfaction that it was abandoned.

"A statement, in detail, of the number issued is now all that is required, and this may be made in any form which suits the convenience of the publisher furnishing it. If notoriously false, it is likely to be disregarded, and, in any event, is liable to receive the critical scrutiny of rivals capable of bringing to bear much positive knowledge on the subject."[①]

Largely through the demands of advertisers and advertising agencies, the situation with reference to circulation figures has been steadily bettered. The most potent force in this direction has been the Audit Bureau of Circulations, a non-profit making corporation, comprising publishers, advertisers, and advertising agents. The A. B. C., as it is popularly called, has formulated and adopted a definition of "net paid circulation" and has also devised a plan whereby the publisher's figures are subjected to independent audit. This insures that all publications belonging to the bureau may be compared on the basis of a common system of rating. Since practically all large newspapers belong to the bureau, misrepresentation of quantity of circulation has been substantially eliminated, so far as the stronger publications are concerned.

In a recent editorial convention, however, the writer heard a country newspaper man seriously ask the question whether actual circulation or claimed circulation should be the basis of certain plans under discussion. The fact that circulation on the smaller papers is frequently misrepresented (though not to the same extent as formerly) is one of the chief reasons why these publications receive but little national advertising. Not a few

---

① Preface, American Newspaper Directory, 1879.

country publishers are still giving the number of copies printed as the actual circulation.

Aside from quantity of circulation, the advertiser or advertising agent must consider quality; that is, he must take into account the buying power and disposition of the persons to whom the paper goes. There is no fixed standard by which to measure quality of circulation, nor would it be practicable to apply such measurement if it existed. It obviously would be impossible to ascertain the income and the wants of every subscriber for a metropolitan daily. The measurement of quality is necessarily somewhat intangible. In soliciting advertising, the newspaper is under obligation to misrepresent in no way the quality of its circulation. Its obligation is to present accurate, unbiased data and to draw honest conclusions therefrom. Any one examining the promotion material sent out by newspapers and magazines, however, cannot fail to suspect that there is exaggeration in the claims of quality circulation. The obligation to maintain accuracy in such claims, however, is generally recognized, at least in theory.

A further obligation rests upon newspapers to exercise no discrimination among advertisers. This does not mean that special rates charged for special positions, or for special types of advertising, or on long-time contracts, are not wholly ethical. It means simply that between two advertisers of the same type of business, utilizing the same amount of space for the same number of insertions, there should be no discrimination as to position or price. It is an application of the one-price principle that has transformed business in the United States from a bargaining basis.

Censorship of advertising arouses perhaps a wider variety of opinions than does any other ethical problem involved in publishing as a business. Like honesty in circulation claims, honesty in advertising is a modern development. The advertiser has been honest no longer than the publisher. Indeed, the growth of honesty in advertising has been stimulated largely by newspaper publishers. The standards of advertising, especially among the large advertisers, are higher than ever before, and are notably higher in this country than in other countries at the present time.

There are still, however, some advertisers who are intentionally dishonest, and others who mislead through excessive enthusiasm, carelessness, or the mistakes of employees. State laws again fraudulent advertising have never worked with thorough effectiveness. The public, being inexpert in merchandising, can be protected against such advertisers most effectively by the publications which carry advertising. Nevertheless, there is a wide variation in the standards of advertising practice enforced by newspapers. At one end of the scale are those publishers, now few in number, who will accept any advertising which will go through the mails and sometimes some which will not. The foreign-language press is, on the whole, the most flagrant example of that tendency in the United States. ① At the other end are those who exercise a strict censorship upon the advertising columns, excluding in block all advertising of certain undesirable classes, such as patent medicines and speculative stocks, and scrutinizing carefully all other advertising submitted.

In some cases the advertising is specifically guaranteed. This practice is less common on newspapers than on periodicals, but the guaranty of a newspaper, when made, is likely to be more iron-bound than that of a magazine. The practice of guaranteeing advertising originated with **The Farm Journal** (Philadelphia) in 1880. In the newspaper field it came into prominence with the militant campaign of **The New York Tribune** against fraudulent advertising, begun in 1914. The financial argument against the guaranty plan, sometimes heard, is not borne out by facts. The actual cost of refunds to customers by a newspaper operating under the plan is not

---

① For statistical data, see Park, *The Immigrant Press and its Control*, pp. 369—373.

likely to exceed one-fifth of one per cent of the advertising revenue. The plan has been employed successfully in small towns as well as in larger cities.

It is often supposed that an advertising guaranty is maintained solely in the interest of the readers. This is not the case. The honest and scrupulous advertiser feels justly that the value of his advertising is diminished if advertising by dishonest or questionable merchants is permitted in the same paper. A specific guaranty enhances the value of all advertising in the paper. If the advertiser knows in advance, as he should be told, all types of advertising accepted by the newspaper, and then inserts his advertisement, he probably has no sound moral justification in complaining of the quality of advertising which the newspaper publishes. From the larger standpoint of service as the basis of business, strict censorship of advertising—with guaranty—on the part of the publisher in the interest of the advertiser, even without considering that of the public, is thoroughly to be commended.

On the other hand, no publisher has any ethical justification for refusing to publish advertising on the sole ground that it competes with the advertising now running in his paper, that it is objectionable for other reasons to some advertiser, or that it is objectionable to the publisher himself, personally. For example, it is wholly unjustifiable for a publisher to sell to a single hardware store the exclusive right to advertise hardware through his paper. The newspapers which declined to run the advertising of Samuel Hopkins Adams's novel, The Clarion, apparently because they were receiving a large advertising revenue from the patent medicine business which Mr. Adams attacked, showed themselves lacking in the ethical principles of ordinary business. The publisher is justified in refusing advertising devoted to attacks upon a competitor of the advertiser, and must, for safety's sake, decline it if it is libelous. On the other hand, there is no justification for a newspaper which publishes so-called publicity advertising representing one side of a controversy, to refuse to publish similar publicity advertising setting forth the opposite side. The moral obligation of the merchant to sell goods to whoever applies for them has been written into law in many places. A similar obligation, although not covered by statute, exists with reference to the newspaper and advertising.

While, as has been pointed out, modern business is based upon the principle of service, no obligation rests upon the newspaper to give to the advertiser any special service, such as investigating markets or aiding the advertiser to obtain distribution of his commodity in the community in which the newspaper circulates. Such activities are perfectly proper on the part of a newspaper, but they rest upon ethical obligation no more than does the case of the dry goods merchant who maintains a rest room as a service to his women customers.

Again, there seems to be no specific obligation on the part of a newspaper to refuse advertising which it is convinced will not pay a profit if run in the particular newspaper concerned. Some few newspapers, notably **The Chicago Tribune**, have adopted this policy for the purpose of promoting the general cause of advertising by making all advertising profitable.

It is still insufficiently recognized that the sale of advertising space is a commercial transaction, in which the advertiser pays a reasonable sum for the privilege of addressing the readers of the paper in a space of given dimensions. Neither legally nor morally is he entitled to any more than this space or to any special privileges to be extended fay the publisher.

Publishing as a business is comparatively young, and there remains a hang-over from the old days when it was a hand-to-mouth trade. It must be remembered that the agate line, as a standard of advertising measurement, was adopted little more than thirty years ago, even on the largest papers. There is consequently a tradition of irregular rates in the mind of the public, including advertisers. Moreover, and still worse, there is a tradition of advertising as a form of charity to the starving printer, or a contribution to avert blackmail, to purchase support in the columns of the newspaper, or at best to help maintain the press, recognized as a desirable institution. These attitudes are found in their frankest form in the smaller places, but points of view based fundamentally upon them are common even in metropolitan centers.

In line with these facts, the merchant in the small town may insist on a free news story whenever he gets in his season's stock, or the banker may call upon the publisher to print as an editorial "canned" material issued by a partisan political agency. A monument company advertising for salesmen, writes: "Should we decide to place this ad. in your paper, we would expect you, in your local news column, to give us a boost and do your best to help our ad secure the man we want." The theaters and motion picture houses are so insistent on free newspaper publicity that many publishers charge them a higher advertising rate than they charge other industries. While the excess allows for the supposedly free copy that is published, the practice is obviously a most undesirable business practice, even though it be assumed—as is not always true—that the reader recognizes the free "puffs" and distinguishes them from legitimate news. In the larger cities, news involving large stores or their owners is sometimes suppressed at the request, or even without the request, of the advertisers. At present this is less common than is popularly supposed, and less common, moreover, than was formerly the case.

It was less than twenty years ago that patent medicine advertisers were inserting in their contracts with publishers a clause making the contracts voidable if any laws restricting the sale of patent medicines were passed, or if any matter prejudicial to the interests of the medicine manufacturer appeared in the paper. In response to demands from the advertisers, newspapers in many parts of the United States requested the legislatures to kill bills providing for the publication of the formulae of patent medicines, and in one state the Press Association passed a resolution opposing such a bill and appointed a committee to fight it. ① Many newspaper readers, having known of this situation in 1904 and 1905, suppose that it still exists.

The increasing tendency of newspapers is to disregard the demands of advertisers in such matters, only partly, it is true, on ethical grounds, partly for purely commercial reasons. Not only is it considered bad policy to permit an advertiser to gain the impression that he "owns the paper," but an accession to one advertiser's request brings scores of similar requests from other advertisers; while, on the other hand, the publication of matter unfavorable to an advertiser pleases his competitors. From an ethical standpoint, the publisher who conforms to the demands of advertisers is cheating his readers, as will be pointed out in greater detail further on, and at the same time he is not playing fair with those advertisers who have purchased their space as a business transaction. Indeed, under these circumstances, no advertiser can be sure, no matter how much free publicity and other illegitimate service he receives, that he is obtaining for his money the same value that other advertisers receive.

The competent and honest newspaper man meets requests of this sort with a courteous but firm refusal, explaining the position of the paper and not infrequently convincing the advertiser. Where the advertiser goes to the extent of withdrawing his advertising, a public explanation in the columns of the newspaper is both ethical and useful. The Enid (Oklahoma) Eagle, a daily in a town of less than twenty thousand people, performed this function courageously early in 1922, when motion picture theaters

---

① Adams, *The Great American Fraud*, pp. 163—164.

withdrew their advertising. The published comment of *The Eagle* follows:

"Meeting of theater owners was held in Enid Sunday and decision reached to withhold all advertising patronage from The Eagle, according to announcement Monday morning.

"Reason for the action is said to be because The Eagle has not suppressed news concerning the immoral doings of movie people, nor kept out of its columns news of the local movement to close the picture shows on Sundays. Particular umbrage is said to have been taken by the theater owners because of an article concerning that distinguished low-brow, Fat Arbuckle, which appeared in the paper Sunday morning.

"The theater owners are well within their rights in withdrawing patronage from The Eagle. It has never been the policy of The Eagle to permit movie show proprietors to dictate its attitude on questions of public morals, nor to censor The Eagle's news columns.

"The local profession, through some misconception of the rights they imagine an advertiser is entitled to, has almost constantly in the past endeavored to dictate the policy of The Eagle concerning every question affecting picture shows and vaudeville. Withdrawal of their patronage from the paper was inevitable."

The Eagle also published a list of the demands made upon it by theater proprietors:

"Suppress news of movements aimed to result in Sunday closing.

"Don't publish complaints of patrons who have felt insulted by indecencies on the stage.

"Use personal influence and the influence of the paper with the mayor to forestall movie legislation.

"Suppress stories showing why the City Censorship Board cannot function.

"Suppress news of activities of the Parent-Teachers' Association, working for cleaner shows.

"Reject all news matter or Forum communications which might be detrimental to the theaters.

"Support candidates for city offices who are endorsed by the theatre owners.

"Write editorials against proposed increases in theatre licenses.

"Suppress news of epidemics, lest the box office receipts of the theaters suffer.

"Print free reading notices and run free cuts with every advertisement.

"Print regularly a portion of the propaganda sent out by press agents of movie stars, which in reality is nothing but thinly veiled advertising.

"Solicit 'co-operative' advertising from other lines of business to be banked around a free advertisement of special attractions in return for one paid ad.

"Suppress news of patrons being bitten by rats or having their furs chewed up by rats while attending a movie."

A similar situation, involving a somewhat more subtle appeal on the part of advertisers to a newspaper, was appropriately handled by **The Chicago Tribune**. A letter, from the representatives of an advertiser seeking political influence in return for the advertising, was published in the correspondence department of the newspaper. On the same page appeared the editorial reply of the newspaper. The letter follows:

"Chicago, Sept. 2.—For several years past your publication has been among those consistently favored with a substantial share of the advertising appropriations of the National Kellastone Company, America's largest producer of magnesite products."

"Doubtless you look upon this advertising account as mighty desirable business, and we feel that therefore you will be interested in learning that under the contemplated tariff on magnesite which is now before the conference committee at Washington, the source of this advertising is seriously threatened with extinction.

"In other words, should the magnesite tariff in its present form be adopted, the business of the National Kellastone Company and of all other concerns dealing in or handling domestic magnesite or its products, will be seriously impaired because of the impossibility of competing in price with foreign magnesite, which, under the new tariff, could be delivered to American seaports at figures which American concerns cannot meet and exist.

"If you have followed the tariff conferences you probably are aware that in the original Fordney tariff bill, a tariff of $10 per ton on crude, and $15 per ton on calcined magnesite of foreign production was placed on this product. This tariff was entirely satisfactory to the American interests concerned, and the bill was duly passed by the house and sent to the senate.

"Meanwhile, importers of foreign magnesite, and representatives of foreign exporters of this product, brought strong influences to bear, with the result that the senate reduced the proposed tariff to $6.25 on crude and $12.50 on calcined magnesite imports.

"Immediately, representatives of American producers appeared before the senate committee, presenting facts and figures to substantiate their claims to the justness of the original tariff. Their pleas were unavailing, however, and the bill, carrying the lower tariff, was turned over to the conference committee, where it now awaits final action.

"Now, as we have already pointed out, should this lower tariff be passed, its adoption means the closing down of many American concerns engaged in the magnesite business. In fact, foreign competition has long been a thorn in the side of this industry. It has already caused the discontinuance of many American magnesite mines whose owners could not pay American wages and American freight rates, and still successfully meet the prices on foreign products.

"The labor employed in the American magnesite industry is among the best paid in the country, and ideal working conditions are maintained. The foreign magnesite which comes to our shores, however, is the product of the cheapest character of labor, produced under miserable conditions, with wages equivalent to about 1 cent per day American money.

"As far as fair and square competition of a foreign source is concerned, American interests have no quarrel. They are perfectly willing that there should be competition, provided it is on a just and equitable basis - provided it is not permitted to prosper at the cost of destruction to an American industry representing millions invested and employing many thousands of American workmen at good American wages.

"Therefore, as the American magnesite producers are seeking1 only a fair fighting chance for existence; and as your publication, an influential factor in the thought of the nation, can do much on the side of fair play, we are writing to urge your endorsement of these claims and to bespeak your cooperation and support in this endeavor to cause the adoption of the higher tariff as provided in the original Fordney bill.

"A letter to your senators and congressmen, in behalf of our client, the National Kellastone Company, and of the industry in general, requesting passage of the original bill will, we are quite hopeful, be of the desired effect, and preserve to our mutual benefit this industry which, although quite large, is still in its infancy.

"Simmonds and Simmonds,
"Per F. M. Simmonds."

This is the editorial answer:

"A THREAT AND AN ANSWER"

"A lengthy letter from Simmonds & Simmonds, an advertising agency, appearing in the Voice of the People today, speaks for itself, in a manner to which newspapers are more or less accustomed, but in a tone less diplomatic and in words more direct than usual. In effect it threatens us with the penalty of withdrawal of advertising if we refuse to work for a high protective tariff on magnesite.

"It says we have been consistently 'favored' with certain advertising appropriations. We might remark truthfully that use of advertising appropriations to place advertisements before *Tribune* readers is no more of a 'favor', to this newspaper than *The Tribune's* acceptance and publication of such, advertisements is a 'favor, to the advertiser. It is a plain business proposition assuring value received on both sides. But that is beside the point.

"The issue is whether we should 'favor' an industry, regardless of its effect upon the country at large, merely to advance our private interests, and under threat. That is the log rolling' method of building tariff schedules and one of which we disapprove. The questions of whether the duty on magnesite should be $10 a ton or $6.25 a ton, of whether the smaller duty will put certain American industries out of profitable business, and of whether the effect of foreign competition will be good or bad for the country in general, are independent questions to be studied and answered by the proper authorities. But they should be decided on their merits, not upon any weight of special influence directed according to the immediate financial returns to those exercising such influence.

"A newspaper which bases its policy on any such influence or is actuated by any such motives is as false to its constituency as a congressman who accepts money for his vote. This newspaper does not and will not conduct either its advertising or its editorial departments in that way,"

A better statement of the function of a newspaper in connection with advertising could hardly be made.

The stand taken by the publishers quoted is obviously the only ethical stand that can be taken in fairness to both readers and advertisers in general. There is possibly no obligation on the part of a newspaper to publish an account of such a controversy; one's judgment in that matter would depend on one's definition of news. In the opinion of the writer, matter of this character is news of interest and significance to readers. Moreover, discussion of the problem is educative to both advertisers and readers, many of whom have never faced the issue involved.

Whether or not publication of the data is made, the fact remains that in few cases can advertisers afford to stay out of a profitable advertising medium for any considerable time. Although there are numerous newspapers in Boston, a boycott of **The Evening Transcript** in the summer of 1920 by a group of shoe concerns because the paper published the facts about the shoe market, ended after seven weeks. In not a few cases, readers have told merchants that they would withdraw their patronage unless advertising were published in their favorite newspapers. Where a newspaper is unable to withstand an attack by advertisers, it is weak in either financial backing or editorial prestige, commonly in both.

It is of course wholly justifiable, and in some cases ethically necessary, to reject advertising which may cause suspicion on the part of readers that other than a strictly commercial transaction is involved. An instance of this, which occurred in 1897, when newspapers generally maintained lower standards than they do now, is related by Elmer Davis,① of ***The New York Times***:

"Some months later all the regular advertising of the city government was unexpectedly offered to ***The Times***. This amounted to about $150,000 a year, a sum which would have made a tremendous difference to ***The Times*** of that period. Moreover, assurances were brought to the management of the paper by a gentleman who was a friend both of the publisher and of the Tammany leaders that this offer was made with absolutely no strings. It was neither the expectation nor the desire of Tammany that ***The Times*** should feel itself influenced in any way, and it was understood that the allotment of the advertising did not in any way involve a modification of ***The Times'*** general hostility to Tammany in local politics. The only reason for this sudden windfall, said the gentleman who brought the news, was the conviction of the Tammany leaders that it was a good thing for the general interests of the Democratic Party to have a conservative Democratic paper maintained in New York City. That paper's feelings about Tammany did not enter into the case.

"The publisher of ***The Times*** had entire confidence in the good faith of the gentleman who gave him these assurances, and saw no need for questioning the good faith of the Tammany leaders. But whether or not their intentions were honorable, their proposal was unacceptable. It was asking too much of human nature to suppose that thereafter when ***The Times*** had reason to attack Tammany, as it certainly would (its exposures of graft payments for gambling-house protection were not very far in the future), the subconscious, if not the conscious minds of those in ***The Times*** office might be affected by the thought that $150,000 was at stake. By that

---

① History of *the New York Times*, pp. 221—223.

time the paper might have got accustomed to living on a higher scale, and would have missed, the $150,000 more than if it had never had it. Moreover, **The Times** was still far behind its rivals in circulation. If this considerable revenue were suddenly awarded to the smallest in circulation of New York morning papers, everybody would believe that Tammany had bought The Times, no matter how pure the motives of the organization or of the paper's management. The shadow was as bad as the substance, in this case; from any point of view the offer was unacceptable."

It is sometimes argued by critics of the press that the comparatively small lineage of advertising carried by the advanced liberal and the radical press is due to advertisers' personal opposition to liberal and radical views. The conservative paper receives advertising, these critics believe, because of conformity to the advertiser's opinions. Thus the conclusion is reached that financial success in publishing is attainable only through subservience to the demands of advertisers.

The fact of the matter is less simple. Among the factors that produce a successful advertising medium is not only buying power but buying disposition on the part of its readers. The readers of many of the radical journals do not possess, in the opinion of advertisers, sufficient buying power to justify the advertising rate that is charged. In the case of liberal and radical publications whose readers possess high purchasing power, advertisers maintain that the buying disposition is destroyed or reduced—except for certain commodities, notably books—by the material which the paper publishes. In other words, the mood which is produced is not conducive to buying merchandise. The advertiser is interested in cash returns rather than in abstract policies. Few if any radical or liberal journals have been influenced in a conservative direction by the policies of advertisers; the newspaper or periodical of this type is usually not dependent on advertising for its support.

In general, it may be concluded that while there is not yet entire freedom on the part of newspapers from direct control by advertisers, there is an increasing tendency in this direction, especially among papers that are financially sound and that present their cases to their readers. The important factor in the entire situation is the reader. He has a sense of fair play. If the newspaper can bring this sense to bear on controversies with advertisers, there can be little question of the outcome. The maintenance of effective ethical standards in the publishing business, as elsewhere, requires not only high principle but the application of psychological laws.

Additional Readings

Adams, *The Clarion*.

Adams, *The Great American Fraud*, pp. 133—185.

Rowell, *American Newspaper Directory*, 1879, Preface.

Audit Bureau of Circulations, *Scientific Space Selection*, pp. 70—90.

Park, *The Immigrant Press and its Control*, pp. 359—411.

Davis, *History of The New York Times*, pp. 219—223, 315—322.

Moses, *The Deadhead Reading Notice*. (Pamphlet of *The New York Evening Post*.)

How Confidence Began. (Pamphlet of *The Farm Journal*, Philadelphia.)

How It Works. (Pamphlet of *The New York Tribune*.)

Lewis, *Guaranteed Advertising*, in *Bulletin of the University of Washington*, General Series No. IOI, pp. 46—51.

Powell, *Building a Circulation*, *University of Missouri Bulletin*, Vol. 15, No. 6, pp. 10—23.

Smith, *Advertising*, in *Civilisation in the United States*, pp. 381—395.

II Journalism as a Profession

Among newspaper men and the reading public, there is a general recognition that journalism is more than simply the business of publishing. It is more than merely selling a commodity. This fact has been realized more or less, not only by newspaper workers but by other classes of the population, from the earliest days of newspapers or their predecessors, the newsbooks and similar publications. The licensing laws governing the press, passed in times when licenses were not required or were required under much less strict provisions for other occupations, indicate that journalism was always recognized as having a certain public or quasi-public function.

Those few persons who in these latter days refer to newspaper work exclusively as a business do not understand its history or its generally recognized function. They are almost invariably men who have grown up in other activities and have turned to journalism as they would turn to the dry goods business, to the selling of real estate, or to any other strictly commercial occupation. These persons, it must be remembered, are relatively few, although their number is slowly increasing. They are confined, for the most part, to great metropolitan dailies, the publication of any one of which calls for an investment too large to be handled by any one but a capitalist. These great dailies are in a small minority among American newspapers, although their greater circulations and their publication in centers of population give them a disproportionate influence.

The owners of most of the smaller newspapers are either professional newspaper men or printers. In both of these occupations there is a tradition of public accountability and public service. Likewise, the men working in all editorial and writing positions on the large dailies are likely to feel strongly that the newspaper is not primarily a business enterprise but a quasi-public institution. The second class mail rates granted to newspapers and periodicals by the government are an indication of the general conviction that newspapers exist to serve the public. The increase made in these rates a few years ago was undoubtedly due in part to a feeling that newspapers were no longer serving this interest as they should serve it. Such a feeling is erroneous. The newspapers are now serving the public interest better than they served it twenty-five, fifty, or a hundred years ago. Their service to the public has not increased as rapidly, however, as the public demand for service, the public conscience, has developed.

Practically all discussions of the newspaper, of which there are many in magazines, books, and public addresses, are founded on the assumption that the newspapers exist primarily to serve a quasi-public function. Schemes to regulate the newspaper, much more far-reaching than schemes to regulate any other occupation, are predicated upon this assumption.

When it comes to the question of what particular public or quasi-public function the newspaper is expected to serve, there is a wide difference of opinion. The newspapers are urged by some to state all the facts without fear or favor. They are besought by others to omit all news which might suggest crime to the criminal, abnormal acts to the psychopathic, or mischief to the children. One critic points to their duty to editorialize in favor of liberal or radical views, another to take a stand in favor of the Constitution as interpreted by the National Security League and similar organizations. One critic would have the newspaper sell fish, coal, or what not, in order to break local monopolies. Still another would have the newspaper devote its attention primarily to getting the good men into office and keeping out the bad.

These differences as to the proper function of the newspaper as related to the public are due, not altogether but largely, to mental confusion. It is only in recent years that the significance of facts has been recognized by anybody. It is now recognized only by a minority. In classical times there were no means of checking the credibility of evidence, even if canons of evidence had been devised. Who was there to dispute Herodotus? —or, for that matter, Julius Caesar, although the dullness of the latter's accounts would seem strong evidence of their honesty? As a matter of fact, it was only in certain exact sciences, such as geometry, that any attempt was made to establish a body of incontrovertible fact. For the rest, a system of abstract philosophy was originated. This held sway in the minds of every one down to the most recent times. It was elaborated in the Middle Ages to extremes of profundity and of absurdity. It is possible to conceive of a system of metaphysics based on observed and substantiated facts, but no such system has ever existed. Systems of metaphysics have commonly been based on tradition, on the supposed word of a god, on popular belief, or purely on the cunningly arranged plans of some theoretical thinker. According to these systems, men arrived at truth or goodness through some mysterious faculties directly or indirectly implanted in them by a creator. St. Paul was convinced of Christ's divinity by what he conceived to be an obvious vision. The farmers, in the opinion of Thomas Jefferson, were sagacious in public affairs because God had mystically endowed them with political wisdom.

With the immense increase in facilities for obtaining and verifying facts, and with the development of the scientific method of arriving at conclusions from definitely ascertained facts, careful thinkers have come to realize that in every avenue of life verified facts are the only sure way to dependable conclusions. The conviction has been reached that the method which has been applied to scientific research may likewise be applied to studies in economics, sociology, and politics, the subjects with which everyday conversation and newspaper stories alike chiefly deal. The corollary follows that conclusions based on anything less than investigation of facts stand an even chance of being wrong, and in practice, probably more than an even chance, because they will be colored by the prejudices and taboos of the race, which are themselves based largely on false rationalization.

This view of the importance of facts has the practical support of an extremely small minority, who are willing to apply it to any of the problems of life. It has the theoretical support of a somewhat larger minority, who practically apply it only to questions on which they have no fixed opinions that they are determined firmly to hold. It has no consideration from the vast majority, who cling to their inherited views and prejudices, precisely as their ancestors have done for untold centuries.

So little consideration has been given in the past to facts that the second minority mentioned is likely to express toward many of them the same feeling that was manifested sixty years ago and is manifested in ignorant circles today, concerning the principle of evolution. This in turn is merely a repetition of the experience of Bacon, Galileo, and other scientists, when confronting their contemporaries with facts that clashed with preconceived notions. The supposedly intelligent capitalist, the supposedly intelligent socialist, the supposedly intelligent single-taxer, is likely to admit theoretically the significance of facts, but may condemn as "immoral" "destructive" "undesirable", or "unbelievable", all facts which do not support his conclusions.

The general public, of course, shows still less intelligence. In America it clings firmly to its cherished beliefs as to the complete superiority of the United States, the immorality of the French, the barbarism of the Russians, and other fond illusions. In other countries the herd has illusions quite as fantastic, but because of a lower proportion of literacy it does not express them so conspicuously.

Trotter's statement of the situation is sound and adequate:

"In matters that really interest him, man cannot support the suspense of judgment which science so often has to enjoin. He is too anxious to feel certain to have time to know. So that we see of the sciences, mathematics appearing first, then astronomy, then physics, then chemistry, then biology, then psychology, then sociology—but always the new field was grudged to the new method, and we still have the denial to sociology of the name of science. Nowadays, matters of national defence, of politics, of religion, are still too important for knowledge, and remain subjects for certitude; that is to say, in them we still prefer the comfort of instinctive belief, because we have not learnt adequately to value the capacity to foretell.

"Direct observation of man reveals at once the fact that a very considerable proportion of his beliefs are non-rational to a degree which is immediately obvious without any special examination, and with no special resources other than common knowledge. If we examine the mental furniture of the average man, we shall find it made up of a vast number of judgments of a very precise kind upon subjects of very great variety, complexity, and difficulty. He will have fairly settled views upon the origin and nature of the universe, and upon what he will probably call its meaning; he will have conclusions as to what is to happen to him at death and after, as to what is and what should be the basis of conduct. He will know how the country should be governed, and why it is going to the dogs, why this piece of legislation is good and that bad. He will have strong views upon military and naval strategy, the principles of taxation, the use of alcohol and vaccination, the treatment of influenza, the prevention of hydrophobia, upon municipal trading; the teaching of Greek, upon what is permissible in art, satisfactory in literature, and hopeful in science.

"The bulk of such opinions must necessarily be without rational basis, since many of them are concerned with problems admitted by the expert to be still unsolved, while as to the rest it is clear that the training and experience of no average man can qualify him to have any opinion upon them at all. The rational method adequately used would have told him that on the great majority of these questions there could be for him but one attitude — that of suspended judgment.

"In view of the considerations that have been discussed above, this wholesale acceptance of non-rational belief must be looked upon as normal. The mechanism by which it is affected demands some examination, since it cannot be denied that the facts conflict noticeably with popularly current views as to the part taken by reason in the formation of opinion.

"It is clear at the outset that these beliefs are invariably regarded by the holder as rational, and defended as such, while the position of one who holds contrary views is held to be obviously unreasonable. The religious man accuses the atheist of being shallow and irrational, and is met by a similar reply; to the Conservative, the amazing thing about the Liberal is his incapacity to see reason and accept the only possible solution of public problems. Examination reveals the fact that the differences are not due to the commission of the mere mechanical fallacies of logic, since these are easily avoided, even by the politician; and since there is no reason to suppose that one party in such controversies is less logical than the other. The difference is due rather to the fundamental assumption of the antagonists being hostile, and these assumptions are derived from herd suggestion; to the Liberal, certain basal conceptions have acquired the quality of instinctive truth, have become 'a priori syntheses,' because of the accumulated suggestions to which he has been exposed, and a similar explanation applies to the atheist, the Christian, and the Conservative. Each, it is important to remember, finds in consequence the rationality of his position flawless, and is quite incapable of detecting in it the fallacies which are obvious to his opponent, to whom that particular series of assumptions has not been rendered acceptable by herd suggestion."①

Human readiness to disregard the importance of facts, even when significant issues are involved, is disclosed again and again in political controversy. This is of special importance in discussing the function of the press, because the newspaper deals to a large extent with what are perhaps not properly but are practically political matters. Moreover, politicians represent greater educational achievement, though not perhaps greater native intelligence, on the average, than the general public to which the daily newspaper makes its principal appeal. The attitude of the reading public toward the facts is no more competent than that of the senator, representative, or other purported student of public affairs.

The attitude of the politician is effectively represented in an incident of a recent Congress, retold by Walter Lippmann:

"At breakfast on the morning of September 29, 1919, some of the Senators read a news dispatch in the Washington Post about the landing of

---

① Reprinted from *Instincts of the Herd in Peace and War*, pp. 35—37, by W. Trotter, by permission of The Macmillan Company, authorized publishers.

American marines —on the Dalmatian coast. The newspaper said:

"FACTS NOW ESTABLISHED"

'The following important facts appear already established. The orders to Rear Admiral Andrews commanding the American naval forces in the Adriatic, came from the British Admiralty via the War Council and Rear Admiral Knapps in London. The approval or disapproval of the American Navy Department was not asked······

"WITHOUT DANIELS' KNOWLEDGE

" 'Mr. Daniels was admittedly placed in a peculiar position when cables reached here stating that the forces over which he is presumed to have exclusive control were carrying on what amounted to naval warfare without his knowledge. It was fully realized that the *British Admiralty might desire to issue orders to Rear Admiral Andrews* to act on behalf of Great Britain and her Allies, because the situation required sacrifice on the part of some nation if D'Annunzio's followers were to be held in check.

"' *It was further realized that under the new league of nations plan foreigners would be in a position to direct American Naval forces in emergencies* with or without the consent of the American Navy Department ······' etc. (Italics mine.)

"The first Senator to comment is Mr. Knox of Pennsylvania. Indignantly he demands investigation. In Mr. Brandegee of Connecticut, who spoke next, indignation has already stimulated credulity. Where Mr. Knox indignantly wishes to know if the report is true. Mr. Brandegee, half a minute later, would like to know what would have happened if marines had been killed. Mr. Knox, interested in the question, forgets that he asked for an inquiry, and replies. If American marines had been killed, it would be war. The mood of the debate is still conditional. Debate proceeds. Mr. McCormick of Illinois reminds the Senate that the Wilson administration is prone to the waging of small unauthorized wars. He repeats

Theodore Roosevelt's quip about 'waging peace.' Mr. Brandegee notes that the marines acted 'under orders of a Supreme Council sitting somewhere,' but he cannot recall who represents the United States on that body. The Supreme Council is unknown to the Constitution of the United States. Therefore Mr. New of Indiana submits a resolution calling for the facts.

"So far the Senators still recognize vaguely that they are discussing a rumor. Being lawyers they still remember some of the forms of evidence. But as red-blooded men they already experience all the indignation which is appropriate to the fact that American marines have been ordered into war by a foreign government and without the consent of Congress. Emotionally they want to 'believe it, because they are Republicans fighting the League of Nations. This arouses the Democratic leader, Mr. Hitchcock of Nebraska. He defends the Supreme Council; it was acting under the war powers. Peace has not yet been concluded because the Republicans are delaying it. Therefore, the action was necessary and legal. Both sides now assume that the report is true, and the conclusions they draw are the conclusions of their partisanship. Yet this extraordinary assumption is in a debate over a resolution to investigate the truth of the assumption. It reveals how difficult it is, even for trained lawyers, to suspend response until the returns are in. The response is instantaneous. The fiction is taken for truth because the fiction is badly needed.

"A few days later an official report showed that the marines were not landed by order of the British Government or of the Supreme Council. They had not been fighting the Italians. They had been landed at the request of the Italian Government to protect Italians, and the American commander had been officially thanked by the Italian authorities. The marines were not at war with Italy. They had acted according to an established international practice which had nothing to do with the League of Nations.

"The scene of action was the Adriatic. The picture of that scene in the Senators' heads at Washington was furnished, in this case probably with intent to deceive, by a man who cared nothing about the Adriatic, but much about defeating the League. To this picture the Senate responded by a strengthening of its partisan differences over the League."①

It is largely the psychological situation that produces the differences of opinion, conscious and unconscious, concerning the quasi-public function of the newspaper. There are the political-minded, who would have the newspaper run in the interest of their particular political views. There are clergymen and others, who hold that the newspaper should be published with a view primarily to the maintenance of morality or some other abstraction — as held by them and not subjected to impartial examination. There are numerous other groups with similar points of view. These hold that the newspaper is primarily "a molder of public opinion," and this molding, according to their view, is not necessarily to be based on actual facts, investigated and proved true, but on assumed facts, un-investigated, plus exhortation based on ethical, political, and other dogmas likewise not subjected to any critical examination.

The Rev. David James Burrell, a prominent clergyman of New York, stated this point of view in a recent sermon, for the text of which he used the words: "As cold water to a thirsty soul, so is good news from a far country." In the course of his address Dr. Burrell said:

"We want a newspaper that shall publish the news. All the news? Well, hardly……

---

① Reprinted from Public Opinion. pp. 17 − 20, by Walter Lippmann, by permission of Harcourt, Brace &. Co., authorized publishers.

"We want a newspaper that shall not merely reflect public opinion, but mold it, and mold it right. Nobody questions the power of the press. Dr. Talmadge made no overstatement when he defined an editor as 'a man who puts a thought on the end of a pen and hurls it to the uttermost parts of the earth.' But that statement is incomplete unless it be yoked up with John Foster's words, 'Power to the last atom is responsibility.' The bended bow of a ready writer may shoot either a message of relief or a poisoned arrow across the walls of a beleaguered city……

"A Christian newspaper? Well, why not? If I throw a handful of iron filings into the air, they descend as harmlessly as thistledown, but, molded into a cannonball, they can sink a man-of-war. There are enough Christians in this community to demand and secure some sort of respect for their convictions; but never, never at the hands of writers who cavil at law and order and common morality, sitting under the cross and casting lots for the garments of our Savior. "It is too much to expect of such men a rational presentation of the underlying forces that make for progress. To us the coming of Christ is 'the one supreme divine event to which the whole creation moves': to them it is nothing. If our Lord were to appear in the clouds of heaven today, what would the morning edition look like tomorrow? Where would the usual headlines be?" ①

This position represents but a slight advance upon that of St. Ambrose in the fourth century: "To discuss the nature and position of the earth does not help us in our hope of the life to come. It is enough to know what Scripture states.'That He hung up the earth upon nothing."② The advance made by the later writer is only in not categorically denying the

---

① *Marble Collegiate Pulpit*, Vol. 32, No. 13, pp. 2 and 8.
② *Hexaëmeron*, 1:6, in Migne's *PatresLatini*, Vol. XIV.

significance of facts.

This view was in general that of newspapers themselves until very recently. In the early newspapers of this country and of other countries, the facts were invariably colored by opinion. Some lip service was given to the doctrine of objective facts, but it was always discounted by the practice of the paper and not infrequently by statements of the editor himself.

At the opposite extreme from the critics heretofore mentioned, stand those who would make the newspaper exclusively a disseminator of objective facts, even to the extent of omitting all editorial comment, all feature material, and everything else that is not strictly news. Few newspaper workers hold this ideal; they know, only too well, that the public demands features as well as significant facts, and they realize that a newspaper cannot be run without public support. Newspaper men generally, however, do hold, theoretically at least, the doctrine that the dissemination of objective facts is the primary if not the exclusive function of the press, and that all other possible functions should be subordinated to this.

This doctrine is based on the modern theory of popular government. Thomas Jefferson, as has been previously pointed out, observed that democracy worked best in rural districts. Temperamentally averse to cities, Jefferson held that the success of democracy in rural communities was due to the superior qualities implanted in rural folk by the Creator. We know now that Jefferson's observation was right but his conclusion wrong. Democracy has ordinarily worked better in rural districts and in small communities because the individual voters are personally familiar with the local conditions and the local personalities. These matters are discussed in detail at town meetings, school district meetings, and other gatherings in which everybody has a voice. The people get the objective facts, then form their conclusions and record their votes, largely on the basis thereof.

As a greater proportion of the population has moved to cities, and as the problems of government have become more complex, the voters have been more and more unable to obtain, through personal observation or investigation: objective facts on which to base their voting, except on the local problems of small communities. Dependence for facts must be placed on the press. It is the only potentially satisfactory agency, existent or proposed, for this purpose. Successful popular government, being dependent on facts, is therefore dependent on the press. Moreover, all the other popular problems, not strictly governmental, have the same twofold dependence. Hence it is maintained, on grounds which can scarcely be successfully assailed, that the fundamental function of the newspaper is to disseminate the objective facts concerning matters of public concern.

While accepted as a practical reality by comparatively few, this ideal of the newspaper is gaining strength rapidly. Among the general public, it is an unconscious standard, but nevertheless a standard. The frequency of such remarks as "You cannot believe that newspaper article" and "That is only a newspaper story," bears witness to a public ideal that the newspaper should present the facts, even though it bears witness also to a common conviction that that ideal is being violated.

Additional Readings

Trotter, *Instincts of the Herd in Peace and War*, pp. 1—41.

Robinson, *The Mind in the Making*, pp. 14—48.

Edman, *Human Traits*, pp. 368—410.

Burrell, *Wanted: A Newspaper. The Marble Collegiate Pulpit*, Vol. 32, No. 31.

Lippmann, *Public Opinion*, pp. 1—32, 253—314.

Lippmann, *Liberty and the News.*

III Public Charges Against the Newspaper

The public as a whole, as has been pointed out, has, consciously or unconsciously, a conception of the newspaper as primarily a disseminator of the objective facts of public significance. Whether this public would actually welcome the complete fulfillment of this function is beside the present problem and will be discussed later.

As is evident to every one, the public believes that the press is not fulfilling its function. Concretely, it charges the newspaper with not telling the truth; or, to put it more exactly, with not publishing the objective facts in an unbiased manner. Closer observers, both writers and speakers, accuse the newspaper of certain specific deficiencies in connection with its function of disseminating objective facts.

One of the fundamental charges is that the newspaper manufactures news. This charge is in general an example of the generally recognized fact that the public, when it sees things going badly in any part of the social system, attributes the difficulties to conditions which have disappeared. The manufacture of news was at one time a common practice. Ben Jonson in the Staple of News accused the journalists of the seventeenth century of barefaced faking. The New York Sun's reputation began with the famous Moon Hoax in 1835. This was a series of pure inventions by Richard Adams Locke purporting to contain important astronomical discoveries made by Sir John Herschel, the noted scientist. The Sun asserted that the fake "hurt nobody" while Edgar Allan Poe Wrote:"From the epoch of the hoax the Sun shone with unmitigated splendor. Its success firmly established the 'penny system' throughout the country, and (through the Sun) consequently we are indebted to the genius of Mr. Locke for one of the most important steps ever yet taken in the pathway of human progress."

Not only was Locke not dropped from the paper when the hoax became known, but he was given further duties on the paper and later became editor of *The Brooklyn Eagle*. The historian of the paper, Frank M. O'Brien, writing as late as 1917, referred to the hoax as "magnificent." [1]

The word "roorback" was added to American language by a fake in 1844, in which a writer credited to a traveler named Roorback a description of the horrors of slavery, including the false statement that James K. Polk, then candidate for the Presidency, had branded forty-three slaves with his initials. Published in several up-state journals in New York, it was exposed by *The Albany Argus* and became a "roorback," reflecting on the integrity of Polk's opponents and helping to bring about his election.

A faked proclamation, purporting to be by Abraham Lincoln, was prepared in 1864 by two young newspaper men, who succeeded in getting it into two newspapers. The young men planned to use it for playing the stock market. The newspapers were temporarily suspended, but were allowed to reopen their offices when the government was convinced that they were not to blame.

A notorious example of faking, or near-faking, took place in the sum-

---

[1] For details of the fake, see O'Brien's *The Story of the Sun*. pp. 64—102.

mer of 1899, when certain well-known insects, including most conspicuously the blood-sucking cone-noses, appeared in somewhat larger numbers than usual and bit a number of persons. Upon this flimsy foundation of fact the newspapers built up a superstructure of misleading stories of injury and death through bites of a so-called "kissing bug." Many of the injuries reported were due merely to bites of the mosquito or of the common horsefly. By means of conscienceless lying, the press of that day caused veritable terror in many American towns and cities, and undoubtedly produced much actual illness among the hysterical. ①

More recently, when Harry K. Thaw was first committed to a hospital for the insane, interviews were faked between Thaw and other noted inmates of the asylum. Another faked story told how Thaw had been appointed superintendent of the chickens at the Mattawan hospital, and quoted rules purported to have been laid down by him for running a chicken farm. Numerous other stories about Thaw had no more foundation than these. In very recent times supposedly humorous stories, to the careful, intelligent reader obviously' fakes, were sent out, or supposedly sent out, from small towns in New York and New Jersey. Newspaper men asserted that these did not deceive the public and were too ridiculous to be accepted as fact. It is probable, however, that some persons did accept them as fact and that many others were prejudiced against the newspaper as an institution by reason of its offering this faked material.

In the latter years of the nineteenth century, as yellow journalism was developing, the practice began of definitely misrepresenting the news in

---

① For discussion of the actual situation, in comparison with newspaper reports, see L. O. Howard, *The Insects to Which the Name "Kissing bug" Became Applied in the Summer of 1899*. United States Department of Agriculture, Division of Entomology, Bulletin 22, New Series, pp. 24—30; also L. O. Howard, *Spider Bites and "Kissing Bugs,"* *Popular Science Monthly*, 56; 31—42.

the headlines. The news stories themselves were reasonably accurate, but over a story dealing with the slight injury of two or three persons in a fire would be printed a head asserting that many had been killed. The obvious purpose was street sales.

In this period, also, faking in connection with pictures was introduced. Pictures were in demand by the sensational press, and were harder to get than they are now. If a prominent personage died and the newspaper lacked a picture, it was not uncommon to get from the files a cut of a person who somewhat resembled the deceased personage and publish this as an actual portrait. In some cases, drawings were made up from imagination and halftones from them were published as from actual photographs.

As late as 1903 Edwin L. Shuman, then literary editor of The Chicago Record-Herald, wrote in explanation of the current journalistic attitude toward facts:

"Newspapers frequently receive important pieces of news that lack the necessary details for presenting them with due dignity of length. It becomes necessary to supply the missing materials in the office. In many cases this can be done with the aid of the 'morgue' or cabinet of biographical and obituary materials that is maintained in every wide-awake newspaper office. Sometimes books of reference will supply much of the needed information. In not a few cases, however, it becomes the duty of the reporter or editor to supply the missing materials from his inner consciousness, drawing much upon his memory or his imagination. So long as he uses his imagination only upon non-essential details the method appears to be permissible.

"This kind of license has become absolutely necessary in writing the reports of events which will be past when the paper appears, but which must be described before they occur. Intense rivalry for the latest news long ago drove editors to the use of the 'journalistic imagination' in such cases. The amount of matter that is prepared in this way, especially for evening papers, probably would surprise the average reader. The fact will account for many of the inaccuracies of the press, but on the whole it is cause for wonder that the newspapers can be as accurate as they are under the circumstances. The ethics of the subject may be left to the individual reader. I merely record the fact that the practice exists to some degree on every enterprising paper."①

The practices heretofore mentioned are no longer those of any considerable number of newspapers. Where they now occur, they are likely to be sporadic, and usually the fault of a dishonest reporter or correspondent, who acts either wholly of his own volition or because of the expressed or implied direction of an editor—himself a subordinate—to get copy regardless of its character. Certain photographic services practice faking. A newspaper knowing this fact assumes risk, if not actual culpability, in buying any photographs from such unreliable sources.

There is, moreover, occasional use of a photograph, apparently by specific design, in such a way as to amount to manufacture of news, as when a sensational metropolitan daily published a picture of Mexican children, standing in water, as evidence that they had been driven to take refuge from bandits who had overrun the country. The same picture had been previously published as representing merely a group of bathing Mexican children. The newspaper which published the picture, it is worthy of note, was endeavoring to persuade the United States to make war upon Mexico.

Regardless of the ethics of the matter, such practices on the part of newspapers are certain to alienate readers and convince them of the dishonesty of the press. *The New York World* tells how, when it published by

---

① *Practical Journalism*, pp. 103—104.

mistake a picture of Newcastle-on-Tyne as one of Hartlepool, a reader wrote in, stating that he recognized the picture and adding the following paragraph:

"You can't fool ALL of the people ALL of the time, and when you do not happen to have on hand an illustration to accompany a news article, for goodness 'sake don't try to hand us something near it. 'Just as good; they won't know any different,' is a policy which is inimical to the boasted fair-play attitude of your paper—and I have read it for a number of years."

In this case, the newspaper was fortunately able to convince its correspondent that the error was wholly unintentional. ①

There of course still remains the temptation to the reporter to fake news, even when he knows his newspaper opposes it. The only safe principle to follow, as it is the only adequate statement of the situation, is: There is no harmless fake. The way in which faking of tremendous social harm develops from the so-called "harmless fake" is well told by Ralph Pulitzer, whose newspaper, *The New York World* was a pioneer in steps looking toward accuracy and fair play:

"The philosophy of faking is worth your attention. The tendency of fake usually begins in some trivial story of a broadly humorous character in which the writer embroiders a comical situation with additionally ludicrous exaggerations which make no pretense to being anything but imaginative. You cannot lay your finger on anything definitely wrong about this story, since it gives its facts faithfully enough and brands its fiction so frankly that no one can be deceived.

"The only thing wrong about it is that it is apt to be the first step to

---

① The incident is discussed in the Biennial Report of The World's Bureau of Accuracy and Fair Play. 1915, pp. 16－17.

worse things. For the writer, congratulated on the brightness of this first story, will possibly, on the next occasion, write a story equally funny, equally frank in admitting to being partially the fabrication of a comic fancy, but a story in which the facts and the fiction blend so together that the reader cannot be sure where the one ends and the other begins. Such a story has crossed the line which divides the enjoyable from the reprehensible. But they say it 'does no one any harm' and is exceedingly droll, and a managing editor with a keen sense of humor is eager to get out a bright paper, and so in it goes.

"Now, the writer's next literary effort is apt to be one in which the humorous facts constitute the merest rudiments of the story, and the story itself as a work of comic fiction could stand unsupported, even if what few facts there were removed. And still those responsible for that story being in the paper may all ask a critic what conceivable harm that story did any one. And at first you can't point to any one that it hurt. But a moment's thought will show you that while this story hurt no one that it was about, it did hurt several other persons and one institution. It injured the reporter who wrote it, the city editor to whom he reported it, the copy reader who edited it, the managing editor who printed it, and the newspaper which published it. It hurt these men by insidiously dulling the keen edge of their sense of accuracy, and it injured the paper by injuring them. For that particular reporter is now ripe to apply the same methods to writing a serious story about serious people and serious events, and instead of using his fancy for the broadening of humor we shall find him using his imagination for the heightening of tragedy, the deepening of pathos, the sharpening of the dramatic. And still on certain papers you will find the excuse that these stories 'do no one any harm. ' And the men who make this excuse do not seem to realize that any harm has been done when the general public uses the term 'newspaper story' - which should be a synonym for facts—as a euphemism for a lie.

"The next step in this Fake's Progress is the descent from embroidering untruths on a background of serious facts to fabricating a serious story out of the whole cloth without a single fact to base it on, but using real persons for characters. About on a level with this last perpetration is the cynical 'stunt' which a very few papers encourage and a few have condoned where the reporter, if he cannot find that a good story has happened, actually hires people to make it happen, let us say to shoot up a saloon in a gang war that has grown lean of news, or to hang a prominent employer in effigy in some strike, as in the story I have already told you.

"The last step of our reporter, now grown hopelessly irresponsible, unscrupulous, and cynical, is a fake that bespatters some honest man's character, or besmirches some virtuous woman's reputation, which ruins spotless lives and has led innocent people to self-inflicted deaths. The reporter who has sunk to this depth of degradation might just as well be a murderer; in fact, there are a good many honest murderers whose boots he is unworthy to lick. But fortunately at this point the libel law, which might well have become effective considerably sooner, is very apt to take a hand in the game; and although our present criminal libel laws have been able to send all too few newspaper crooks to jail, yet heavy money damages are likely to visit a partial retribution on the offending paper, and when the pocket nerve, which is the nearest approach to a conscience which such a paper possesses, begins to ache, the reporter who lost this paper some of its money is apt to walk the plank. And there you have the whole progress, from the bright little flight of the imagination that was so laughable and harmless, down to the criminal piece of work that wrecked innocent lives, brought a rotten reporter to final ruin—and lost an unscrupulous paper a fraction of its ill-earned dividends.

"As the fake varies in viciousness, so the responsibility of the newspaper varies in degree. For some fakes, which a paper prints, plausible stories sent in from distant correspondents whose accuracy it has no reason for doubting and no means of corroborating, it would be grossly unjust to blame that paper. All it can do in a case like this is promptly to discharge the guilty correspondent, but this it should do ruthlessly. Fortunately, most of the fakes-charged against the press belong to this class. For other fakes that get printed, neither newspapers nor reporters are responsible. These are the fabrications exploiting everything from rapid-transit systems down to chorus girls which the pernicious press agent is constantly plotting to worm into a newspaper. Experienced editors are generally equipped with a sixth sense for the detection of the press agent yarn, but, nevertheless, these wretched concoctions do quite frequently slip in, and the newspapers get the blame.

"Then there is the case where the newspaper innocently prints a fake by one of its reporters or correspondents and subsequently fails through good nature, weakness, or a blunted sense of accuracy to discharge the writer. Here the paper immediately assumes a large share of responsibility for the fake. It not only encourages that particular reporter to gain extra space rates by further faking of one-stick items into one-column stories, but it tempts other honest reporters to do likewise.

"The last case is where the paper itself deliberately stimulates faking in its writers or actually engineers a fake itself. This fortunately is exceedingly rare. There are papers which cynically avow their motto to be: 'Facts merely embarrass us!' But you can pretty well count all of them in this country on the fingers of your two hands. They may be enjoying the fleeting prosperity that even a monstrosity at a side show can enjoy, but they are evanescent. They are built on slime instead of on rock. Any institution that flourishes on an appeal to morbidness by the aid of mendacity can have but a precarious hold on prosperity or even on life itself.

"I am afraid that in the last few minutes I have drawn a dark picture, but fortunately it applies to few papers. And the number of these papers is growing smaller from year to year. I don't think anyone who knows his newspaper history will question the fact that the striving for accuracy is steadily growing keener and more widespread. Newspapers are spending more and more money and efforts in the verification of news. It has been estimated that a responsible paper, for every four dollars that it spends on originally getting a piece of news, spends six dollars on verifying it."[①]

The gradual disappearance of faking is due partly to the fact that news is now easier to obtain and to verify because of the increased organization of newspapers and press associations, partly to the growing realization of the value of news and the growing sense of the dignity and honor of their profession on the part of practicing newspaper men. In the case of less scrupulous journalists, the disapprobation and contempt manifested by the public toward fakes have had their influence.

The extensive faking in times past, however, has crystallized into a public belief that they still are the common methods followed by newspapers. Not only the general public, but experienced observers, believe that such practices are common. For example, Roland G. Usher, professor of history in Washington University, St. Louis, recently asserted: "The cable news you read is not written on the other side except in rare instances. The cost of cabling such lengthy accounts would be prohibitive. That news is sent in dispatches of from eight to ten lines and is expanded by the re-write men into two columns of stuff." Professor Usher's charges were answered by Frederick Roy Martin, general manager of the Associa-

---

① Pulitzer, *The Profession of Journalism: Accuracy in the News*. pp. 12—15. Reprinted by permission.

ted Press, who pointed out that in the cable dispatches "the only omission is a few small words like the, and, etc., where the meaning is perfectly plain and which in no way abbreviates the plain context of each sentence and line and of' the dispatch as a whole." The daily cable report was given by Mr. Martin as containing about 10,000 words. ①

C. V. Van Anda, managing editor of *The New York Times*, presented figures showing more than 9,000 words daily by cable and wireless from correspondents of his paper.

The long persistence of charges after the basis for them has largely or even wholly disappeared makes it of utmost importance for the newspaper to deal as fairly as possible with its public. Dishonesty or unfairness today will be quoted by publicists and by the general public twenty-five years hence.

None of the other charges which are generally made against the newspaper have been superseded so fully by changes in newspaper practice as has the charge of manufacturing news. There has been a gradual improvement in newspaper practice, although it is by no means sufficient to acquit the newspaper of charges made against it.

For example, while the complete manufacture of news has practically disappeared, the practice of putting "hokum" into the news still exists. "Hokum" is sure-fire stuff. Every nation has its own varieties, determined by the taste and interests of the mass of the population. The use of "hokum" in the movies and in popular fiction has probably stimulated its employment in the newspapers.

"Hokum" in the United States is sentimental, mixed up with a certain vapory idealism and at the same time with a devotion to financial and business success. From the days of *The Log Cabin Boy Who Became President*

---

① *The Editor and Publisher*. February 17. 1923.

to the days of Harold Bell Wright, the taste of the dominant middle-class public in "hokum" has only slightly wavered. That riches come to the righteous and God-fearing, that nevertheless there are other things, such as true love, which are superior to financial considerations, and that the great are invariably kind to dumb animals—these are a few of many bits of "hokum" which are firmly fixed in the middle-class mind.

Newspaper men know the public taste for "hokum" and they frequently add to news stories matter which they have invented in order to make the facts appear to conform to the public ideas. For example, not long ago a young woman, heiress to an estate of some millions of dollars left her by a relative, was married to her childhood sweetheart. The facts of the case were that the young woman and the young man had grown up in the same town. Her parents were not wealthy, even according to the standards of the place. His people, on the other hand, had considerable means, owning stores not only there, but in several other towns. His interests at the time of his marriage to her amounted to perhaps a quarter of a million dollars. He is a pleasant young business man, a member of the various local booster and social clubs. Upon their marriage they went to live in a country house owned by him, containing perhaps twenty rooms and situated in the midst of a considerable estate.

In the actual facts of the case there was little, which could arouse the sentimental interest of a middle-class reader. Ingenious reporters developed a wholly different story. The young man was a poor boy but idealistic. It was discovered by the reporters that he had some slight talent in drawing and that some years before he had made a series of political cartoons for a small paper in his state and had done more or less other desultory work with his pen. This made him, according to the reporters' story, a struggling young artist who had given up the possibility of making a living by business in order to follow his art. Moreover, when he found that his beloved had become heir to millions he was represented as having been unwilling to ask her to marry him, but she, magnanimous in the possession of a fortune and in the knowledge that love for her was mingled with idealistic devotion to art, brought it about that they were married. Thereupon they went to live in a little cottage by the river, the same twenty-room home heretofore mentioned. Thus the public was again given touching evidence that dollars cannot stay the progress of true love and that love and art will live happily together in the meanest hovel.

A more sinister use of "hokum," approaching the out-and-out fake, is reported by Isaac D. White of *The New York World*:

"In a factory town in a neighboring state a young woman was drowned one evening while out boating with one of the mill hands. The latter, drenched to the skin and badly frightened, was the first to give word of the tragedy. He explained that while changing seats the boat had been upset accidentally about one hundred yards from shore, and that after trying vainly in the darkness to reach the woman, he, being a poor swimmer, with difficulty managed to save himself. The boat and oars were found adrift in the lake next morning, and later the body of the girl was dragged from the bottom near the spot pointed out by her companion. There were no marks or bruises on the body, and the cause of death was shown to be drowning.

"The unfortunate victim of what was so clearly an accident was a prostitute, in personal appearance most unprepossessing. She had a harelip, was tongue-tied, and had been half-witted from her birth. She was the boon companion of the most notorious woman in the town. Every New York newspaper had hurried men to the scene, and the facts connected with the drowning and the young woman's reputation were promptly made known to the reporters by the local police. And yet readers of one New

York newspaper were led to believe that 'a beautiful young society girl' had been drowned while 'defending her honor'; that the entire community was aroused and indignant over the failure of the authorities to arrest her companion; that some unknown and mysterious influence was protecting him in open defiance of law and justice. The community was indignant, right enough, but the indignation was directed toward the reporter who had deliberately lied about the town and its officials. This faker continued to send out lying reports from the town for a week, and then capped the climax of his faking by inducing an ignorant relative of the dead girl to sign a petition to the Governor of the State denouncing the local authorities and praying His Excellency to interfere to the end that justice might be done. The reporter published the petition in his paper before mailing it to the Governor." ①

Another type of "hokum," more common because it can be practiced with less ability, consists merely in attaching to persons who appear in the news certain stereotyped titles to make them more interesting to the reading public. A man, who chances to be arrested while in evening clothes, may be referred to as "a popular clubman" or as "a prominent man about town." A woman accused of immorality is not uncommonly spoken of as "pretty" or "beautiful" regardless of her actual appearance.

The tolerant but cynical attitude often taken by newspaper men toward this form of misrepresentation is illustrated in the humorous story published in 1917 in The Chicago Herald, in which the "Old Reporter" offers some questions for examining aspirants for reporters' licenses. Some of the questions asked were these:

---

① White, *Fairness and Accuracy in Journalism*, *The New York World*, December 22, 1912.

"How many high-balls does it take to turn a prominent clubman into a well-known figure in the city's night-life?

"How many pink teas does it take to turn a social leader into a queen of the exclusive set?

"How does a scion differ from a rich man's son?

"How much must a father leave before his daughter may be called an heiress, and how long after forty-two may she still be young and beautiful?

"Write a sentence with the words 'It is alleged' in such a manner that the reader will have no doubt the allegation is true.

"Describe the wedding romance of a wealthy and prominent teamster and a beautiful young heiress of Goose Island.

"On what page must the story of a fire be printed so that it may be spoken of as a conflagration?

"How long after a woman is arrested for shoplifting does she become a former actress?

"Would you refer to the deceased parents of a deceased politician as having been poor but honest, or would you not better call them immigrants who came to the land of golden promise to make their way in the New World across the sea?

"What do you know about campus beauties? Are they also pulchritudinous co-eds or only rah-rah girls?" ①

It is argued by reporters who engage in the practice of manufacturing "hokum" that in most cases it is harmful to nobody. The story of the young married couple pleased a vast circle of readers and confirmed them in their sentimental views of life. It presumably amused the persons concerning whom it was written and possibly pleased them, because it placed them be-

---

① Quoted by *The Literary Digest*. Vol. 54, pp. 1021—1022.

fore the world in a semi-heroic light, and being heroic is distasteful to very few. The story is simply fiction "founded on fact," as stories in our childhood days used to be headed.

But what of the people who had lived in the town and region where this couple had lived since childhood? What was the effect of the story upon them? Precisely the same effect that is produced by every such story. It added further evidence to their conviction that nothing published in a newspaper can be depended upon. Persons who know of this and similar circumstances will view with the same suspicion a truthful story dealing with international relations or any other subject of vast public importance.

To a considerable extent the belief also prevails that where news exists it is falsified, or misrepresented, with or without design on the part of newspapers, before it reaches the public. Any unprejudiced observer finds evidence of falsification in such a matter as the handling of the news during and after the Russian Revolution. When a newspaper itself publishes cartoons satirizing the news stories relating to the "death," "imprisonment," and other vicissitudes that did not happen to Premier Lenin, there can be no room for doubt as to the extent of falsification of the Russian situation. Again, the quotations made by Messrs. Lippmann and Merz in *A Test of the News* show a considerable amount of absolute falsification. Headlines announced the "smashing" of the Bolshevist army, the burning of Petrograd, and, later, the capture of Petrograd by Yudenitch's army! [1]

Falsification of the news is, however, much less common than the average reader probably believes. At the present time, no matter recorded with a reasonable degree of certainty is likely to be falsified. No newspaper would think for a moment of falsifying the result of an election, the quota-

---

[1] *A Test of the News*. pp. 30 and 33. This study, published as a supplement to *The New Republic* of August 4, 1920, analyzes all news about Russia in *The New York Times*, chosen as an outstanding newspaper, from March, 1917, to March, 1920.

tions on the stock exchange, or the verdict of a jury, even if it were not in competition with other newspapers which would furnish the facts to the public. Falsification occurs most often where the actual facts are difficult to obtain and rumor and belief are accepted in their stead. ①The simpler and more honest plan, of course, would be to publish no news when there is none that the editors consider dependable. This plan newspapers refuse to adopt, maintaining that competition compels them to print a certain amount of news about any given event or supposed event. They salve their consciences and attempt to protect themselves against complaining readers by the use of such expressions as "it is rumored," "it is believed," "high officials assert," which are held by the courts, certainly not in advance of public conscience, to be no defense in suits for libel. If the publication of rumors, even labeled as such, can harm the individual to such an extent that he can recover damages the same as if they were stated as facts, their publication, even when not libeling any individual, must certainly be held by enlightened public opinion to be subversive of that clear view of human affairs which the press should give and upon which the citizen should act.

---

① Mr. Lippmann seems to the writer to go too far, however, in his discussion of the relation between the certainty of news and the system of record (Public opinion. pp. 342—345). He lays insufficient stress on the possibility of carelessness, laziness, or some less common psychological trait in the reporter or copy-reader. For example, in reporting the famous speech of Senator La Follette on September 20, 1917, The Associated Press inserted the word "no" in such a way that a sentence reading, "We had grievances," was altered to "We had no grievances." The error was apparently unintentional on the part of the editor who prepared the story, and was ascribed by the Associated Press in its apology to lack of care. The writer, however, would raise the question whether it is not one of those errors which modern psychology has shown to be determined by the unconscious of the individual making them. The editor, opposed to Mr. La Follette, might unconsciously insert in a story matter which would naturally produce an unfavorable impression of the speaker. More attention might wisely be given to problems of this character in the study of journalism.

Another common charge against the newspaper is that the news is often suppressed. In the average small town it is not a difficult matter to persuade an editor to suppress a piece of news that may be distasteful to an advertiser or, more commonly, simply a friend and subscriber. In the larger towns and cities such suppression is less common. [①] Certain newspapers, too, suppress news that is unfavorable to views that the paper holds. For example, when several hundred thousand dollars was subscribed by members of the New York trade unions for support of the steel strike at a meeting to which New York papers gave front-page position, Pittsburgh newspapers omitted all reference to the subscriptions or the meeting. [②]

The problem of news suppression is complicated by the fact that no newspaper of considerable size can print nearly all the copy that comes to it. There must be a process of selection. Some news must be suppressed. What critics of newspapers mean when they assert that news is suppressed by the papers is, of course, that news of public significance is suppressed. The matter is in part a question of judgment, but unfortunately injudicial bias often creeps in. The newspaper desirous of retaining the respect of its constituency for itself and for newspapers generally will be sedulous to avoid suppressing news which it might be assumed would be to its interest to suppress.

Again, it is charged against the newspapers that news is colored by the policy of the paper. Examples of this are quoted from headlines and

---

① The example of this most often quoted-which, however, occurred a number of years ago-is that of the Philadelphia newspapers which unanimously suppressed the story of the suicide of a prominent Philadelphia advertiser in New York when caught in disgraceful circumstances. (See Ross.) The Suppression of Important News, in Bleyer's The Profession of Journalism, p. 84, and Sinclair, *The Brass Check*. p. 227.

② Interchurch World Movement, Commission of Inquiry, Public opinion and the Steel Strike. pp. 150－151.

from news stories themselves. The coloring of news, where it takes place, is ordinarily in the interest of the policy of the paper or what reporters and editors on the paper conceive to be its policy, although there is some coloring by reporters because of personal prejudice, due not infrequently to the attitude of persons in the news toward reporters. Numerous examples of the coloring of news may be found in any industrial controversy on the part of papers representing both sides. The coloring of news on the part of the conservative press is aired more frequently because conservative papers are in the majority. Examination of radical newspapers, however, will show a similar amount of coloring in behalf of their side of any controversy. For example, the Federated Press, which professes to "report objectively," ends a news story concerning a critic of Upton Sinclair thus:

"There is no special reason apart from orders higher up why Carter should rush to the defense of the colleges, since, according to his own story; he never went beyond the district school."[①]

There is likewise much coloring of the news in the interest of sensationalism, partly as a policy of newspapers, partly by reporters of their own volition. Discussing a recent divorce suit, Edwin W. Booth, editor of *The Grand Rapids Press*, published in the place where the case was tried, said of the treatment of this case in certain Chicago and Detroit newspapers: "If a verbatim report of the trial had been given to the public the public might have fairly judged of the merits of the case, but, following the rule, the charges against Trotter were played up and his defense played down. Though adjudged innocent by the court, at the bar of public opinion Trotter's reputation was so damaged that I personally question whether his work will ever be the same, not only in this city, but in other cities where

---

① The Federated Press Bulletin. Vol. 5, No. 9, p. 4.

the unfair news was carried."①

The coloring of news by means of headlines is the subject of well justified criticism. Many persons doubtless read only the headlines or get from the headlines an attitude toward the news which even an unbiased story following the head will not erase. The practice of expressing opinion in heads is increasing, to the distinct lowering of the value of the press as a disseminator of objective facts. Following, for example, are eleven heads used over the same letter written by President Harding to Stephen E. Connor, secretary of the Federated Shop Crafts of the Central Railroad of New Jersey:

HARDING REBUKES ROADS THAT FAIL TO SETTLE STRIKE—STUBBORN MINORITY IS DECLARED RESPONSIBLE FOR COAL SHORTAGE AND FREIGHT CONGESTION.

——New York World.

HARDING BLAMES RAIL STRIKERS FOR SUFFERING-WRITES JERSEY CENTRAL SHOP LEADERS HE REGRETS REFUSAL OF MINORITY OF MEN TO RETURN TO THEIR JOBS-FEARS WORSE CONDITIONS-CRITICIZES THEM FOR HOLDING UP COAL DELIVERIES AND DEMORALIZING INDUSTRY.

——New York Tribune.

HARDING DEMANDS END OF RAIL STRIKE-HIS LETTER ON SHOP CRAFTS TROUBLE STIRS NEW JERSEY CENTRAL-HE HELPS RELIEF FUND-HOLDS MINORITY OF INTERESTS RESPONSIBLE FOR FAILURE TO SETTLE-RAILWAY ENTERS DENIAL—ASSERTS POLICY HAS BEEN IN ACCORD WITH

---

① Addresses and Proceedings of the Fourth Annual Meeting of the University Press Club of Michigan p. 101.

PRESIDENT's PROCLAMATION.

———New York Herald.

RAIL SHOPMEN ARE REBUKED BY PRESIDENT -NO REASON FOR STRIKE OF LAST YEAR TO DRAG LONGER, MR. HARDING DECLARES.

———Buffalo Express.

SHOP STRIKE UNJUSTIFIED-HARDING SAYS- MINORITY BLAMED FOR TRAFFIC CONDITIONS.

———Cincinnati Enquirer.

HARDING EAGER FOR END OF R. R. SHOPMEN STRIKE-SEES NO REASON FOR MEN HOLDING OUT.

———Chicago Tribune.

BARRING OF SHOPMEN SCORED BY HARDING- PRESIDENT BLAMES UNCOMPROMISING RAIL- ROADS IN PART FOR SHORTAGE OF COAL-HE SEES NO JUSTIFICATION-IN LETTER TO NEW JERSEY UNION LEADER HE SAYS MINORITY ROADS SHOULD FOLLOW LEADS OF BIG LINES.

———New York Time.

HARDING ADVISES SHOPMEN TO YIELD-SEES NO REASON FOR FURTHER DELAY IN REACHING FULL SETTLEMENT-WRITES UNION OFFICIAL.

———Philadelphia Public Ledger.

HARDING ASSAILS RAILROAD STRIKE-PRESI-DENT SEES NO REASON FOR FAILURE OF MINORITY TO EFFECT PEACE-BLAMED FOR CONGESTION-INTERRUPTED COAL DELIVERIES, TOO, ASCRIBED TO FAILURE TO END WALKOUT.

———Baltimore Sun.

HARDING RAPS STRIKERS-PRESIDENT TELLS RAIL SHOP-MEN ALL SHOULD BE BACK AT WORK-BLAMES THOSE WORK-

ERS OUT FOR INTERRUPTION OF COAL DELIVERIES.

——Chicago Daily News.

HARDING ASKS ALL SHOPMEN TO END STRIKE-PRESIDENT SEES NO REASONS FOR PROMULGATING OF RAIL UNION WAR.

——Rochester Democrat-Chronicle.

It will be observed that of these eleven newspapers several assert that the president blames certain railroads for failing to settle the strike and others that he blames the strikers for continuing the difficulty. Still others show a certain degree of prejudice in one direction or the other. Only two, *The Cincinnati Enquirer and The Baltimore Sun*, treat this news in a strictly objective manner. It is a significant fact, as showing the attitude of interested parties toward the unbiased handling of news, that the clip sheet of the American Federation of Labor, known as the International Labor News Service, spoke disparagingly of the head in The Cincinnati Enquirer, which it characterized as "meaning nothing at all," and that in The Baltimore Sun. which, it asserted, "is as meaningless as The Cincinnati Enquirer."

Less significant, so far as direct effect upon public life is concerned, but much more widely noticed, is the inaccuracy which marks the columns of American newspapers. Every reader of newspapers knows of instances in which errors have been made to his knowledge. He knows that his friend's name or his own has been misspelled. He has seen an item in his daily newspaper referring to a "Stratibury" violin or has seen *The Mind in the Making and The Americanization of Edward Bok* referred to as "popular works of fiction."Or he has seen Edna St. Vincent Millay referred to as "Edna Stevincent Hillay" in a newspaper popularly reputed to be one of the best edited in America.

In one newspaper of the writer's acquaintance the following head appeared on the first page: SENATE REJECTS YAP TREATY BY 50 TO 23 VOTES. ①The lead of the story follows:

"Washington. Feb. 28.-Dividing virtually on party lines, the senate refused to amend the Yap treaty today in the first test of strength on any case affecting the international covenants negotiated at the arms conference. Vote was 50 to 23."

In this case the incompetence or laziness of the copy-reader was such as no reporter, however ignorant, could have excelled.

In point not only of accuracy but of the other desiderata in which the press is subject to criticism, it is evident to any unprejudiced student that the newspaper does better than would the average intelligent observer of events. Anyone who has heard testimony by unbiased and careful witnesses as to the most readily observable matters has inevitably been struck by the disparities among the various stories. Likewise, everyday conversation makes it obvious that the average individual regularly alters facts to suit his opinions. He may indulge in this consciously or unconsciously.

On the other hand, this is not an argument sufficient to justify the present practices of the press, although it is often presented as such. It only introduces mitigating circumstances. As an argument in itself, it has little more value than the insistence of a barber that he is competent because he can cut hair better than the average citizen who has never worked at the barber's trade. The newspaper is supposed to be written by persons trained and experienced in fulfilling the function of the press. In his professional capacity, a journalist is to be compared not with the general public but with the best journalists elsewhere.

---

① The Leavenworth Times. March 1, 1922.

Additional Reading

Lippmann, *Public Opinion*, pp. 338—357.

Macy, Journalism, in *Civilization in the United States*, pp. 35—51

Ross, *The Suppression of Important News*, in Bleyer's *The Profession of Journalism*, pp. 79—96.

Sinclair, *The Brass Check*, pp. 228—313.

Lee and Sinclair, Discussion of *The Brass Check*. The New York Globe and Commercial Advertiser, June and July, 1921.

Holt, *Commercialism and Journalism*, pp. 1—49.

Sullivan, *National Floodmarks*, pp. 160—166.

Interchurch World Movement, Commission of Inquiry, *Public Opinion and the Steel Strike*, pp. 87—162.

Salmon, *The Newspaper and the Historian*, pp. 138—157, 412—467.

Gladden, *Tainted Journalism, Good and Bad*, in Thorpe's *The Coming Newspaper*, pp. 27—50.

Lippmann and Merz, *A Test of the News*, Supplement to *The New Republic*, August 4, 1920.

IV Deficiencies of the Press: The Materialistic Indictment

Almost everyone who makes charges against the press has an explanation for the deficiencies of which he complains. The explanations commonly given and generally believed are in line with certain tendencies of the popular mind, manifest in its attitude in all subjects of public concern.

To begin with, there is in the popular mind what may be termed "an atrocity habit." Every trouble that arises appears to be result of an atrocity perpetrated on democratic government, on morality, on civilization, or on something else that intensely matters. Or, perhaps, the trouble itself seems to be the atrocity. Closely associated with this is the conspiracy habit of mind, a feeling that some group of persons is constantly plotting the ruin of what is to the best interests of the public. Atrocity, conspiracy—these two ideas stir the public from lethargy.

This is no new phenomenon in American history. The Boston Tea Party was the result of an atrocity complex. For a number of years the Anti-Masonic Party existed on the basis of atrocity and conspiracy complexes, and these became so powerful that in Vermont, according to historians, every Masonic lodge surrendered its charter. In the Civil War, an atrocity complex was dominant in the North and a conspiracy complex in the South. Every Southerner was a brutal slave-driver, while every Northerner was a scheming Yankee enrolled in a conspiracy to destroy the resources of every state below Mason and Dixon's line. The Populist Party throve on the atrocities of the older parties. One of its principal apologists urged the necessity of raising "less corn and more hell." The Progressive Party owed its rise and also its downfall largely to the two habits of mind. It was the idea of busting the trusts and imprisoning their officers that roused the crowd. Complexes feed on themselves, and when the Progressive leaders ran out of dragons to exhibit before execution the people sought other atrocities and conspiracies and other men to denounce them.

With the appetite of the American citizen so whetted for atrocities and conspiracies, it is no wonder that he was fed on them during the recent war, by superpatriots on the one hand and by radicals—when the administration gave them a chance—on the other. It still continues. The Communist Party, the I. W. W. , the Socialists, union labor, and scores of other bodies are asserted to be in a conspiracy to commit atrocities against "Americanism."From the stand point of the radicals, there is a capitalistic conspiracy, definitely organized and heavily supported, to suppress every suggestion of change in the status quo.

The public attitude toward the newspaper, expressed in general conversation and in printed books and articles, accepts the atrocity and conspiracy theories. Not infrequently the suggestion is made that the proprietors of a given newspaper ought to be arrested. The typical article on the subject proposes a law of some sort to govern the press. The explanations commonly given for the deficiencies of the press are in accord with this point of view. One of the reasons often presented for the failure of newspapers to present the news accurately and fairly is that sensational handling of the news builds circulation. It is true that certain newspapers have built up their circulations while pursuing a sensational policy and have used this policy as a circulation argument. In some cases they may have adopted a sensational policy as a means of getting circulation. The most conspicuous examples of ultra-sensational journalism, the Hearst newspapers, have generally followed the practice of building their circulations among groups of the population that were not previously reading any newspapers. Getting newspaper circulation is always expensive, but this is the cheapest way to get it. It is easier to persuade a person not taking any paper to take one—particularly if you offer him a green glass butter dish or a picture of Daniel among the lions—than to persuade some one already taking a paper to stop that one and take yours. In the latter case a good deal of time-consuming and consequently expensive argument must be added to the butter dish or the picture. The people who were not newspaper readers when the Hearst organization made its big campaigns belonged to the relatively unintelligent. An interesting divorce case loomed larger to them than a serious international problem. They could understand divorce where they could not understand international relations. The newspaper that appealed to them had to be sensational. There is still a question, however, whether the newspaper became sensational in order to appeal to them or the newspaper, being sensational to begin with, made a natural appeal.

As to American newspapers in general, the theory that they become sensational in order to attract readers is not tenable. A study of circulation figures, as given by the Audit Bureau of Circulations, shows that in the average city which contains one or more "yellow" newspapers, one or more conservative (in handling of news, not in political theory), and one or more that lie between the two, the biggest circulation is held by a moderate paper, a "yellow" paper stands second, while conservative papers trail along toward the end.

On any newspaper of size, however, circulation is merely a means to an end, that end being advertising. As already stated, a large newspaper seldom gets enough from subscribers and newsstand buyers to pay its paper bills. An extremely large circulation means a quantity circulation; that is, a circulation which appeals to the advertiser mainly on the ground of its size. A small circulation, if among the rich or well-to-do, is a quality circulation. Rates for advertising are invariably compared on the basis of the amount charged per agate line or per inch for each unit of circulation. The rate on, a quantity circulation is always very low. On a quality circulation it is very high. The minimum rate ranges on daily newspapers in large cities from $1.08 per milline (quantity papers) to $7.31 per milline (quality papers). ①It follows that a newspaper may be very profitable financially on an exceedingly small circulation.

Another reason given by many for the deficiencies of the press is that the support of newspapers may be purchased for cold cash and thus enlisted in the support of certain corporations, politicians, or even criminals. When a newspaper is supporting what appears directly contrary to the public welfare, it is often surmised that its support has been bought as a business transaction.

Those cases of direct bribery have taken place, there is no doubt. Fremont Older, in *My Own Story*, ②gives details of such transactions. The writer personally knew one publisher—fortunately, for the welfare of journalism, now dead—whose support, he is convinced, could be bought for any measure. Though this publisher had the only newspaper in his city, a franchise which he had vigorously supported, making use of numerous

---

① The milline rate is the rate per agate line per 1,000,000 of circulation. For data on specific papers, see the *Standard Rate and Data Service*.
② pp. 23—30.

dishonest tactics, was defeated five to one. Every member of his own staff voted against the franchise. This was the culmination of long years of attempted betrayal of the public trust. So thoroughly did the public finally become aroused that the publisher sold his paper and left the city. Old newspaper men will all recall reporters who accepted bribes personally.

Direct bribery of newspapers or newspapermen is now, the writer is convinced, extremely rare; it is doubtful if it ever was common. It has disappeared along with direct bribery of public officials and individual voters. The public, though apathetic and long-suffering, at last revolted against bribery of all sorts. With the public vigilant and strongly opposed to bribery, those who would corrupt officials, the electorate, or the press, have found that even where takers of bribes can be found, the expected results cannot be delivered.

Those who do not hold that newspapers are bribed directly, often maintain that they are bribed indirectly by the promise to give or the threat to withhold advertising. Like direct bribery, this practice is less common than it once was. It has always been attempted by advertisers more often than it has succeeded. Some years ago, when bicycles were becoming popular, all the bicycle advertising was withdrawn from one of the New York dailies because it pointed out that bicycles were being sold at from five to six times their manufacturing cost. Again, the department stores of the same city withdrew their advertising from a newspaper because of its attitude on the tariff, and even stopped the credit accounts of customers who took the newspaper's side in the controversy. [1] More recently, as mentioned earlier in this work, *The Boston Evening Transcript* lost a great quantity of shoe advertising because it printed the actual news about the

---

[1] The two incidents, with numerous others, are treated in Holt's *Commercialism and Journalism*, pp. 66—68.

shoe industry in Massachusetts. In each of the cases mentioned, the advertisers eventually came back to the newspapers.

Numerous instances might be given of newspapers that have acceded to the requests of advertisers to suppress this or that. In every such case, of course, the demands of the advertisers steadily increased. Requests for suppression or publication of certain statements come to every newspaper from advertisers—and from non-advertisers—who in most instances probably do not realize the dishonorable and anti-social character of their requests.

Large papers, on the whole, are not so much affected by promises or threats on the part of advertisers as are smaller papers. It is regarded as poor business to let the advertiser gain the impression that he controls the papers. In any case, as has been often shown, he cannot stay out of a good advertising medium for long. There is, however, a tendency, even on large papers, to show a kind of gratitude to (or at least consideration for) the advertiser by accommodating him (usually without his request) in news matters which affect him. Such is commonly the impelling motive when newspapers omit the names of department stores in which accidents, cases of shoplifting, and other unpleasant incidents take place. Gratitude for advertising is obviously a ridiculous motive on the part of a strong newspaper. The sale of advertising is purely a business transaction, in which the advertiser expects to receive a profitable return from the space which he has purchased. Any disposition of gratitude to the advertiser is a relic of days when newspaper circulations were small, advertising rates were wholly unstandardized, and advertising was inserted largely as a charity to the publisher. It behooves no publication today to put advertising on a charity basis.

In the case of newspapers that have not strong financial backing, the temptation to please advertisers is strong. The average newspaper obtains only 35 per cent of its revenue from circulation, and this proportion is much smaller in the metropolitan daily. Slight as it is, circulation revenue fluctuates greatly. Except in the case of small country weeklies on which subscriptions are paid by the year, the reader is under no obligation to continue the paper from week to week or even from day to day. Every issue must sell itself to the reader's interest. In addition to the fact that they furnish the bulk of the revenue of a newspaper, advertisers tend to be more constant in their patronage than do readers.

That the financial problem is a real one is well known to any one familiar with the publishing business. An investigation made ten years ago in Kansas showed that 82 per cent of the newspaper plants in that state were operating under mortgages. ① Dr. Talcott Williams, who is probably as well-informed as any other man about metropolitan journalism, states that there are few if any American dailies which have not gone on the "red" in the past fifty years, so far as their yearly profit and loss account is concerned. ② As a business, publishing a newspaper is precarious.

The extent of influence of the advertiser upon the news in the press cannot be definitely stated. Doubtless it is much less than is commonly supposed. One realistic factor, commonly overlooked, which influences strongly against special favors to advertisers is the fact that advertisers are competitors. What pleases one may displease a score of others, and vice versa. Moreover, in the mass of news the advertiser has little if any personal interest. While undoubtedly it has its influence, advertising cannot be considered a principal reason for the deficiencies of the press.

This does not mean, of course, that the influence of advertising in this direction is to be disregarded as of no significance. Every effort should

---

① Thorpe, *The Coming Newspaper*, p. 13.
② *The Newspaperman*, p. 146.

be made to put advertising on a strictly commercial basis. The stronger newspapers are resorting to various means of accomplishing this. One well-known newspaper which endeavors to maintain its standards of fact in the news and its definite policies in the editorial columns even when they are unpopular, for years has carried a heavy reserve investment in a distant part of the country in order to be assured of sufficient funds in case the attitude of the paper results in financial loss. Financial independence, it cannot be too strongly urged, is likely to be necessary to ethical independence in the case of any institution which derives its revenue from private sources but owes responsibility to the public.

Again, as explanation of the deficiencies of the press, it is stated that newspapers are strongly influenced by business connections, such as ownership by capitalists or inter-locking directorates between the newspaper and a railway or other public service corporation, a great farming enterprise, or a land speculation scheme. As a matter of fact, not many newspapers have such connections. When the connections do exist, there is evidence of their effect. Of similar character is the effort of bankers to influence the policy of weak newspapers by granting or withholding loans. Personal ambitions of a publisher, in politics, social life, or business, may likewise lead the newspaper astray. The explanations that have been presented represent the causes commonly assigned for the deficiencies of the American newspapers, for their failure to maintain a higher standard of objective fact. The explanations involve both the atrocity and the conspiracy. They represent an essentially materialistic view of the press. Embodying all of them is a prevalent feeling that the newspaper has become essentially a prostitute, and after the manner of prostitutes has allied herself with other sinister interests. Many persons express agreement with Upton Sinclair when he says:

"What is the Brass Check? The Brass Check is found in your pay-envelope every week—you who write and print and distribute our newspapers and magazines. The Brass Check is the price of your shame—you who take the fair body of truth and sell it in the marketplace, who betray the virgin hopes of mankind into the loathsome brothel of Big Business. And down in the counting-room below sits the 'madame' who profits by your shame; unless, perchance, she is off at Palm Beach or Newport, flaunting her jewels and her feathers."①

It is natural that this point of view should be widely accepted. As has been stated, some evidence can be found in support of it. It is simple. It agrees with the atrocity and conspiracy habits of mind which are so widespread.

If, however, this were an adequate explanation, one would expect to find in the radical press, which is bitterly opposed to capitalism, the accuracy, fairness, and absence of bias which it is alleged are thwarted in the rest of the newspapers by capitalistic conspiracy. Instead, one finds in the radical press substantially the same deficiencies as in the conservative press. The deficiencies of the press are explained to no considerable extent by any materialistic theory.

Additional Materials

    Sinclair, *The Brass Check*, pp. 32—38, 221—249, 258—310.
    Holt, *Commercialism and Journalism*.
    Belloc, *The Free Press*.
    Williams, *The Newspaperman*, pp. 145—151.
    Older, *My Own Story*.
    Adams, *Success*.
    Adams, *The Clarion*.

---

① *The Brass Check*, p. 436.

Thorpe, *The Coming Newspaper*, pp. 1—26.

Angell, *The Press and the Organization of Society*, pp. 11—75.

Anderson, *The Blue Pencil. The New Republic*, December 14, 1918, pp. 192—194.

V   Deficiencies of the Press: A Realistic Explanation

The materialistic view of the newspaper heretofore presented, is, as has been pointed out, in relatively small part true. The principal causes for the failure of the American newspaper to fulfill its primary function are not those which are commonly alleged, but are to be found much more deeply imbedded in American life. They are subtle, slow-working, and intertwined with many other characteristics of our civilization.

Not corruption, but ignorance, inertia, and fear—the same type of ignorance, the same type of inertia, and the same type of fear that permeate American life—are the fundamental causes for the failure of American newspapers in giving the public the facts which the public has a right to demand.

Persons who come to this country from Europe, familiar with the better of the newspapers there, are astonished at the ignorance displayed by American reporters and copyreaders about the simplest matters, though their astonishment is always tempered when they discover the same sort of ignorance among high school and college students. Common geographical and historical facts, the names of well-known persons, to say nothing of economic, political, and artistic terms, are ludicrously twisted by reporters, and the copy-readers often enough pass the errors by.

Such ignorance, though lamentable, would not present so serious a face were it not for the fact that the average reporter does not seek enlightenment. He is afflicted with inertia, such as keeps a voter from seeking to understand political issues or even from voting at all. Given an assignment on an unfamiliar subject, the reporter will start out cocksure without consulting a reference book or even a more intelligent member of the staff of his paper. He will return and write his story without even looking into a dictionary. The story is currently told of a city reporter, sent out to interview John Burroughs, whom he fatuously supposed to be the inventor of the adding machine. After some minutes of conversation with the naturalist, the reporter began to feel some doubt as to the mechanical knowledge of the man he was interviewing, and blurted out:

"You'll pardon me, Mr. Burroughs, but what line of business are you in?"

A reporter of the writer's acquaintance on a widely quoted daily, who had finally got sufficiently perplexed over a religious story to turn to the despised reference book, attempted to look up the name of Mary Magdalene in *Who's Who in America*.

Circumstances of this sort make the American newspaper undependable in its reports of technical matters and to a less but still considerable extent in its ordinary news. In most cases the errors made do not directly affect the public judgment on significant issues. They are, however, a distinct discredit to American journalism.

On the other hand, when a reporter is placed on an important international story, he can do much damage by ignorance. Not a little of the misrepresentation of European conditions during and after the war was due to ignorance of history, geography, and economics on the part of American correspondents. The Warsaw correspondent who conveyed the impression that Vilna is historically Polish was, in all probability, simply ignorant and too lazy to ascertain the facts. The same excuse would hold for American editors who printed his story without verification.

In economic affairs, the ignorance of the typical American newspaper man is most marked. Here, again, he merely reflects the ignorance of the American public; indeed, he is less ignorant than the vast majority of his readers. Members of the British Labour Party and of the French trade unions have a familiarity with economic history and current economic problems such as shames the American college graduate. The various directions in which economic change has been brought about in Europe, in Australia, in other parts of the world, the very terms, which are in common use in modern economics, are unknown to, or misunderstood by, the average journalist in this country. It is not surprising that he stamps as "bolshevistic" "radical" socialistic, or "anarchistic"—he uses all these and many other terms with fine disregard of their meaning—all plans for altering the *status quo*, or that he utterly confuses the news relating to such plans.

Quite as serious is the ignorance of the American reporter concerning what constitutes evidence. Evidence is not an easy matter to deal with practically; the experience of the courts is sufficient proof of this fact. Nevertheless, there are some fundamental principles that the reporter should, but frequently does not, recognize. For example, it is a well understood principle that nothing should be accepted as fact on the uncorroborated statement of a single individual. So important is this that even in scientific investigation, where men of special training and presumably impersonal zeal for the truth are engaged, it is a common practice for individual records to be kept by to persons. Yet reporters—and perhaps news editors even more readily—accept as fact or something very close to fact what is at best uncorroborated testimony of one person and at worst mere rumor.

The acceptance as fact of statements by persons high in official life, in the United States or in other countries, or by persons who claim, without actually possessing, some special knowledge of a subject, is especially common among reporters. This is in part mere credulity on the reporter's part. In part, however, it represents inertia. There is no easier way to get news than to obtain it from some single individual. Again, there is no easier way to handle such news than to accept it as fact without examining its intrinsic probability, the actual qualifications of the individual giving it to speak with authority on the subject, or the freedom of this individual from official or personal bias which may lead him, intentionally or unconsciously, to misrepresent the facts.

The misinterpretation of the Russian situation from the time of the Revolution on was due to a considerable extent to the credulity and ignorance of American reporters. While it is true that the actual conditions in Russia during this confused period are far from clear now, it is at the same time evident that the news furnished by American correspondents, especially during the counter-revolutionary campaigns, was notoriously unreliable. The comment made by Messrs. Lippmann and Merz on the credulity of reporters in this severe test is illuminating:

"The analysis shows how seriously misled was The Times by its reliance upon the official purveyors of information. It indicates that statements of fact emanating from governments and the circles around governments as well as from the leaders of political movements cannot be taken as judgments of fact by an independent press. They indicate opinion, they are controlled by special purpose, and they are not trustworthy news.

If, for example, the Russian Minister of War says that the armies of Russia were never stronger, that cannot be accepted by a newspaper as news that the armies of Russia are stronger than ever. The only news in the statement is that the Minister says they are stronger. By any high journalistic standard, the Minister's statement, if it deals with a matter of vital importance, is a challenge to independent investigation.

"The analysis shows that even more misleading than the official statement purporting to be a statement of fact, is the semi-official and semi-authoritative but anonymous statement. Such news is fathered by such phrases as:

"'Officials of the State Department'

"'government and diplomatic sources'

"'reports reaching here'

"'it is stated on high authority that'

"Behind those phrases may be anybody, a minor bureaucrat, a dinner table conversation, hotel lobby gossip, a chance acquaintance, a paid agent. Dispatches of this type put the editor at home and the reader at the mercy of opinion that he cannot check, and it is time to demand that the correspondent take the trouble to identify his informants sufficiently to supply the reader with some means of estimating the character of the report. He need not name the individual source but he can 'place' him······

"The analysis indicates also that even so rich and commanding a newspaper as *The Times* does not take seriously enough the equipment of the correspondent. For extraordinarily difficult posts in extraordinary times, something more than routine correspondents are required. Reporting is one of the most difficult professions, requiring much expert knowledge and serious education. The old contention that properly trained men lack the "news sense" will not stand against the fact that improperly trained men have seriously misled a whole nation. It is habit rather than preference which makes readers accept news from correspondents whose usefulness is about that of an astrologer or an alchemist. Important as it is for the press to read lessons in efficiency to workingmen, employees, and politicians, it is no less important for the press to study those lessons itself. Measured by its responsibility and pretensions, the efficiency of the newspapers is not what determined men could make it."[1]

When the ignorance of the American journalist, and specifically the American reporter, is mentioned, the argument is often advanced that greater knowledge is impossible. The error of this conclusion may readily be seen if one will compare the articles about Russia published in 1920 in the better dailies of the United States with those of Mr. Arthur Ransome, published in The Manchester Guardian. Knowledge of general conditions and readiness to investigate with meticulous care in order to get specific data are manifest in the work of this English reporter. For examples, Mr. Ransome's articles stated such pertinent facts as these: The proportion of manufactured goods imported into Russia prior to the Revolution; the exact number of available locomotives in the country each year from 1914 on; the number of horses mobilized in Perm Government for timber production; the monthly output of coal per man in each of a number of coal mines; the proportion of the nominal working hours kept in the state metal-working factories; the precise membership of the Communist party; the details of organization that secured for this party, with its small membership, actual dominance.

These data, with numerous others, are brought together in such a way as to give a clear picture of economic conditions. While much of Mr.

---

[1] *A Test of the News*, pp. 41—42.

Ransome's information is not news, in the sense of dealing exclusively with immediately contemporaneous happenings, it comprises those objective facts which are so closely related to events as to make the latter unintelligible without a knowledge of the former. ①

To take an example nearer home, American newspapers frequently sensationalize, ridicule, or ignorantly misrepresent scientific conventions. In 1922, however, *The New York Times* sent to cover the annual meeting of the American Association for the Advancement of Science Alva Johnston, who was fitted by temperament and training to handle the facts of science. Dealing with an enormous variety of scientific subject matter, Mr. Johnston, by reason of his prior knowledge and his care as to the exact facts, produced daily during the convention a group of news stories which for accuracy, clearness, and interest could hardly be surpassed. The award of the Pulitzer Prize to these stories as the best example of a reporter's work during the year is evidence of a growing concern for newspaper writing of indubitable reliability. ②

The instances cited show clearly that sufficient mental equipment and energy in seeking facts are by no means unattainable on the part of the reporter. Ignorance and inertia exist on newspapers simply because knowledge is not demanded. "A good story" is the most common expression in many a newspaper office. The exact truthfulness of the story is too seldom called into question. There is a prevalent feeling in newspaper offices that the public demands "good stories" and is not concerned much with their accuracy.

Well-written stories, based partly on facts, semi-humorous leads written in by copy-readers, and florescent, artificial heads (developed, it

---

① Much of Mr. Ransome's material is reprinted in his book, The Crisis in Russia, which will be especially useful where files of *The Guardian* are inaccessible.
② The articles appear in The New York Times, December 28 to 30, 1922.

is true, as an exigency of newspaper makeup), make such a combination as may well drive considerations of clear-cut knowledge completely out of the reckoning.

Real knowledge of modern economics is less likely to gain promotion for a reporter on the average paper than the ability to write an interesting but largely untruthful story about a street fight over the ownership of a custard pie. The public, the editor says, is more interested in the humor of custard pies than in economics.

Closely related to ignorance and inertia, but even more powerful in its influence against complete and impartial truth-telling by newspapers, is fear. Fear is a characteristic not simply of newspapers; it is a characteristic of the American people. It is not a physical fear; Americans have shown courage and endurance times without number. It is rather an intellectual and spiritual fear, based on nothing tangible, on nothing which affords a reasonable basis for fear. It takes most conspicuously the form of fear of and deference to the herd, the whole body of people within the nation. Necessary for preservation of the race in some distant period of its history, it remains today as an anomaly.

It is to be admitted at once that because of man's gregarious nature there is everywhere a natural desire—slowly diminishing, however—on the part of the individual to identify himself with the herd with respect to his conviction and opinions. While he may not desire, or may even actively shrink from, the approbation of the great mass of people, he will nevertheless seek the approval of a small body, "a herd within a herd," with which he conforms in matters of opinion. [1]On the other hand, there is an excessive deference to and fear of the herd, which prevent intellectual and,

---

[1] For a detailed discussion of this phenomenon, see rotter, *Instincts of the Herd in Peace and War*, pp. 23−41.

to a considerable extent, other progress. This attitude has long been recognized as one of the dangers of democratic government.

In his treatise On Liberty,① John Stuart Mill pointed out that if either of two opinions "has a better claim than the other not merely to be tolerated but to be encouraged and countenanced, it is the one which happens at the particular time and place to be in a minority." Going on with his discussion, Mill stated that tyranny of established ideas tends to "a dead uniformity of taste and opinion and method of life that will finally lead to a more than Chinese stagnation." In the United States, the development of excessive deference to the herd is due not only to the natural tendency of democracy but also to the fact that in early times the unity of the nation, such as it was, was based on common antipathies more than on common sympathies.

So far as fear is concerned, it is obviously useless. As Dr. Freud says, "everything that happens would be consummated just as well and better without the development of fear."② The general recognition of the uselessness of fear probably accounts in part for the fact that it masks or rationalizes itself in other guises. No individual is willing to admit, even to himself, that he is a coward. The fear complex is inhibited by the psychic censor, and manifests itself in indirect and devious ways. Conduct actually inspired by fear is explained by the individual on the basis of various false rationalizations.

Hence, fear, though carrying none of the moral stigma which attaches to corruption, is much more devastating. Corruption presents a clear-cut issue of right and wrong, of honesty and dishonesty. There is always the chance that the crook will see this issue and determine to try to follow

---

① Chapter 2.
② *A General Introduction to Psychoanalysis*, p. 341.

the right. Fear involves no dear-cut issue of any sort. Unadmitted as a motive by the person who is actuated by it, fear undermines every intellectual, ethical, and emotional resistance.

Fear in journalism begins with the reporter and permeates every part of the newspaper organization up to the publisher. Conversation with many reporters has convinced the writer that the vast majority are fundamentally honest. It likewise has convinced him that the vast majority are either liberals or radicals, though in many cases unintelligent ones. If, however, one picks up the average newspaper today and reads the stories written by these men, one will find a certain bias toward conservative and reactionary policies and against liberal and radical policies. Presumably, if these men unconsciously varied from strict objective truth in writing their stories, they would vary in the direction of their own convictions; namely, in a liberal or a radical direction. What is the explanation of their varying in exactly the opposite direction?

The average critic of the newspaper, unfamiliar with newspaper practices, attributes this to instructions issued by the publisher to his staff that matter must be written with a certain bias. In some cases, such orders are issued-practically always, however, by publishers who are in no sense professional journalists but are rather business men running newspapers as they would run factories. On most papers run even by men of this type, there are no such orders. Most instruction sheets issued to the members of newspaper staffs urge the importance of accuracy and fairness. ①

A new managing editor comes to a newspaper. He calls the members of the staff together and says to them:

"Boys, the thing I want you to do is to get the news. We want all the news and we want it accurately. We don't care what it's about or whom it

---

① See examples of such sheets in Appendix A, pp. 211−238.

hits. There are going to be no sacred cows on this paper so long as I'm managing editor. If I see a sacred calf coming on, I'm going to choke it before it grows up."

The boys listen, then they go out smiling to themselves, and write the same old stories with the same old bias. What is the trouble?

Fundamentally, it is fear on the part of the reporter and employees immediately above the reporter. All, or nearly all, the newspapers that the reporter has seen, including the one on which he is working, have exhibited a conservative bias in handling the news. He believes that the publisher wants only stories with a conservative bias and that if he writes an important political or economic story showing no bias or showing radical or liberal bias, the story will not be printed and he may be fired. If nothing more, he feels that the story will be so altered by the copy desk as to maintain the conservative bias. The statements of the managing editor have not removed his fears. That functionary is considered by the reporter to have been "letting off steam," "trying to kid himself," or "just making a speech." The reporter is perhaps encouraged in his beliefs by the city editor and the copy-readers—men who have grown old and cynical in the newspaper office and who could not readily find employment outside of it. There is instilled into the young newspaper man's mind the feeling that the publisher is involved in various capitalistic enterprises, that his business and social associates are all capitalists, and that he is publishing the newspaper in the interests of capitalism.

Thus is formed a hapless circle. Because of what newspapers he has read and because of what older newspaper men have told him, the young newspaper reporter gives a bias to what he writes. Other reporters, coming after him, will have read what he has written, will perchance listen to his talk, and will follow his example.

The same reasoning applies to such an organization as the Associated

Press. As has heretofore been intimated, critics such as Mr. Upton Sinclair① hold that the Associated Press is essentially corrupt, maintained in the interests of capital. The situation rather is like this: Except where a special bureau is maintained, the Associated Press paper in each town—practically always a politically conservative paper—is, by virtue of its membership, the Associated Press correspondent for that town. The actual handling of the correspondence is, as a rule, turned over to some bright young man on the paper. This bright young man knows that there are other bright young men on his paper who would be glad of the job. Consequently, he is not going to do anything to cause a chance of his losing the position. He follows the beaten path of conservative bias in writing the news which he sends to the Associated Press. Quite beside the mark is the possibility that material written in a wholly definite way might be acceptable. The point is that the reporter disbelieves this, it may be for excellent reasons, and is actuated by the fear of losing his job.

The morale of the reporter may be further broken down by such circumstances as the fact that occasionally a "yellow" newspaper may keep a man to engage in dishonorable activities, such as picture-stealing, browbeating of witnesses, and even bribery. A man of this type is usually a partial invalid, a drunkard, a dope fiend, or a man weakened by some other form of dissipation. Reporters see the activities of a man of this sort and, knowing that he can be relied upon to do anything he is asked to do, think it not worthwhile to fight hard for such ideals of journalistic ethics as intellectually they may retain.

The natural result of such situations is to produce in the reporter the cynical attitude that a newspaper is a purely commercial enterprise, and that it does not pay to try to be honest upon it. The newspaper comes to

---

① *The Brass Check*, pp. 353—376.

occupy, in his estimation, the same position as a store selling groceries or dry goods. It sells what the people want, or what the proprietor thinks the people want, or what, for some other reason, the proprietor is determined to sell. There is developed in the reporter the psychological phenomenon known as dissociation of consciousness. In one compartment of his mind he keeps his convictions about truth-telling and his liberal or radical ideas. In another compartment he keeps the commercial principles which he is convinced are those of the journalistic world. His attitude is the same as that of the deacon who cheats his customers on weekdays on the conviction that business is business. Neither the reporter nor the deacon is necessarily a conscious hypocrite.

The responsibility for this statement must not be laid wholly upon the reporter. The belief of the reporter that his paper demands biased news may not be based on any instructions from the publisher. When, however, in the face of such belief, the publisher remains silent or speaks half-heartedly, the public concludes that the fear on the part of the reporter is justified. A publisher can make it clear that unbiased reporting is the only acceptable reporting on his paper. He can, if necessary, discharge all editors and copy-readers who persist in conveying the opposite impression.

In most cases, the publisher does not face the issue at all. For one thing, in the large city he is more than likely not to be a professional journalist, but rather a businessman, who has come up through the advertising department and who calls himself a "newspaper maker" rather than a newspaper man, an editor, or a journalist. He sees the newspaper as a business enterprise; intended to interest and please the public sufficiently to build a circulation which will bring in advertising. If he were asked categorically, he would say he wanted his paper to be honest, and he would mean it. He turns the editorial side of the paper over to competent men, to whom he gives few instructions. He assumes that they will run the paper satisfactorily, and so long as they do so he sees no reason for interfering with them. He reads his paper every day, and it seems to him a good, honest paper. His friends tell him it is a good, honest paper. The utter dishonesty of misrepresenting the news by means of giving it a specific bias has never been a concern of his.

In case the paper is corporately owned and managed by a board of directors, the truthfulness of the news becomes a matter of still less concern. A group of this character is always more cautious, less ready to interfere so long as things seem to be going fairly well, than any individual in the group.

The consolidation of papers under single ownership, individual or corporate, is likely to lead to equally unfortunate results.

The publisher or publishers, moreover, are subject to intellectual and spiritual fear-fear of the herd and deference to the herd. This is a factor more potent than any fear of the publisher on the part of the employees of the newspaper. Fear of the herd permeates newspaper workers from the publisher to the youngest cub reporter.

The newspaper, as at present constituted, is essentially a herd institution; and the herd in the United States constitutes much more clearly a mass formation than in any other great country. It is held together by a definiteness of faith unequaled except in a supposedly infallible Church. A long list of taboos—sexual, political, economic, and social—are dogmas of the American faith. Like the dogmas of an infallible Church, the dogmas of American faith are subject to no critical examination. The person who holds them may be able to give no more satisfactory reason for his belief than the believer in justification by faith or justification by works. Yet questioning of the dogmas convinces their holder that if you are not a heretic you are at least a vulgar fellow. Even those who profess willingness to test their beliefs usually approach them with a favorable prepossession, and merely attempt—unconsciously, it is true—to find logical ground for continuing to hold the doctrines. There is no genuine self-doubting.

Obviously devotion to the truth, for its own sake or as the sole guide to conduct, is not encouraged by a dogmatic system. Indeed; the people of the United States are notorious for their ostrich like attitude toward all truths which will not climb up on their shoulders and purr. A motion picture censorship board recently barred from a widely known film the words, "It's a boy," and substituted "The boy is better," thus protecting American modesty against the unfortunate truth that children are born. Like the little girl in her attitude toward the boys, the American people do not like truths; they like "nice" truths.

The herd dogmas constituting the American deposit of faith are ingrained in newspaper folk, from the proprietors down. The sympathy with the mass of people demanded by the contemporary newspaper with the emphasis on "human interest" often brings with it the masses' view of life. Devotion to absolute truth being in nowise encouraged by the dogmatic system, the tendency, in the absence of any set policy whatsoever, is to exclude from the papers anything, however true, which violently conflicts with herd dogmas.

For many years news of women and women's organizations was treated flippantly by newspapers, the serious facts of the subject being excluded or misrepresented. This is no longer the case. Some have ascribed the change to the fact that women not only have the vote but also determine what paper the family shall take. This is a shallow explanation. The real reason for the change is that the herd attitude toward women has changed, a general conviction having developed to the effect that women are people, and newspaper men have changed—in large measure unconsciously—with the herd.

The news concerning Russia, so far as it was not influenced, as previously pointed out, by ignorance and lack of understanding of the ordinary canons of evidence, was colored not through actual corruption of the press but because of the feeling of the press that the herd tradition was against Soviet Russia. And so it was. It is true that the herd tradition in this direction was directed in large measure by the newspapers, but they in turn had accepted propaganda from official and semi-official sources. This propaganda was skillfully prepared so as to bring the doctrines of Soviet Russia into apparent conflict with such American beliefs as the outward sanctity of marriage, democratic government, and private ownership of property. Again to quote from the study by Messrs. Lippmann and Merz:

"The news as a whole is dominated by the hopes of the men who composed the news organization. They began as passionate partisans in a great war in which their own country's future was at stake. Until the armistice they were interested in defeating Germany. They hoped until they could hope no longer that Russia would fight. When they saw she could not fight, they worked for intervention as part of the war against Germany. When the war with Germany was over, the intervention still existed. They found reasons then for continuing the intervention. The German Peril as the reason for intervention ceased with the armistice; the Red Peril almost immediately afterwards supplanted it. The Red Peril in turn gave place to rejoicing over the hopes of the White Generals. When these hopes died, the Red Peril reappeared. In the large, the news about Russia is a case of seeing not what was, but what men wished to see.

"This deduction is more important, in the opinion of the authors, than any other. The chief censor and the chief propagandist were hope and fear in the minds of reporters and editors. They wanted to win the war; they wanted to ward off bolshevism. These subjective obstacles to the free pursuit of facts account for the tame submission of enterprising men to the objective censorship and propaganda under which they did their work. For subjective reasons they accepted and believed most of what they were told by the State Department, the so-called Russian Embassy in Washington, the Russian Information Bureau in New York, the Russian Committee in Paris, and the agents and adherents of the old regime all over Europe. For the same reason they endured the attention of officials at crucial points like Helsingfors, Omsk, Vladivostok, Stockholm, Copenhagen, London, and Paris. For the same reason they accepted reports of governmentally controlled news services abroad, and of correspondents who were unduly intimate with the various secret services and with members of the old Russian nobility."[1]

In incidents such as these, newspapermen in part are themselves influenced to believe what the herd believes, because they are essentially of the herd, while in part they consciously publish through fear what they believe the herd wants—as they say, they "give the public what it wants."

In addition to the common herd instincts of the people of the United States, there exist the specific herd instincts of the several economic classes. The rich, the middle class, the proletariat, or laboring class, have each distinctive herd instincts. By inheritance, tradition, education, and associations, newspaper men and women usually belong to the middle class, which is fundamentally a trading class and hence interested chiefly in commercial affairs. The owner of a newspaper, even in the few instances in which he is a rich man, is likely to hold the standards, instincts, and ideals of the middle class.

There are few more striking phenomena in the United States than the contempt of any class for the class or classes below it and the snobbish re-

---

[1] Test of the News, p. 3.

gard of any class for the class or classes above it. Nowhere, moreover, are these qualities more manifest than in the middle class. With the attitude of the middle class what it is, the newspaper man—publisher and reporter alike—is annoyed if he is called a "bolshevik" or a "radical" even in a joking way. He may assert that he believes in radical doctrines, but in his unconscious mind there still exists the desire to stand among the sober members of his class, who never deny or thwart its herd instincts.

Moreover, in the rare instances in which he has got rid of his unconscious deference to his class and the class above him, he has a certain fear of them. They are articulate. The proletariat has herd instincts, just the same, but it is largely inarticulate. The newspaper need have no fear of it. And the ideal of truth is no part of the herd instincts of any class, rich, middle, or poor, any more than it is a part of the herd instincts of the people as a whole.

The smaller the community, the more pronounced is deference to the herd. The large city, by reason of its very size and lack of curiosity, affords protection to him who differs from the herd. The vast majority of the newspapers of the United States are published in small towns, and these newspapers are more carefully read and are more influential with their readers than are the city dailies. At the same time, they display less independence of the herd.

A single example will make this clear. It is a common practice of small newspapers to omit the names of persons arrested for ordinary crimes and misdemeanors, although in a small community these undeniably constitute news. The reason regularly given for omission of these names is that publication of them would cause sorrow to the innocent relatives of the offenders. It is obvious that this is a false rationalization, produced according to well-known psychological laws, to account for what is really the product of fear of the herd.

The fear of the herd is in part an unconscious phenomenon. This invisible censor is not only invisible to the average newspaper man; its very existence is unknown to him. If told that he is governed largely by deference to the herd, he would deny it. He would give a variety of excuses for what he does, chief among them that he is governed by his best judgment.

Now and then, when a paper does publish facts which tend to conflict with herd dogmas, the herd—or part of it—manifests its shock of horror and resentment. It is not uncommon for subscribers to cancel their subscriptions or for advertisers to withdraw their advertising because a newspaper has published matter, usually undeniable facts, which they dislike. Those who do not break off their financial connections with the paper are prone to write letters of denunciation. In these latter days mobs of self-styled patriots have demanded of newspapers that the facts be misrepresented in the interest of private propaganda. In the smaller cities and towns, individuals and organizations bring pressure to bear to have printed as news, matter which at its best is editorial comment and at its worst plain misrepresentation of facts. In all these cases, naturally, pressure comes from the articulate sections of the community. Such incidents lend weight to the contention, often advanced by cynical newspaper men, that the American public prefers always a pleasant lie to an unpleasant truth. And one may venture the further conclusion that the cold objectivity of the truth is of itself unpleasant to those who have grown accustomed to warm, cozy lies.

Nevertheless, although essentially part of the herd, maintaining a herd institution, and showing constant fear of and deference to herd instincts, many a newspaper publisher of today considers himself essentially superior to the herd. In some cases he speaks as if he were divinely appointed a molder of public opinion and a leader of the herd. At the same time, he has a conscious distrust and physical fear of the herd, quite different from his unconscious intellectual and spiritual fear of and deference to the herd.

His distrust and fear of the people manifest themselves in conscious unwillingness to give the people the facts. Such unwillingness is, of course, no new thing; Governmental opposition to newspapers in ages long past was due to governmental opposition to giving the people the facts—particularly the facts concerning government. In England it was at one time permissible to publish only foreign news, this being regarded as relatively safe for the people to read. When the regulations were relaxed and news of England could be published in English papers, concealment of the facts from the people was aided, partly by statutory enactment, partly by the judicial ruling that the greater the truth, the greater was the libel. This fine piece of judicial casuistry was justified on the ground that the truth is more likely to provoke disturbance of the peace than is false hood. In those days, the opposition to publication of facts came from kings, from landed aristocracies, from wealthy merchant groups-minorities conscious of present power but fearful of their future ability to maintain themselves in the face of the numerical majority. Newspaper publishers stood out, even in the face of prison sentences, for the right to publish the facts.

There can be seen a certain justification for the attitude of the rulers of those times. They did not profess to believe in popular government; nobody, except a few inconsequential fanatics, professed to believe in it. The government was not a government of the people, nor did it intend to be. Why should the people have any concern with it?

Today newspapermen seriously maintain their right to withhold facts from the people, and have thus taken the place of those monarchs and lords and rich traders whom they vanquished generations ago. Yet the newspaperman who would withhold facts from the people lacks the justification which those old-time rulers had. He professes to believe in popular government. He is fond of referring to the Declaration of Independence, the Constitution, and the principles of democracy. At the same time, he is ready to withhold from the people the facts—and facts are the only basis on which the people can form sound, dependable judgments.

This development has been produced by a combination of factors. Important among these has been the increasing tacit acceptance, in American political, civic, and commercial life, of the doctrine that the end justifies the means—no new doctrine, but one which would have been frowned upon by the sturdier democrats of the early days of the Republic. There has also been an expansion of that specious motto, "Our country ... may she ever be in the right; but, right or wrong, our country," until it has reached the depths of absurdity, easily apparent in the addresses of "boosters," as "Right or wrong, our town" and even "Right or wrong, our club."

To the growth of such sentiments newspapers have lent their aid. Every one knows how news of serious disease in a town is often suppressed or "played down" lest the reputation of the place—created by the local Chamber of Commerce—as "the healthiest city within five hundred miles in any direction" should be shattered. People still remember the attitude of California newspapers toward the earthquake and fire in San Francisco. Many other examples might be mentioned.

The growth of the tendency to conceal the facts because of distrust of the people was immeasurably assisted during the World War. Beginning with the suppression of the facts in the possession of the administration in the autumn of 1916 in order to make effectual the specious plea that the President "kept us out of war," the practice was followed throughout the war of giving to the public only such facts as it was believed would aid in winning the war or in bringing credit to American diplomacy. The so-called "voluntary censorship," on the one hand, and the Espionage Act, on the other, showed plainly the governmental attitude toward giving the facts to the public. No one doubts the desirability of keeping wartime secrets from reaching the enemy, but it is exceedingly questionable whether anything is added to the morale of a democracy by concealing all facts which are not optimistic in their import. Certainly such a practice means immeasurable harm to the future intellectual integrity of that democracy.

This was an exceedingly favorable time to fix upon the newspapers the practice of concealing the facts. In war practically every newspaper, in deference to the herd if for no other reason, wants to appear completely patriotic and a supporter of the government in its every activity. With the administration committed to the policy of presenting to the people only such facts as it held the people should know, the newspapers not unnaturally followed the same practice—a practice, however, in which to a less extent many of them had, it must be remembered, been previously engaged. The practice became a more or less honored tradition in many newspaper offices, and with the passing of the war it has continued. The question is asked, time after time, "Is it safe to give the people all these facts?" The young reporter, ignorant and inexperienced, asks the question of himself before he writes a story. It is noteworthy, moreover, that the facts which are omitted are not commonly details of crime and vice, interest in which might be criticized as morbid, but facts of political, economic, and social significance.

In the United States there is no phenomenon more threatening to popular government than the unwillingness of newspapers to give the facts to their readers. No more serious indictment can be presented against any public or quasi-public institution than that it ever questions the wisdom of giving the people the facts. It may be asserted that the people are unintelligent, swayed by prejudice and unreason, and that they should be supplied with only such facts as will cause them to think and act wisely; i. e. , in the way in which a given newspaper—or even editor or reporter—considers it wise for them to think and act. But what is making them unintelligent if not the newspaper which adopts such a policy? And who shall say that the people, possessed of all the facts, will prove less capable of judgment than the staff of the average American newspaper?

The only other argument advanced in favor of this practice is even less worthy of serious consideration. It is that certain newspapers will suppress some facts and other newspapers other facts and that thus the people will get all the facts. As if a reader could legitimately be expected to go through a process comparable to the examination of witnesses in court, in order to discover the facts about public affairs! The only chance for actual popular government is for all the available facts to be given to the people clearly and objectively. The people may not always be wise, but they can gain no wisdom save through experience. Any person—or any institution—which seeks to keep from the public any facts of public concern shows thereby that he has at heart no belief in popular government. If he professes such belief, he is either consciously a deceiver or irretrievably self-deceived.

Additional Readings

Ransome, The Crisis in Russia.

Press releases and other copy furnished by Science Service.

Articles on the convention of the American Association for the Advancement of Science. The New York Times. December 28—30, 1922.

Trotter, Instincts of the Herd in Peace and War, pp. 23—41.

Freud, A General Introduction to Psychoanalysis, pp. 340—355.

Mill, On Liberty.

Salmon, The Newspaper and the Historian. pp. 114—137, 195—248.

Hackett, The Invisible Censor, pp. I—10.

Lippmann and Merz, A Test of the News, Supplement to The New

Republic, August 4, 1920.

Ghent, False Testers of the News. The Review 4:488—489, 509—511.

Hapgood, Journalism, in Every-day Ethics, pp. I—I5.

Bliven, Newspaper Morals. The New Republic 35:17_19.

VI The Principle of Objectivity Applied: Balance and Proportion

In the foregoing chapters, it may be pointed out, there has been laid down a somewhat elaborate philosophy of journalism, a philosophy which presents objectivity in the dissemination of facts as the primary ideal of the press. Now, granted that every one theoretically agrees with this philosophy and would like, moreover, to see it carried out in actual practice, how is this to be accomplished? Are there not certain practical applications to be made which involve at times most difficult adjustments?

It must be admitted at once that the practical application of this philosophy-as indeed of any philosophy-does involve difficulties. The press is a human institution, and no human institution ever conforms precisely to a consistent ethical or philosophical theory. That newspapers generally are moving gradually toward the goal that has been presented, however, there can be little doubt. Nor can it be doubted that still more rapid progress would be made were the ideal of objectivity more tenaciously and realistically held by journalists. The advance made in the natural sciences since they abandoned the chiefly speculative and adopted the investigative method is evidence of what may be accomplished in a human institution even against the most implacable opposition.

Among the definite problems which must be met and settled by the press-not once for all, but time after time in the work of a single day-is that of proportion and balance. This problem involves what is commonly referred to by the layman as "the suppression of news."It involves also to a considerable extent the problem of sensationalism, a charge frequently brought against the press by persons interested primarily in preserving certain ethical standards in life.

In the small town the problem of proportion and balance does not cut a large figure. The newspaper has ample space for covering the news of its community. Where a piece of news remains unpublished, the suppression may be assumed to be deliberate an attempt on the part of the publisher to conceal facts from his readers. Like- wise, there is little question as to the news value of any specific local event. The problem remains relatively simple.

This is not true of a larger paper, and the larger the paper, the more perplexing becomes the problem. Reporters on metropolitan dailies turn in many times as much copy as could be printed in the space available. In addition, a great deal more copy could be obtained through more detailed investigation. Obviously there is a large quantity of material of some news value that does not get into the papers. A great deal of news must be "suppressed"- simply in the sense of being omitted from the newspapers. This, of course, is not the sense in which the term is commonly used by critics of the press. When they say that news is "suppressed," they imply that matter of public importance is concealed for unworthy reasons.

A difficult problem thus comes before the editors of any large newspaper for solution. Not only does the suppression of news for unworthy reasons exist in actual practice, 'out it is generally supposed to exist to a larger extent than is really the case. Moreover, there must be considered the real importance of all events and the interest of the readers of the newspaper in them, though the latter point is overemphasized on most newspapers. These matters all enter in when an editor is considering the balance to be given to the day's news, how much space is to be devoted to certain stories, whether certain other stories shall be cut down or left out altogether.

However objective a man (or woman) may strive to be, he is likely to be misled at a critical moment by his own philosophy of life or his own private interests unless he is guided by some definite standard. Consequently, in order to insure fairness in handling and balancing the news, some newspapers have-and probably all should have-specific rules as to what sort of news must be printed. In a large city all cases filed in a court of a certain rank must, according to such rules, be dealt with m the news columns. The smaller the city, the lower the jurisdiction of the court whose proceedings must be chronicled. In the small town, however, there is a strong tendency for the editor to suppress unpleasant news altogether, on the specious ground that publication will do harm to the individual involved or more often to the individual's family, but in reality, as was pointed out in a previous chapter l because the editor is afraid.

The rationalization offered in this attitude is well answered by William Allen White in discussing a specific case, that of the drunkard: "The man who fills up with whiskey and goes about making a fool of himself, becomes a public nuisance. If permitted to continue it, he becomes a public charge. The public has an interest in him. Publicity is one of the things that keeps him straight. His first offense is ignored in The Gazette, but his second offense is recorded when he is arrested, and no matter how high or low he is, his name goes in. We have printed this warning to drinkers time and again; so when they come around asking us to think of their wives and children, or their sick mothers or poor old fathers, we always tell them to remember that they had fair warning, and if their fathers and mothers and wives and children are nothing to them before taking, they are nothing to us after taking." 1

A frequent argument in favor of suppression of the news of crime or vice in a small town is that its publication destroys the reputation of the town outside, and, furthermore, stirs up ill feeling in the town itself. The same argument would, if carried to a logical conclusion, prevent a clergyman from preaching against evil and even a court from punishing it. It is based, consciously or unconsciously, on the doctrine that whatever is concealed can do no harm. It is, moreover, the argument regularly advanced by the friends and supporters of professional gamblers, thugs, and other criminals in endeavoring to prevent a city from being cleaned up. Newspapers which adopt this reasoning are merely playing into the hands of criminal and degenerate elements of the public.

As Mr. White points out, news of crime or misdemeanor is a public matter and publicity is a deterrent to evil-doing.

Furthermore, particularly in the small town, publicity affords a measure of protection to the evil-doer himself against exaggeration of the evil that he has committed. If the facts are left unpublished, town gossip will exaggerate them out of all proportion to their actual state, The publication of the exact facts enables the public to obtain a correct understanding and to draw fair conclusions from it[①].

In certain small towns and even in large cities, news is sometimes suppressed because of the prominence of the persons involved. In the cities, however, newspaper competition has largely eliminated this condition

---

① Quoted by J. S. Myers in The Journalistic Code of Ethics, p. 30.

and most metropolitan dailies will publish the news of a minor offense of which a prominent person is accused, while omitting reference to the same offense if committed by an obscure individual. The reason is that the doings of persons of prominence are held to be of public interest and in some degree of public importance. While this point of view is open to question, there is some argument to justify it.

Any prominence which a person has attained, he has attained through society. Recognition obtained by wealth, by family position, or by ability, is obtained from society and by reason of living in a state of society. Society may be said to possess a greater interest in the individual whom it has thus recognized than in the person who has achieved no prominence.

Many newspapers have rules providing for the omission of certain matters of news. These may be divided into two classes: (1) Matters which are suppressed out of consideration for the individual concerned; and (2) matters suppressed for the general interests of society.

Under the first head come offenses of women and children. Many papers have a rule against publishing the proceedings of juvenile courts with the name of the individuals involved, unless the proceedings involve a sentence to a reform school or some other place of correction. Justification for this is given by a statute in many states, such statutes making the juvenile court a partly judicial tribunal, while in part the juvenile court stands in loco parentis to the child, giving advice and counsel and even administering corporal punishment. For this reason, the hearings of juvenile courts are often made private by statute, the reason for public court trials, the preservation of the integrity and reputation of the judiciary, being not here involved. Where no sentence is imposed, it is obviously better for the child and in no way harmful to society that his playmates should not have the opportunity to ridicule him or to make a hero of him. Childhood is essentially sensitive, and to it the wages of sin may not properly be publicity.

Cases involving women involve a somewhat similar point of view. While clear-thinking people recognize that it ought not to be so, the fact remains that in our present civilization a woman finds it difficult to regain a reputation lost through lack of chastity. Even where no want of chastity on the part of the woman herself is involved, she is often affected by being involuntarily involved in some unfortunate situation, as in the case of the girl referred to in Master's Spoon River Anthology. For this reason hearings in the so-called morals courts of cities are not infrequently private. Practically all newspapers enjoin greater care in dealing with the reputation of women, and many of them have a specific rule that the names of women shall not be mentioned in cases involving apparent want of chastity unless the woman is a prostitute or the case presents other aspects of importance. In respect to all other crimes and offenses, women stand on the same plane as men so far as publication of news in the average paper is concerned. Possibly the average reporter exercises a little more care-in some cases his paper instructs him to do so-in dealing with news about women. This, of course, is an unjustifiable position, for he should exercise the maximum of care in dealing with news about all persons.

In the other class of details commonly omitted are included such matters as the names of poisons used in committing suicide, the specific methods employed by burglars in executing their crimes, and the salacious details of abnormal crimes. The reason for the suppression of these facts is simply that they are likely to be suggestive to the psychopathic or the criminal. It has been found that the publication of stories of the use of a certain poison for committing suicide is followed by a large number of suicides in the same manner. The evidence as to criminal acts is less definite.

That not all newspapers suppress details of this sort is evident. For instance, a metropolitan daily purported to tell how a young burglar had bungled in committing his first job and how he might have avoided capture①. Presumably in this case the young reporter was merely anxious to air his supposititious knowledge of the tactics of burglars or to be amusing and the item slipped past the copy desk unchanged.

Certain newspapers lay great stress on language as an ethical matter. The writer knows of one newspaper which flagrantly colors its news, in some cases completely misrepresenting the facts, but which makes a great point of barring from its columns all profanity, even such words as "damn." Many newspapers, in an effort to appear moral, use words which the middle class assumes represent better ethical standards. For example, a woman is always said to "disrobe," never "undress," although the latter word is both colloquially and in literature practically universal. Such practices simply represent a confusion of morality and convention.

About the foregoing matters definite rules can be laid down. So far as real progress is concerned, they are relatively unimportant. They are the more trivial matters of news.

In the larger matters of news no set rules can be laid down. As matter falls into more definite classes and is more efficiently recorded, the problem of suppression will grow less. A sound ethical rule that the newspaper can follow at present with reference to suppressing matter is never to suppress any matter because of its connection with a private interest, because of its unpleasantness to the editor, because of doubt as to whether the public should have the information, or for any other reason than a conviction that it is of less importance than other news available. In the balancing of the news is a great test of the journalist's objectivity of vision. It is here in particular that the journalist who is full of opinion instead of fact will unconsciously betray his public. Against this no. one can guard him care-

---

① See story, Tried to Rob Uncle's Home, The Kansas City Star, February 25, 1920.

fully, for there is no one but is prone to lapses from objectivity.

Additional Readings

Bennett. What the Public Wants.

symposium:Giving the Public What is Wants, in Thorpe's

The Coming Newspaperman,pp. 223—247.

Willian Rockhill Nelson: The Story of a Man, a Newspaper, and a City. pp. 115—133.

Lippmann, Public opinion, pp. 338—357.

VII   The Principle of Objectivity Applied: Sensationalism

Sensationalism in the press, particularly the daily press, presents as acute practical problems to the editor as does any phase of giving due proportion to the news. Sensationalism is in part a phase of proportion in the news, for if it does nothing else, it emphasizes certain news facts to the exclusion or the minimizing of others. Again, the problems of sensationalism involve the business interests of the newspaper even more directly than does any problem of news suppression, for the readers of not a few newspapers, trained to care for sensational journalism, have little taste for anything better. There also is involved in sensationalism the ethical question as to the desirability of "playing up" criminal, vicious, or sordid sides of life.

Certain common factors of sensationalism are simple matters. The manufacture of news, misrepresentation, coloring, are to be condemned outright. They are as reprehensible when used for sensational purposes, merely to titillate the nerves of readers, as when used for the definite purpose of conveying false information about important affairs. There is no ethical difference between lying about a divorce case in order to arouse the sensational interest of readers and lying about a strike in order to protect private interests. Direct misrepresentation for the purpose of being sensational is not so common as it once was, but it is still too common.

The war with Spain in 1898 was to a considerable extent attributable to the efforts of sensational newspapers. Their desire for war was apparently based neither on a conviction that the United States had a righteous cause nor on a desire to increase the profits or prestige of America. Their desire seemed to be mainly to write good stories, which a war would enable them to do. In July, 1919, according to the Chicago Commission on Race Relations, The Herald-Examiner published a story about several thousand men breaking into the Eighth Regiment armory to seize guns and ammunition, with police action and casualties. The Commission states that there were no weapons in the armory, that it was not broken into, though some windows were broken, and that there was no such lash with the police[1]. Other Chicago papers were criticized by the Commission for sensational and inflammatory reports of the rioting that occurred in the summer of 1919 between negroes and whites.[2] While the difficulty of obtaining accurate news at the time is recognized, the increased responsibility of the press in periods of popular hysteria is stress.

Not infrequently misrepresentation is the fault of reporters who, in the absence of instructions from their paper or even counter to such instructions, write sensational stories in the hope, often justified, that it will enhance their value to the paper. Such reporters have no sense of honor, and their superiors too often excuse themselves by laying the whole

---

[1] The Negro in Chicago, p. 29.
[2] Idem, pp. 25—33.

blame upon the reporter while accepting the reporter's story.

The invasion of privacy for sensational reasons is another practice which cannot be condoned. It is necessary, of course, to consider carefully what proper privacy is. The young reporter is often too willing to refrain from writing justifiable news because he is persuaded by some person of prominence that it is none of the paper's business. Matters which are of importance to the public welfare are the public's business and the reporter has a right to obtain them in any honorable way he can. He is under no obligation to wait until some interested person has used these facts for his private gain and has then determined to release them officially to the press. Indeed, he is under obligation not to wait until that time, provided he can get the facts in an honorable manner with a certainty that they are facts. Most of the facts which are of concern to the public, persons directly concerned with them are unwilling to reveal or are willing to reveal only equivocally or inadequately. No one objects to the revelation of such facts except those who desire to conceal from the public those facts to which it is entitled.

The invasion of privacy to which objection is justifiably made by all right-thinking persons is that which drags into the limelight of publicity persons, particularly women, who are indirectly connected with news of sensational interest. For example, a young woman of doubtful reputation is murdered. The authorities announce that they plan to question a wealthy and prominent married man who was intimately acquainted with her. Under pressure from the press the authorities reveal the name of this man. So far the press has performed a service. The public is entitled to know who this man is and the authorities are properly compelled to act as representatives of the people and not as private inquisitors seeking to protect individuals because of their wealth and position. Following this, however, newspapers seek out the wife of this man, attempt to subject her to questioning which can have no possible concern to the public, even spy upon her home to such an extent that it is necessary for her to post guards to obtain ordinary privacy. The papers publish what they can obtain about her, including her photograph. The purpose of this is purely to appeal to the morbid and sentimental curiosity of a certain group of readers. In doing this the newspaper has deserted its function as a purveyor of accurate news and has become a cheap society gossip. It is a happy augury that an incident of precisely this character was vigorously condemned recently by *the Editor and Publisher*, which represents the best newspaper standards of the country[①].

The practice complained of, however, is common even among newspapers which are not ultra-sensational. The publication of photographs of relatives of criminals, the use of interviews with persons whose only connection with news is through some other individual, and many similar practices may be observed in the press every day.

So much for such factors in sensationalism as are not justified from any point of view. Nobody justifies them, not even those who perpetrate them.

Eliminating misrepresentation of all kinds and invasion of privacy, the problem of sensationalism resolves itself largely into a question of balance. As has been pointed out before, it is utterly unjustifiable to carry out the process of news selection either in the paper as a whole or in individual stories in such a way as to conceal from the people facts of importance to their welfare. Even without any intention of concealment, however, a newspaper may adopt widely varying policies with reference to selecting news.

The newspaper which appeals to intellectual people makes its selection primarily on the basis of importance. At the opposite pole are the ul-

---

① And They Called It Journalism, Editor and Publisher. March 31, 1923, p. 34.

tra-sensational newspapers which make their selection on the basis purely of interest-what is popularly termed "human interest," the same interest that causes people to turn to popular novels and to see melodrama on the stage. The development of the theory of "human interest" as a criterion in news selection came chiefly with the building of large circulations by sensational newspapers, particularly the earlier Hearst papers, in the great cities. These papers built their initial circulations among groups of the population which previously had not read any newspaper. These people belonged to the working class and were not more than a generation or two removed from Europe. They had little knowledge of political, economic, or social problems in the United States. Their interests were narrowed to their homes, their shops, and a few familiar haunts. A sensational criminal trial aroused their attention much more than a war between Japan and Russia or a steel strike in Pennsylvania. Give them what they want, the newspaper publishers decreed, and thus the "human interest" newspaper developed.

While it may be said in behalf of the sensational news-papers that they educated a relatively ignorant group of the population in the practice of newspaper reading, it is also true that the sensational press has influenced every section of American journalism. W. R. Nelson, the veteran publisher of The Kansas City Star, used to assert that the trouble with most editors is that they allow Mr. Hearst to run their papers.

The influence of the sensational journals on other sections of the press has been most marked in two respects. One of these has been overemphasized by critics to an extreme extent. That is the development of the large headline. This does not necessarily have any ethical import whatsoever, and care must always be taken to distinguish between ethics and taste. The only possible harm that the large headline may intrinsically do, from an ethical stand point, is to crowd out news that otherwise would be printed. The large headline was devised by sensational newspapers to attract readers. It is used today for the same purpose by all newspapers that use it at all. It possesses particular commercial value for street and newsstand sales. It is not necessarily a mark of sensationalism. Some newspapers that are very conservative in their investigating and writing of news use large headlines. Some other newspapers that treat stories in a highly sensational manner put small head-lines over them-in some instances for the probable purpose of impressing the conservative-minded but ignorant reader, who because of the early use of scare-heads by "yellow" journals draws conclusions as to the accuracy of the story in inverse proportion to the size of the head. So far as indicating the relative importance of news stories is concerned, this can be accomplished by the relative size of the heads, irrespective of the actual type sizes employed. It may be questioned, moreover, whether indication of the relative importance of news stories is really desirable, since it constitutes essentially an interpretation on the part of the editor and removes the reader one step further from strict objective facts. Contemporary readers, accustomed to spending but a small amount of time on their newspaper, [1] would doubtless be unready, however, for this practice to be changed.

The other form of influence of sensational journalism on the American press in general is much more significant, although less attention has been paid to it by critics. That influence is in the direction of emphasizing interest rather than importance as a test of news. In doing this, the sensational newspapers simply appeal to an ancient and powerful instinct. As John Macy says, "Everybody likes a story, and there are only a few souls in the

---

[1] An investigation conducted by Walter Dill Scott indicated that the typical Chicago business or professional man spent fifteen minutes a day reading local newspaper. See Scott, the psychology of advertising, pp. 375－394.

world who yearn at breakfast for information." ①The sinister side of the situation is found in the fact that sensational newspapers and the other journals that followed their example merely took, for the most part, the stories that lay ready to their hands, which meant the trivial, the purely entertaining, the ephemeral. The effect of this practice is seen in the manner in which the Dempsey-Gibbons fight and the convention of the National Education Association were covered by the press of the United States in the summer of 1923. The newspapers of representative American cities on July 5 devoted the following number of column inches to the two events respectively: ②

	Fight	Convention
New York	1,425 3/4	93 1/2
Chicago	1,353 1/2	1 3/4
Washington	405	8

What American newspapers might have done in the past, and what they may still do, is to make the really important so thoroughly intelligible that it cannot fail to be of interest. That this can be done is shown by the experience of Science Service in making scientific material, usually considered the height of dullness, interesting to the average reader. It is not easy to make the important intelligible, and perhaps the chief harm that has been done by sensationalism consists in its regularly having taken the easiest way to the interests of readers. If the practice grows of making the important interesting, the ultimate influence of sensational journalism will

---

① *Civilization in the United States*, p. 45

② Figures from *The Christian Science Monitor*, July 6, 1923. In Boston *The Monitor* and *The Transcript* devoted respectively 0 and 25 1/2 inches to the fight, 227 and 40 inches to the convention. The Post, The Globe, and The Herald ignored the convention but gave a total of 942 1/2 inches to the fight.

prove a happy one, in that it will be found to have been the indirect cause of creating an interest in the important in the large body of persons who read only for interest and entertainment.

In justice to the sensational press, one should recognize the fact that it has done some good in stimulating reporting. It has made investigation by reporters a part of the day's work. While the investigations undertaken by sensational newspapers have not always been of the right character, they have shown the opportunity and duty of the press as an investigating force. On no paper of consequence is the reporter any longer merely a listener.

There is further to be considered the fact of sensationalism in its influence upon the ethical standards and practices of newspaper readers. The treatment of the news of crime and vice affords a fair opportunity to examine different standards of policy and practice on the part of the press as respects sensationalism. At one extreme stand those who would exclude all, or practically all, news of crime and vice on the ground that it can do no possible good to the readers to have these things brought to their attention. This view finds few supporters among members of the profession of journalism. Its only newspaper representative in this country is The Christian Science Monitor, which, moreover, does not absolutely exclude all news of crime. Furthermore, this paper differs from other newspapers in being not primarily a local but an international paper. The Christian Science Monitor, the bulk of whose circulation is outside the vicinity of Boston, where it is published, stands in a relation wholly different from the ordinary newspaper whose circulation, even in the case of the most conspicuous American papers, is confined largely to the trading area of its city. Next there is a group of newspapers, small in number, represented by such a paper as The Boston Evening Transcript, which deal very briefly with news of crime. A sensational murder in Boston received in The Transcript two inches of type under a two-deck head, as against more than three columns, under a streamer head and illustrated by two photographs, in a sensational Boston newspaper. It is argued in behalf of The Transcript's way of handling news of crime that the public is entitled to the news and that it is a safeguard to the ethical welfare of the community and the administration of justice that publicity be given to crime, but that extensive details of crime are demoralizing and debasing.

The bulk of the larger newspapers of the country belong to two other groups, one of them giving news of crime in detail but balancing it with other news to varying extent, the other "playing up" the news of crime with sensational and often suggestive details. In behalf of both of these practices and more particularly the latter, the argument is advanced that while the prevention and punishment of crime are the responsibility of the public the public must be startled into attention to crime. It is to be feared that in most instances this argument is a rationalization invented to account for playing up crime in order to appeal to the morbid sensibilities of the reader, of the writer, or of both. In cases where the newspaper might perform a service by publishing detailed news of crime, it commonly destroys its effectiveness by adopting the psychology and clamor of the mob. For example, when sex crimes occur, the average newspaper and the average reader shout such terms as "fiend" and "degeneracy." They feel the common repugnance to the unnatural or the abnormal, and see in persons guilty of sex crimes a willful moral guilt. As a matter of fact, sex crimes are almost invariably the result of definitely recognized psychopathies.

It is an astounding fact that in the various trials in which Harry K. Thaw was involved and concerning which certain newspapers published such revolting details that they were threatened with criminal prosecution, no newspaper or magazine, to the writer's knowledge, published a sound, understandable explanation of the sexual psychopathy with which Thaw was and is afflicted, or discussed the means of guarding against the menace of this condition in human life. Again, in all the stories that appeared in Kansas City papers in 1921 concerning a "vice ring" in that city, there was line after line of suggestive material that might easily cause a boy or girl to wish to delve further into the type of vice represented, but there was not a line in any newspaper in that city that gave a rational explanation of the sexual inversion with which the leaders of this ring were afflicted, or the proper psychiatric method of handling such cases. Without such explanation, the news was really incomplete.

Whether sensational news in general is to any considerable extent promotive of crime or vice is a debatable question, with the direct evidence largely negative. On the other hand, it is often argued by moralists that sensational news produces a general weakening of the moral fiber and a general lowering of ethical standards. In opposition to this point of view, it is pointed out that such weakening and lowering, if they exist, are as probably the causes as the results of sensationalism. Again, it must be borne in mind that much of the objection to sensationalism is esthetic rather than ethical, even though considered by the objectors to be the latter.

It is evident that sensational news crowds out other news, often of much greater importance. Not only the emphasis on crime and vice, but the attention to trivialities, characteristic of sensational journalism, means less space for significant news. If a paper devotes a column to describing the contents of forty-seven trunks of clothing owned by a musical comedy star or to telling how firemen spent half an hour rescuing a cat marooned on a telephone pole, international and national news is bound to suffer. The newspaper, of course, must be interesting if it is to attract readers, and unless it attracts readers it serves no social purpose. On the other hand, it must convey facts of importance if it is to be of public value. How far the public is naturally devoted to the trivial and sensational, and to what extent it has been turned in these directions by newspaper efforts, is an open question, as is also the problem of how far any given newspaper can go in eliminating the trivial and continue to please the general reader, to whom the average newspaper must make its appeal. There is an occasional city in which there is a sufficient clientele of well-educated, cultured readers to support an almost purely informative newspaper. This is not true of the average American city or town. There are few places in which a paper like The Boston Evening Transcript, with no sensational news, with a circulation slightly in excess of 30,000, and with an advertising rate of 20 cents per agate line, could be successfully run.

On the other hand, it is not necessary to maintain a sensational newspaper in order to compete successfully with the sensational press. This is merely the easiest thing to do. The public prefers the material with which the sensational press deals because it is easy to understand and because it furnishes an emotional outlet, through its human interest. Human interest and emotional quality can, however, be put into news of importance. The relation of the important to everyday life can be made clear. The reason why this is not generally done is that most authorities on subjects of importance are dull speakers and writers, while few newspapers have reporters or editors who can so translate this material as to make an intellectual and emotional appeal to the general public. The growth of The Kansas City Star, one of the most striking in American journalism, was due largely to its owner's policy of selecting from other publications matters of importance and at the same time of public interest. Under this policy the paper, largely devoid of sensationalism, competed successfully with highly sensational publications and maintained a larger subscription list and a heavier run of advertising.

In the small town the problem of sensationalism does not enter to any considerable extent. The small town newspaper is tending to become more and more a local publication. Its telegraph service, if any, is meager. Readers who desire the sensational obtain it in metropolitan dailies published in a city nearby. Little that is of itself sensational occurs in the average small town. When it does happen, it is not likely to be sensationally treated. This is due partly to lack of training in sensational writing on the part of local newspapermen. It is in part due to lack of public demand for the sensational. Moreover, the individual in the small town is likely to see the importance to himself of matters of public interest in the community. Public attention, so far as the newspapers are concerned, is therefore centered its matters of some significance. Furthermore, the backyard gossip, which occupies a considerable place in sensational dailies in metropolitan centers is retailed in the small town by word of mouth-which of course is no improvement over its publication by a news-paper except that the latter practice gives it a seemingly more vital relation to the social structure.

Unquestionably, the tide of sensationalism has begun to recede. The demand for a saner ideal for the press is manifest among both newspapermen and readers. For ex-ample, the women of Los Angeles started early in 1923 a movement for less emphasis on crime and scandal in the newspapers of southern California.[①] As an instance of the attitude of editors and publishers may be cited the resolution adopted by the Oregon Editorial Association in 1922:

"Whereas, we believe that the newspaper profession is one of the most honorable, the most influential, and most important of the professions and should therefore be the most careful of all of them in maintaining high ideals of service, promoting a high consideration for public and private morals; and

---

① See news story, *300,000 California Citizens Demand Cleaner Newspapers*, and editorial, The Call for *Clean Journalism*, *The Christian Science Monitor*, January 6, 1923.

"Whereas, we are convinced that too much stress laid upon scandals, crimes, and stories of immorality has a bad influence upon the public mind, especially upon those minds that are young and impressionable; therefore, be it

"Resolved, that while we recognize the duty devolving upon a newspaper to publish the news, in reference to these matters, yet we urge that salacious details be not overemphasized and we especially urge the various press associations to refrain from unduly emphasizing this class of news in their dispatches."

Additional Readings

Chicago Commission on Race Relations, The Negro in Chicago, pp. 436—594.

Street. The Truth About the Newspaper. Chicago Tribune. July 25, 1999.

Fenton, The Influence of Newspaper Presentation, upon, the Growth of Crime and Other Anti-Social Activity. American Journal of Sociology 16:342—371,538—564.

Alger, Sensational Journalism and the Law, in Bleyer's The Profession of Journalism, pp. 167—180.

Lloyd, Newspaper Conscience-A Study in Half-Truths. American Journal of Sociology 27:197—210,

Gladden, Tainted Journalism:Good and Bad, in Thorpe's The Coming Newspaper,pp. 27—50.

And They Called It Journalism. Editor and Publisher. March 31, 1923,p- 34.

Scott. The Psychology of Advertising, pp. 375—394

The Call for Clean Journalism and 300,000 California Citizens Demand Cleaner Newspapers. The Christian Science Monitor, January 6,

1923.

Williams, Presidential Address, in *The Press Congress of the World in Hawaii*, pp. 70—77.

VIII The Principle of Objectivity Applied: Editorial Leadership

With the emphasis that has been laid on objectivity as the primary ideal of the newspaper, the question naturally arises: Is there no place in modern journalism for editorial leadership?

Few journalists or students of public opinion would now maintain that a newspaper is under any obligation to furnish editorial guidance of any sort to its readers. They hold that the ideal of molding public opinion has been largely supplanted by the ideal of disseminating objective facts. Some, perhaps, chiefly among the older men, look back with regret to the old days. Others, holding very modern, realistic views, question whether any molding of public opinion is desirable in a country maintaining a popular government.

The majority, while not regarding editorial guidance as by any means the most significant function of the press, maintain that it still occupies a place among the proper functions of journalism. Few papers are ready to abandon it. There are, however, a number of country weeklies without editorial pages, and there is occasionally a country weekly with an editor of sufficient courage to publish an editorial only when he feels he has something definitely worth saying to his community. Practically no newspapers of metropolitan dimensions are without editorial pages.

The influence exerted by the press through editorial comment appears to be diminishing. Observers point to elections in New York City in which candidates were elected against the opposition of all the newspapers or against the opposition of all but two or three. They point to similar conditions in Kansas City. They note that the two most recently elected governors of Oklahoma and Kansas were chosen against the advice of an overwhelming majority of the newspapers. No one who has taken account of conditions like these can believe that the editorial influence of the press is as potent as its wide distribution might make plausible.

One reason for the waning editorial influence of the press is the fact that the public has become convinced that in controversial matters, especially partisan politics, the news furnished by the press is not dependable. The public reasons that if the press will lie in its news columns the reasoning in the editorial columns cannot be depended upon. It is true that considerations of this sort do not affect the great body of partisan voters, who cling to their own party with an inertia which nothing can overcome. It does, however, influence the independent voters, who are almost always a minority but who are in sufficient numbers in most places to hold the balance of power in elections.

A further reason for the defeat of the press in elections and the waning public confidence which this indicates is the fact that the press is disposed to critical comment chiefly at election times. This convinces the public that the presses is interested in winning elections rather than in advocating policies of public benefit. A newspaper which steadily, in season and out of season, advocates the policies in which it believes and calls attention to acts of public officials for and against these policies, has a much better chance of being influential with American voters.

It is often asserted that the editorial page of a newspaper is less read than was formerly the case. If one considers the proportion of readers who consult the editorial page, the statement is true; if one considers the actual number, it is untrue. Early newspapers were taken by a small minority of the public. At the close of the War of 1812 no New York newspaper had a circulation of more than 2,000.① In those days practically all the subscribers read every- thing in the paper. The paper was small enough and subscribers had leisure enough to permit of this. The news-paper readers of that day, however, represented an extremely small minority of the voting public, although probably they had greater influence than a similar group would have today. Today practically every literate citizen living where a daily paper is readily available reads one. The majority give little or no attention to the editorial page. The common estimate is that twenty per cent of the readers of a metropolitan daily read the editorials, while a somewhat larger proportion take some interest in the editorial page as a whole. They may care for the humorous column, for the correspondence department, or for some other editorial page feature. It still remains true that the more intellectual and influential persons read the editorials, although they are tending to accept the guidance of the weekly journals of opinion rather than that of the newspapers. The number of these readers in proportion to the population is much greater than it was one hundred or even fifty years ago. The editorial department of the paper is getting as wide a hearing as ever and, for the most part, among precisely those persons who are independent in their voting and their views. In an effort still further to enlarge the circulation of readers of editorial matter, a number of newspapers have a-

---

① Lee, History of American Journalism, p. 142.

dopted the policy of ' publishing editorials on the front page, either regularly, as with the columns contributed by Arthur Brisbane to the Hearst newspapers, or occasionally, as with the editorial published on the front page in The Kansas City Star at times when the staff of the paper feels that there is an issue which deserves this position.

A number of papers are publishing signed columns ex-pressing personal editorial convictions. It is somewhat questionable whether the signed editorial exerts any more influence than the unsigned one. Precisely those papers which use signed editorials are well known to the public to represent specific private ownership. Everyone who would be influenced by the signature at the bottom of an editorial knows that the Hearst newspapers represent the personality and views of Mr. Hearst, even though they may be technically owned by a corporation. Even if they did not know this fact, the probability is that the public would not be any more influenced by the signature of a writer, unless he was nationally known, than by an expression of opinion on the part of the paper. It is true that newspaper editors, if they signed their editorials, would become better known among the reading public and this would probably be advantageous for newspapers. Certainly it would be desirable, from the reader's point of view and probably the news-paper also, to print the names of the editorial council at the masthead of the paper. The journals of opinion now do this, with much enhancement of prestige thereby.

There are certain advantages, however, in a newspaper's speaking as an institution. The larger metropolitan dailies all have editorial councils which meet daily. At these meetings all possible subjects for editorials are discussed, and it is decided what editorials shall be written. Except on the most highly technical matters the general position to be taken is also determined, after considerable discussion. The decision may be made by vote or, more commonly, by the official head of the paper. Assignments of editorials to be written are then made to the various editorial writers. No writer is ever asked to write an editorial which does violence to his own convictions. If the writer to whom a particular editorial would normally be assigned feels that he cannot conscientiously write it in accordance with the decision of the editorial council, it is assigned to some one else. Such a situation, of course, rarely arises, because the members of the editorial council of a newspaper are likely to have similar views; the news-paper employs men who are in general accord with its policy. A conservative newspaper has an editorial council made up of conservatives; and in like manner, the editorial council of a liberal journal is regularly made up of liberals. The editorials resulting from an editorial council, while they are written by individuals, do not represent merely individual views, but these views modified and added to by the convictions of other members of the council.

On the smaller papers, where all the editorial writing is done by one person, that person may come into conflict often enough with the publisher of the paper unless, as rarely happens, he and the publisher have precisely the same notions of public policies. On a British newspaper the editor would be supreme. ① On an American newspaper, unfortunately, this is not the case. But any editorial writer had better resign than write what he considers to be false. By writing editorials in which he does not believe, he betrays his employer by turning out copy that does not have the ring of conviction, and the public by misrepresenting what he conceives to be the actual situation.

On the still smaller papers, where the publisher writes his own editorials, he is responsible only to his own conscience as a public servant. In most cases he is insufficiently qualified to discuss national or international

---

① This is the time-honored practice. But, in contrast, see Belloc's The Free Press.

issues intelligently, but he may effectively lead his community in community affairs. In contrast to metropolitan dailies, a small-town daily or weekly is often the greatest single influence in the community. Here are both responsibility and privilege.

The editorial writer, on whatever paper, should have as his primary function clarifying facts and helping readers to draw dependable conclusions from the facts. More and more is it being recognized that the editorial is an interpreter more than an advocate. It combines in one the parts of public prosecutor, public defender, and judge What a responsibility rests upon it, therefore, not to misrepresent in the slightest degree any fact which it may have obtained from the news or elsewhere and to make use of no specious arguments in drawing its conclusions. That such arguments are used by editors, there is no doubt. On the other hand, in many cases they are employed unconsciously. The writer is misled by his prejudices, his fears, and his hopes, or perhaps he is incapable, as many reasonably competent writers are, of sound, logical reasoning.

In many instances an integral part of the newspaper's editorial influence is found in so-called "editorial campaigns." These, because of the iteration that they involve, produce more apparent results, at least for the time being, than do editorial efforts in general. Examples are the crusade of The Chicago Tribune for a sane Fourth of July, begun by James Keeley in 1899 and brought to fruition in recent years in the all-but-universal ban on private use of fireworks [1]; and the campaign of *The New York Tribune* to stamp out fraudulent advertising, which was not carried on vigorously for a sufficient time to bring as notable results.[2] Like other editorial

---

[1] See The W. G. N., p. 60, for details.
[2] The methods of the campaign are discussed in the Tribune pamphlet, How It Works, and examples may be found by consulting the files of The Ad-Visor column in The Tribune in 1914—1916.

leadership, such campaigns in general do not constitute an ethical obligation of the press; a newspaper is free to be a "crusading newspaper" or not, as it chooses.

It is not true, however, that there are no circumstances under which the fundamentals of a campaign are strictly matters of news and consequently facts which a newspaper is ethically bound to present to its readers. This was the situation when The New York Times, not normally a "crusading newspaper," exposed the Tweed Ring in 1870—71. Less obviously a matter of news, though still very close to it, was the expose by *The Detroit News* of fake race track gambling in 1922. It must be apparent here that the writer holds a somewhat broader view of news than is held by some critics, notably Mr. Walter Lippmann, who maintains that "the function of news is [exclusively] to signalize an event."① While there is much justice in his contention that news is too often regarded merely as another word for truth and consequently impossible demands are made of the press, hardly any journalist of adequate experience in dealing with news would be willing to restrict the term as Mr. Lippmann does. The practiced journalist realizes that at times the absence of an event is as important news as an event itself. In the case of the Tweed Ring, the campaign of *The New York Times* really began with publication of the fact that the financial accounts of the city were being concealed in spite of the law making them public property. The failure of the municipal officials to publish any financial statement was, in the opinion of the writer, news. A critic with Mr. Lippmann's point of view would doubtless maintain that no news existed until some citizen should, for instance, bring mandamus proceedings to compel the opening of the books to the public. With the multiplicity of efforts made to conceal from the press what is obviously news, it seems

---

① *Public Opinion*, p. 358

hardly practicable for the reporter to desert the investigative function. If he does desert it, the published news will become more and more inconsequential.

In the fact that matters commonly assigned to the province of the "crusade" are often closely associated with news, there is an element of danger to sound ethical practice.

Whenever an institution, such as the press, or, for that matter, an individual, embarks on a campaign for what is conceived to be for human betterment, there appears the tendency to emphasize facts that support the desired end, to minimize facts that seem to oppose it, and even to falsify the actual situation altogether. At present these practices are evident in newspapers which are campaigning for the abandonment or reduction of prohibition and likewise in journals which are advocating "bone-dry" measures. In any campaign in which it is interested, and particularly in any which it has itself inaugurated, a newspaper must walk delicately and circumspectly if it is not to be condemned as a follower of the doctrine that the end justifies the means.

Apart from news matters, the ethical position which one will take on campaigns by a newspaper will depend largely on his views on social institutions generally. The journalist is likely to see in such service a certain danger to the supremacy of news in the function of the press. He has observed that papers which devote great 'attention to crusades commonly devote correspondingly less space and attention to news. Even if campaigns did not interfere with news in this respect, they would nevertheless tend, he feels, to distract the citizens attention from so digesting objective facts as to be able to accomplish for himself, by ballot and other legitimate means, what the newspaper attempts to do for him.

Loose, sentimental idealism, both within and without the newspaper office, is inclined naturally toward a vast number of campaigns and a vast amount of special service of all sorts. "Anything that is for the public good should be done by the press," represents fairly this undiscriminating attitude. The sensational press has emphasized campaigns and other special service to readers, partly, no doubt, for commercial reasons, partly because of a desire to put "human interest" into the newspaper, to make it, in the words of a prominent exemplar of this type of journalism, "a paper with a heart and a soul." It cannot be denied that special service does put readers into human touch with the newspaper. The same is true of any conspicuous editorial leadership. The development of such a situation is useful to the publication both in giving weight to its editorial utterances and in establishing credence for its news. The average person takes his views, and even his "facts," from those whom he admires. As Dr. Sigmund Freud says:

"Faith repeats the history of its own origin; it is a derivative of love and at first requires no arguments. When they are offered by a beloved person, arguments may later be admitted and subjected to critical reflection. Arguments without such support avail nothing, and never mean anything in life to most persons. Man's intellect is accessible only so far as he is capable of libidinous occupation with an object." ①

The fact here brought out should make the newspaper which has attained public confidence and affection by special service or any other means, doubly careful not to violate that confidence by misrepresentation of news or specious editorial argument.

Closely allied to editorial leadership on the part of a newspaper, one is likely to find the expression—as distinguished from the molding—of public opinion. The correspondence column, by whatever name called, offers this opportunity. It serves a less important function than many suppose, for

---

① A General Introduction to Psychoanalysis, p. 385

contributions come to it from an extremely small minority of the public, not infrequently those whose opinions are highly colored by the fact that their personal interests are involved in the points at issue.

In the handling of letters submitted for publication the honest editor is scrupulously careful. He is under no obligation to print a letter because some reader writes it. He has the right to use his own judgment. He is under obligation, however, to correct any error which he has made and which has been brought by a reader to his attention. He is unfair to his readers if, in publishing letters in his correspondence department, he does not give fair balance to the various sides represented. It is wholly unethical for him to publish numerous letters which commend his own point of view and to omit those letters which differ from that point of view.

Still more unethical is it for an editor so to edit or head a letter that it will convey an impression opposite to or even different from that which the writer intended. It is frequently complained that editors do this. For example, Professor Alfred H. Lloyd calls attention to an incident in which he himself figured:

"Not long ago I sent a communication to a paper of different political views from my own. The letter was an experiment. It called attention to a certain public man's opportunism and inconsistencies, quoting his speeches at different times. I wondered if the paper would publish the letter and face the exposure. It did publish the letter, but with saving headlines, and I have to add, with editorial omissions of essential sentences, so that a shifting and truth-careless politician was made to seem a patriot! I was, of course, helpless. The paper had a right, at least a legal right, so long as newspapers are not common carriers or public servants, not to publish at all, but it had no right either to its headlines or the editorial changes."[①]

---

① The American Journal of Sociology. vol. 27, p. 03.

Not infrequently, of course, a letter containing material that a newspaper would like to publish is too long. Condensation is always dangerous. Elisions are less dangerous if made with care and honesty. No newspaper may justifiably cut a letter without indicating the places at which it made elisions. The danger in honest elision is that unconsciously the editor may omit significant material and thus commit an unethical act, or may omit passages which are not really significant but which the writer of the letter thinks are, and may thus gain with that writer and among his friends a reputation for unethical conduct, which is just as detrimental to the standing of a newspaper as unethical conduct itself. A plan sometimes suggested is for the editor to send back to the writer any letter that he proposes to shorten, with a statement of the omissions to be made, and allow the writer to decide whether he wishes it to be published in this form. Objection has been raised to this plan on the ground of impracticability.

A newspaper is often enabled to add to its circulation and general financial strength by the more spectacular forms of editorial leadership or even of representing and enforcing public opinion. One is not justified in concluding even from the exclusively financial standpoint, however, that "a journalist can never succeed unless he is fathering popular or moral causes."[1] The recent history of such newspapers as *The Boston Transcript* and *The New York Times* proves the contrary. Even if financial strength can be most readily obtained in this way, it is too dearly purchased in case it interferes in any way with the function of the newspaper as a disseminator of objective facts.

Additional Readings

Villard, *Some Newspapers and Newspapermen*.
Davis, *History of The New York Times*, pp. 81 — 116.
O'Brien, *The Story of The Sun*, pp. 304—312.

Heaton, *The Story of a Page*.

The *W. G. N.*, pp. 53—79.

Scott, *The Manchester Guardian: A Century of History*.

The Race Track Graft. Pamphlet of *The Detroit News*.

Lippmann, *Public Opinion*, pp. 358—365.

Leupp, *The Waning Power of the Press*, in Bleyer's *The Profession of Journalism*, pp. 30—51

IX Setting Professional Standards: Legal Measures

Whenever any scandal or even unpleasantness arises to ruffle the composure of the average American citizen as to government, civilization, or any such matter, he promptly fixes upon some individual or group of individuals whom he holds to be responsible, and asserts indignantly, "They ought to be put in jail." Or, in the event he realizes that there is no legal means whereby the culprits may be hurried to prison, he is prone to start his discussion, "There ought to be a law."

The faith of the American people in law is a problem for the psychologist rather than the journalist. That it exists as one of the facts of life in this country is not to be denied and must be faced by every public or quasi-public institution.

With this reliance of the public upon law it is not surprising that various laws have been proposed for the purpose of improving the press. Laws already in existence relate chiefly to libel, to obscene writing, and to the exclusion of certain types of advertising. ① In general these, as interpreted by the courts, are fair to the newspaper and to the public. The principal exception is in the case of laws relating to obscene writing, which have been stretched in some instances to cover works of great literary significance, but this has affected magazine and book rather than newspaper publishers. Contempt proceedings against newspaper workers by sensitive judges have been unfair to the persons directly involved and have at the same time rendered it difficult for the press to perform its rightful function.

Further proposals for legal restriction of journalism are intended to compel newspapers to be accurate and fair by process of law. The most drastic of such suggestions is a plan devised to secure "compulsory veracity" in newspapers. The proposer of this plan is Edward Paul, who advocates his plan in the following words:

"Compulsory veracity in the newspapers is no more an infringement on our democratic rights than compulsory purity in foods. In maintaining that a pure news act would be interfering with the 'freedom' of the press, the press leads us to infer that Democracy is more interested in a healthy body than in a healthy mind. A healthy mind is dangerous to Democracy only in so far as that Democracy is shielding a minority in the enjoyment of privileges it is not worthy of enjoying. A healthier public mind would send more of such men to Washington as are now making things disagreeable for the packers and for those interests that thrive on the intimate friendship of railroads. The people having gained the vote, the last resort of Privilege is to deceive the voter, as it did last November. We have almost reached the *caveat lector* stage of social evolution. "It is of considerable importance that steps be taken before many years to bring about compulsory veracity

---

① 1For a detailed discussion of laws governing the press, see Hales, *The Law of the Press*.

in the newspapers. The pressure of economic circumstances may at any time make the masses aware of the fact that they cannot trust the organs for the dissemination of news. When they realize that, they are likely to inquire what sort of government it is which permits the overwhelming majority of the people to be tricked, while that majority, engaged in labor, has its back turned."[1]

To obtain absolute accuracy a law is proposed that "whoever shall publish in a newspaper or other periodical a statement willfully misrepresenting the facts, or shall publish as facts statements known to them to be untrue or erroneous through gross carelessness, shall be guilty of a misdemeanor."

In addition to this law there would be reserved in every paper a column for a public literary defender "elected by the people, who could give due importance to buried news and supply the point of view frequently omitted."

"With this system in vogue," asserts the editor of The Arbitrator, the paper responsible for the plan, "it would be possible to retain the freedom of the press. For there should be no objection to the appearance of any startling opinions of the editor, provided the correct ideas were given equal prominence in the same paper.

If the policy of the paper was to oppose the conscription of men or of wealth, every issue could also contain the reason why such opinions were untenable and objectionable in the eyes of the government official answerable to the people."

"Another way," this writer goes on to say, "would be to have all complaints against the press submitted to various local commissions ap-

---

[1] This and the following quotations are from The Arbitrator for July, 1919 (Vol. 2, No. 2).

pointed for the purpose of punishing by fine, suspension, etc., the periodical which printed lies, or of compelling the offender to print a denial in a prominent column. Such a commission would not only relieve the courts, but the term of office and personnel could be so arranged as to secure justice for the public." While to the practicing journalist or the careful student of journalism such suggestions are obviously absurd, they are gaining adherents constantly among those who do not understand newspaper conditions and who are prone to grasp at legal solutions of all problems. The proposed law making it a misdemeanor to misrepresent the facts might be employed effectively in cases where there is certainty of record but where reporters disregarded the facts and published invented material of their own. This rarely happens, however, except through carelessness. Reports of cases in court, of municipal records, of legislative and executive proceedings, are reasonably accurate as to facts, and a reporter who habitually misrepresented in such matters through carelessness or design would not be retained on any important paper.

On other matters there is frequently room for difference of opinion as to what facts really are until some plan is devised whereby they can be carefully and competently investigated. With widely conflicting testimony presented, as would certainly be the case, a jury would rarely, if ever, convict. The same would hold true in the event of a prosecution for carelessness. Any one who has had experience in court knows that juries are exceedingly ready to accept extenuating circumstances, and carelessness would readily be adopted as such in a newspaper case, as it is accepted today in many court proceedings.

Already laws exist in certain states to punish all persons who knowingly and willfully transmit to any publication false and untrue statements of fact. Such a law exists in New York as Section 1353 0f the Penal Code. It has been very seldom invoked. So innocuous has it been that many newspaper men do not know of its existence. When a similar law was passed by the Minnesota legislature recently, certain New York newspapers referred to it as if it were a new legal departure. A Massachusetts statute, passed in 1922, imposes fine or imprisonment for publishing false statements about candidates for public office. ① Granted that the proper means of establishing the veracity of the press is by law, it is obvious that the law proposed would be ineffectual. It would doubtless result in a number of prosecutions, mostly based on unimportant matters. These prosecutions would cover a short period of time after the law was adopted. Thereafter, the statute would become a dead letter, never invoked except for spite or in case of some flagrant violation, such as, however, is now covered by the laws punishing libel.

The suggestion of a public literary defender is still more absurd. Any one who has had experience as a newspaper man in dealing with public officials, from village councilmen to high officials of the United States, knows how little reliance can be placed upon their objectivity of view or their fairness in any matter in which their personal interests or the interests of their party are concerned. It may be urged that a public literary defender would represent the point of view of a majority of the people on contested questions. In this country, however, the number of contested issues is so great that no elected officials necessarily represent the point of view of a majority of the people upon these issues. These officials were elected by a combination of factors. Some voters cast their ballots on one issue, others on another issue. Furthermore, as has been previously pointed out, the public is not always—perhaps is never—seeking the complete objective facts, the dissemination of which is the highest function of the newspaper. The proposer of the office of literary defender naively admits this in referring to

---

① *General Laws of Massachusetts*, Chapter 55, Section 34a.

"the correct ideas."Manifestly, he belongs to that group of careless thinkers who consider that correctness of opinion is to be established by majority vote. In considering this point of view, one may well reflect on what support the ideas of Socrates, of Galileo, of Darwin, to take but a few examples, had from the majority opinion of their times.

A still more drastic legal provision is suggested by W. T. Colyer,[①] who advocates that every paper should be compelled to devote at least half a column in every issue to answering questions about its stockholders, employees, or contributors. He would make a requirement also that every paper print in each issue a list of the letters submitted for publication but not intended to be published, with a summary of the letters. It is evident, of course, that such proposals as Mr. Colyer's tend simply to confuse the issue of accuracy by introducing the question of personal bias on the part of editors or owners of the paper and by representing the newspaper to be a public forum, which, under the most widely social interpretation of its function, it is not. There is no obligation upon a newspaper to publish a letter which it receives, any more than there is an obligation upon the owner or lessee of a hall to open the platform for a reply to an appointed speaker. There is, of course, an obligation to correct errors of fact when brought to the newspaper's notice by letter or otherwise.

Upton Sinclair naturally urges law for the government of newspapers. He proposes in *The Brass Check*[②] a law providing that newspapers shall not publish an interview with any one that has not been O. K.'d or concerning which they have not the permission of the person interviewed to publish it without an O. K. In point of fact certain newspapers make this requirement in the case of important matters. In not a few cases persons

---

① *Obligatory Answers*, in *The Arbitrator*, Vol. 2, No. 2, pp. 12—13.
② p. 404

who know they will be interviewed on a matter prepare statements to be submitted to the newspapers to express their views. The Kansas Newspaper Code of Ethics, adopted in 1910, advocated the same proceeding that Mr. Sinclair advises. ①

Generally speaking, the rule which is thus urged would be impracticable because of limits of time in modern newspaper work. Suppose a reporter interviews a man in the Bronx in New York, then goes downtown to write his story or telephone it to the office to be written. In either event the sending of a messenger from downtown New York to the Bronx to obtain an O. K. on the interview would cause editions to be missed. Moreover, it would result in heavy expenditures of money which the importance of the matter would usually not justify. In some cases, for example, criminal matters, disappearance of the person interviewed would make an O. K. Impossible.

Furthermore, the requirement of an O. K. on interviews would cause many written interviews, perfectly correct, to be destroyed and others to be altered, because upon reading them the person interviewed would feel that what appeared in black and white, while perfectly true, was contrary to his private interests. While undoubtedly interviews are sometimes faked or partly faked, every newspaperman knows that a considerable proportion of those concerning which complaint is made represent the actual statements of the persons interviewed. An individual denies the interview merely because upon its publication he has felt it to be unpopular or contrary to his own interests. Certain high officials have been notorious among newspaper reporters for denying interviews concerning which there was no question.

Mr. Sinclair also suggests "a law providing that when any newspaper

---

① See Appendix A, p. 206.

has made any false statement concerning an individual and has had its attention called to the falsity of this statement, it shall publish a correction of the statement in the next edition of the publication and in the same place and with the same prominence given to the false statement." [1]

The French practice[2] with reference to corrections of errors and answers to attacks in newspapers is of interest here. The French law provides that when the official actions of public officers have been incorrectly reported or distorted, a newspaper is required to publish on the first page an answer of not more than twice the length of the injurious article. This answer must appear in the first issue following notification by the interested party. In case the answer is more than twice as long as the original, the newspaper may charge for the excess at the rate provided for legal notices.

With reference to private individuals named or designated in an untruthful news story, a newspaper must publish within three days after receiving it an answer twice as long as the original article. The answer must appear in the same place in the paper where the original article was published, and must be printed in the same type.

In practice, the law is seldom invoked, as newspapers regularly publish the answers sent to them without waiting for any form of legal notice.

Another law advocated by Upton Sinclair is one putting the distribution of news to American newspapers under public control. Mr. Sinclair, who believes the Associated Press to be a monopoly, desires that any one who wishes to publish a newspaper in any American city or town may receive the Associated Press service without any formality whatever except the filing of an application and the payment of a fee to cover the cost of the

---

① *The Brass Check*, p. 405.
② The writer is indebted to Professor P. de Bacourt of Columbia University for authoritative data on the French law and practice.

service. [1] In view of the fact that Mr. Sinclair believes the public opinion of America to be "poisoned at the source"[2] by this organization, it would seem anomalous that he should wish to extend its service. Laws of the sort advocated by Mr. Sinclair already exist in Kansas and Kentucky but have never been enforced, the handling of news being an interstate matter. Newspaper men, of course, know that the Associated Press is not a monopoly, the United Press and the International News Service being vigorous general competitors, and several other services being competitors in limited fields.

None of the foregoing suggestions represents the serious thought of any one practically experienced in journalism. The only proposed law which does represent the point of view of the professional journalist to any extent is the suggestion of a state board of journalism which should issue and revoke licenses to practice the profession of journalism. Such a law would be intended to introduce into the journalistic profession standards similar to those now existing in the legal and medical professions. One of the earliest suggestions of this character was made by Barratt O'Hara, a practicing newspaper man, formerly lieutenant governor of Illinois. Mr. O'Hara's plan, proposed in 1913, contained the following provisions, according to the author's own statement:

"A license should issue:

"1. When the applicant had reached legal age;

"2. Completed the equivalent of a high school education.

"3. Studied two years in a recognized college of journalism, or passed the same period of time in a newspaper office as an apprentice reporter;

---

[1] *The Brass Check*, p. 406.

[2] *The Brass Check*, pp. 362—376.

"4. Furnished the Board with positive proof of good moral character; and

"5 Successfully passed an examination, in writing, conducted by the State Board at regular intervals.

"Adequate provision was made for the beginner. who might receive, on application to the Board and proof of good moral character and an education equivalent to that of the ordinary high school, a certificate as an Apprentice Reporter. As such he might perform the usual work of a cub reporter, but would be disqualified from passing final judgment on his own and other persons' copy. That is, he might write the items, but the same would be read and possibly revised by a licensed journalist before reaching the printer. Two years of such training and restriction, with the natural looking forward to the examinations ahead and the constant preparing for them, could scarcely fail to bring out the very best newspaper qualities in the young aspirant. Or the same period might be spent with equal profit in an approved and practicable school of journalism.

"A license, on the other hand, should be revoked:

"1. Automatically, on the practitioner's conviction of a felony; or

"2. After due filing of charges and trial by a jury of his fellow practitioners for willful misrepresentation, malicious writing of scandal, acceptance of money or other prize tendered as bribe for the deliberate and unjustified coloring of news items, or other conduct unprofessional, reprehensible, and dishonest."

A somewhat similar bill was proposed in the Oklahoma legislature in 1923. It was strongly opposed by the newspapers of the state generally, which believed that it was inspired by a spirit of revenge rather than by a desire to improve journalistic conditions. The bill was defeated. The bill provided that the board should consist of the President of the State University, the Dean of the School of Journalism of the State University, and three members to be appointed by the governor. All of the appointed members were required to have had at least five years' active experience as newspapermen in Oklahoma. The revocation of licenses was made conditional on the following facts:

"(a) When it shall be ascertained that any applicant made any false statements or representations in procuring his license.

"(b) When any licensee is convicted of a crime against the laws of the State of Oklahoma involving moral turpitude.

"(c) When any licensee becomes a habitual drunkard.

"(d) When any licensee prints or causes to be printed, or permits the printing and publication of any story or news article about any citizen of this state or nation which is not true.

"(e) When any licensee prints, or causes to be printed. Or permits the printing and publication of any news article, story or editorial, which either directly or by insinuation, falsely charges any citizen of this state or nation with an act which hurts the standing or reputation of such citizen in the community or state or nation, either in a business or social way.

"(f) When any licensee prints, causes to be printed or permits the printing and publication of any news item, editorial, or story which is immoral or degrading."

Similar bills have been introduced in the legislature of Connecticut and possibly those of other states.

It is altogether probable that in time admission to the profession of journalism will be made conditional upon passing certain requirements. This will come, however, as the result of a demand from practicing journalists rather than from the outside. In accordance with the practice in every profession, any examining board would be composed of members of the profession. Until the ethical standards of the profession are more definitely established than they are today, the tendency of examinations and other acts of the board might conceivably be to preserve the present status of journalism and to hinder development of higher standards. A professional consciousness and the ethical and social implications flowing from this are necessary before any legal enactment can improve the status of journalism as a profession.

Additional Readings

Hale, *The Law of the Press*.

Angell, *The Press and the Organisation of Society*, pp 76—89.

Sinclair, *The Brass Check*, pp. 403—407.

The Arbitrator, Vol. 2, No. 2, July, 1919.

O'Hara, *A State License for Newspaper Men*, in Thorpe's *The Coming Newspaper*, pp. 148—161.

Oklahoma Press Bill Is Doomed. Editor and Publisher, March 17, 1923, p. 18.

X Setting Professional Standards: Organizations of Journalists

Among practicing journalists one of the most hopeful signs for the general betterment of the professional is the growth—through slow—of a professional spirit and of desire for a respect-commanding organization. Schools of journalism, economic factors, and the realization that all is not well with the press are influences in this direction. Too many newspaper men, however, still regard their work not as a profession, but merely as a job—and frequently as a steppingstone to something else. They leave it for positions ranging from publicity agent for a religious society to salesman of blue-sky stock. This is not surprising, in view of the low salaries paid in newspaper work and the paradoxical situation which subjects the reporter to a measure of contempt but at the same time places him in direct contact with the influential in business, social, and political life.

Other countries have made more progress than the United States in organizing journalists and a glance at their methods is enlightening. Particularly in England has such progress been made that today practically every reporter and subeditor in the country now belongs to one of the three organizations of journalists.

The oldest of these organizations is the Institute of Journalists, which was established by royal charter in 1889. The outgrowth of a smaller organization of progressive young men which was known as the National Society of Journalists and which was confined to provincial papers, it embodies the aspirations of idealistic youth and has made marked progress in many directions. It maintains an unemployment fund which provides benefits for thirteen weeks, a defense fund for the purpose of giving legal advice and dealing both in and outside the courts with literary and journalistic disputes in which the members become involved, a fund which assists the orphans of journalists, and another fund which provides insurance at low cost. An employment register free to all members is kept.

While the Institute has set no examinations or other special tests for prospective members, it expects eventually to adopt some such plan. This is provided for in the charter of the Institute, which also makes provision for various projects, some of which have not yet been undertaken but which are upheld as ideals before the members. The principal objects named in the charter are these:

"Devising measures for testing the qualifications of candidates for admission to professional membership in the Institute by examination in theory and in practice or by any other actual and practical tests.

"The promotion of whatever may tend to the elevation of the status and the improvement of the qualifications of all members of the journalistic profession.

"The ascertainment of the law and practice relating to all things connected with the journalistic profession and the exercise of supervision over its members when engaged in professional duties.

"The collection, collation, and publication of information of service or interest to members of the journalistic profession.

"Watching any legislation affecting the discharge by journalists of their professional duties and endeavoring to obtain amendments of the law affecting journalists, their duties, or interest.

"Acting as a means of communication between members, or others, seeking professional engagements and employers desirous of employing them.

"Promoting personal and friendly intercourse between members of the Institute; holding conferences and meetings for the discussion of professional affairs, interests, and duties; the compilation, constant revision, and publication of lists and registers of journalists and of records of events and proceedings of interest to journalists.

"The formation of a library or libraries for the use of members of the Institute.

"The encouragement, establishment, or development of a professional journal for journalists.

"The promotion, encouragement, or assistance of means for providing against the exigencies of age, sickness, death, and misfortune.

"The acquisition by the Institute of a hall or other permanent place of meeting and of other places of meeting.

"Securing the advancement of journalism in all its branches and obtaining for journalists, as such, formal and definite professional standing.

"The promotion by all reasonable means of the interests of journalists and journalism."

The Institute has subsidiary associations all over the British Empire. In the larger centers it has branches devoted to special types of journalism, such, for example, as trade journalism. In all its work it aims not only to lay down sound, ethical principles but to create opportunities for beneficial intercourse among journalists. It has been a potent force in developing professional consciousness among the newspaper men and women of England.

The National Union of Journalists, the other leading British organization of newspaper workers, was founded in 1906 as a trade union. It is affiliated with the Printing and Kindred Trades Federation of Great Britain. It has made rapid progress and in the spring of 1923 had a membership of 4,200, which it claims is more than three times that of any other organization of British journalists.

The National Union of Journalists consists exclusively of journalists dependent on their own work. It does not admit newspaper proprietors, directors, or managers, but the holding of shares in a newspaper company does not necessarily bar an otherwise eligible journalist from membership. It includes not only members of the staffs of newspapers but persons who in this country would be called freelance writers. For example, H. G. Wells is a member of the Union.

The objects of the society, stated in its amended rules, are:

"1. To defend and promote the professional interests and status of its members with regard to salary, conditions of employment, tenure of office.

"2. The establishment of out-of-work, benevolent, and superannuation benefits.

"3. To deal with questions affecting the professional conduct of its members.

"4 To be an Approved Society within the meaning of the National Health Insurance Acts, and to transact business under the Acts, and to do all things required by the Acts, and by the Ministry of Health for the purpose of so being an Approved Society and of transacting such business.

"5. To carry out the provisions of the Unemployed Insurance Act, 1920."

Marked attention has been given to the salary question. Salaries of newspaper workers in England had been shockingly low, due to a variety of causes, among which was the considerable number of persons of independent income in the profession. As the war raised prices, many journalists were faced with practical starvation. The Union, by this time strong enough to act, took steps to change these conditions, not only because of the economic necessity but because of the greater professional independence that is always secured to a man who is receives a living income.

The agreements made by the Union with newspaper proprietors in London and the provinces have increased salaries 100 to 200 per cent above the pre-war figures. Before the war some competent journalists were working in Fleet Street for as little as £3 a week. At present (1923) the minimum London rates range from £6.6s. for reporters on trade papers to £9.9s. on dailies and Sunday newspapers. On provincial weekly papers the minimum wage is £4.7s. 6d. and on provincial dailies £5.3s. In London fixed maximum working hours have also been established. These are 38 1/2 hours a week for sub-editors or copy-readers, as they would be called in the United States,—44 hours for reporters and photographers, and 48 hours for photo printers, who in England are classified as journalists. The Union has also obtained a three weeks' vacation each year for journalists in London.

Most of these accomplishments have been obtained by trade union action with the support of the mechanical workers in the printing industry.

The Union has standing honorary counsel, who advises on questions relating to journalists' rights and privileges. The Union has fought cases arising out of radius agreements, copyright of written matter and photographs, wrongful dismissal due to insufficient notice, and payment of salary during sickness, and his recovered large sums of money for members. Every case fought by the Union has been won.

The Union maintains a register and also pays benefits to unemployed members, £2 a week for the first thirteen weeks and £1 a week for the next thirteen weeks. The Union is an approved society under the National Health Insurance acts of Great Britain. It is represented on the London University Journalism Committee and on the Joint Industry Council for the Newspaper Industry.

The other organization of working journalists in England is the Society of Women Journalists. Women are not barred from the other societies, but a number of them have organized in this society to deal with their own specific problems.

In Australia, New Zealand, and South Africa journalists are organized on the union basis. Indeed, the British National Union of Journalists has newspaper agreements with the organizations in the colonies. In Australia and New Zealand agreements between representatives of employing newspapers and of working journalists are in effect under the trade union laws of these colonies. These agreements provide for hours, wages, including a minimum rate per line for material furnished by correspondents, and other details.

In the United States no organization exists comparable to those in English-speaking countries abroad. There are a number of organizations of newspaper publishers, concerned to a large extent with business problems. There was recently organized the American Society of Newspaper Editors, which is concerned largely with ethical problems. It has adopted an admirable code of ethics. It is composed, nevertheless, exclusively of men holding high positions on newspapers, and only 124 0f them, although these papers possess special significance by reason of belonging to the metropolitan group. The various state press associations, which devote their attention to both business and professional problems, are likewise made up almost exclusively of newspaper proprietors. While it is highly desirable that there be organizations of this character, it is evident that they cannot represent the profession as a whole, since owners of newspapers are in a small minority. The professional interest of journalism must be supplied fundamentally by the mass of working journalists.

A number of national organizations of journalists have been attempted in this country. Most of them have made no marked headway. There are three reasons for this: (1) Lack of money to promote organization; (2) the individualism of newspaper workers; (3) hostility of newspaper publishers. Certain publishers, even of those professing to be liberal, have fought steadily all organization among their employees, preventing even the formation of such wholly social bodies as press clubs. Their reasons are obvious. On the other hand, opposition of that sort would be much less effectual were newspapermen themselves more ready to act collectively.

At present the field is open for a definite organization of newspaper workers. Among the most effective organizations now existing are Sigma Delta Chi and Theta Sigma Phi, respectively men's and women's professional journalism fraternities. These are but a few years old and their membership is relatively small, although it is rapidly growing in both numbers and influence. It includes, however, only college men and women, except such practicing journalists as may be admitted as associate members, and thus excludes the vast majority of actual newspaper workers in this country. Furthermore, election to membership is dependent on the same sort of ballot as in a lodge or social fraternity, and sometimes persons of marked ability and character fail of election. Steps in the direction of a more inclusive organization are under consideration by Sigma Delta Chi. There are in existence several other journalistic organizations such as the American Journalists' Association. Their membership is small.

Here and there American journalists have affiliated with the trade union movement. In doing this they become members of the International Typographical Union, but an effort is now in progress to obtain from the American Federation of Labor recognition for a journalists' union.

The trade union plan of organization is looked upon with disfavor by most of them—and perhaps with some justice, since it suggests that journalism is a trade rather than a profession. On the other hand, there is nothing in the trade union idea that should essentially bar professional workers. The argument that the newspaper man should not affiliate with a labor organization because it will impair his impartiality overlooks the fact that newspaper men as such join Chambers of Commerce, Rotary Clubs, and similar organizations, without any protest on the part of those who look with horror on a trade union connection.

In Australia and New Zealand the same opposition arose when the movement began. Of the change in attitude, Dr. Walter Williams, who made a personal investigation, says:

"While the introduction of the wages-board or trade-union principle to journalism in these countries was opposed, sometimes with bitterness, by a majority of the employers and by a small minority of the employed, it has apparently resulted in considerable good. The objections urged against it in advance of its adoption were that it would lower the dignity of journalism, decrease the opportunities for the best journalists, level down salaries, and take from journalists the incentive which the professional rewards had given. These objections do not seem to have been well-founded. The employing publishers and chief editors of Australia are not unanimous in condemning the law. A few do condemn, but the great majority assert the law has not been in existence long enough to prove itself either good or bad, while a few express the opinion that it has resulted for the best interests of all parties. On the other hand, the working journalists, members of the Australian Journalists' Association, contend—and with show of truth—that wages have been increased, holidays have been granted, and, with a resulting improvement in the character of work done, the professional spirit has not diminished, while financial independence and permanence of employment have helped toward better writing and better newspapers."

In England the situation was somewhat different. The trade union movement there is far in advance of that in the United States and has the active opposition of no important portion of the population. Moreover, the young graduates of the universities are more and more embracing the labor cause, many of them being active in the Labour Party. It is not surprising, therefore, that the National Union of Journalists should have received the commendation of Lord Northcliffe and other widely known publishers.

There is a further difference between the American and the British situation which makes the wage question there paramount. In England the editor is in control of his paper, regardless of whether he owns a share of stock or not. This is the age-old tradition. Consequently, the problem of the journalist in conflict with a publisher determined, through ignorance or dishonesty, to misrepresent the news is not a significant issue in England. There are signs of its development, however. The journalistic organizations already existing will possibly prevent its gaining a strong foothold.

In all probability the outlook for the distinctively professional organization of newspaper men and women is most favorable in the United States in the near future. It would perhaps follow to a considerable extent the plans of the British Institute of Journalists.

An organization embracing practically all working journalists could fix high standards of entrance into the profession, could establish a sound and workable code of ethics, and could insure adequate salaries in the profession. In all of these, of course, it would need public sympathy and cooperation. From the work of such an organization might develop eventually laws for examining and licensing journalists. There would also be a tendency toward the elimination of one of the most unfortunate features of the press, editorial control of newspapers by men who have had no professional training or experience in journalism and who consider journalism merely a business.

Additional Readings

Williams, *The World's Journalism*, *University of Missouri Bulletin*. Journalism Series 9. pp. 20—29.

Angell, *The Press and the Organisation of Society*, pp. 76—123.

Labour Research Department, *The Press*, pp. 35—43.

Sinclair. *The Brass Check*, pp. 415—428.

Bullen, The English Substitute for the License Plan, in Thorpe's *The Coming Newspaperman*, pp. 162—170.

News Writers' Union Local No. 1. *The New Republic* 20: 8—9.

American Bar Association, *Canons of Professional Ethics*.

American Medical Association, *Principles of Medical Ethics*.

XI Setting Professional Standards: The Newspaper's Part

Those who maintain that the press is essentially and consciously corrupt look for no improvement in the conditions of journalism from within the press itself. If they are sufficiently realistic in point of view to recognize the futility of legal measures as a corrective of evils in journalism, they are nevertheless prone to seek some other remedy, the impetus for which comes from outside the profession of journalism. Such an origin does not necessarily mean that a given proposal is unwise, but should lead the unprejudiced observer to regard it with caution, since it can hardly be presumed that any institution is wholly unwilling to be improved or unable to improve itself.

Aside from laws governing a privately owned press, the two suggestions most commonly made call respectively for endowed newspapers and for newspapers owned by the government, federal, state, or municipal.

Against both the endowed newspaper and the government-owned newspaper, one objection is commonly urged by practicing journalists;

namely, that they would be too dull to appeal to the general public. Weight is given to this objection by a reading of government publications in general. Few of them possess interest except to the technical reader. The Official Bulletin, issued by the United States government during the recent war, was, although edited by a professional newspaperman, one of the dullest publications ever circulated. There are in this country no endowed newspapers, in the strict sense of the word, so that one cannot definitely pass judgment as to the probable interest of such publications. There are several magazines of opinion, however, which are practically endowed. However enjoyable and stimulating these may be to the intellectual reader, their small circulation proves their lack of appeal to the general public. If a publication is supported by the government or by private endowment, the staff does not feel strongly the necessity of interesting a large number of readers. While this might be beneficial in eliminating the ultra-sensational from a newspaper, it would at the same time reduce the value of the publication as a means of disseminating facts.

As to the endowed newspaper, another objection arises. Endowments are likely to be instituted for the purpose of advancing a particular cause rather than for the purpose merely of disseminating objective facts. Moreover, no matter how much care is taken to prevent it, there is a tendency for endowments to represent and perpetuate the mental attitude of the donors regardless of what the stated purpose of the endowment may be. This fact has been complained of time and again in the case of educational institutions, justly and unjustly; there is no reason to assume that the same complaints would not arise in the case of endowed newspapers. Once the complaint developed, whether well founded or not, much of the influence of the newspaper would be lost.

The government-owned newspaper is open to the objection that it would certainly be used for propaganda. Indeed, it seems astonishing that government newspapers should be seriously advocated by those who are familiar with the politician's attitude toward facts, and particularly by those who complain of current political conditions. The unreliability of purported facts furnished to newspapers by government officials has been emphasized again and again. The inability to reason from facts to conclusions and the practice of basing opinions purely on preconceived notions are apparent to any one who will read The Congressional Record or listen, as a newspaper reporter, to the press statements made by executive officials.

The theory that politicians would not take advantage of the opportunity of a government-owned newspaper to advance their own fortunes and those of their groups and parties, is untenable. The attempts of politicians to influence newspapers, privately owned, to misrepresent or suppress the facts, afford sufficient clue to what would happen were these same politicians in control of the financial support of the press. The method of the politician, even when he evidently considers he is acting for the best interests of the country, is illustrated by the following circular, issued when both Canada and the United States were engaged in the World War:

Circular No. C. P. C. 57a.

CONFIDENTIAL CIRCULAR FOR CANADIAN EDITORS

(Not for Publication.)

(I) Owing to the shortage of agricultural labourers in Canada, consequent upon the absence of such a large proportion of Canadian manhood on military service, and in view of the supreme importance of securing the highest possible production in natural products, the Government is making an effort to bring in from the United States to the Western Provinces as much farm labour as possible. Editors are asked to suppress references to this particular matter, as it is feared that publicity may seriously interfere with the plan.

ERNEST J. CHAMBERS,

Chief Press Censor for Canada.
Office of the Chief Press Censor for Canada,
Department of the Secretary of State,
Ottawa, January 19, 1918.

Where the private interests of the politician or his party, rather than apparently those of his country, are involved, he employs much less obvious, but for that reason more sinister, methods.

Furthermore, unless the government newspapers were given exclusive rights, they would fail of their purpose. The best journalists would still be found on privately owned papers, and the public would prefer the latter. This was found to be true when even semiofficial newspapers existed in Washington, in the first half of the nineteenth century. To give exclusive rights to government newspapers would restore the abuses of seventeenth-century England, when the government endeavored to control all dissemination of news and all expression of opinion on public matters. At that time, of course, there was a clandestine press, just as there was in Belgium during the German occupation in 1914—1918, and eventually government control was done away with. The same thing would undoubtedly occur in the United States were the government to attempt to take over the press.

The one thing which can be done by the government to improve the press is to develop certainty of record on a greater number of matters, comparable to the certainty of record that now exists on court proceedings, the acts of legislative bodies, and some other events. Particularly may this be wisely developed in social and economic problems. Mr. Lippmann's suggestion of intelligence bureaus, organized to supply facts but neither to render decisions nor to take action, presents a plan which, if efficiently carried out, would mean a decided advance for the newspaper in its capacity as a disseminator of objective facts. Such a system would have to be removed from direct political control, and it should, in turn, have no control over politics or over the press, but should be exclusively a fact-finding agency, as distinguished from a fact-disseminating, a policy-advocating, or an executive agency.

So far as other governmental steps are concerned, they would in all probability be worse than useless. A government-controlled press would be essentially a propaganda press, whereas one of the chief accomplishments which newspapers of themselves can hope to make is freedom from propaganda.

The problem of propaganda is serious. Propaganda is practiced by every type of institution, from the patent medicine trade to the governments of important nations. Stimulated tremendously by the war, where its effectiveness was made manifest to the most skeptical, propaganda has obtained, by payment of large salaries, the services of exceedingly skillful thinkers and writers, commonly ex-journalists. Several years ago, there were 1,200 professional press agents and publicity experts in New York City alone. Today the number is doubtless much greater. A large newspaper will receive daily as much as 150,000 words from publicity bureaus of various sorts.

The purpose of the publicity agent, of course, is to get a favorable hearing for his side. He may adopt devious methods to accomplish his purpose. He may fake news; he may stage events for the purpose of "creating" news; he may "dress up" or even directly misrepresent news; he may endeavor to suppress news—all in order to produce a favorable impression of the cause that he is trying to advance. These are the abuses, embodying, in the person of a non-journalist, practically every charge that is made against the newspapers themselves. On the other hand, the publicity worker may be entirely honorable in his methods; he may merely present to the newspaper facts concerning his cause that otherwise might be overlooked. In this he does formally only what is done informally by every one who comes into contact with the press, and only in a limited sense is he a propagandist.

The danger of the propagandist to the press is partly in the abuses in which he often is involved, partly in the mere fact that he is a propagandist, and so skillful a propagandist that it is difficult for the journalist to obtain a fair view of situations into which professional propaganda has entered. Too, the presence of the press agent, or publicity expert, frequently keeps the investigating reporter from actual contact with the persons from whom he could obtain adequate information. Under such circumstances, reporting becomes a matter of accepting typed statements from the various persons connected with a news event, and these statements tend frequently to disguise rather than clarify the matters under consideration.

In behalf of the press agent, it must not be forgotten that in at least two ways newspapers have stimulated the professional development of propaganda. In the first place, reporters have so often misquoted speeches and otherwise misrepresented individuals that the latter in self-defense have turned to publicity bureaus as a means of placing exact statements in the hands of the newspapers. In the second place, reporters have failed to seek out news and have given most space to persons who would furnish them with typed copies of speeches, ready-prepared interviews, and similar material.

Although newspapers are in general fighting the growing tendency to propaganda, particularly where it clearly seeks to influence public opinion, they still display a disposition, when criticized, to throw the blame upon the persons or organizations involved in the news, and thus to invite further propaganda. For example, when the press was criticized for the slight space devoted to the convention of the National Education Association as compared with that devoted to the Dempsey-Gibbons fight, the *Editor and Publisher* asserted of the association that "with a subject of interest to every home in the land it has not been able to put enough human interest into it to compete in a news sense, with a professional brawl in an out-of-the-way town on the plains of Montana." The inference is plain: Education is important, but journalists cannot be expected to make the important interesting to the reader. The one who is involved in the news must put human interest into it. The easiest way, obviously, is through an expert press agent. This viewpoint is recognized by The Christian Science Monitor, which, in discussing the same matter, writes an editorial entitled *A Wider Field for the Press Agent*, in which it treats of "the indifference of the promoters" of education "to methods of awakening journalistic interest."

That the function of the publicity agent, by whatever name called, will soon disappear under pressure of the newspapers, is extremely unlikely, especially in view of their recognition in some cases, as just detailed, of his desirability. Until greater specialization, more marked investigative skill, and more pronounced readiness to go to trouble in obtaining news, are general among journalists, the publicity agent is likely to retain his place. What newspapers may practicably do toward freedom from propaganda is to accept the aid of the publicity agent only in supplying indubitable facts and in putting into popular language the technical details of specialized fields. Newspaper also may wisely refuse to accept any copy of any sort from any publicity agent who has once proved unethical in his conduct. The general practice of newspapers is in this direction. However blindly they may at times attack the problem, journalists realize essentially that the only press worth anything is a free press.

Aside from reducing the amount of propaganda, what, if anything, can the press as an institution do, toward raising the standards of journalism? The first step is to recognize that not all is well with the profession. This step has already been taken. While the universal tendency of the professional man to defend his profession against the laity still exists in journalism, the number of editorials in newspaper trade journals and even newspapers themselves about the faults of the press proves that the intelligent editor is not complacent. Too many publishers, who are not themselves editors, are complacent, but they are not likely to remain so indefinitely.

The second step is self-analysis. This is not an easy matter. The best plan, manifestly, would be an analysis of representative examples of the American press by a committee of whose objective-mindedness, fairness, and familiarity with journalistic practice there could be no doubt. Such an investigation should cover various sections of the country and should include various types of newspapers, from the metropolitan daily to the country weekly. The few studies that have been made cover only large city dailies, whereas the vast majority of American newspapers and probably the weight of journalistic influence are found in the papers published in small towns. Furthermore, reports made by persons strongly opposed to the press or strongly in sympathy with it are useful in drawing public attention to conditions, but do not carry great evidential weight; indeed, in most cases they contain too little authenticated evidence to sustain any conclusions. An investigative project such as has been suggested would require a large endowment, but the results would more than justify it. The mere publication of the findings of the investigators would put the indubitable concrete facts about American journalism into the arena of public discussion, and this of itself would result in a speedy improvement. If a group of public-spirited publishers—or for that matter a group of any sort—would endow such an investigation, it would produce incalculable results for the betterment of journalism.

Until this is done, each newspaper must make its own analysis. A few papers are already doing so. *The Detroit News* employs an editorial secretary whose duties include investigation of the accuracy of statements in the paper. In 1913, Ralph Pulitzer established the Bureau of Accuracy and Fair Play of *The New York World*. The purpose, as stated by the founder, is "to promote accuracy and fair play, to correct carelessness, and to stamp out fakes and fakers." Every complaint made concerning an item in The World is investigated. If the complaint is justified, a correction is published, and the blame for the error is also fixed. The complainant is invariably informed of the results of the investigation. Faking or gross carelessness on the part of a reporter or correspondent subjects him to dismissal. Some other newspapers follow similar practices on a less formal and elaborate scale. The better newspapers quite generally correct errors that are called to their attention, some in a "Beg Your Pardon" column established for the purpose, others in the regular news columns. This is a marked advance over the older practice of refusing to make corrections on the ground that they destroyed confidence in the press. There are still, it should be remarked in passing, newspapers which refuse to make corrections except of matters which they deem "important", and thus lead the public to utter disbelief in their integrity.

While it may seem at first glance that these methods constitute merely a negative method of self-analysis on the part of the newspapers, reflection will show that a publication could hardly initiate investigation of all the stories that it publishes, because of their vast number and the numerous lines of investigation that must be followed in tracing down the accuracy or inaccuracy of each. A newspaper might, however, initiate investigation of a certain number of stories each week, choosing those written by various members of the staff. A newspaper might also, still more practicably, publish in a prominent place in each issue an invitation to readers to complain of inaccuracies in any story. Undoubtedly many errors occur to which attention is never called but which would perhaps be brought to the notice of the paper were readers assured of the desire for their cooperation in the promotion of accuracy.

The third step that may be taken by the newspaper, the attempt to eliminate the faults which self-analysis shows, is illustrated in the practice of The New York World here, heretofore mentioned. So far as the reporter is concerned, he will in most cases try to be accurate and fair if he knows that accuracy and fairness are wanted, and particularly if he knows that a penalty will be exacted for their violation. Many newspapers publish codes of ethics for the guidance of their staffs, which fact alone indicates a genuine interest in improving journalism. The same thing may be said of codes adopted by state press associations and similar bodies. Unless the code is enforced, however, unless the reporter or other staff member, indeed, feels that there is behind it a rigorous, moral purpose, it is likely to lead to few results. It is of course to be recognized that any code of ethics represents ideals rather than merely contemporary practice, but if the code is to be useful the practice must make an effort in the direction of actual conformity with the ideals set up.

So much for the newspapers as newspapers. Can the newspaper worker, reporter, copy-reader, or editorial writer, himself accomplish anything in the direction of maintenance of sound standards? He cannot, of course, do as an individual what a powerful organization of journalists could do. But he can do something. He can adopt a practical working code of ethics for himself. He can decide, for instance, that he will never intentionally write anything untrue or unfair, that he will never use any dishonorable means in securing news, that he will never violate a confidence, that he will never accept money or any other gratuity for writing or refraining from writing any item, that he will never knowingly give readers a false impression concerning any matter, however trivial. Having adopted a code, he can stand ready to be "fired" rather than violate it.

He is not, it is true, very likely to be "fired," for intentional, studied dishonesty on the part of newspapers, it has been pointed out, is not the chief reason for their deficiencies. Such betterment of conditions as can be accomplished by the various individualistic means suggested reaches mainly, it is evident, the more casual deficiencies of the press-inaccuracy, general carelessness, so-called "harmless" faking, and the like. The underlying causes can be reached by no such application of palliatives. They will be eliminated slowly, chiefly by organization and educational agencies in cooperation with the press itself.

Additional Readings

Payne, *History of Journalism in the United States*, pp. 230—239.

Williams, *A History of British Journalism to the Foundation of the Gazette.*

Massart, *the Secret Press in Belgium.*

Lippmann, Public Opinion, pp. 369—410.

Sinclair. The Brass Check, pp. 408—414, 438—443.

Brown, The Menace to Journalism, The North American Review, 214:610—618.

Brownell, Publicity and its Ethics, The North American, Review, 215:188—196.

Brown. A Comment. The North American Review, 215: 197—199.

Chafee, Freedom of Speech, pp. 1—228.

Blythe, Pro Bono Publicity. The Saturday Evening Post, August 4, 1923, pp. 20—21.

Biennial Reports of The New York World's Bureau of Accuracy and Fair Play.

Files of The Official Bulletin.

XII Setting Professional Standards: Educational Agencies

The progress of society has always depended largely on education under the leadership of persons of creative intelligence. Improvement in journalism will come in the same way. Ignorance, inertia, and fear—psychological phenomena all of them—are, it has been observed, the principal causes for the deficiencies of American newspapers in respect to their primary function of presenting objective facts to the public. Psychological factors are eliminated, sublimated, or otherwise controlled, in the mass as in the individual, only by means of education. By the same means, the conscious factors that play a certain part in keeping the press from fulfillment of its functions may be done away with; education of the right type is one of the best guaranties against antisocial acts.

The education necessary for these purposes is not simply schooling. It is not the supplying of ready-made theories and conclusions to students. Persons who have had much schooling are often ignorant, lazy, and pathologically timid. At the same time, we must depend on the general school system plus such other aids as can be enlisted. The school system is established, it has public support-even if lukewarm at times, — and it is susceptible of practical improvement. What, then, may be done for the betterment of journalistic practice by the schools of the United States?

What may they accomplish toward the elimination of conscious antisocial tendencies in the press, and, more important, of ignorance, inertia, and fear as factors in journalism?

In discussions of education in relation to journalism, the school of journalism must occupy a significant place. There are twenty institutions in the United States offering degree curricula in journalism, while more than 200 0ther colleges and universities offer some instruction on the subject. The number of students now making professional preparation for journalism in institutions of higher learning is not less than 2,500, while the number of practicing journalists is estimated at under 60,000. The proportion of college students of journalism to practicing journalists is greater than was the proportion of college students of law and of medicine to practicing lawyers and physicians, respectively, forty years ago. The young men and women now studying journalism in schools designed for the purpose will be an important factor—perhaps the most important factor—in American newspaper work not many years hence.

The instruction, the purposes, and the ideals of schools of journalism thus become a matter of deep public concern. There are two distinct conceptions of the schools of journalism, and each has its supporters among the schools themselves. One conception is that the function of the school of journalism is to produce reporters who can write "good stories." Advocates or this conception are prone to argue publicly that newspapers want only reporters and that if the school can produce reporters they can learn in the newspaper office all else that they need to know about "the game." A school of this type emphasizes above everything else newspaper technique.

This is the trade-school method, and it turns out graduates who have the competency which a trade school gives. They are facile, self-confident, and outwardly efficient. In their first year out of school, they give good accounts of themselves as reporters go on American newspapers.

The school of this type is run frankly to furnish reporters for American newspapers—the same sort of reporters, with perhaps a little added polish, tact, and suavity, for the same sort of American newspapers that is current today. The schools commended by copy-readers, city editors, and even publishers for giving sound, practical teaching —" none of this theoretical stuff on rights and responsibilities and ethics." "By God!" such a publisher exclaims, "all the ethics a reporter needs is loyal to his paper. I want men who'll he as loyal to this paper as they are to the flag." And from the trade school the publisher gets the men who will swear by his variant.

The other conception of the school of journalism is that journalism is a profession and that the school of journalism is a professional school. It admits that the school must give technical training in newspaper writing, but maintains that this technical training could be obtained in a very brief course and that the primary function of the school is rather to give the student such an intellectual and ethical training and background as will best enable him to serve the public through the press.

Like the trade school, the professional school of journalism aims to train reporters, for it realizes that capable, honest reporters are the foundation stone of a dependable press. But its conception of a reporter is not a man who can write "a good story." It is rather a trained investigator seeking the objective facts.

If such a school is even to approximate its practice to its ideals, it must encourage men and women of the proper natural qualifications to study for journalistic careers and must discourage those who lack the necessary qualifications. Aside from integrity, intelligence and objective-mindedness are the qualities most needed. Tact, ability to meet people pleasantly, interest in humanity, and many other qualities are desirable, but not of supreme importance. Without intelligence, however, the work of a journalist is essentially futile. He may go through various professional motions, but he will never know what he is doing or why he is doing it. Without objective-mindedness on the part of journalists, the press will invariably fail to fulfill its principal function. The sincerity of a reporter may beyond question, but if his head is always full of opinions instead of facts he can do nothing but harm to his profession.

In a school maintaining professional ideals, there must also be such a curriculum as will still further develop the journalists and will dispel the ignorance characteristic of college students and graduates. This means the introduction of such special courses, dealing intelligently and freely with current events, as often are not offered elsewhere in the college or university. It requires the development of realistic courses in politics, economics, and sociology, instead of the academic courses which deal only with the theory and never with the actual workings of institutions. It must supply the scientific basis for understanding the vast technical developments of contemporary civilization. It must furnish training in what constitutes evidence, in order that the future reporter may not he misled by intentional or unintentional attempts to deceive him. In every subject that it presents, such a school aims to develop in the student complete intellectual honesty, the acceptance of no doctrine because it is held by the herd, or because it is professed by the newspapers, or for any other reason than that after straightforward thinking he is convinced of its truth.

The professional school of journalism, moreover, shows an increasing tendency to encourage its students to specialize in specific phases of modern life—in international affairs, in commerce, in labor, in agriculture, in politics, and in other important fields—in order that in their newspaper work they may be prepared the better to serve civilization. The general public depends upon the newspapers for understanding of contemporary life. Contemporary life is complex, and no one person is qualified to deal with many phases of it. The old conception of the pretended omniscience of the journalist has disappeared, and more and more the public demands newspaper men and women who not only can write but know the fields about which they write.

The school of journalism which maintains these conceptions and standards has an uphill job, but not an impossible one. For most of the schools of journalism are making definite progress along precisely these lines. But they are making progress against odds.

In the first place, they have sometimes the opposition of newspaper publishers. There is developing in the United States a theory that certain institutions of learning or certain departments within them exist primarily for the selfish benefit of those to whose vocations their work is most closely related. One tries to serve the physician, another the business man, another the engineer, another the farmer. These men regard the schools or departments as in a measure their property. The newspaper publisher frequently looks upon the school of journalism as designed primarily to serve him, to prepare men to do what he wants them to do on his newspaper. The strictly professional school of journalism, on the contrary, takes the position that the purpose of every educational institution is to serve all humanity by means of the truth. Specifically with reference to journalism, it holds that the young man or woman going out to work on a paper is not primarily a servant of that paper, but rather a servant of humanity. It maintains that while the man who serves his publisher at the expense of humanity may win his publisher's praise, he nevertheless is a traitor to civilization. The professional school of journalism wants the suggestions and advice of newspaper men, but it wants them with the understanding that the interests of humanity and not the preservation of the status quo in journalism are paramount.

Not only does the professional school of journalism run counter sometimes to the wishes of newspaper men; it also must resist the pressure, brought to bear on all educational institutions by the rich, by politicians, by clergymen, and by other groups of the population, to accept without investigation the dogmas of the herd. The public, which the school is striving to serve, is often ungrateful, especially where the service involves the discovery and presentation of unwelcome truth.

Every citizen who is interested in the fulfillment by newspapers of their primary function of presenting the objective facts, may wisely interest himself in the professional school of journalism; in its battle with ignorance and fear it offers genuine hope for the future. The trade school of journalism, on the other hand, deserve no support, except, perhaps, from newspapers that want to employ its graduates.

Along with the trade school of journalism should be abolished all high school courses professing to teach journalism as a vocation. A resolution opposing such courses was unanimously adopted by the National Council of Teachers of English in 1920, and since such courses are commonly offered in connection with the English work, only the fatuity of school administrators or the pressure of newspapers seeking cheap and impressionable employees is likely to cause the retention of such courses. They offer merely cheap journalistic technique; giving the student none of the intellectual and ethical preparation necessary to a proper professional career. Their very existence makes it practicable for a newspaper proprietor whose employees leave him because of his dishonest or unfair practices, to fill their places with boys and girls who have neither the intelligence nor the courage to resist domination. Vocational high school courses in journalism are, of course, to be carefully distinguished from those courses in which training in news writing is used merely as a means of motivating and making practical the instruction in English composition.

In all colleges, regardless of what conceptions are maintained in the teaching of journalism, a gain will be made for democratic civilization, in the writer's estimation, if faculty censorship of news contained in student papers or sent to other newspapers by student correspondents is abolished. The writer makes this statement advisedly, after careful thought, after some years of experience in both journalism and teaching, and with a considerable knowledge of journalistic conditions in American colleges. Collegiate censorship, where it exists, is not a censorship for eliminating papers one may find ridiculous inaccuracies and statements which would justify submission to a jury in a suit for libel.

The censorship exists primarily for the purpose of keeping from the public, within or without the college, such facts as the authorities of the institution feel that the public ought not to know. It is, in short, a convenient device for suppressing the truth. The recently retired president of one in institution with which the writer is acquainted permitted students of the college to hold dances, although the Church whose members largely support the institution is opposed to dancing. The president, a clergyman of this Church, forbade the college newspaper to mention dancing, stipulating that in its columns dances must always be referred to by other names. In discussing this matter with a student editor he said frankly that supporters of the college would cause much trouble if he did not conceal the fact that he permitted dancing. One need not sympathize with the prejudices of the college supporters in order to recognize the ethical character of the example set by the college president.

The argument in favor of censorship in colleges is two-fold: First, that students lack judgment; second, that suppression of the facts is often for the "higher good." The first argument is perfectly true, —but students learn judgment only by exercising it, and any editor, student or other, is sobered by responsibility for everything he does. Moreover, the ill effects of censorship far outweigh the difficulties and embarrassments that may result from the unsound judgment of students. No university or college can honorably make use of the second argument. There is no higher good than the truth, to the discovery and dissemination at which all honest education is dedicated.

The effect of such casuistry as has just been discussed is to impress students with the conviction that truth is not the highest good and may properly be concealed or misrepresented in order to gain ends which are thought desirable. The principle back of this is the same physical fear and distrust of the people which, as has been observed, actuate newspaper men in deciding that certain facts are not good for the public to know. Not only students directly concerned with the college publications, but all the students who know of the system, are affected. They go into journalism active supporters of news suppression and mis-representation, and into other walks of life passive apologists for it. Unconsciously, through precept and example, they have been made fundamental disbelievers in government by the people, in that they uphold the principle of withholding from the people that which alone makes the people capable of government.

While considering education, one must not overlook the account for the deficiencies of the American newspaper are not to be found exclusively in journalism. On the contrary, they permeate American life. Consequently, a program of education for the improvement of the press must not stop with the education of future journalists or even with college students in general. A more thorough-going process must be devised.

The newspapers are read more extensively than any other publication in the United States. Is it not an anomaly that in most schools—even most high schools and colleges—the newspaper is not mentioned from September to June? Would one not be astounded if the judiciary or the legislative branch of the government were not mentioned in the schools? Yet for knowledge of the doings of their courts and of their legislative bodies the people must depend on the newspapers. For the very information which enables them to decide whom they want for their elected judges and whom for their representatives, they must depend on the newspapers. From the time when the child is old enough to be able to read until he is graduated from the university, the newspaper should be brought to his attention and studied as a social phenomenon. He should be made to understand that without a truthful press a successful popular government is impossible and that without the cooperation of the public a truthful press is impossible. He should be brought to see that any attempt by any individual or group of individuals to cause a newspaper to suppress, falsify, color, or misrepresent in any manner any fact is a blow at the truthfulness of the press and consequently at popular government. Let the youth once be brought to esteem as a traitor to popular government any man or woman who attempts to influence the press to depart from its obligation to print the facts, and such treason to popular government will become rare.

If general education is to aid in making the press more useful in a democratic society, it must also recognize and make clear the fact which Mr. Lippmann points out, that every human being is surrounded by two environments, one of them real, the other composed of "the pictures in our heads" which we assume to be the real environment and upon which we act. While it is desirable to remove as far as possible the contradictions between these two environments, it is not practicable altogether to introduce into our minds a true and complete picture of the real environment. In a complex civilization there must be certain stereotypes, certain generalities; not everything can be seen in detail. The schools must recognize this situation, and must emphasize the necessity of humility about one's beliefs, ability to recognize stereotypes as such, and readiness to modify or discard them as may be necessary to conform to discovered facts.

Education in this direction will tend toward elimination of fear as a characteristics of the public mind and consequently of the press. In particular, the unconscious fear of the herd will tend to disappear once it is clearly understood that opinion is merely opinion and that no belief, however universal, is immune from evidential examination. Likewise, fear of facts in any phase of life will be seen to be ridiculous when they are used, not to bolster up preconceived opinion, but to test all opinions and to arrive at new conclusions.

The process of attaining this condition of affairs may not be a short one; it will doubtless seem unnecessarily long to those who believe that righteousness will immediately triumph if but given the aid of a few new laws or at most a new social and economic system. Yet, when one considers the progress made in the natural sciences in a relatively brief time against great odds, one may well wonder if perchance the accomplishment of similar ends in journalism may not come sooner than is commonly expected. Whatever the rate at which results may be attained, it is certain that there is no more significant field for effort. Every effort toward better journalism forms a part of the struggle against ignorance, inertia, and fear. Conversely, every step which is taken to release the American people from bondage to these forces of hopelessness is a step toward releasing also the American newspaper. For ignorance, inertia, and fear are the unchanging foes of the one thing which makes the newspaper useful, and genuine popular government possible—truth.

Additional Readings

Proceedings of the American Association of Teachers of Journalism,

1921 and 1922.

Hornaday, Education for Journalism in the United States, in Williams's The Press Congress of the World in Hawaii, pp. 115—155.

Lee, Instruction in Journalism in Institutions of Higher Education.

Harrington, Journalism as a Part of College. The Forum 67:476—484

Harger, Journalism as a Career, in Bleyer's The Profession of Journalism, pp. 264—277.

Williams, The Newspaperman, pp. 114—144.

Lippmann, Liberty and the News, pp. 69—104.

Lipmannn, Public Opinion, pp. 3—32, 79—156

Appendix A Codes of Ethics and Rules Adopted by Organizations of Journalists and by Newspapers

CODES OF ETHICS ADOPTED BY ORGANIZATIONS OF JOURNALISTS

CANONS OF JOURNALISM[1]

The primary function of newspapers is to communicate to the human race what its members do, feel, and think. Journalism, therefore, demands of its practitioners the widest range of intelligence, of knowledge, and of experience, as well as natural and trained powers of observation and reasoning. To its opportunities as a chronicle are indissolubly linked its obligations as teacher and interpreter.

To the end of finding some means of codifying sound practice and just aspirations of American journalism these canons are set forth:

---

[1] Written by the Committee on Ethics (Harry J. Wright, Chairman), American Society of Newspaper Editors, and adopted by the Society in 1923.

I

Responsibility. The right of a newspaper to attract and hole readers is restricted by nothing but considerations of public welfare. The use a newspaper makes of the share of public attention it gains serves to determine its sense of responsibility, which it shares with every member of its staff. A journalist who uses his power for any selfish or otherwise unworthy purpose is faithless to a high trust.

II

Freedom of the Press. Freedom of the press is to be guarded as a vital right of mankind. It is the unquestionable right to discuss whatever is not explicitly forbidden by law, including the wisdom of any restrictive statute.

III

Independence. Freedom from all obligations except that of fidelity to the public interest is vital.

1. Promotion of any private interest contrary to the general welfare, for whatever reason, is not compatible with honest journalism. So-called news communications from private sources should not be published without public notice of their source or else substantiation of their claims to value as news, both in form and substance.

2. Partisanship in editorial comment which knowingly departs from the truth, does violence to the best spirit of American journalism; in the news columns it is subversive of a fundamental principle of the profession.

IV

Sincerity, Truthfulness, Accuracy. Good faith with the reader is the foundation of all journalism worthy of the name.

1. By every consideration of good faith a newspaper is constrained to be truthful. It is not to be excused for lack of thoroughness or accuracy within its control or failure to obtain command of these essential

qualities.

2. Headlines should be fully warranted by the contents of the articles which they surmount.

V

Impartiality. Sound practice makes clear distinction between news reports and expressions of opinion. News reports should be free from opinion or bias of any kind.

1. This rule does not apply to so-called special articles unmistakably devoted to advocacy or characterized by a signature authorizing the writer's own conclusions and interpretations.

VI

Fair Play. A newspaper should not publish unofficial charges affecting reputation or moral character without opportunity given to the accused to be heard; right practice demands the giving of such opportunity in all cases of serious accusation outside judicial proceedings.

1. A newspaper should not invade private rights or feelings without sure warrant of public right as distinguished from public curiosity.

2. It is the privilege, as it is the duty, of a newspaper to make prompt and complete correction of its own serious mistakes of fact or opinion, whatever their origin.

VII

Decency. A newspaper cannot escape conviction of insincerity if while professing high moral purpose it supplies incentives to base conduct, such as are to be found in details of crime and vice, publication of which is not demonstrably for the public good. Lacking authority to enforce its canons, the journalism here represented can but express the hope that deliberate pandering to vicious instincts will encounter effective public disapproval or yield to the influence of a preponderant professional condemnation.

THE WASHINGTON CODE OF ETHICS[①]

I Will Be

Truthful in News

Truthful in Editorials

Truthful in Advertising

True to all My Obligations

Honest with My Competitors

True to the Ideals of Journalism

Mindful to the Value of Sincerity

Faithful to Community, State, Nation

Firm in Publication of Clean News

Honorable in all of My Dealings

Thorough in all of My Studies

Unselfish in all My Services

Faithful to all My Friends

Fair to all My Critics

THE OREGON CODE OF ETHICS FOR JOURNALISM[②]

"Not only all arts and sciences but all actions directed by choice aim at some good."

——Aristotle, Nicomachean Ethics, I. 1.

PREAMBLE

We believe in the teaching of the great ethicists that a general state of happiness and well-being is attainable throughout the world; and that this

---

① Written by Chapin D. Foster and others and adopted by the Washington State Press Association in 1923.

② Written by Dean Colin V. Dyment, University of Oregon, and adopted by the Oregon State Editorial association in 1922.

state is the chief end-in-view of society.

We recognize an instinct in every good man that his utterances and his deeds should make a reasonable and continuous contribution toward this ultimate state, in the possibility of which we reiterate our belief, however remote it may now seem.

We believe that men collectively should also follow the principles of practice that guide the ethical individual. For whatever purpose men are associated, we believe they should endeavor to make the reasonable and continuous contribution that distinguishes the ethical man. And all the agencies and instrumentalities employed by men, singly or collectively, should be based upon the best ethical practice of the time, so that the end-in-view of society may thereby be hastened.

Of all these agencies the printed word is most widely diffused and most powerful. The printed word is the single instrument of the profession we represent, and the extent to which it is shaping the thoughts and the conduct of peoples is measureless. We therefore pronounce the ethical responsibility of journalism the greatest of the professional responsibilities, and we desire to accept our responsibility; now and hereafter, to the utmost extent that is right and reasonable in our respective circumstances.

Accordingly, we adopt for our guidance the following code, which shall be known as the Oregon Code of Ethics for Journalism.

I. SINCERITY; TRUTH

The foundation of ethical journalism is sincerity. The sincere journalist will be honest alike in his purposes and in his writings. To the best of his capacity to ascertain truth, he will always be truthful. It si his attitude toward truth that distinguishes the ethical from the unethical writer. It is naturally not possible that all writing can be without error; but it can always be without deliberate error. There is no place in journalism for the dissembler; the distorter; the prevaricator; the suppressor; or the dishonest thinker.

The first section of this code therefore provides that we shall be continuously sincere in professional practice; and sincerity as journalists means, for example, that:

1. We will put accuracy above all other considerations in the written word, whether editorial, advertisement, article, or news story.

2. We will interpret accuracy not merely as the absence of actual misstatement, but as the presence of whatever is necessary to prevent the reader from making a false deduction.

3. In an ethical attitude toward truth, we will be open at all times to conviction, for the sincere journalist, while fearless and firm, will never be stubborn; therefore we will never decline to hear and consider new evidence.

4. If new evidence forces a change of opinion, we will be as free in the acknowledgment of the new opinion as in the utterance of the old.

5. We will promote a similar attitude in others toward truth, not asking or permitting employees to write things which as sincere journalists we would not ourselves write.

II. Care; Competency; Thoroughness

Inaccuracy in journalism is commonly due more to lack of mental equipment than to willfulness of attitude. The ill-equipped man cannot be more competent as a journalist than he can as a doctor or engineer. Given an ethical attitude, the contribution that each journalist makes to his community and to society is nearly in ratio to his competency. We regard journalism as a precise and a learned profession, and it is therefore the second part of this code that:

6. By study and inquiry and observation, we will constantly aim to improve ourselves; so that our writings may be more authentic, and of greater perspective, and more conducive to the social good.

7. We will consider it an essential in those we employ that they not merely be of ethical attitude, but reasonably equipped to carry out their ideals.

8. We will make care our devotion in the preparation of statements of fact and in the utterance of opinion.

9. We will advocate in our respective communities the same thoroughness, sound preparation, and pride of craft, that we desire in ourselves, our employees, and our associates.

10. We are accordingly the active enemies of superficiality and pretense.

III. Justice; Mercy; Kindliness

Liberty of the press is, by constitution, statute, and custom, greater in the United States than anywhere else in the world. This liberty exists for our press so that the liberty of the whole people may thereby be guarded. It so happens that at times the liberty of the press is exercised as license to infringe upon the rights of groups and of individuals: because custom and law have brought about certain immunities, it happens that in haste or zeal or malice or indifference, persons are unjustly dealt by. Yet the freedom of the press should at all times be exercised as the makers of the constitution, and the people themselves through their tolerance, have intended it. The reputations of men and women are sacred in nature and not to be torn down lightly. We therefore pronounce it appropriate to include in this code that:

11. We will not make "privileged utterance" a cloak for unjust attack, or spiteful venting, or carelessness in investigation, in the cases of parties or persons.

12. We will aim to protect, within reason, the rights of individuals mentioned in public documents, regardless of the effect on "good stories" or upon editorial policy.

13. We will deal by all persons alike so far as is humanly possible, not varying from the procedure of any part of this code because of the wealth, influence, or personal situation of the persons concerned, except as hereinafter provided.

14. It shall be one of our canons that mercy and kindliness are legitimate considerations in any place of journalism; and that if the public or social interest seems to be best conserved by suppression, we may suppress; but the motive in such instances must always be the public or social interest, and not the personal or commercial interest.

15. We will try so to conduct our publication, or to direct our writing, that justice, kindliness, and mercy will characterize our work.

IV. MODERATION; CONSERVATISM; PROPORTION

Since the public takes from the journalist so great a proportion of the evidence upon which it forms its opinions, obviously that evidence should be of high type. The writer who makes his appeal to the passions rather than to the intellect is too often invalid as a purveyor of evidence because his facts are out of perspective. By improper emphasis, by skillful arrangement, or by devices of typography or rhetoric, he causes the formation in the reader's mind of unsound opinion. This practice is quite as improper as and frequently is more harmful than actual prevarication. Through this code we desire to take a position against so-called sensational practice by acceptance of the following canons:

16. We will endeavor to avoid the injustice that springs from hasty conclusion in editorial or reportorial or interpretative practice.

17. We will not overplay news or editorial for the sake of effect when such procedure may lead to false deductions in readers' minds.

18. We will regard accuracy and completeness as more vital than our being the first to print.

19. We will try to observe due proportion in the display of news to the

end that inconsequential matter may not seem to take precedence in social importance over news of public significance.

20. We will in all respects in our writing and publishing endeavor to observe moderation and steadiness.

21. Recognizing that the kaleidoscopic changes in news tend to keep the public processes of mind at a superficial level, we will try to maintain a news and an editorial policy that will be less ephemeral in its influence upon social thought.

V. PARTISANSHIP; PROPAGANDA

We believe that the public has confidence in the printed word of journalism proportion as it is able to believe in the competency of journalists and have trust in their motives. Lack of trust in our motives may arise from the suspicion that we shape our writings to suit non-social interests, or that we open our columns to propaganda, or both. Accordingly we adopt the following professional canons:

22 We will resist outside control in every phase of our intellectual freedom in journalism.

23. We will rise above party and other partisanship in writing and publishing, supporting parties and issues only so far as we sincerely believe them to be in the public interest.

24 We will not permit, unless in exceptional cases, the publishing of news and editorial matter not prepared by ourselves or our staffs, believing that original matter is the best answer to the peril of propaganda.

VI. PUBLIC SERVICE AND SOCIAL POLICY

We dispute the maxim sometimes heard that a newspaper rather than try to lead it. We do not expect to be so far ahead of our time that our policies will be impractical; but we do desire to be abreast of the best thought of the time, and if possible to be its guide. It is not true that a newspaper should be only as advanced in its ethical atmosphere as it conceives the average of its readers to be. No man who is not in ethical advance of the average of the community should be in the profession of journalism. We declare therefore is follows:

25. We will keep our writings and our publications free from un-refinement, except so far us we may sincerely believe publication of sordid details to be for the social good.

26. We will consider all that we write or publish for public consumption in the light of its effect upon social policy, refraining from writing or from publishing if we believe our material to be socially detrimental.

27. We will regard our privilege or writing for publication or publishing for public consumption as an enterprise that is social as well as commercial in character, and therefore will at all times have an eye against doing anything counter to social interest.

28. We believe it an essential part of this policy that we shall not be respecters of persons.

VII. ADVERTISING AND CIRCULATION

We repudiate the principle of "letting the buyer beware." we cannot agree to guarantee advertising, but we assume a definite attitude toward the advertising that we write, solicit, or print. We believe that the same canons of truth and justice should apply in advertising and circulation as we are adopting for news and editorial matter. We therefore agree to the following business principles:

29. We will cooperate with those social interests whose business it is to raise the ethical standard of advertising.

30. We will discourage and bar from our columns advertising which in our belief is intended to deceive the reader in his estimate of what is advertised. (This clause is intended to cover the many phases of fraud, and unfair competition: and the advertising of articles that seem likely to be harmful to the purchaser's morals or health.)

31. We will not advertise our own newspaper or its circulation boastfully, or otherwise, in terms not in harmony with the clauses of this code of ethics. (This is intended to cover misleading statements to the public or to advertisers as to the whole number of copies printed, number of paid-up subscribers, number of street sales, and percentage of local circulation.)

32. We will not make our printing facilities available for the production of advertising which we believe to be socially harmful or fraudulent in its intent.

To the foregoing code we subscribe heartily as a part of our duty to society and of our belief that the salvation of the world can come only through the acceptance and practice by the people of the world of a sound and practical ethical philosophy.

SOUTH DAKOTA CODE OF ETHICS[1]

We of the profession of journalism, especially of that department which has to do with the publication of newspapers, deem it fitting that a code of ethics be set down to embody those ideals of service and that sense of propriety and honor which should imbue the motives and guide the actions of all who enter upon this profession.

This code of ethics is founded upon the basic principle of truth and justice. It is to be kept as nearly inviolate as is possible in the alignment of human aspirations with the golden rule of conduct, "whatsoever ye would that they do unto you, do ye so unto them."

SERVICE

The profession of journalism occupies the place of an essential service in its relations to the public. Its implied contract with the reader invites

---

[1] Written by a committee composed of J. H. Mckeever, H A Sturges. Paul W Kieser, and J. A Wight, and adopted by the South Dakota Press Association in 1922.

trust and accepts the responsibility of dependence. To merit this mutuality of interests the newspaper owes and must give adherence to high standards and these recognized ideals of motive, heart, and conduct.

TRUTH AND HONESTY

The foundation stone of the profession of journalism is truth. Unwavering adherence to "whatsoever things are true, whatsoever things are honest," must be the constant aim of men and women who publish newspapers.

News should be uncolored report of all vital facts accurately stated, insofar as it is possible to arrive at them.

Editorials should be sincere discussion based upon true statements in the premises from which honest argument may be developed by orderly deduction.

Advertising should be decent and honest in its selling intent and free from misleading or untrue statement.

FAIRNESS AND ACCURACY

The profession of journalism must be fair in all its dealings with the public. Society exists and our laws are made under a government deriving its powers from the people continued existence.

To the end that this continue to be justly so, it is of first importance that the whole people be kept fully and fairly informed.

The printed word is the most widespread and useful medium of contact with the human mind, and the newspaper the most powerful agency for broad-casting information. Upon those who practice this profession rests the sacred duty of keeping these mighty means of communication among mankind pure at the source, undefiled of intent, and free of bias.

The profession of journalism is the greatest force in influencing human judgment. It is of first importance therefore, that judgments be formed after a fair presentation of all facts, accurately stated. This accuracy is not only to be an absence of misstatement, but the orderly presence of all the pertinent truths.

In accuracy partisanship or the taint of propaganda has no part and cannot be present in fair journalism.

SINCERITY AND DECENCY

Sincerity of purpose as well as of writings characterizes the ethical journalist, honest convictions inspire his written words. Back of them is the sincerity of desire that actuates all high intent.

With full realization of this, the members of the South Dakota Press Association accept their responsibility in truthfully reporting, in directing the thoughts, and shaping the conduct of society. In all sincerity and to the utmost extent that is right and reasonable in our respective communities, we pledge our efforts to this end.

Guaranteed the freedom of its press, the profession of journalism recognizes liberty is not license. It therefore reserves to itself the right of decision in what shall be printed and what shall be omitted.

This is done to safeguard our publications from un-refinement, to protect within reason the rights and reputations of individuals, and to free our papers from sordidness, except as we sincerely believe publication to be for the good of society.

We deem suppression to be a righteous function of ethical journalism to enforce omission of undue matter based upon an honorable intent to serve public good, and not selfish purpose.

Advertising, indecent in word or motive, the aim of which is to defraud, or which serves no useful purpose, has no part in the publications of the sincere member of the profession.

HONOR

The honor of the profession is above the publication of an untruth upon an unworthy motive or upon a biased discussion based upon the false premise of a half-truth entered upon for personal gain or party advancement.

The honor of the profession should be dear to all in a realization that individual character and conduct reflect good or ill upon the profession. If then, private honor the profession remains unsullied.

RECOMPENSE AND RESPECT

As the Servant is worthy of his hire, journalism is entitled to fair recompense in proportion as it serves. This must be evidenced by a demand which should be sufficient to establish all useful publications upon a sound business basis.

This is a prime essential because it is a fact that the publication, successful through honest endeavor and free of entanglements of financial obligation and political debt, has broader scope toward service, freer acceptance of its opinions and a larger opportunity for usefulness. Success in service is the end sought. And it is only to be obtained rightfully through integrity, industry, and a clear vision of the function of the true journalist.

As the profession of journalism demands of its members that they are honest, fair, and just to all, they in return shall demand fair treatment, justice, and respect from those with whom they deal.

MISSOURI DECLARATION OF PRINCIPLES AND CODE OF PRACTICE[①]

PREAMBLE

In America, where the stability of the government rests upon the approval of the people, it is essential that newspapers, the medium through which the people draw their information, be developed to a high point of

---

① Written by William Southern, Jr, and adopted by the Missouri Press Association in 1921.

efficiency, stability, impartiality, and integrity. The future of the republic depends on the maintenance of a high standard among journalists; such a standard can not be maintained unless the motives and conduct of the members of our profession are such as merit approval and confidence.

The profession of journalism is entitled to stand side by side with the other learned professions and is, far more than any other, interwoven with the lines of public service. The Journalist can not consider his profession rightly unless he recognizes his obligation to the public. A newspaper does not belong solely to its owner and is not fulfilling its highest functions if devoted selfishly. Therefore the Missouri Press Association presents the following principles as a general guide, not as a set form of rules, for the practice of journalism.

EDITORIAL

We declare as a fundamental principle that Truth is the basis of all correct journalism. To suppress the truth, when it properly belongs to the public, is a betrayal of public faith.

Editorial comment should always be fair and just and not controlled by business or political expediency. Nothing should be printed editorially which the writer will not readily acknowledge as his own in public.

Control of news or comment for business considerations is not worthy of a newspaper. The news should be covered, written, and interpreted wholly and at all times in the interest of the public. Advertisers have no claim on newspaper favor except in their capacity as readers and as members of the community.

No person who controls the policy of a newspaper should at the same time hold office or have affiliations, the duties of which conflict with the public service that his newspaper should render.

ADVERTISING

It is not good ethics nor good business to accept advertisements that are dishonest, deceptive, or misleading. Concerns or individuals who want to use your columns to sell questionable stocks or anything else which promises great returns for small investment should always be investigated. Our readers should be protected from advertising sharks. Rates should be fixed at a figure which will yield a profit and never cut. The reader deserves a square deal and the advertiser the same kind of treatment.

Advertising disguised as news or editorial should not be accepted. Political advertising especially should show at a glance that it is advertising. It is just as bad 'to be bribed by the promise of political patronage as to be bribed by political cash.

To tear down a competitor in order to build up one's self is not good business, nor is it ethical. Newspaper controversies should never enter newspaper columns. Good business demands the same treatment to a competitor that one would like for the competitor to give to one's self. Create new business rather than try to take away that of another.

Advertising should never be demanded from a customer simply because he has given it to another paper. Merit, product, and service should be the standard.

SUBSCRIPTION

The claiming of more subscribers than are actually on the paid list in order to secure larger advertising prices is obtaining money under false pretenses. The advertiser is entitled to know just what he is getting for his money, just what the newspaper is selling to him. Subscription lists made up at nominal prices or secured by means of premiums or contests are to be strictly avoided.

OUR CODE

In every line of journalistic endeavor we recognize and proclaim our obligation to the public, our duty to regard always the truth, to deal justly and walk humbly before the gospel of unselfish service.

KANSAS CODE OF ETHICS[1]

FOR THE PUBLISHER
IN ADVERTISING

Definition. —Advertising is news, or views, of a business or professional enterprise which leads directly to its profits or increased business.

News of the industrial or commercial development of an institution which in no way has a specific bearing upon the merits of its products is not advertising.

Besides news which leads to a profit, advertising also includes communications and reports, cards of thanks, etc. , over the space of which the editor has no control. Charges for the latter become more in the nature of a penalty to restrict their publication.

Responsibility. —The authorship of an advertisement should be so plainly stated in the contract or at the end that it could not avoid catching the attention of the reader before he has left the matter.

Unsigned advertisements in the news columns should either be preceded or followed by the word "advertisement" or its abbreviation.

Freedom of space. —We hold the right of the publisher to become a broker in land, loan, rental, and mercantile transactions through his want and advertising columns, and condemn any movement of those following such lines to restrict this right of the publisher to the free sale of his space for the purpose of bringing buyer and seller together.

This shall not be construed to warrant the publisher as such in handling the details, terms, etc. , of the trade, but merely in safeguarding his freedom in selling his space to bring the buyer and seller together, leaving

---

[1] Written by Willis E. Miller and adopted by the Kansas Editorial Association in 1910 — apparently the earliest code of ethics adopted by any association of journalists.

the bargaining to the principals.

Our advertising is to bring together the buyer and the seller, and we are not concerned whether it is paid for and ordered by the producer, the consumer, or a middleman.

Acceding to any other desires on the part of traders is knocking the foundations out from under the advertising business-the freedom of space. We hold that the freedom of space (where the payment is not a question) should only be restricted by the moral decency of the advertising matter.

We hold that the freedom of space denies us the right to sign any contract with a firm which contains any restrictions against the wording of the copy which we may receive from any other firm, even to the mentioning of the goods of the first firm by name.

Compensation. —We condemn the signing of contracts carrying with them the publication of any amount of free reading matter.

We condemn the acceptance of any exchange articles, trade checks, or courtesies in payment for advertising, holding that all advertising should be paid for in cash.

We condemn the giving of secret rebates upon the established advertising rate as published.

Rates. -All advertising rates should be on a unit per thousand basis and all advertisers are entitled to a full knowledge of the circulation, not only of the quantity but also of the distribution. Statements of circulation should show the number of bona fide subscribers, the number of exchanges, the number of complimentaries, and the number sold to newsdealers, and if possible the locality of distribution, in a general way.

Position. —Position contracts should be charged a fixed percentage above the established rate of the paper, and no contracts should be signed wherein a failure to give the position required results in a greater reduction from the established rate than the position premium is greater than the established rate.

Comparisons.—We consider it beneath the dignity of a publisher to place in his columns statements which make invidious comparisons between the amount of advertising carried or the circulation of his paper and that of his competitor.

Press Agents and Unpaid Advertising.—The specific trade name of an article of commerce, or the name of a merchant, manufacturer, or professional man with reference to his wares, products, or labors should not be mentioned in a pure news story.

We condemn as against moral decency the publication of any advertisement which will obviously lead to any form of retrogression, such as private medical personals, indecent massage parlor advertisements, private matrimonial advertisements, physician's or hospital's advertisement for the care of private diseases, which carry in them any descriptive or suggestive matter of the same.

IN CIRCULATION

Definition.—Circulation is the entire list of first-hand readers of a publication and comprises the paid readers, complimentary readers, exchange readers, and advertising readers.

Compensation.—Subscriptions should be solicited and received only on a basis of cash consideration, the paper and its payment being the only elements to the transaction.

News-dealers.—The purchase of a quantity of papers should be made outright, allowing for no return of unsold copies.

Gambling.—We condemn the practice of securing subscriptions through the sale or gift of chances.

Complimentaries.—Complimentary copies should not be sent to doctors, lawyers, ministers, postal clerks, and police or court officials for news or mailing privileges.

IN ESTIMATING

Definition. —Estimating is the science of computing costs. Its conclusion is the price.

Basis. —We do not favor the establishment of a minimum rate card for advertising which would be uniform among publishers, but we do favor a more thorough understanding of the subject of costs, and commend to our members the labors of the American Printers' Cost Commission of the First International Cost Congress recently held in Chicago. Let us learn our costs and then each establish a rate card based upon our investment and the cost of production, having no consideration for the comparative ability of the advertisers to pay, or the semi-news nature of the advertisement.

Quantity Discount. —We consider it unwise to allow discounts greater than 10 per cent from the rate of first insertion for succeeding insertions.

News

Definition. —News is the impartial report of the activities of mind, men, and matter which do not offend the moral sensibilities of the more enlightened people.

Lies. —We condemn as against truth:\

(1) The publication of fake illustrations of men and events of news interest, however marked their similarity, without an accompanying statement that they are not real pictures of the event or person, but only suggestive imitations.

(2) The publication of fake interviews made up of the assumed views of an individual, without his consent.

(3) The publication of interviews in quotations unless the exact, approved language of the interviewed be used. When an interview is not an exact quotation it should be obvious in the reading that only the thought and impression of the interviewer is being reported.

(4) The issuance of fake news dispatches, whether the same have for their purpose the influencing of stock quotations, elections, or the sale of securities or merchandise. Some of the greatest advertising in the world has been stolen through news columns in the form of dispatches from unscrupulous press agents. Millions have been made on the rise and fall of stock quotations caused by newspaper lies, sent out by designing reporters.

Injustice. —We condemn as against justice:

(1) The practice of reporters making detectives and spies of themselves in their endeavors to investigate the guilt or innocence of those under suspicion.

Reporters should not enter the domain of law in the apprehension of criminals. They should not become a detective or sweating agency for the purpose of furnishing excitement to the readers.

No suspect should have his hope of a just liberty foiled through the great prejudice which the public has formed against him because of the press verdict slyly couched in the news report, even before his arrest.

We should not even by insinuation interpret as facts our conclusions, unless by signature we become personally responsible for them. Expositions, explanation, and interpretation should be left to the field of the expert or specialist with a full consciousness of his personal responsibility.

(2) The publication of the rumors and common gossips or the assumptions of a reporter relative to a suspect pending his arrest or the final culmination of his trial. A staff of reporters is not a detective agency, and the right of a suspect to a fair and impartial trial is often confounded by a reporter's practice of printing every ill-founded rumor of which he gets wind.

Indecencies. —Classification: For the sake of clearness and order, crimes with which we will be concerned may be divided into those which offend against the public trust (such as bribery, defalcation, or embezzlement by a public official); those which offend against private institutions or employers (which are also often defalcations and betrayals of confidence), and crimes which offend against private morality, most often centering around the family relation.

(1) In dealing with the suspicions against public officials or trustees we urge that only facts put in their true relation and records be used in the news reports.

No presumption or conclusion of the reporter should be allowed to enter, even though it has all the elements of a correct conclusion.

Conclusions and presumptions should be placed in interviews with the identity of their author easily apparent.

If an editor desires to draw a conclusion on the case, let him sign it. Do not hide behind the impersonality of the paper with your personal opinions.

(2) In dealing with the suspicions against agents of private institutions, facts alone, put in their true relation, should again be used.

But in this class of stories suspicions and conclusions should be confined to those of the parties directly interested, and no statement of one party to the affair reflecting upon another should be published without at the same time publishing a statement of the accused relative thereto.

The comment of those not directly involved should not be published previous to the arrest or pending the trial.

(3) In dealing with the offenses against private morality, we should refuse to print any record of the matter, however true, until the warrant has been filed or the arrest made, and even then our report should contain only an epitome of the charges by the plaintiff and the answers by the defendant, preferably secured from their respective attorneys.

No society gossips or scandals, however true, should ever be published concerning such cases.

However prominent the principals, offenses against private morality should never receive first-page position and their details should be eliminated as much as possible.

Certain crimes against private morality which are revolting to our finer sensibilities should be ignored entirely; however, in the event of their having become public with harmful exaggerations, we may make an elementary statement, couched in the least suggestive language.

In no case should the reckless daring of the suspect be lionized,

(4) Except when the suspect has escaped, his picture should never be printed.

FOR THE EDITOR

VIEWS

Definition. —Views are the impressions, beliefs, or opinions which are published in a paper, whether from the editorial staffs of the same, outside contributors, or secured interviews.

A Distinction. —We hold that whenever a publication confines the bulk of its views to any particular line of thought, class of views, or side of a moot question, it becomes to that extent a class publication, and insomuch ceases to be a newspaper.

An Explanation. —You will note by our definition of news that it is the impartial portrayal of the decent activities of mind, men, and matter. This definition applied to class publications would be changed by replacing the word impartial with the word partial,

In this section we will deal with impartiality in the presentation of the decent activities of the mind of the community-with the views or editorial policy of a paper.

Responsibility. —Whereas a view or conclusion is the product of some mind or minds, and whereas the value and significance of a view is dependent upon the known merit of its author or authors, the reader is entitled and has the right to know the personal identity of the author, whether by the signature in a communication, the statement of the reporter in 'an interview, or the caption in a special article, and the paper as such should in no wise become an advocate.

Influence (Editorial). —We should avoid permitting large institutions or persons to own stock in or make loans to our publishing business if we have reasonable grounds to believe that their interest would be seriously affected by any other than a true presentation of all news and free willingness to present every possible point of view under signature or interview.

Influence (Reportorial). —No reporter should be retained who accepts any courtesies, unusual favors, opportunities for self-gain, or side employment from any factors whose interests would be affected by the manner in which his reports are made.

Deception. —We should not allow the presumed knowledge on the part of the interviewed that we are newspaper men to permit us to quote them without their explicit permission, but where such knowledge is certain we insist upon our right to print the views unless directly forbidden.

Faith With Interviewed. —An interview or statement should not be displayed previous to its publication without the permission of the author.

Bounds of Publicity. —A man's name and portrait are his private property and the point where they cease to be private and become public should be defined for our association.

EXTRACTS FROM RULES AND SUGGESTIONS PREPARED BY NEWSPAPERS FOR THE GUIDANCE OF THEIR STAFFS[1]

THE BROOKLYN EAGLE

EAGLE POLICY

1. The Brooklyn Eagle is primarily a home newspaper. It prints all the news, but aims to emphasize what is helpful rather than harmful. It believes in enterprise, but not in sensationalism. As a' 3-cent newspaper it must uphold the highest standards of newspaper making. In particular it must always be truthful, accurate and fair.

2. "Brooklyn First" is a cardinal principle of Eagle policy. This newspaper is a Brooklyn institution. It is also a public service institution. Whatever helps Brooklyn helps The Eagle. The more you know about Brooklyn and about The Eagle the better you will serve both.

3. The Eagle ranks as one of the world's greatest newspapers. The world is its province and its interest extends to the activities of human-kind everywhere. It is through being liberal and cosmopolitan that you can best contribute your share to preserving The Eagle's reputation as a broadly representative newspaper.

GENERAL RULES

The cardinal principle of good newspaper work is accuracy. The Eagle demands it and will insist on getting it. Verify your facts. Don't depend on some one's say-so, but go to the reference books.

Get names right. Nothing does a newspaper more harm than misspelled names. A list of names frequently used in The Eagle is included in

---

[1] A number of newspapers have no such published rules, but depend on tradition and oral instruction.

this book. Supplement this with a list of your own. Carelessness in this connection always bars promotion and has led to dismissal.

Be fair. The Eagle wants to make friends, not enemies. Don't suppress any part of the truth for fear of spoiling a good story. Get both sides. Don't let anyone use The Eagle to vent a grudge. Give the man or institution under attack a chance to make out a case.

When a person is charged with crime or has done something immoral or discreditable do not intrude the names of prominent relatives who are in no way involved. In writing obituaries do not emphasize unfortunate incidents in the lives of well-reputed persons.

Beware of the seekers after free publicity. Remember that space in The Eagle is worth twenty-five cents a line. What you give away The Eagle cannot sell. Don't help press agents cheat the advertising department.

Always hesitate to write anything that will offend the members of a race or sect. You may offend 20,000 Eagle readers with a single word. Do not mention the nationality or religious belief of a person under arrest unless that is an essential and inevitable feature of the story. Don't emphasize locality in fire or burglary stories or in news reports which give a special section an unsavory reputation.

Read *The Eagle* from the first page to the last. Only in that way can you become familiar with its style, its policy, and its special hobbies. If you discover errors, report them; if you have suggestions, make them. Read the other local papers and note how they handled your story. If you notice any important difference of fact, length or emphasis, call it to the City Editor's attention. To be known as a "live wire" is to be in line for promotion.

Beware of your own prejudices. Your personal likes or dislikes have no place in a news story. If you feel strongly on some subject try your hand at an editorial or write a letter for the Forum Page. But keep your news reports free from editorial comment.

Never promise to suppress a news story. News which you secure as an Eagle employee is The Eagle's property, and your superiors are the final judges of what shall or shall not be used. Requests for suppression or omission must always be carefully reported and reasons given, but your answer to the request must be nothing more than the promise that you will transmit it.

Always accept news items or suggestions from outsiders gratefully. Some may be worthless, but an attitude of encouragement ultimately wins help that will prove invaluable to you and to The Eagle.

THE CHRISTIAN SCIENCE MONITOR

1. Good English. —A feature of The Monitor is the wide field covered in its news service and the various departments, therefore space in its columns is valuable—each word should be to the point and tell its own story.

2. Terse, crisp writing is not necessarily devoid of the picturesque, and is far more forceful. In three words, "boil it down."

3. Aim at simplicity; express your thoughts so clearly "he that runs may read."Faulty construction, long, involved sentences, in which the original subject and predicate are hopelessly entangled in a labyrinth of modifying phrases and clauses, and the pronouns have become of doubtful lineage-all these are faults to be avoided. Use words of one syllable rather than those of many-the latter may serve to show off your learning, but the average reader hasn't a dictionary at his elbow or the time to use it.

4. You are writing for an English-reading public, of whom only a minority are college-bred men and women—don't lose sight of the majority. It often happens that the exact shade of meaning-it may be the pith of your "story"—can be conveyed only in the original tongue-use it then, by all means, but as a rule only such foreign words and expressions as by long

and familiar usage have become a part of the English language have any place in the columns of a daily paper.

5. Nauseating words. —Never use expressions that suggest nauseating ideas; as "burned to a crisp," "gutted."

6. Avoid such tautological expression as "marriage nuptials," "funeral obsequies," "suffocated to death," etc.

7. Slang. —Slang is undoubtedly a large element in colloquial language, yet it must be excluded from the columns of The Christian Science Monitor. Even in interviews it must not be used unless sanctioned by the EDITOR-IN-CHIEF. When the paper speaks for itself the use of slang is prohibited. This caution is given the second time that all may mark its imperative nature.

8. News, not Opinions. —The news columns are for news; not for opinions except as these are reported as news. Attempts on the part of the reporters or correspondents to usurp the editor's functions and pass judgment upon the merits of propositions should be suppressed, no matter how big a hole the omission makes in the story.

9. Beware of imputations of wrong-doing in connection with mysterious disappearances. Comment is not justifiable unless public interests are involved, and then good authority should be had for any statements made.

10. Reports of failures or anything affecting commercial credit should never be used upon hearsay.

11. Accuracy. —Editors and reporters in preparing their "copy" must write PROPER NAMES so plainly that they NEED NOT BE mistaken, and also when possible should use printed matter in the casts of plays and programs. One of the primal points in satisfactory performance of duty for The Christian Science Monitor is accuracy. This is made possible in the various departments by competent work in the editorial and reportorial branches. Write out in full both the first and last names of persons; initial for

middle name.

12. Verify all quotations, especially from the Bible, whenever time will permit.

13. Heads.-Indicate style of head by number. Make careful count, so that the head as written may fit the style. Head-lines must be an index to the story, not a characterization of it; descriptive, not opinionated; concrete, not abstract, and alliteration, claptrap, and sensationalism are PROHIBITED. General headings such as "Held for Court," "Sent to Jail," "Sued for Damages," will not be tolerated. Avoid such headings as "Killed Her Own Children"; "Frantic Mother's Horrible Deed"; "Lake Steamer Lost in Storm", "Wild Waves Gather a Harvest of Death."

15. Above All.-Remember that you are preparing copy for a Christian Science publication whose standard is Truth and whose policy is absolutely devoid of sensationalism.

THE SPRINGFIELD REPUBLICAN

INTERVIEWING

Never put within quotation marks in your copy what people say to you in an interview without,

First—An understanding with them that they are to be quoted.

Second—Letting them know just what words you attribute to them.

This is the only safe rule to follow when the subject is at all controversial or involves private or personal interests.

When people are quoted, the paper is placed in the position of assuring its readers that the quoted passages were literally spoken; consequently, inaccuracy in quotation is unpardonable.

Direct quotation in an interview, unless permission is given to use that form, can be avoided ordinarily by using indirect discourse. For instance, you may write: Mr. Smith, in discussing the subject, said in effect that-etc.

Reports of public addresses should never be put within quotation marks unless the exact language of the speaker is reproduced.

Before interviewing a person, decide on a series of questions on the subject about which you wish to inquire. If the person interviewed talks willingly, follow him through. If he does not, stick to your original questions. If the assignment presents difficulties, before you attempt it consult the city editor about the best method to pursue. Try to familiarize yourself as much as possible with the subject about which you are to talk with him.

OBITUARIES

Be very careful about writing obituaries. Make every possible effort to get the facts and write them accurately. Omit reference to aspects of the dead person's life, unless the circumstances are exceptional, which would pain or aggrieve the surviving relatives and friends. Good will may be cultivated for the paper by writing appreciatively of the dead person's good qualities and achievements.

MISCELLANEOUS INSTRUCTIONS

Read over your article so as to be sure the reader will get the picture you have in mind.

Do not depend on the editor to correct your mistakes; correct them yourself.

Never try to write a humorous article on the suffering or death of an animal, nor, in the case of human beings, where the incident involves disgrace, humiliation, or sorrow to them, their relatives, or friends.

Carefully estimate every piece of news you get. There is ample space for important news. Unimportant news should be disposed of as briefly as possible.

Wrong things will from time to time be done and wrong conditions will develop in this as in every other community. It is the function of an honest newspaper to print the news without fear or favor. Publicity brings correction. But no report should be so written that it can be interpreted as revealing a petty malice on the part of the reporter or the paper in attributing wrongful acts to any person. The Republican has been published in Springfield for nearly 100 years; it believes, with pride, that, the standards of the community are high and that it has contributed to their maintenance by a fearless news policy. The Republican, however, is not out to "get" anybody in order to gratify animosities. The paper wants friends, not enemies.

THE SPRINGFIELD UNION

1. The Union aims to be a newspaper worthwhile, a newspaper that will make you feel that you have rendered the public some measure of service.

2. Strive to be accurate and fair in your statements, that The Union may print the truth without bias.

3. Write nothing as a journalist that you would not write as a gentleman.

4. Seek to get news of real public interest. Give to it the space it is actually worth and a heading that will indicate its relative importance.

5. Remember, this is a busy world and few persons have the time or inclination to read verbose accounts of happenings, however important.

6. Tell what you have to tell in clear, concise English, attaching to words their true meanings.

7. Do not dwell on human frailties, or try to make sensations out of things that are not sensational. If you cry wolf when there is no wolf, the public will not believe you when the wolf comes. Public confidence is the best asset a newspaper can have, and it is your best asset also.

8. Avoid all that is yellow in journalism, but emulate the enterprise

that characterizes the yellow journalist.

9. Regard as especially valuable news concerning the world's progress-news of discoveries in the arts and sciences, news of inventions likely to work important changes, news of enterprises in which labor is interested, news of financial institutions and large corporations, news of railroads and all other public utilities, news of real estate transactions, news relating to public improvements, news of outdoor and indoor sports and pastimes, news concerning well-known persons, news pertaining to educational and religious topics, news of a political nature-in short, all news that naturally appeals to wholesome-minded people desirous of being informed of what is going on around and about them.

10. Put yourself in the reader's place and ask "Will this interest the average reader, and if so, how many of him?" Your judgment of your readers will be reflected in the way your story is written, in the amount of space you give to it and in the heading that you put on it.

11. To be on the safe side try to get as many different items as possible into The Union, remembering that The Union, is read by many people of varying tastes.

ACCURACY AND FAIRNESS

Accuracy! The Union demands it and will insist on getting it. Every correspondent, every reporter, every copy-reader, every editor, must learn to be accurate. And it is not enough merely to be accurate. It is quite as essential to be fair. Partial truths are worse than lies. Tell the truth, the whole truth, and nothing but the truth.

Don't accept anybody's say-so for the facts. See everybody concerned; get all sides. Something may seem to be so, probably is so, but you will not know whether it really is so until you have found out for yourself. Don't supply details from your imagination.

Nothing in all the world is so interesting as facts. If you write facts and write them fairly you can laugh at libel suits.

The Union makes due allowances for mistakes; it realizes that they occasionally will occur, but it expects every member of its staff to profit by his mistakes and not repeat them. Chronic carelessness invariably will result in dismissal. If you can't get things right The Union, doesn't want you.

Inaccuracy does serious injury to innocent persons, it hurts your chances of promotion and it destroys the public's confidence in the newspaper. The Union wants its reader to feel that they can believe everything it prints.

Be accurate.

Be fair.

Get facts.

SOME OF THE UNION S POLICIES

1. *The Union* aims to be a constructive, not a destructive newspaper. Get the news, but be charitable.

2. In politics *The Union* is Republican, but not narrowly so. It believes in the broad underlying principles of the Republican Party, but does not feel in any way bound to support every measure advocated by that party nor every candidate running on the Republican ticket. It puts the common good ahead of party or other considerations. It aims to deal fairly with all political parties, to give the news regardless of its own opinions, and to keep its columns always open. It is a newspaper absolutely free from entangling alliances of any sort.

3. The Union does not print the names of children who get into trouble with the police nor give publicity to cases that come before the juvenile court, unless the circumstances are such as to afford abundant justification for so doing.

4. The Union does not publish the names of persons arrested for drunkenness, nor of "drunks" who are fined nominal amounts by the court, unless the arrest and appearance in court were attended by unusual circumstances. Give them a chance to reform.

5. The Union does not mention the nationality of a person that commits a crime or other discreditable act, except as that may be an essential detail of the affair. The name itself usually conveys sufficient information and other persons of the same race quite properly resent the added emphasis that mention of the nationality gives.

6. It is The Union's policy to report cases of suicide in the briefest manner possible, unless the circumstances are very extraordinary or the person is of particular prominence. If death was accomplished by poison, do not name the kind of poison used. If with a revolver, do not tell where the bullet struck. If by hanging, do not describe the method. Do not make the account suggest to those who may be contemplating self-destruction how they may go about it.

7. In automobile accidents do not give the name of the car, nor in shooting cases the make of weapon used.

8. Do not advertise anything in the news columns. Articles offered for free publication are always to be regarded with suspicion. Generally they are clever attempts to get advertising for nothing. Don't help publicity agents to cheat the advertising department.

THE DETROIT NEWS

The paper should be:

Vigorous, but not Vicious.

Interesting, but not Sensational.

Fearless, but Fair.

Accurate as far as human effort can obtain accuracy.

Striving ever to gain and impart information.

As bright as possible, but never sacrificing solid information for brilliancy.

Looking for the Uplifting rather than the Depraved things of Life.

We should work to have the word reliable stamped all over every page of the paper.

The place to commence this is with the staff members: First getting men and women of character to do the writing and editing, and then training them in our way of thinking and handling news and other reading matter.

Nothing here is intended as a reflection on the present staff or the paper we have been getting out; we have a good staff and a good paper; the aim is to improve both as much as possible.

If you make an error, you have two duties to perform: One to the person misrepresented and one to your reading public. Never leave the reader of The News misinformed on any subject. If you wrongfully infer that a man has done something that he did not do, or has said something that he did not say, you do him an injustice-that's one. But you also do thousands of readers an injustice, leaving them misinformed as to the character of the man dealt with. Corrections should never be given grudgingly. Always make them cheerfully, fully, and in larger type than the error, if any difference.

If a reporter gets drunk, the people do not say, "There goes So-and-So," calling him by name, they say, "There goes a News reporter."That reflects on the entire staff, that robs the paper of a certain amount of its standing, of a certain amount of its reputation for reliability. No one has confidence in the work of a drunken man. Any one on the editorial staff who gets drunk once or who willfully prints a misstatement of any kind should not be retained on the staff a minute.

The American people want to know, to learn, to get information. To quote a writer: "Your opinion is worth no more than your information." Give them your information and let them draw their own conclusions. Comment should be more along the line of enlightenment by well-marshalled facts, and by telling the readers what relation an act of today has to an act of yesterday. Let them come to their own conclusions as far as possible.

No issue is worth advocating that is not strong enough to withstand all the facts that the opposition to it can throw against it. Our readers should be well informed on both sides of every issue.

Kindly, helpful suggestions will often direct officials in the right, where nagging will make them stay stubbornly on the wrong side. That does not mean that there should be any lack of diligence in watching for, and opposition to, intentional crooks.

A staff can only be good and strong by having every part of it strong. The moment it becomes evident that a man, either by force of circumstance or because of his own character, does not fit into our organization, you do him a kindness and do justice to the paper by letting him know, so he can go to a calling in which he can succeed, and he will not be in the way of filling the place with a competent man.

Make the paper good all the way through, so there will not be disappointment on the part of a reporter if his story is not found on the first page, but so he will feel it must have merit to get into the paper at all. Avoid making it a "front-page paper."

Stories should be brief, but not meager. Tell the story, all of it, in as few words as possible.

Nature makes facts more interesting than any reporter can imagine them. There is an interesting feature in every story, if you will but dig it out. If you don't get it, it is because you don't dig deep enough.

The most valuable asset of any paper is its reputation for telling the truth, the only way to have that reputation is to tell the truth. Untruth, due to carelessness, or excessive imagination, injures the paper as much as though intentional.

Everyone with a complaint should be given a respectful and kindly hearing; especial consideration should be given the poor and lowly, who may be less able to present their claims than those more favored in life. A man of prominence and education knows how to get into the office and present his complaint. A washerwoman may come to the door, timidly, haltingly, scarcely knowing what to do, and all the while her complaint may be as just as that of the other complainant, perhaps more so. She should be received kindly and helped to present what she has to say.

Simple, plain language is strongest and best. A man of meager education can understand it, while the man of higher education, usually reading a paper in the evening after a day's work, will read it with relish. There is never any need of using big words to show off one's learning. The object of a story or an editorial is to inform or convince, but it is hard to do either if the reader has to study over a big word or an involved sentence. Stick to plain English all the time. A few readers may understand and appreciate a Latin or French quotation, or one from some other foreign language, but the big mass of our readers are the plain people and such a quotation would be lost on the majority.

Be fair. Don't let the libel laws be your measure as to the printing of a story, but let fairness be your measure. If you are fair, you need not worry any about libel laws.

Always give the other fellow a hearing. He may be in the wrong, but even that may be a matter of degree. It wouldn't be fair to picture him as all black when there may be mitigating circumstances.

It is not necessary to tell the people that we are honest, or bright, or alert, or that a story appeared exclusively in our paper. If true, the public will find it out. An honest man does not have to advertise his honesty eternally.

Time heals all things but a woman's damaged reputation. Be careful and cautious and fair and decent in dealing with any man's reputation, but be doubly so-and then some-when a woman's name is at stake. Do not by direct statement, jest, or careless reference, raise a question mark after any woman's name if it can be avoided-and it usually can be. Even if a woman slips, be generous; it may be a crisis in her life. Printing the story may drive her to despair; kindly treatment may leave her with hope. No story is worth ruining a woman's life-or man's either.

Keep the paper clean in language and thought. Profane or suggestive words are not necessary. When in doubt, think of a 13—year-old girl reading what you are writing.

Do not look on newspaper work as a "game," of pitilessly printing that on which you are only half-informed, for the mere sake of beating some other paper, but take it rather as a serious, constructive work in which you are to use all the energy and diligence needed to get all the worth-while information for your readers at the earliest possible moment at which you can do so and have it reliable.

Nothing should ever be taken from another publication without giving full credit. Merely crediting a piece of writing to "Exchange" is not fair.

Elections coming on Tuesday, no candidate or party should be permitted to print new charges or statements later than the Friday before election. No paper should print anything about anybody without allowing ample time for an answer.

The hardest lesson the journalist must learn is the development of the impersonal viewpoint. He must learn to write what he sees and hears, clearly and accurately, with never a tinge of bias. His own views, his personal feelings, and his friendships should have nothing to do with what he writes in a story.

The ideal reporter would be a man who could give the public facts about his bitterest enemy even though such facts would make the man he personally hated a hero before the public.

THE HEARST NEWSPAPERS[1]

ADVERTISING

The principles and policies governing the advertising department of our newspapers should be just as firmly established and just as well known to every one in the business office as the news and editorial departments.

News and editorial character are built only on reliability of statement. We cannot hope to build advertising on any other basis. No man who misrepresents facts must be allowed on our newspapers. Honesty is a form of common sense.

Employ men of brains, breeding and acquaintance. Character counts in advertising as in all other things.

Our newspapers must sell advertising only by their printed rate card. If your rate card is wrong, change it. If it is right, live up to every letter of it. There should be no double standard of morality involving buyer and seller of advertising. Cut rates, special concessions and secret rebates are boomerangs, which return to cripple progress when they are least expected. Men who make "gentlemen's agreements" are not wanted.

Do not accept any advertising which is detrimental to the public welfare. Questionable financial, objectionable medical, clairvoyants, spiritualists, fortune tellers and fake advertising of any and every description have no place in the Hearst newspapers. Our readers trust us. We would

---

[1] The selections are from the personal instructions given by William Randolph Hearst to his newspapers.

not deceive them in our news or editorial columns. We must not allow others to deceive them in our advertising columns.

NEWS

Make the paper accurate and trustworthy.

Compare statements in our paper with those in other papers and find out which are accurate.

Get rid of reporters and copy-readers who are persistently inaccurate. Reward those who are trustworthy as you reward those who are valuable in other respects.

Don't allow exaggeration. It is a cheap and ineffective substitute for real interest. Show appreciation for reporters, who can make the truth interesting. Eliminate those who can not.

Be fair and impartial in the news columns at least. Don't make a paper for Democrats, or Republicans, or Independence Leaguers. Make a paper for all the people, and give unbiased news of all creeds and parties. Try to do this in such a conspicuous manner that it will be noticed and commented upon.

Condense the news when necessary to get it in. Much of the news is better when intelligently condensed.

Make your departments complete and reliable, so that the reader will know, first, that he can find a thing in the paper, and, second, that he can find it right.

Make the paper thorough; print all the news. Not only get all the news into the office, but see that it gets into the paper.

Select the best stories in the paper and feature them— i. e., emphasize them in a way to make them stand out and give life and character to the paper.

If your feature is big enough, it must get display, regardless of everything; but mere display does not make a feature.

It is not necessary to cover a page with a story in order to make it a feature. A page feature generally looks heavy and is heavy. A story should be made to stand out by appreciation of the interesting points and emphasis of those points in typography and phraseology. A feature can be made interesting in a column, and it may be made stupid in a page.

Make a paper for the best kind of people. The masses of the reading public are better and more intelligent than newspapermen seem to think they are.

Don't print a lot of stuff that nice people are supposed to like and do not, but omit things that will offend nice people.

Avoid coarseness and slang and a low tone. The most sensational news can be told if it is written properly.

Don't use the words "murder," "scandal," "divorce," "crime," and other rather offensive phrases when it is possible to tell the story without them. Murder stories and other criminal stories are not printed merely because they are criminal, but because of the 'mystery, or the romance, or the dramatic qualities in them. Therefore, develop the mystery, or the romance, or the dramatic qualities, and avoid the offensive qualities.

Make the paper helpful and kindly and pleasing.

Don't scold and forever complain and attack in the news columns.

An occasionable justifiable crusade or exposure will be all the more effective if this rule is maintained.

Please sum up your paper every day at a conference and find wherein it is distinctly better than the other papers. If it is not distinctly better, you have missed that day. Lay out plans to make it distinctly better the next day.

THE SACRAMENTO BEE

The Bee demands from all its writers accuracy before anything else.

Better lose an item than make a splurge one day and correct it next.

Equally with that, it demands absolute fairness in the treatment of news. Reports must not be colored to please a friend or wrong an enemy.

Don't editorialize in the news columns. An accurate report is its own best editorial.

Don't exaggerate. Every exaggeration hurts immeasurably the cause it pretends to help.

If a mistake is made, it must be corrected. It is as much the duty of a Bee writer to work to the rectification of a wrong done by an error in an item as it is first to use every precaution not to allow that error to creep in.

Be extremely careful of the name and reputation of women. Even when dealing with the unfortunate, remember that so long as she commits no crime other than her own sin against chastity, she is entitled at least to pity.

Sneers at race, or religion, or physical deformity, will not be tolerated. "Dago," "Mick," "Sheeny," even "Chink" or "Jap," these are absolutely forbidden. This rule of regard for the feelings of others must be observed in every avenue of news, under any and all conditions.

There is a time for humor and there is a time for seriousness. The Bee likes snap and ginger at all times. It will not tolerate flippancy on serious subjects on any occasion.

The furnisher of an item is entitled to a hearing for his side at all times, not championship. If the latter is ever deemed necessary, the editorial department will attend to it.

Interviews given the paper at the paper's request are to be considered immune from sneers or criticism.

In every accusation against a public official or private citizen, make every effort to have the statement of the accused given prominence in the original item.

In the case of charges which are not ex officio or from a public source, it is better to lose an item than to chance the doing of a wrong.

Consider The Bee always as a tribunal that desires to do justice to all; that fears far more to do injustice to the poorest beggar than to clash swords with wealthy injustice.

THE SEATTLE TIMES

The following rules of decency are published for the guidance of all concerned:

(a) Remember that young girls read The Times.

(b) The physiology of conception and childbirth and all matters relating thereto will not be discussed in the columns of The Times.

(c) All scandalous matter will be omitted, excepting where competent orders are given to the contrary.

(d) When it is necessary to refer to improper relations between the sexes, the limit permitted in *The Times* is some such statement as: "The couple were divorced," or "The couple separated," or "Various charges were made not considered fit for publication in the columns of *The Times*."

(e) The use of the words, "rape," "adultery," "indecent exposure," "incest," "assault" (in this connection), or any word, phrase, or sentence, similar or having like meaning, is prohibited.

(f) As far as practicable, any news bearing upon events that depend upon the commission of crimes of sex will be omitted from the paper. Where a person is lynched for a crime against a woman or child, the cause of the lynching will not be given, and for it will be substituted some such statement as "The victim of the mob was accused of injuring a woman."

(g) Reference to expectancy of motherhood or physicians' certificates in connection with establishment of the innocence of a woman charged with a sexual crime, or any other subject that in the remotest degree is of a similar character, will be omitted.

(h) In connection with accidents where persons are injured or killed, all unpleasant details of suffering or maiming will be omitted. In this connection the word "mangle" is forbidden, and this prohibition should carry with it by inference anything of a similar nature.

THE KANSAS CITY JOURNAL-POST

There are two sides to every story. GET BOTH.

The best story is simply told and told simply.

Be truthful.

Get the facts.

The Journal-Post will play its politics on the editorial page. Write political stories impartially.

Treat religious matters reverently.

Avoid heaping ignominy on innocent men, women, and children.

The Journal-Post's ideals are high-truthfulness, toleration, fairness, decency, and cleanliness.

ALWAYS VERIFY NAMES!

THE MARION STAR[①]

Remember there are two sides to every question. Get them both.

Be truthful.

Get the facts. Mistakes are inevitable, but strive for accuracy. I would rather have one story exactly right than a hundred half wrong.

Be decent. Be fair. Be generous.

Boost-don't knock. There's good in everybody. Bring out the good and never needlessly hurt the feelings of anybody.

---

① Written by the late President Warren G. Harding when editing The Star.

In reporting a political gathering, get the facts; Tell the story as it is, not as you would like to have it.

Treat all parties alike. If there is any politics to be played, we will play them in our editorial columns.

Treat all religious matters reverently.

If it can possibly be avoided, never bring ignominy on an innocent man or child, in telling of the misdeeds or misfortunes of a relative. Don't wait to be asked, but do it without the asking.

And, above all, be clean. Never let a dirty word or suggestive story get into type.

I want this paper to be so conducted that it can go into any home without destroying the innocence of any child.

THE JOURNALIST's CREED

By Walter Williams

I believe in the profession of journalism.

I believe that the public journal is a public trust; that all connected with it are, to the full measure of their responsibility, trustees for the public; that acceptance of lesser service than the public service is betrayal of this trust.

I believe that clear thinking, and clear statement, accuracy, and fairness are fundamental to good journalism.

I believe that a journalist should write only what he holds in his heart to be true.

I believe that suppression of the news for any consideration other than the welfare of society is indefensible.

I believe that no one should write as a journalist what he would not say as a gentleman; that bribery by one's own pocketbook is as much to be avoided as bribery by the pocketbook of another; that individual responsibility may not be escaped by pleading another's instruction or another's dividends.

I believe that advertising, news, and editorial columns should alike serve the best interests of the readers; that a single standard of helpful truth and clearness should prevail for all; that the supreme test of journalism is the measure of its public service.

I believe that the journalism which succeeds best-and the best deserves success-fears God and honors man; is stoutly independent, unmoved by pride of opinion, or greed of power; constructive, tolerant, but never careless; self-controlled, patient, always respectful of its readers, always unafraid; is quickly indignant at injustice; is unswayed by the appeal of privilege, or the clamor of the mob; seeks to give every man a chance, and, as far as law and honest wages and recognition of human brotherhood can make it so, an equal chance; is profoundly patriotic, while sincerely promoting international good will, and cementing world comradeship; is a journalism of humanity, of and for today's world.

Appendix B A Selective Bibliography

Books and Parts of Books

Adams, Samuel Hopkins. *The Clarion*. Boston: Houghton Mifflin Company. 1914.
 A novel dealing with the newspaper and the patent medicine business.

Adams, Samuel Hopkins. *The Great American Fraud*. Chicago: American Medical Association. 1906.
 Articles on the patent medicine business and its influence on the press.

Adams, Samuel Hopkins. Success. Boston: Houghton Mifflin Company. 1921.
 A novel of newspaper life, bringing out many ethical problems.

American Bar Association. Canons of Professional Ethics. Baltimore: American Bar Association. 1917.
 A statement of the ethical standards of the American bar.

American Medical Association. *Principles of Medical Ethics*. Chicago: American Medical Association. 1914.

A statement of the ethical principles held in the medical profession in the United States.

Angell, Norman. *The Press and the Organisation of Society*. London: Labour Publishing Company. 1922.

A study of the press in relation to social organization, from the intellectual labor point of view.

Audit Bureau of Circulations. Scientific Space Selection. Chicago: Audit Bureau of Circulations. 1921.

A detailed explanation of the basis of the sale of advertising space, with data on its evolution.

Belloc, Hilaire. The Free Press. London: George Allen & Unwin. Ltd. 1918.

An analysis of the effects of commercialism on the British press, and a discussion of the "free press" as a means for making the truth known.

Bennett. Arnold. What the Public Wants. New York: George H. Doran Company. 1911.

A play dealing with an English newspaper proprietor who has no ideal above that of pleasing the public.

Bleyer. Willard Grosvenor. editor. The Profession of. Journalism. Boston: Atlantic Monthly Press. 1918.

Essays on various phases of journalism, by various writers, originally published in -Dze Atlantic Monthly.

Chafee, Zechariah, Jr. *Freedom of Speech*. New York: Harcourt, Brace and Howe. 1920.

A discussion, by a distinguished professor of law, of the historic meaning of freedom of speech and of recent departures from that meaning.

Chicago Commission on Race Relations. The Negro in Chicago. pp. 436—574. 6eg-639, 650—65r. Chicago: University of Chicago Press. 1922.

Data on the handling of race riot news by the press, and recommendations with reference to public opinion on the negro problem.

Cook, E. T. *The Press in Wartime*. New York: The Macmillan Company. 1920.

A detailed discussion. by a British writer, of the situation of the press in war.

Dana, Charles. *The Art of Newspaper Making*. New York: D. Appleton and Company. 1895.

Three Lectures giving the views of the distinguished nineteenth-century editor on ethical and other problems of journalism.

Davis, Elmer. *History of The New York Times*. 1851—1921. New York: The New York Times. 1921.

A history of one of the greatest newspapers in the United States, by a member of its editorial staff.

Eastman, Max. *Journalism Versus Art*. New York: Alfred A. Knopf, Inc. 1916.

Criticism of the influence of journalism against significant art.

Edman, Irwin. *Human Traits and Their Social Significance*. Boston: Houghton Miffiin Company. 1920.

A discussion of human traits in the contemporary social environment.

Every-day Ethics. pp. 1—15. New Haven: Yale University press. 1910.

An address on ethical problems in journalism, delivered by Norman Hapgood at the Shefileld Scientific School.

Freud, Sigmund. *A General Introduction to Psychoanalysis*. New York: The Macmillan Company. 1922.

A work devoting much attention to the place of the emotions in the formation of beliefs.

Gibbs, Sir Philip. *Now It Can Be Told*. New York: Harper & Brothers. 1920.

A recital of facts about the Great War, showing the part. played by untruthful propaganda.

Hackett, Francis. *The Invisible Censor*. New York: B. W. Huebsch, Inc. 1921.

A book of essays, some of which have special reference to journalism and public opinion.

Hale, William G. *The Law of the Press*. St. Paul: West Publishing Co. 1923.

A thorough discussion of the various laws governing the newspaper in the United States.

Hart, Bernard. *The Psychology of Insanity*. Cambridge, England: University Press. 1916.

A work on mental conflict, making clear the problems of fear, dissociation of consciousness, and the like.

Heaton, John L. *The Story of a Page*. New York: Harper & Brothers. 1913.

A history of the editorial influence of *The New York World* under Joseph Pulitzer.

Holt, Hamilton. *Commercialism and Journalism*. Boston: Houghton Mifflin Company. 1909.

An address delivered at the University of California.

Interchurch World Movement, Commission of Inquiry. *Public Opinion and the Steel Strike*. New York: Harcourt, Brace & Company. 1921.

Reports of investigators on the manipulation of public opinion, by newspapers and other means, in the steel strike of 1919.

Labour Research Department. *The Press*. London: Labour Publishing Company. 1922.

A survey of the newspaper industry as a part of the economic development of England.

Lee, James Melvin. *History of American Journalism*. Boston: Houghton Mifflin Company. 1917. Second Edition (revised), 1923.

A history containing innumerable quotations from newspapers and other valuable reference data.

Lippmann, Walter. *Liberty and the News*. New York: Harcourt, Brace and Howe. 1920.

Three essays analyzing the nature of modern liberty and its relation to the press.

Lippmann, Walter. *Public Opinion*. New York: Harcourt, Brace and Company. 1922.

The best and most modern realistic presentation of 'the formation of public opinion.

Locard, Edmond. *L' Enquête Criminelle et les Méthodes Scentifiques*. Paris: Ernest Flammarion. 1920. i

A work showing among other things, the inability of the average witness to describe objectively.

Lowell, A. Lawrence. *Public Opinion in War and Peace*. Cambridge: Harvard University Press. 1923.

A discussion, by the president of Harvard University, of factors influencing opinion and of the reciprocal influence of opinion upon these factors.

Massart. Jean. *The Secret Press in Belgium*. New York: E. P. Dutton & Company. 1919.

A history of the maintenance of a pro-Belgian press throughout the war despite the efforts of the German army to suppress it.

Masters, Edgar Lee. *Spoon River Anthology*. New York: The Macmillan Company. 1914.

A series of poems in which reference is made to newspapers and public opinion in a village.

Migne, Jacques Paul, editor. *Patres Latini*. Volume XIV. Paris: Garnier Frères.

St. Ambrose's *Hexaëmeron*, which expresses the traditional attitude toward objective facts, is found in the volume cited.

Mill, John Stuart. *On Liberty*. New York: Henry Holt & Company. 1882.

A discussion, perhaps the best in the English language, on the subject of liberty, by the great economist.

Mills, William Haslam. *The Manchester Guardian, a Century of History*. New York: Henry Holt and Company. 1922.

An interpretative history of the great Liberal daily of England.

Nevins, Allan. *The Evening Post: A Century of Journalism*. New York: Boni & Liveright. 1922.

The history of one of the oldest and most highly respected dailies in the United States.

O'Brien, Frank Michael. *The Story of The Sun*. New York: George H. Doran Company. 1918.

A history of one of the most distinctive of American newspapers.

Older, Fremont. My Own Story. San Francisco: The Call. 1919.

An account of the experiences of the veteran Pacific coast journalist on San Francisco newspapers.

Park, Robert E. *The Immigrant Press and Its Control*. New York: Harper & Brothers. 1922.

A survey of the foreign language press, with data on the manner in which much of it has been subsidized.

Payne. George Henry. *History of Journalism in the United States*. New York: D. Appleton and Company. 1920.

An interpretation of events in the history of the American press in the light of contemporaneous political happenings.

Ransome, Arthur. *The Crisis in Russia.* New York: B. W. Huebsch, Inc. 1921

Examples of highly competent reporting in a difficult field, from The Manchester Guardian.

Robinson, James Harvey. *The Mind in the Making.* New York: Harper & Brothers. 1921.

A realistic account of the development of human thought.

Rogers, J. E. *The American Newspaper.* Chicago: University of Chicago Press. 1909.

A study of the space devoted to various kinds of news in newspapers fifteen years ago.

Rowell, George P. *American Newspaper Directory.* Boston: George P. Rowell. 1879.

An old directory, containing suggestions of interest on the publishing practices of its time.

Salmon, Lucy Maynard. *The Newspaper and the Historian.* New York: Oxford University Press. 1923.

A study of the excellencies and the deficiencies of the press as a source of historical material.

Scott, Walter Dill. *The Psychology of Advertising.* pp. 375 — 394 Boston: Small, Maynard & Company. 1908.

Results of a questionnaire on the time spent in reading newspapers.

Scott-James. R. G. *The Influence of the Press.* London: S. W. Partridge & Company. Ltd. 1914.

A discussion of the development of newspaper influence, referring chiefly to England, but treating the American press to some extent.

Shuman, Edwin L. *Practical Journalism.* New York: D. Appleton & Company. 1903.

One of the earlier works on journalistic practice, containing material on the tendencies of the press at the time when the book was written.

Sinclair, Upton. *The Brass Check*. Pasadena, Cal. : Author. 1919.

An attack on the American press, which the author holds has prostituted itself to capitalism.

Stearns. Harold E. , editor. *Civilization in the United States*. pp. 35—52. 381—396. New York: Harcourt. Brace and Company. 1922.

Essays on journalism and advertising, by John Macy and J. Thorne Smith respectively. as part of a general inquiry into American life.

Sullivan, . Mark T. *National Floodmarks*. New York: George H. Doran Company. 1915.

Editorials, some of them on journalistic problems, from Collieds Weelzty.

The W. G. N. Chicago: *The Tribune*. 1922. .

A history of The Chicago Tribune, published in commemoration of its seventy-fifth birthday.

Thorpe, Merle, *editor*. *The Coming Newspaper*. New York: Henry Holt and Company. 1915.

Addresses at the 19i4 Newspaper Week, University of Kansas.

Trotter, W. *Instincts of the Herd in Peace and War*. New York: The Macmillan Company. 1916.

An examination of herd instinct in its relation to contemporary civilization.

Villard. Oswald Garrison. *Some Newspapers and Newspapermen*. New York: Alfred A. Knopf, Inc. 1923.

A discussion of prominent American daily papers and editors, by the editor of The Nation.

Watterson, Henry. "*Marse Henry*," *An Autobiography*. New York: George H. Doran Company. 1919.

The journalistic and other experiences of the great editor of *The Louisville Courier-Journal*.

White, Lee A. The Detroit News: 1873 — 1917. Detroit: The Evening News Association. 1918.

The history of a great Middle Western daily newspaper.

William Rockhill Nelson. The Story of a Man, a Newspaper, and a City. Cambridge: The Riverside Press. 1915.

The history of the work of the late distinguished editor of The Kansas City Star.

Williams. J. B. *A History of British Journalism to the Foundation of the Gazette.* Oxford: University Press. 1908.

A work showing the restricted conditions of the press in the seventeenth century.

Williams. Talcott. *The Newspapermen.* New York: Charles Scribner's Sons. 1922.

A presentation of the opportunities and defects of journalism as a vocation.

Williams, Walter, editor. *The Press Congress of the World in Hawaii.* Columbia, Mo. : E. W. Stephens Publishing Company. 1922.

Proceedings of an international journalistic gathering, including several papers on ethical problems of the press.

Addresses and Proceedings of the Fourth Annual Meeting of the University Press Club of Michigan. Ann Arbor. 1922.

Biennial Reports, Bureau of Accuracy and Fair Play. New York: The World.

Constitution and rules, Institute of Journalists. Tudor Street, London, E. C. 4.

Constitution and rules, National Union of Journalists. 180 Fleet Street, London. E. C. 4.

Appendix B   A Selective Bibliography   **421**

Constitution and rules, Society of Women Journalists. Sentinel House, Southampton Row, London, W. C. 2.

Cook. Waldo C. *Character in Newspapers*. University of Iowa Extension Bulletin No. 62. Iowa City. 1920.

Ethical Aspects of Journalism, Bulletin of the University of Washington. General Series No. 101. Seattle. 1916.

How Confidence Began. Philadelphia: The Farm Journal.

How It Works. New York: The Tribune.

Lee. James Melvin. *Instruction in Journalism in Institutions of Hihgher Education*. Washington: United States Bureau of Education. 1918.

Moses. Bert. The Deadhead Reading Notice. New York: The Evening Post

Myers, Joseph S. *The Journalistic Code of Ethics*. Ohio State University Bulletin, Vol. 26. No. 8. Columbus, Ohio. 1922.

Powell, j. B. *Building a Circulation*, University of Missouri Bulletin. Vol. 15, No. 6. Columbia, Mo. 1914.

Proceedings of the American Association of Teachers of Journalism. 1921 and 1922. Minneapolis: R. R. Barlow, University of Minnesota. *Some Newspaper Problems as Seen in the State of Washington*, Bulletin of the University of Washington. General Series No. 111. Seattle. 1917.

Supplementary Lectures in Journalism, Bulletin of the University of Washington. General Series No. 103. Seattle. 1916.

The Better Newspaper, Bulletin of the University of Washington. General Series No. 81. Seattle. 1914.

The Race Track Graft. Detroit: *The News*. 1922.

Williams, Walter. The World's Journalism. University of Missouri Bulletin, Journalism Series No. 9. Columbia, Mo.

Appendix C INDEX

Accuracy, 80, 83, 164, 183, 188—189, 196, 211—212, 218, 220, 221, 230233, 237, 238

Adams, Samuel Hopkins, 12

Advertisers, boycotts by, 21, 68—69; discrimination among, 9; obligations to, 5—24

Advertising, 3, 5—24, 67, 193, 196, 197, 200, 202—204, 229—230, 239; censorship of, 10; fraudulent, 10—11; guaranty of, 11, 193; laws concerning, 133

Agate line, 13

Albany Argus. 40

American Association for the Advancement of Science, 80

American Federation of Labor, 61

American Journalists' Association 152

American Newspaper Directory, 7—8

American Society of Newspaper Editors, 151, 183

Americanism, 65

Anti-Masonic Party, 64

Arbitrator. 134—135
Aristotle, 187
Associated Press, 49, SS n., 85, 141
Atrocity habits of mind, 64
Audit Bureau of Circulations, 8
Australia, journalistic conditions in. 150—153
Bacon, Roger, 29
Balance and proportion, 99—106
Baltimore Sun. 60, 61
Bankers, 72
Beg-Your-Pardon columns, 165
Bias in news, 83—85
Bok, Edward, 61
Booth, Edwin W., 58
Boston Globe. 113 n.
Boston Herald, 113 n.
Boston Post, 113 n.
Boston Tea Party, 64
Boston Transcript. 21, 69, 113 n., 115, 117, 132
Boycotts by advertisers, 21, 68—69
Bribery, 68, 142
Brisbane, Arthur, 124
British Labour Party, 76, 154
Brooklyn Eagle. 40, 211—213
Buffalo Express, 59
Bureau of Accuracy and Fair Play, 164
Burrell. David James, 35
Burroughs, John, 75
Business ethics, 3—24

Buying power and disposition, 9, 23

Cable reports, 48—49

Caesar, Julius, 27

Campaigns by newspapers, 126—130

Canons of Journalism, 183

Capitalism, 65, 71, 72—73Care, 189

Carelessness, 74—76, 167

Censorship, 10, 96, 174—175

Chambers of Commerce, 152

Charges against newspaper, 39—63

Chicago Commission on Race Relations, 108

Chicago Daily News, 60

Chicago Herald, S3

Chicago Herald-Examiner, 108

Chicago Record-Herald, 42

Chicago Tribune. 13, 17—20, 59, 127

Children, offenses of, 103—104, 222

Christian Science Monitor. 113 n. ,114, 11S, 119 n. ,162, 214—216

Cincinnati Enquirer, 59, 60, 61

Circulation, 3, 4, 7, 9, 66—67, 123,193, 201, 204—205

Civil War. 64Codes of ethics, 139, 151, 166, 183—240Coloring of news, 57—61, 107

Colyer, W. T. , 138

Communist Party, 6S

Competency, 189

Compulsory veracity, 134

Congress, 32—34

Congressional Record, 158

Connor, Stephen E. , 58

Appendix C INDEX **425**

Conservatism, 191

Consolidation of newspapers, 87

Conspiracy habits of mind, 64

Contempt of court, 134

Contests, 6

Correction of errors, 140, 165, 185,225—226

Corruption, 71—73, 82

Crime, news of, 26, 114—117, 193,207—209

Cynicism in journalism, 53, 86

Davis, Elmer. 21

de Bacourt, Paul, 140 n.

Decency, 185

Deficiencies of the press, 39—98

Democracy, 37

Dempsey-Gibbons fight, 113, 162

Detroit News, 127, 164, 224—228

Discrimination among advertisers, 9

Dyment, Colin V. , 187

Economics, 171

Editor and Publisher, 110, 162

Editorials, 121—132, 196, 199—200,209—210, 239

Editorial leadership, 121—132, 23f

Education, 168—179

Election News, 228

Emporia Gazette, 102

Endowed newspapers, 156—1S7

England, journalistic conditions in, 145—154

Enid Eagle, 15—17

Environment, 177—178

Espionage Act, 96

Estimating, 205

European newspapers, 74

Evidence, 76—77, 90, 171, 191

Exaggeration, 9, 230, 233

Extra copies, sale of, S

Fairness, 18S, 186, 196, 221, 226,230, 233, 237, 238, 239

Faking, 39—49, 107, 167, 206

Farm Journal, 11

Fear, 74, 81—98

Federated Press, 57

Financial relations of press, 210

First newspapers, 229—232

Foster, Chapin D. , 186 n.

Fraudulent advertising. 10—11

Freedom of the press, 183, 190, 197

Freud, Sigmund, 82, 129

Galileo, 29

Gambling, 20S

Government-owned newspapers, 156—159

Grand Rapids Press, SS

Hale, William G. , 133 n.

Harding, Warren G. , 58, 238 n.

Headlines, 42, 58—61, 111—112, 184,216

Hearst, William Randolph, 66, 111, 124, 229 n.

Herd instincts, 29—35, 81—98, 172

Herodotus, 27 Herschel, Sir John, 40

High school journalism, 173—174

"Hokum," 49—54

Holt, Hamilton, 69 n.
Honesty, 195
Howard, L. O., 41 n.
Human interest, 111—118
Ignorance, 74—76
Impartiality, 183
Inaccuracy, 51, 61, 74, 80, 83, 167
Income of newspapers, 70
Independence, 183
Individual standards. 166—170
Industrial Workers of the World, 65
Inertia, 74—76
Institute of Journalists, 145—148,154
Integrity, 171
Intelligence, 171
Inter-Church World Movement, 56 n.
Interlocking Directorates, 71
International Labor News Service, 61
Interviews, 75, 139—140, 206, 210,217, 234
Invasion of privacy, 108—110
Jefferson, Thomas, 28, 36—37
Jonson, Ben, 39
Johnston, Alva, 80
Journalists' Creed, 239—240
Justice, 190
Kansas City Journal-Post. 297
Kansas City Star. 105 n., 111, 118,124
Kansas Code of Ethics, 139, 202—210
Keeley, James, 127

Kieser, Paul W., 195 n.

Kindness, 190

Kissing-bug scare, 40—41

Labor unions, 76

La Follette, Robert M., 55 n.

Language, 105, 214—215. 231

Laws, 10, 133—144

Leavenworth Times, 61 n.

Lee, James Melvin, 123 n.

Lenine, Nikolai, 54

Letters from readers, 130

Libel, 133, 226

Liberal press, 23

Licensing laws, 25, 141

Lincoln, Abraham, 40

Lippmann, Walter, 32—34, 54—55, 77, 90, 127—128, 160, 177

Lloyd, Alfred H., 131

Locke, Richard Adams, 39

Macy, John, 113

Manchester Guardian, 79—80

Manufacture of news, See Faking

Marion Star, 238

Martin, Frederick Roy, 49

Mary Magdalene, 75

Masters, Edgar Lee, 104

Mercy, 190

Merz, Charles, 54—55, 77, 90, 195 n.

Mill, John Stuart, 82

Millay, Edna St. Vincent, 61

Miller, Willis E., 202 n.

Milline rates, 67

Missouri Declaration of Principles and Code of Practice, 199—201

Moderation, 191 Moon Hoax, 39—40

Mortgaged newspaper plants, 70

Motion picture theaters, 14—17

Myers, Joseph S., 102 n.

National Council of Teachers of English, 174

National Education Association, 113,162

National Society of Journalists, 146

National Union of Journalists, 148—150

Nelson, W. R., 111

New Republic, 55 n.

News, coloring of, 57—61, 107; of crime, 26, 114—117, 193, 207—209; of suicide, 223 ; suppression of, 14—24, 56—57, 69—70, 92, 100,103—105, 197. 207—209, 213, 235—236, 239

New York Herald, 59

NEW York Sun, 39, 40

New York Times, 21—22, 49, 55 n., 60, 77—79, 80, 127, 128, 132

New York Tribune, 11, 59, 127

New York World, 44, 51—52, 58, 164, 166

New Zealand, journalistic conditions in, 150—153

Northcliffe, Viscount, 154

Objectivity, 99—132, 171, 213, 215,218, 221, 228, 233, 237, 238

O'Brien, Frank M., 40

Obscene writing, 133

Offenses of children, 103—104, 222

Offenses of women, 104, 227, 233

Official Bulletin, 156

O'Hara, Barratt, 141

Older. Fremont, 68

Oregon Code of Ethics for Journalism, 187

Oregon Editorial Association, 119

Organizations of journalists, 145—155

Ownership of newspapers, 25—26, 71, 87

Park, Robert E., 10 n.

Partisanship, 192

Patent medicines, laws concerning, 14—15

Paul, Edward, 134

Payne, George H., 132 n., 159 n.

Philadelphia Public Ledger, 60

Pictures, faking of, 42—43

Poe, Edgar Allan, 40

Politicians, 32—35, 159

Politics, 171

Polk, James K., 40

Populist Party, 65

Premiums, 6

Press agents, 47, 160—163

Privacy, invasion of, 108—110

Progressive Party, 65

Propaganda, 5, 13—14, 160—63, 192, 204, 212, 223

Proportion, 99—106, 191

Public literary defender, 135—137

Public opinion, expression of, 80—81, 130

Publicity, 13—14

Publisher, 86—87

Pulitzer Prize for reporting, 80

Pulitzer, Ralph, 44

Quality circulation, 9, 23, 67

Quantity circulation, 9, 23, 67

Radical press, 23, 72—73

Ransome, Arthur, 79—80

Rationalization, 82

Responsibility, 183

Rochester Daily Chronicle, 60

Roorback, 40

Rotary Clubs, 152

Rowell, George P., 7—8

Rumor, 207

Russia, news about, 54—55, 77, 89—91

Sacramento Bee, 231—234

St. Ambrose, 36

St. Paul, 28

Salaries, 149

Schools of journalism, 169—173

Science Service, 114

Scott, Walter Dill, 112 n.

Self-analysis by the press, 163—165

Sensationalism, 66—67, 107—119, 185,193, 207—208, 216, 220, 235—236

Shuman, Edwin l., 42—43

Sigma Delta Chi, 152

Sincerity, 183, 188, 197

Sinclair, Upton, 57, 72, 85, 138—139,141

Slang, 215, 231

Sociology, 171

Steel strike, news of, 56

Sturges, H. A. , 195 n.

Social policy, 193

Socialists, 65

Society of Women Journalists, 150

South Africa, journalistic conditions in, 150—153

South Dakota Code of Ethics, 195

Southern, William, Jr. , 199 n.

Spanish-American War, 108

Springfield Republican, 217—219

Springfield Union, 220—223.

Suppression of news, 14—24, 56—57, 69—70, 92, 100, 103—105, 197, 207—209, 213, 235—236, 239

Subscriber, obligations to, 4

Subscriptions, solicitation of, 4

Suicide, news of, 223

Taboos, 88

Tact, 171

Thaw, Harry K. , 41, 116

Theaters, 14—17

Theta Sigma Phi, 152

Thoroughness, 189

Trotter, W, 29—31

Truth, 183, 186, 188, 195

Tweed Ring, 127, 128

Unemployment benefits 148—150

Union labor, 65

Unions of journalists, 148—150, 152—153

Appendix C INDEX **433**

Usher, Roland G., 48—49
Van Anda, C. V., 49
War of 1812, 123
Washington Code of Ethics, 186
Wells, H. G., 148
White, Isaac D. 51—52
White, William Allen, 101
Williams, Talcott, 70
Williams, Walter, 153, 239
Women, offenses of, 104, 227, 233
World War, 95—96, 158
Wright, Harold Bell, 50
Wright, Harry J., 183 n.
Wright, J. A., 195 n.

A PARTIAL LIST OF BORZOI TEXTS
—EARLY CIVILIZATION:
AN INTRODUCTION TO ANTHROPOLOGY

By Alexander A. Goldenweiser, Lecturer on Anthropology and Sociology at the New School for Social Research. New York

Large 8vo, Cloth, XXIV 424 pages

While offering an elementary text for the beginner in anthropology, this volume is mainly designed as a sourcebook of information and suggestion for students of sociology who may wish to amplify their familiarity with modern social phenomena by an inquiry into the nature of early civilization and the workings of the primitive mind.

SECRET HISTORY OF THE ENGLISH OCCUPATION OF E-GYPT

By Wilfrid Scawen Blunt

Large 8vo, Cloth, 450 pages

This book makes a clear the varying motives-imperialistic, economic, and personal-which brought about the English occupation of Egypt. Based on personal records and con-temporary documents, its statements and conclusions have a profound interest and importance for students of history in general and of English history in particular.

THE GERMAN CONSTITUTION

By Rene Brunet. Professor of Constitutional Law at the University of Caen (translated from the French by Joseph Gollomb, with an Introduction by Charles A. Beard)

8vo, Cloth, XIV 339 pages

This is a critical discussion of the new German Constitution, the actual text of which is included, in English, as an appendix. It gives a lucid and unbiased account of the German Revolution, describes the conflict of forces which ended in the establishment of the Republic, a d concludes with a systematic analysis of the new plan of government.

THE FOUNDATIONS OF SOCIALS SCIENCE

By James Mickel Williams. Professor of Economics and Sociology in Hobart College

Large 8vo, Cloth XVI 494 pages

A comparative study of the psychological aspects of the social sciences. It treats of the relation of social psychology to political science, jurisprudence, economics, history and sociology, analyzing the psychological assumptions underlying the behavior of men living in social relations.

PRINCIPLES OF SOCIAL PSYCHOLOGY

By James Mickel Williams. Professor of Economics and Sociology in Hobart College

Large 8vo Cloth, XII 459 pages

This book represents the first attempt that has been made to explain society concretely in psychological terms. It describes the essential processes that extend throughout the social organization, analyzing the conflict of the different types of behavior in all human relations.

THE HISTORY OF SOCIAL DEVELOPMENT

By Franz Carl Müller-Lyer (translated from the German by E. C. and H. W. Lake. with Introductions by L. T. Hobhouse and E. J. Urwick)

8vo. Cloth, 362 page

This volume is mainly designed as a text for beginners in social studies. It surveys broadly the various phases of man's origin and progress. coordinating the general facts of social evolution from the earliest times and indicating the probable trend of future developments.

HUMAN NATURE IN POLITICS

By Graham Wallas. Professor of Political Science in- London University

8vo, Cloth, 320 pages

This is a slightly revised edition, with a new Preface, of Professor Walla's famous work first published in England, in 1908, and for some time out of print. It offers a clear and forceful analysis of the psychological progresses which underlie political thought and action, laying special emphasis upon the application of social psychology to politics.

HOW ENGLAND IS GOVERNED

By Rt. Hon. C. F. G. Masterman

8vo, Cloth, XVI 293 pages

An introductory study of the working of the British Constitution, written from the standpoint of one who has had actual experience of the working of the political machinery of England. Students of politics and government will find in this volume a most interesting and valuable source of information.

FACING OLD AGE

By Abraham Epstein. Formerly Director of the Pennsylvania Commission to Investigate Old Age Pensions

8vo, Cloth. XVI 352 pages

This book offers a scientific examination of the social and economic problems presented by the aged. Frankly a plea for social action, it presents in a most thoro and lucid manner the latest available data bearing upon this interesting and important question.

12mo, Cloth, 280 pages

OUR WAR WITH GERMANY

By John Spencer Bassett. Professor of American History in Smith College

Large 8vo, Cloth, 398 pages

This is a compact but complete account of the part played by the United States in the World War. It is in no sense a mere record of military events, but an analytical account of the political, economic and military events that marked the period of the war.

CONSUMERS' COOPERATIVE SOCIETIES

By Charles Gide. Professor of Economics at the University of Paris (translation from the French, edited by Cedric Long)

8vo, Cloth, 300 pages

This translation of Professor Gide's famous work is intended to meet the needs of American students of Distributive Co-operation. The first three chapters are devoted to an elucidation of the meaning and history of the co-operative movement while the bulk of the volume deals with the practical problems of organization, administration and development of consumers' societies themselves.

THE ETHICS OF HERCULES

By Robert Chenault Givler

12mo, Cloth 210 pages

A strictly behavioristic treatment of ethical values. Not only is human conduct the result of external and internal stimuli upon the human body, but even our notions of right and wrong are derived from the reactions of our nerves and muscles to the various stimuli which excite them.

THE ETHICS OF JOURNALISM

By Nelson Antrim Crawford

8vo, Cloth 270 pages

A clear-cut, objective exposition and analysis of contemporary journalistic practice with reference to advertising, news, and editorial, carefully documented. Here is a pioneer book on a subject which is attracting keen attention especially among practicing and prospective journalists.

THE BASIS OF SOCIAL THEORY. By Adam G. A. Balz. with the collaboration of William S. A. Pott

12mo, Cloth 253 pages

The writers of this book take the position that a science of Human Nature is requisite for the progress of all the social sciences, that Social Psychology is failing to accomplish its fundamental purpose of clarifying the uncertainties and ambiguities concerning the nature of social facts and causes.

THE TREND OF ECONOMICS

By Various Writers (edited by Rexford G. Tugwell)

8vo, Cloth 550 pages

A series of monographs contributed by thirteen outstanding American economists of the younger generation designed to set forth the present tendencies of economic thought and inquiry in the light of their historical development

图书在版编目(CIP)数据

新闻伦理学 /（美）纳尔逊·安特宁·克劳福德著；江作苏，王敏译. —北京：中国传媒大学出版社,2018.3
（新闻学与传播学经典丛书. 大师系列）
书名原文：The Ethics of Journalism
ISBN 978-7-5657-2113-7

Ⅰ.①新… Ⅱ.①纳… ②江… ③王… Ⅲ.①新闻学—伦理学 Ⅳ.①G210-05

中国版本图书馆CIP数据核字(2017)第201911号

新闻学与传播学经典丛书·大师系列

新闻伦理学
XINWEN LUNLIXUE

著　者	[美]纳尔逊·安特宁·克劳福德
译　者	江作苏　王　敏
策划编辑	司马兰　姜颖昳
责任编辑	曾婧娴　司马兰
封面设计	运平设计
责任印制	阳金洲
出版发行	中国传媒大学出版社
社　址	北京市朝阳区定福庄东街1号　邮编：100024
电　话	010-65450532 或 65450528　传真：010-65779405
网　址	http://www.cucp.com.cn
经　销	全国新华书店
印　刷	三河市东方印刷有限公司
开　本	880mm×1230mm　1/32
印　张	14.25
字　数	403千字
版　次	2018年3月第1版　2018年3月第1次印刷
书　号	ISBN 978-7-5657-2113-7/G·2113　定价 68.00元

版权所有　翻印必究　印装错误　负责调换

The Ethics of Journalism by Nelson Antrim Crawford
Copyright © 1924 by Alfred A. Knopf